...d States, in Order to form a more perfect Union, ...establish... ...the general Welfare, and secure the Blessings of Liberty to our... ...ted States of America.

...Congress of the United States, which shall consist of a Senate and H...

...s chosen, every second Year by the People of the several States, and the... ...Branch of the State Legislature.

...the Age of twenty five Years, and been seven Years a Citizen of the United... ...d be chosen.

...States which may be included within this Union, according to their respec... ...including those bound to their service for a Term of Years, and excluding... ...made within three Years after the first Meeting of the Congress of the Unit... ...by Law direct. The Number of Representatives shall not exceed one f... ...until such enumeration shall be made, the State of New Hampshire sh... ...Plantations one, Connecticut four, New York six, New Jersey four, Penns... ...h Carolina five, and Georgia three.

...utive Authority thereof shall issue Writs of Election to fill such Vacancie... ...and shall have the sole Power of Impeachment.

...from each State, chosen by the Legislature thereof, for six Years, and ...

...er a ...they shall be divided as equally as may be into three Classes... ...may be at the Expiration of the fourth Year, and of the... ...next Year, and if Vacancies happen by Resignation, or otherwise, durin... ...y temporary appointments until the next Meeting of the Legislature, which shall then...

...thirty Years, and been nine Years a Citizen of the United States, and wh...

...shall have no Vote, unless they be equally divided.

...e, in the absence of the Vice President, or when he shall exercise the Off...

...ting for that Purpose they shall be on Oath or Affirmation. When the... ...t ... should the Concurrence of two thirds of the Members pre... ...s... ...er and ... Office, and disqualification to hold and enjoy any Office... ...ve had, and subject to Indictment, Trial, judgment and Punish...

...nators and Representatives, shall be prescribed in each State by the Legis...

NOVUS
ORDO
SECLORUM

NOVUS ORDO SECLORUM

THE INTELLECTUAL ORIGINS OF THE CONSTITUTION

FORREST McDONALD

University Press of Kansas

© 1985 by the University Press of Kansas

ALL RIGHTS RESERVED

Published by the University Press of Kansas (Lawrence, Kansas 66045), which was organized by the Kansas Board of Regents and is operated and funded by Emporia State University, Fort Hays State University, Kansas State University, Pittsburg State University, the University of Kansas, and Wichita State University

LIBRARY OF CONGRESS CATALOGING IN PUBLICATION DATA

McDonald, Forrest.
  Novus ordo seclorum.

  Bibliography: p.
  Includes index.
  1. Political science—United States—History—18th century.
2. United States. Constitutional Convention (1787) I. Title.
JA84.U5M43   1985   320′.0973   85-13544
ISBN 0-7006-0284-4   ISBN 0-7006-0311-5 (pbk.)

Printed in the United States of America

CONTENTS

PREFACE

FASHIONS IN HISTORICAL INTER-
pretation come and
go. In 1958 I published a work called *We the People: The Economic Origins of the Constitution,* which was primarily concerned with testing Charles A. Beard's *Economic Interpretation of the Constitution*—then the prevailing version. Because the results of that test were essentially negative, I wrote in the preface that the purpose of my book was to "clear the decks" and that I intended to follow the volume with two more, "in which I shall attempt to write something meaningful about the making of the Constitution."

My timing in publishing *We the People* was fortunate: Robert E. Brown and several other scholars were just then attacking Beard's thesis, and the mood of the historical profession was ripe for something new. The result was that Beard's book was all-but-unanimously pronounced defunct. My timing (1965) in publishing the first of the two sequel volumes, *E Pluribus Unum,* was considerably less happy. That work focused upon the wheeling and dealing and the interplay between politics and economics which enabled hard-nosed practical men to establish the Constitution; several reviewers described it as "neo-Beardian." That sort of analysis was no longer in season: students of the Revolution and of the early national period, led by Bernard Bailyn and J. G. A. Pocock, had turned their attention to the role of ideology in the founding of the nation. During the remainder of the sixties and through most of the seventies a host of works in the ideological vein appeared, and there emerged something of a consensus that neoclassical republican ideology, traceable from Machiavelli to the eighteenth-century English Opposition, underlay the founding.

I admire much of the work of the ideological school but find it ultimately unsatisfying. It fails to distinguish among the several kinds of republicanism that were espoused by various Americans, which by and large reflected regionally different social and economic norms. Those ideological historians who have concentrated on the tradition of civic humanism have all but left the influential Scots thinkers out of account, and in their eagerness to downplay the influence of John Locke—once greatly overrated—they have neglected the importance of theories of natural law and natural rights. They have largely disregarded the law and legal institutions. In the whole corpus of the ideological literature there is scarcely a mention of what used to be called social, political, and economic "reality," or of such practical men of affairs as George Washington and Robert Morris, without whom, arguably, there might have been no founding. Finally, though the ideological historians have delineated the tensions between republican virtue and luxury/vice, they have inadequately addressed the counterpart tensions between communitarian consensus and possessive individualism and those between the concepts of liberty *to* participate in the governing process and liberty *from* unlimited government.

Because of these shortcomings, but also because the solid contributions of the ideological school provide indispensable building blocks, I have at last been moved to write this final volume in the series that I proposed long ago. There is another reason as well: I have become convinced that the late Douglass Adair was right when he opted to give *E Pluribus Unum* two cheers but not three. The cheers, he wrote, were for my "sophisticated picture of the dynamic interrelationships of avarice and American politics" at both the national and the state level; his reservation was

that I had left out the intellectual dimension and had failed
to take into account the passion for fame among the
founders. I hope that in this work I may win a posthumous
third cheer from that great historian.

It could be, of course, that my timing is once again bad.
The ideological school has come under attack from some
quarters and is being ignored by the many who have gone
on to psychohistory, family history, cliometrics, and other
exotica. Nonetheless, it is now possible, as it was not a
mere twenty-seven years ago, to make a reasonably comprehensive survey of the complex body of political thought
(including history and law and political economy) that went
into the framing of the Constitution, and I here venture to
undertake it.

A few words regarding methodology seem germane. It
is with reluctance that I have used the word *origins* in my
subtitle, for tracking down the sources of an idea or the
means by which it is transmitted is a tricky business. Let me
illustrate the difficulties with one of the ideas contained in
the Declaration of Independence. That the central argument of the Declaration is based mainly upon John Locke's
Second Treatise is indisputable, I believe, whatever ancillary
bodies of thought were also of influence; but Jefferson, as is
well known, departed from Locke's trinity of "life, liberty,
and estate" and substituted "the pursuit of happiness" for
the third of these. Whence did he derive the concept, or did
he think of it independently? It seems evident that the first
eighteenth-century philosopher to have developed the idea
was Jean Jacques Burlamaqui, but it is not certain that
Jefferson had read Burlamaqui's *Principles of Natural and
Politic Law*. Gilbert Chinard pointed out many years ago
that Jefferson had copied into his commonplace book
extensive extracts from James Wilson's 1774 pamphlet,
Considerations on the . . . Authority of the British Parliament,
and that that pamphlet draws heavily upon Burlamaqui.
The phrase in question, however, was not among the
passages that Jefferson copied from Wilson. Alternatively,
Jefferson might have drawn the idea from Sir William
Blackstone, whose treatment of natural law was based

upon Burlamaqui's work, or from Emmerich de Vattel, who studied under Burlamaqui at Geneva.[1] Again, Jefferson might have taken it from John Adams's *Thoughts on Government*, written in January of 1776 and circulated among the Virginians in Congress, or from the Virginia Declaration of Rights, drafted by George Mason and adopted on June 12, 1776. Jefferson might even have found it where Burlamaqui did—in Aristotle.

There are those who would regard all this as proof that any effort to understand a past intellectual world is inherently futile. I regard it as the opposite. It is true that we cannot be sure where Jefferson acquired the idea, or even that he did not conceive it on his own without reference to other thinkers. Yet we can say, with measured confidence, that here was an Aristotelian idea which had figured in no major way in the classical revival in seventeenth-century England but was popularized by Burlamaqui and his followers amidst the eighteenth-century enthusiasm for natural law. We can also say that it somehow spread rapidly in America and that it was, by 1776, in common currency among Patriots.

Some scholars, of course, regard such observations— and indeed the whole enterprise of intellectual history—as unverifiable "impressionistic" history and hold that we can never know how other people think or thought. That seems to me to violate common sense (in the twentieth-century signification of those words, not in the eighteenth), for we think in the patterns of others as a matter of daily routine. College students, for example, frequently encounter professors who teach from points of view that the students do not share; and when that happens, students in pursuit of grades are usually able and willing to write the essays and give the answers that the teacher wants to hear. What is involved is this: thinking takes places in symbolic codes or languages, and we can learn to think in languages that are

[1] The foregoing is developed at length in Ray Forrest Harvey, *Jean Jacques Burlamaqui: A Liberal Tradition in American Constitutionalism* (Chapel Hill, N.C., 1937), 114–116, 123–124, and passim.

not native to us, whether these be Latin, music, mathematics, legalese, or eighteenth-century English.

In thinking in eighteenth-century English, I suggest three main guiding principles. First, one must pay close attention to meanings of even the most ordinary words, for these have changed in myriad ways. For instance, *discover* meant, not *uncover* or *find*, but *disclose* or *reveal*; *nervous* meant, not *worried* or *jittery*, but *strong* or *vigorous*; *awful* meant, not *extremely bad*, but *that which inspires to awe and reverence*; *natural* had many of its present meanings, but it also meant *discoverable by reason* as opposed to *revealed by God*, *illegitimate* as opposed to *legal*, and simply *an idiot*. Two necessary tools are Samuel Johnson's *Dictionary* and the *Oxford English Dictionary*, but these are insufficient if one is not sensitive to shades of meaning implicit in etymology, grammar, syntax, and context. In these regards, a rudimentary knowledge of Latin is highly useful; after all, every educated Englishman and American knew Latin, English words were generally closer in meaning to their Latin originals than they are today, and sometimes, as with the use of the subjunctive, it is apparent that an author is accustomed to formulating his thoughts in Latin. (Passages in Daniel Defoe's novels, for example, often read like literal translations from Latin.)

The second principle is that one must seek out the "buzz words" or "code words" that are identifiable with particular ideologies or bodies of thought. This point can perhaps best be illustrated with phrases employed in current political discourse. If one hears or reads the phrase "right to life" or the aphorism "If guns are outlawed, only outlaws will have guns" or the facetious remark "Nuke the whales," one is fairly safe in assuming that the speaker or writer did not vote for Walter Mondale in the 1984 presidential election. In similar fashion, clusters of words and ideas were, in the eighteenth century, sometimes shorthand clues to entire mind sets, and one can find them if one looks for them. There is nothing arcane about unraveling such clues. Any careful student of the period, upon encountering a speech or an article in which, for example, the word *bloodsuckers* is used to describe traders in public securities, can fill in the rest of the piece, complete with undertones and overtones and harmonic variations.

Third, while one employs the most modern techniques of analysis, one must be cautious in bringing to bear concepts and information that were not available to the eighteenth-century subjects. Thus, in my judgment, it is a grave mistake to try to understand eighteenth-century Americans through Freudian or other twentieth-century modes of psychiatric analysis. They had their own models of normal and abnormal behavior, and if one is to pry into their psyches, those models alone are relevant. As for information, it is readily demonstrable that eighteenth-century Americans were sometimes uninformed or misinformed about the past, including their own past, but they acted on the basis of their own knowledge and understanding, not ours. A prime case in point concerns English law and legal history. Modern scholarship has demonstrated that Blackstone was mistaken on a number of counts, but few if any Americans knew that, and it was Blackstone whom they read on the subject. Accordingly, in discussing English legal practice, I have usually followed Blackstone, though I have occasionally pointed out instances in which modern scholars have shown that Blackstone was wrong.

One final comment. The American founders left an enormous quantity and variety of written materials, informing us from many points of view what they did, what they read, what they believed, and what they thought. It is a central part of the plan of this book that the notes be set at the foot of the page, so that the reader can see for himself just what a rich store of materials the founders bequeathed to us. To aid the reader further, I have included a list of delegates to the Constitutional Convention and a copy of the Constitution in appendixes.

I am grateful to Richard Ware and the Earhart Foundation for financial support; to A. Neil McLeod and Charles King of the Liberty Fund for encouragement and assistance in a variety of ways; to Professors Lance Banning, M. E. Bradford, Elizabeth Fox-Genovese, J. H. Hexter, Michael

Kammen, Harvey Mansfield, Jr., and Michael Mendle for keen critical readings of the manuscript; and to Ellen Shapiro McDonald, for everything.

Coker, Alabama
January 25, 1985

FORREST MCDONALD

I

THE PROBLEM

SORELY DIVIDED AS AMERICANS WERE IN regard to independence, the Patriots among them, at least in principle, were nearly unanimous in their understanding of what independence entailed. The short-range necessity was to win on the battlefield what they had proclaimed in the halls of Congress. The longer-term necessity, in the language of the Declaration, was "to institute new Government, laying its Foundation on such Principles, and organizing its Powers in such Form, as to them shall seem most likely to effect their Safety and Happiness."

The latter task appeared, with some reason, to pose no difficulty. Almost to a man, Patriots were agreed that the proper ends of government were to protect people in their lives, liberty, and property and that these ends could best be obtained through a republican form. They had had abundant experience—probably more Americans had participated directly in government at one level or another than had any other people on earth—and if their experience turned out to be inadequate, enough of them were familiar witʳ the theoretical works of Aristotle and Polybius, of Machiavelli and Harrington, of Locke and Hume and Montesquieu, to see them through.

But it proved to be far less simple than they had anticipated. In an article published in 1781, not long before the decisive battle at Yorktown, young Alexander Hamilton

(who, as General Washington's aide-de-camp, had witnessed the army's tribulations resulting from the "imbecility" of government) diagnosed what had gone awry.
Most Americans who had had political experience beyond
the local level, Hamilton wrote, had become Loyalists, and
thus Americans "began this revolution with very vague
and confined notions of the practical business of government." Accordingly, in the drafting of the Revolutionary
state constitutions and the Articles of Confederation, as
well as in the management of civil and military affairs,
"there have been many false steps, many chimerical pro-
jects and utopian speculations." The nub of the problem, in
Hamilton's view, was the "extreme jealousy of power" that
is "the attendant on all popular revolutions, and has
seldom been without its evils."[1]

He elaborated this proposition at length. "History," he
said, "is full of examples, where in contests for liberty, a
jealousy of power has either defeated the attempts to
recover or preserve it in the first instance, or has afterwards
subverted it by clogging government with too great precautions for its security, or by leaving too wide a door for
sedition and popular licenciousness." If liberty is to en-
dure, as much attention must be paid to giving "a proper
degree of authority, to make and execute the laws with
vigour" as to "guarding against encroachments upon the
rights of the community." An excess of power leads to
despotism, whereas "too little leads to anarchy, and both
eventually to the ruin of the people."[2]

The perception that energetic government is necessary
to the security of liberty and property—for, as James
Madison put it in the Constitutional Convention, "the
more lax the band," the more easily can the strong devour
the weak—was a crucial step toward becoming able to
devise a viable system of free political institutions.[3] Earlier,

[1] "Continentalist No. I," July 12, 1781, in *The Papers of Alexander Hamilton*, ed.
Harold C. Syrett et al., 26 vols. (New York, 1961-1979), 2:649-650.
[2] Ibid., 2:651.
[3] *The Records of the Federal Convention of 1787*, ed. Max Farrand, 4 vols. (New
Haven, Conn., 1937), 1:448.

Patriots had tended to view the problem as having only one dimension, that of preventing oppression by government. Now they could see a second dimension. As Benjamin Rush said, "In our opposition to monarchy, we forgot that the temple of tyranny has two doors. We bolted one of them by proper restraints; but we left the other open, by neglecting to guard against the effects of our own ignorance and licentiousness."[4] This was the perspective that the Framers brought to bear when they convened in 1787 to reconstitute the Union.

In the undertaking, they were guided as well as limited by four sets of considerations, none of which was so clear as subsequent (or even contemporary) writing would lead one to believe. The first was inherent in their purpose, that of providing protection for the lives, liberty, and property of the citizenry. They repeatedly voiced their agreement about their goals. Charles Pinckney declared that to extend "to its citizens all the blessings of civil & religious liberty . . . is the great end of Republican Establishments" and that "the *landed interest* . . . are and ought ever to be the governing spring in the system."[5] Madison said that "we ought . . . to provide every guard to liberty that its preservation cd. require" and that "the primary objects of civil society are the security of property and public safety."[6] Roger Sherman insisted that government was "instituted for those who live under it. It ought therefore to be so constituted as not to be dangerous to their liberties."[7] Hamilton said that "one great objt. of Govt. is personal protection and the security of Property."[8] George Mason and Luther Martin concurred.[9]

Only four delegates diverged from the consensus, three of them just slightly. Gouverneur Morris, John Rutledge,

[4]Rush, "An Address," Philadelphia, 1787, in *Principles and Acts of the Revolution in America*, ed. Hezekiah Niles (New York, 1876), 234. See also James Madison, *Federalist* number 51, in *The Federalist*, ed. Edward Mead Earle (New York, 1937), 337.

[5]Farrand, *Records*, June 25, 1:402.

[6]Ibid., June 26, 1:423; Pierce's notes, June 6, 1:147.

[7]Ibid., June 26, 1:423.

[8]Ibid., June 18, 1:302.

[9]Ibid., June 26, 1:428; June 27, 1:440.

and Rufus King put the protection of property ahead of liberty as the main object of society.[10] James Wilson alone departed entirely from the consensus: rejecting the idea that the protection of property was "the sole or the primary" purpose of government, he asserted that "the cultivation & improvement of the human mind was the most noble object" of government and society.[11]

All this—except for Wilson's comment—would at first glance appear to constitute an unambiguous set of aims; but though the concept of life was straightforward enough until the advent of modern medicine, the other two terms, *liberty* and *property*, were cloudy in the extreme. Indeed, the fact—rarely taken into account by scholars[12]—is that the vocabulary of political discourse was, during the eighteenth century, in a state of flux. Many pivotal words were new and not yet in general usage, and others had not even been coined. For example, *society*, in the sense of an abstract whole, had first been employed in the late seventeenth century and still most often connoted its earlier meaning of a narrow, specially constituted association of people with an identity and interest different from those of the whole. Similarly, the concept of an "economy" as an entity having a life of its own was just emerging; and though *capital*, in its economic meaning, had been in use for several decades, the word *capitalist* was novel and *capitalism* had not yet been minted. And thus, as we shall see, though virtually every American believed that *property* and *liberty* were both *natural* and *civil rights*, it transpired during the Constitutional Convention that delegates had different understandings of all five of the words set here in italics.

The same was true of the second governing and limiting consideration, the commitment to republicanism. A few of the Framers questioned the desirability of adhering to a republican form of government, thinking that form to be less compatible with liberty than limited monarchy was, but

[10] Ibid., July 5, 1:533, 534; July 6, 1:541.
[11] Ibid., July 13, 1:605.
[12] Increasing numbers of scholars are studying eighteenth-century political vocabulary; see, e.g., the works of J. G. A. Pocock and Garry Wills.

none believed that any other form would be acceptable to
the American electorate. And yet, though the Framers
shared the commitment in the abstract, they were far from
agreed as to what republicanism meant, apart from the
absence of hereditary monarchy and hereditary aristocracy.
For example, Hamilton, who had inherited almost nothing,
was wont to define a republic as any government in which
no one had a hereditary status; whereas his friend Madison, who had inherited the status of freeman amidst
slavery and whose blacks had inherited their status as
slaves, preferred a definition that would avoid the sticky
question of status and merely considered as republican any
system in which governmental power derived from the
consent of the "public." Moreover, no matter how republicanism was defined, the concept—again as we shall see—
carried with it a number of implications that were not
entirely consonant with most Americans' ideas about liberty and property.

The third guiding and limiting factor was history, in
several senses of the term. One concerned history in the
conventional sense: most of the Framers were versed in the
history of ancient Greece and Rome, of confederations and
republics, and of England at least since Elizabethan times.
Moreover, most of them thought historically and used
references to history to support or illustrate their reasoning.
During the first three weeks of the convention, for instance,
delegates buttressed their arguments with historical examples at least twenty-three times, not counting references
drawn from British or colonial or recent American history,
inclusion of which would treble that total. John Dickinson,
Pierce Butler, Benjamin Franklin, George Mason, James
Madison, James Wilson, Alexander Hamilton, and Charles
Pinckney delivered to their colleagues mini lectures and
lectures that sometimes lasted for several hours on the
lessons to be drawn from ancient or modern history.[13]

[13] Farrand, *Records*, Dickinson, June 2, 7, 1:87, 153; Butler, June 5, 11, 1:125,
204; Franklin, June 4, 1:103; Mason, June 4, 1:112; Madison, June 6, 7, 16, 19,
1:135, 151–152, 254, 317, 319; Wilson, June 6, 7, 18, 1:137 (143), 254, 305;
Hamilton, June 18, 1:285, 290; Pinckney, June 25, 1:399, 401–402.

Another sense was that of history as legacy, which means mainly English political institutions and the common law as received and adapted selectively by the thirteen American political societies. Again considering just the first three weeks of the convention, on more than twenty separate occasions the delegates cited British constitutional practice as being instructive concerning the tasks at hand. Interestingly, in light of the vehemence with which Americans had rejected British "tyranny" in 1776, only a handful of delegates—Elbridge Gerry, James Wilson, Edmund Randolph, Pierce Butler—argued against using British constitutional practice as a guide, and for the most part these did so in regard to the relevance of the British constitution to an immediate question before the convention.[14]

The delegates were acutely conscious of history in yet another sense, that of their place in its ongoing flow. From the outset of the Revolution, public men in America had shared this awareness. "You and I, my dear friend," John Adams had written to Richard Henry Lee in 1777, "have been sent into life at a time when the greatest lawgivers of antiquity would have wished to live. How few of the human race have ever enjoyed an opportunity of making election of government . . . for themselves or their children."[15] By 1787 the joy that Adams had expressed had given way to a sense of urgency. It was "more than probable," Madison said in the convention, that the delegates "were now digesting a plan which in its operation wd. decide forever the fate of Republican Govt."[16] Hamilton agreed, adding that "if we did not give to [the republican] form due stability and wisdom, it would be disgraced & lost among ourselves, disgraced & lost to mankind for ever."[17] Franklin said that if the convention failed, "mankind may hereafter from this unfortunate instance, despair of establishing Governments by Human Wisdom and leave

[14] Ibid., May 31, June 1, 7, 13, 1:50, 65, 66, 153, 233.

[15] *Fame and the Founding Fathers: Essays by Douglass Adair*, ed. Trevor Colbourn (New York, 1974), 21; and *Letters of Members of the Continental Congress*, ed. Edmund C. Burnett, 8 vols. (Gloucester, Mass., 1963 reprint), 1:526, 2:67, 228.

[16] Farrand, *Records*, June 26, 1:423.

[17] Ibid., June 26, 1:424.

it to chance, war and conquest."[18] Rufus King said that his fears were "more agitated for his Country than he could express, that he conceived this to be the last opportunity of providing for its liberty & happiness."[19] And even after the convention had successfully completed its work, Washington declared, in his Inaugural Address, that "the sacred fire of liberty and the destiny of the republican model of government" were deeply and irrevocably staked "on the experiment intrusted to the hands of the American people."[20]

Finally, the Framers had a large body of political theory at their disposal. To be sure, most of them were prone to dismiss such "speculative" theory lightly. ("Experience must be our only guide," said John Dickinson, for "Reason may mislead us.")[21] Yet it formed a greater part of their understanding and of their perceptive apparatus than they always realized or were willing to admit. Several times in the convention, Hamilton and Madison quoted or paraphrased David Hume without acknowledging that they were doing so. Luther Martin cited several theorists of natural law. George Mason gave a speech that might have been taken directly from James Harrington's *Oceana*. The contract and natural-rights theories of John Locke were repeatedly iterated without reference to their source. Six delegates cited Montesquieu, and the spirit of that philosopher (and, through him, Bolingbroke) permeated the debates; and though Blackstone was mentioned only twice, his work was also pervasive.[22]

Given all this and given the common goal of the Framers and the common material with which they had to work, one might suppose that the outcome of their deliberations

[18] Ibid., June 28, 1:452.
[19] Ibid., June 30, 1:490.
[20] *Documents of American History*, ed. Henry Steele Commager, 7th ed. (New York, 1963), 152.
[21] Farrand, *Records*, Aug. 13, 2:278.
[22] Ibid., June 4, 1:110–114; Wilson, June 1, Sept. 6, 1:71, 2:530; Hamilton, June 18, 29, 1:308, 472; Butler, June 23, 1:391; Madison, June 30, July 17, 1:485 (497), 2:34; Randolph, July 11, 1:580; Pinckney, app. A, 3:109; Dickinson, Aug. 29, 2:448.

in Philadelphia—provided that a few compromises regarding conflicting interests could be reached—was more or less a foregone conclusion. But there was a catch, just one. The ingredients were incompatible.

II

THE RIGHTS OF ENGLISHMEN

IN 1786 THE *Providence Gazette & Country Journal* proudly reprinted the following item from a London newspaper: "There are 775,300,000 people in the World. Of these, arbitrary governments command 741,800,000, and the free ones (including 10 million Indians) only 33½ million. Of these few, 12½ million are subjects or descendants of the British Empire—⅓ of the freemen of the world. On the whole, slaves are three and twenty times more numerous than men enjoying, in any tolerable degree, the rights of human nature."[1]

The anonymous author of these calculations did not specify what he meant by freedom—he doubtless assumed that his readers needed no instruction on the matter—and yet the statement itself contains (in addition to the sexism) at least six implicit and not altogether consistent comments upon the nature and origins of liberty. The first two are definitions in terms of opposites. Freedom is the opposite of slavery: these two conditions alone are possible, and all people are either slaves or freemen. Again, freedom is the opposite of arbitrary rule: it is life under a government of laws, wherein rulers govern according to known and fixed principles. The other four comments concern the theoretical origins of liberty. First, freedom originates in natural law, deriving from "the rights of human nature." Second, it

---

[1] *Providence Gazette and Country Journal*, Nov. 11, 1786.

exists in a state of nature, inasmuch as Indians, living in a state prior to the organization of political society, are numbered among the free. Third, whatever the means by which governments are instituted among men, the vast majority of governments illegitimately deny the people their natural right to liberty. And fourth, more than half the people who live freely in organized political societies have their liberties by virtue of the English constitutional tradition.

At the time of independence a great many Americans believed, with this anonymous author, that liberty or freedom required no definition. Liberty trees could be planted, liberty poles could be erected, chapters of the Sons of Liberty could be formed, and Patrick Henry could declaim, "Give me liberty or give me death"—all without having to give deep thought to what was involved in the concept. Henry, for example, had lifted his eloquent words from a popular play, Joseph Addison's *Cato*.[2] But an astonishing number of Americans did devote deep thought to the subject. Indeed, it is no great exaggeration to say that for two decades prior to the meeting of the Constitutional Convention, American political discourse was an ongoing public forum on the meaning of liberty. And there was a wide range of opinion: almost the only thing generally agreed upon was that everybody wanted it. Everything else—what liberty was, who deserved it, how much of it was desirable, how it was obtained, how it was secured— was subject to debate.

Similarly, when the Framers of the Constitution said that the protection of property was a (or the) fundamental purpose for submitting to the authority of government, they understood that the word *property* had more meanings than one. In its older and more general sense it was related to the word *proper*, derived from the Latin *proprius*, meaning particular to, or appropriate to, an individual person. John

[2]Colbourn, *Fame and the Founding Fathers*, 284 n–285 n. Charles L. Cohen discusses the origin of the remark in an excellent article, "The 'Liberty or Death' Speech: A Note on Religion and Revolutionary Rhetoric," *William and Mary Quarterly* 38 (1981): 702–717.

Locke usually (though not invariably) used the term in that way. In the more restricted and more common usage, by the late eighteenth century property had come to be related to the idea of dominion, derived from the Latin *dominus*, meaning lordship, and ultimately from *domus*, meaning house. Sir William Blackstone used the term thus in his celebrated definition: "that sole and despotic dominion which one man claims and exercises over the external things of the world, in total exclusion of the right of any other individual in the universe."[3]

Under English law, every such dominion originated in, was dependent upon, and was held of some superior lord; it ultimately originated in grants made by the king. The varieties of tenure were myriad, and so were the obligations that accompanied them. Scholars in the seventeenth and eighteenth centures disagreed, as have scholars of more recent vintage, in regard to the historical sources of the system (common lawyers were curiously unwilling to recognize the fact of the Norman Conquest). The crucial point, however, is that by law, custom, and usage, every legitimate title to "real" property derived ultimately from a grant by the king, whatever the source of his authority may have been.[4]

American property law evolved from English law, differing from the original mainly in being less encumbered with relics of the past. The establishment of a hereditary barony had been attempted with the seventeenth-century Carolina grants, but that experiment had shortly been abandoned. By the middle of the eighteenth century— except for the proprietary holdings of the Penns in Pennsylvania and of the Calvert heirs in Maryland, the Fairfax estate in Virginia, the Granville holdings in North Carolina,

[3] Sir William Blackstone, *Commentaries on the Laws of England,* 12th ed., 4 vols. (London, 1793–1795), 2:2. For the development of earlier definitions see G. E. Alymer, "The Meaning and Definition of 'Property' in Seventeenth-Century England," *Past and Present* 86 (1980): 87–97.

[4] Blackstone, *Commentaries,* 2:69ff.; J. G. A. Pocock, *The Ancient Constitution and the Feudal Law: English Historical Thought in the Seventeenth Century* (New York, 1967), passim; J. H. Baker, *An Introduction to English Legal History* (London, 1971), 121ff.

and the estates held under Dutch patents in New York—landholding in America was essentially unencumbered. To be sure, the law of primogeniture and entail still nominally prevailed in some states even after independence, but it was rapidly being abolished; and though the term *fee simple,* which was of feudal origin, was used to describe American land tenure, landholding in America was more nearly what on the Continent was described as *allodial.* Even so, American property law was essentially English property law, and title to every foot of land that was legally held in the United States derived its legitimacy from a grant by the Crown or the Crown's assignees or successor or successors as sovereign.[5]

To understand the concepts of liberty and property in America, it is therefore necessary to understand, at least in general terms, how American law differed from but was similar to English law. This, for a beginning, entails a recognition of certain fundamental principles of both bodies of jurisprudence. One was that personal liberty and private rights to property were normally beyond the reach of the king and could be taken from the individual only as provided by the law of the land. This principle was deeply rooted in the English common law, had been confirmed by Magna Carta in the thirteenth century and by parliamentary enactment in the fourteenth, and had been reconfirmed by act of Parliament as recently as 1773. It had been incorporated into the laws of the Maryland General Assembly in 1639, the Massachusetts Body of Liberties in 1641, the West New Jersey Charter or Fundamental Laws in 1676, the

[5] Blackstone, *Commentaries,* 2:44–518; James Kent, *Commentaries on American Law,* 3d ed., 4 vols. (New York, 1836), 3:487–514; Julius Goebel, Jr., *History of the Supreme Court of the United States* (New York, 1971), 1:47; C. Ray Keim, "Primogeniture and Entail in Colonial Virginia," *William and Mary Quarterly* 25 (1968): 545–586. Interestingly, the 1776 Virginia act abolishing entail on estates, in *The Statutes at Large: Being a Collection of All the Laws of Virginia . . . ,* comp. William W. Hening, 13 vols. (Richmond, 1809–1823), 9:226–227, offers as a charge against the practice of entail that it "does injury to the morals of youth, by rendering them independent of and disobedient to their parents," in addition to discouraging fair traders and improvements of land. For an account of primogeniture and entail in the northern colonies see Percy Wells Bidwell and John I. Falconer, *History of Agriculture in the Northern United States, 1620–1860* (New York, 1941), 59, 66.

New York "Charter of Libertyes and privilidges" in 1683, several Revolutionary state constitutions after 1776, and the Northwest Ordinance of 1787.[6]

The other principles were interrelated. The concepts of liberty and private property carried with them a large body of assumptions, customs, attitudes, regulations both tacit and explicit, and rules of behavior. Thus neither liberty nor property was a right, singular; each was a complex and subtle combination of many rights, powers, and duties, distributed among individuals, society, and the state. Together, these constituted the historical "rights of Englishmen" of which eighteenth-century Americans were so proud—at least until 1776, when they abandoned their right to call themselves Englishmen.

Blackstone's sweeping definition of the right of property overstated the case; indeed, he devoted the succeeding 518 pages of book 2 of his *Commentaries*, entitled "Of the Rights of Things," to qualifying and specifying the exceptions to his definition. The broadest set of limitations upon private ownership involved rights that were reserved to the public in its corporate or governmental capacity. These included the power to regulate economic activity in the public interest and the power, inherent in sovereignty, of taking private property for public use, according to the law of the land. Under English and American law, the taking power, generally speaking, could be exercised in three main ways: through forfeiture, through eminent domain, and through taxation.[7]

[6]Blackstone, *Commentaries*, 1:139–140; Emmerich de Vattel, *The Law of Nations, Or, Principles of the Law of Nature, Applied to the Conduct and Affairs of Nations and Sovereigns* (Philadelphia, 1817, from the revised Neuchâtel ed., 1773), bk. 1, chap. 20, sec. 244, p. 112; Kent, *Commentaries*, 2:338–340; *Puritan Political Ideas, 1558–1794*, ed. Edmund S. Morgan (Indianapolis, Ind., 1965), 180–181; *The Federal and State Constitutions, Colonial Charters, and Other Organic Laws . . .* , ed. Francis N. Thorpe, 7 vols. (Washington, D.C., 1909), 5:2549 and passim; Robert Allen Rutland, *The Birth of the Bill of Rights, 1776–1791* (Chapel Hill, N.C., 1955), 14, 21.

[7]Vattel used the term "eminent domain" to cover all the rights reserved by the sovereign in private property, including all the various forms of taking (*Law of Nations*, bk. 1, chap. 21, secs. 244–245, pp. 112–113). Leonard W. Levy, in *The Law of the Commonwealth and Chief Justice Shaw* (Cambridge, Mass., 1957), 120 and n.,

The "regulatory power" was not a term usually employed by the great commentators; it is used here to cover a variety of powers that restricted private rights to property. Some of these powers, exercised under what Blackstone called laws prohibiting "offenses against public trade"—for example, laws against usury, forestalling the market, regrating, and engrossing, and laws regulating the assize of bread—restricted property rights by prohibiting lawful owners of property from using it to maximum advantage. If a man has money to lend and another man is willing to pay twelve percent interest on the loan in a free and voluntary transaction, a law prohibiting the lending of money at interest above six percent deprives the first party of the full use of his property. Similarly, the assize of bread—that is, published scales of prices at which bread of various quality and size could be sold, which were common throughout England and British America—deprived grain growers, millers, and bakers of the full enjoyment of their property and labor. But the crucial fact is that ownership did not include the absolute right to buy or sell one's property in a free market; that was not a part of the scheme of things in eighteenth-century England and America.[8]

mistakenly suggests that the concept was novel in the 1830s and that the term was first popularized by Kent, though it had been used in a South Carolina court in 1796 in the case of *Lindsay* v. *Commissioners*. Arthur Lenhoff, "Development of the Concept of Eminent Domain," *Columbia Law Review* 42 (1942): 598. The idea, of course, is much older: Vattel's use of the words "eminent domain" in the 1758 edition had been preceded by Grotius's "Eminens Dominum" a century and a half earlier. See Milton Colvin, "Property That Cannot Be Reached by the Power of Eminent Domain for a Public Use or Purpose," *University of Pennsylvania Law Review* 78 (1929): 1. What was novel in the nineteenth century was the narrower, more restricted, usage.

   [8] Blackstone, *Commentaries,* 4:154–159. *Forestalling* the market was "buying or contracting for any merchandize or victual coming in the way to market"; *regrating* was buying commodities "in any market, and selling it again in the same market"; *engrossing* was acquiring "large quantities of corn or other dead victuals, with intent to sell them again"—all of which practices were prohibited by law in England. Vattel did use the term *regulation* to refer to exercises of the police power, and he cited examples, conformable to natural law, of regulating what could be planted, of controlling what could or must be bought or sold, and of placing bounds on spending by prodigals (*Law of Nations,* bk. 1, chap. 20, secs. 254–255, pp. 115–116). For colonial examples of the kind of regulation mentioned here see Michael G. Kammen, *Colonial New York: A History* (New York, 1975), 56–57, 189; Sydney V. James, *Colonial Rhode Island: A History* (New York, 1975),

A second form of regulation that limited private property rights consisted of sumptuary laws, those governing personal morality. Properly and historically speaking,

157; William B. Weeden, *Economic and Social History of New England, 1620–1789,* 2 vols. (New York, 1890), 1:99, 118–119, 132, 178, 189, 200, 406, 2:524–526; Richard L. Bushman, *From Puritan to Yankee: Character and the Social Order in Connecticut, 1690–1765* (Cambridge, Mass., 1967), 113; Lewis Cecil Gray, *History of Agriculture in the Southern United States to 1860,* 2 vols. (Gloucester, Mass., 1958), 1:103, 163, 2:583. For an attempt in colonial Virginia see Niles, *Principles and Acts,* 273; and for colonial complaints against engrossers and forestallers see "presentments of the Jury, S.C., 1776," ibid., 335.

During the Revolution a regional attempt by four New England states to regulate prices (William Ellery to the Governor of Rhode Island, Jan. 30, 1777, in Burnett, *Letters,* 2:227 and n. 2) was favorably commented on by John Adams, Feb. 7, 1777: "The attempt of New England . . . is extremely popular in Congress, who will recommend an imitation of it to the other States" (ibid., 2:237). The debate in Congress is instructive (Feb. 14, 1777, ibid., 2:250–253), particularly the objections on practical grounds made by Benjamin Rush. These objections, and especially that price regulation creates scarcity, were voiced later by John Witherspoon (Jan. 27, 1778, ibid., 3:57). (The reality of scarcity because of regulation is seen in *The Life and Correspondence of Rufus King . . . ,* ed. Charles R. King, 6 vols. [New York, 1894–1900], 1:25.) For a congressional recommendation of price regulation see *Journals of the Continental Congress, 1774–1789,* ed. W. C. Ford et al., 34 vols. (Washington, D.C., 1904–1937), 15:1288–1293. The course of wartime regulation was not smooth, as can be seen in Burnett, *Letters,* 3:125 and n. 3, 198, 202, 212, 278, 4:485, 537, 550; the final failure of the attempt is seen in John Armstrong's letters of Jan. 12, 24, Feb. 16, 1780, ibid., 5:7–8, 13–14, 37–39. The failure can also be seen in *A Study in Dissent: The Warren-Gerry Correspondence, 1776–1792,* ed. C. Harvey Gardiner (Carbondale, Ill., 1968), 102–103, 108, 114.

The animosity toward engrossing was consistent; see Burnett, *Letters:* Richard Henry Lee, 3:438, 8:231, 620; Elbridge Gerry, 3:483; Committee of Congress, 3:490, 493; Henry Laurens, 3:500; Thomas Burke, 3:543; Committee of the Commissary of Maryland, 4:35; James Duane, 5:477–478; William Grayson, 8:95–96; David Howell, 8:106. See also Congress to the inhabitants of the United States, May 26, 1779, in Niles, *Principles and Acts,* 405. Local mobs articulated this animosity against "those Vermins the Speculators"; see Burnett, *Letters,* 4:232 and 4:239–240 (the latter includes Charles Carroll's desire for effectual laws to stop engrossers).

On the state level, regulation appeared in various forms. Calls were sometimes for particular regulation, as in Niles, *Principles and Acts,* 224. For general regulations see the New York act to regulate "wages of mechanicks and labourers, the prices of goods and commodities and the charges of innholders," passed on Apr. 3, 1778, in *Laws of the State of New York, 1778,* 1st sess. (Albany, 1886), vol. 1, chap. 34; the Virginia "act to amend the act [1777] for preventing forestalling, regrating, engrossing, and publick vendures," Oct. 1778, in Hening, *Laws of Virginia,* 9:581–583; and the Pennsylvania act, Oct. 8, 1779, "for the more effectually preventing engrossing and forestalling, for the encouragement of commerce and the fair trade . . . ," in *Statutes at Large of Pennsylvania from 1682 to 1801,* comp. James T. Mitchell and Henry Flanders, 17 vols. (Harrisburg, 1896–1915), 9:42–43, especially sec. 15, regarding "The wicked arts of speculators . . . who infest every part of the country." See also Burnett, *Letters,* 5:4, 23.

sumptuary laws related only to restrictions against luxury or extravagant expenditures on clothing, jewelry, and food, which were deemed to be socially harmful. The term later came to designate laws comprehended under the police power, such as those regulating or prohibiting gambling, alcoholic beverages, prostitution, and the like. As to activities encompassed in the broadened definition, none of the commentators doubted the justice or prudence of appropriate legislation, but there was disagreement over the efficacy of sumptuary laws in the stricter sense. Sir Edward Coke tended to favor them. Blackstone remarked that enthusiasm for them came and went, and expressed his own opinion that they were bad unless they accomplished some useful general purpose. To make the point, Blackstone singled out a statute of Edward IV that prohibited gentlemen from wearing shoes with high heels or platforms; this law, said the commentator, "savoured of oppression; because, however ridiculous the fashion," restraining it "could serve no purpose of common utility." By contrast, the statute of Charles II that required woolen dress for the dead was "consistent with public liberty; for it encourages the staple trade, on which in great measure depends the universal good of the nation." During the reigns of Edward III (1327-1377), Edward IV (1461-1483), and Henry VIII (1509-1547), a multitude of sumptuary laws had accumulated in England. These remained on the books until most were repealed in one sweep by a statute passed during the first year of the reign of James I; new ones soon began to accumulate. In America, every colony exercised the power of passing sumptuary legislation, though in their extreme forms such laws were uncommon except in New England and though in all their forms their applicability varied with the social status of the individual. The point here is that in any of its forms, sumptuary legislation restricted private rights to property, for it required persons to buy some things and prohibited them from buying or selling other things, whether they wanted them or not.[9]

[9]Blackstone, *Commentaries*, 1:126, 4:170; Sir Edward Coke, *The Institutes of the Lawes of England, In Four Parts*, 15th ed. (London, 1794), 3:199. For examples of

Another variety of regulation was involved in the granting of monopoly privileges. Contrary to a prejudiced belief that was widespread in eighteenth-century America and was not uncommon in England, many of the monopoly trading companies that were created under the Tudors and some of those created by the Stuarts were not restrictive; for rather than taking away anyone's property rights, they authorized particular companies of persons to conduct certain kinds of trade that had been previously forbidden to all. Thus they constituted a limited expansion of the rights of property. Nor did the granting of a corporate charter as

New England sumptuary legislation see the 1675 Massachusetts statutes in Morgan, *Puritan Political Ideas*, 226–233; Weeden, *Economic and Social History*, 1:106–107, 223–224, 226–227, 286; Bushman, *Puritan to Yankee*, 5–6, 26. The Fundamental Constitutions of East New Jersey (1683) mandated sumptuary laws, as did the Pennsylvania Concessions and Frame of Government, 1681 and 1682 (Thorpe, *Constitutions*, 5:2580, 3046, 3063). The Virginia Association of 1774, which was subsequently endorsed by the First Continental Congress, employed vigilante tactics to enforce sumptuary measures (see Edmund Cody Burnett, *The Continental Congress* [New York, 1941], 56–57).

There was a considerable sentiment in favor of sumptuary legislation throughout America, arising from Montesquieu's dictum that luxury was fatal to republics (*Spirit of the Laws*, bk. 7, chaps. 2 and 4). The cry against "luxury" can be seen in the "Proceedings of the People assembled at Annapolis, respecting the importation of British goods," 1769, and David Ramsay's "Oration," July 4, 1778, in Niles, *Principles and Acts*, 255, 375; in the *Virginia Gazette*, May 21, 1785; in the *Boston Gazette*, Apr. 18, May 9, 1785; in the letters of James Warren, in Gardiner, *Study in Dissent*, 129, 134, 182; in Jefferson to John Page, to James Madison, to James Monroe, in *The Papers of Thomas Jefferson*, ed. Julian P. Boyd et al., multiple vols. (Princeton, N.J., 1950–), 9:445–446, 8:40, 10:612. As John Adams remarked, "The very mention of sumptuary laws will excite a smile . . . but the happiness of the people might be greatly promoted by them," in *The Works of John Adams*, ed. Charles Francis Adams, 10 vols. (Boston, 1850–1856), 4:189–202; see also his desire to banish certain luxury items as expressed in his letter to Abigail, June 3, 1778, in *Familiar Letters of John Adams and his wife Abigail Adams, during the Revolution*, ed. Charles Francis Adams (Boston, 1875), 334.

For a resolution of the Continental Congress against theater, vice, idleness, and dissipation see the letters of Samuel Adams, Oct. 16, 17, 1778, in Burnett, *Letters*, 3:451–452. See also A Committee of Congress to the Several States (Nov. 11, 1778, ibid., 3:491–492) against the distilling of liquor; a Nov. 1780 proposal by Timothy Matlack for sumptuary legislation (ibid., 5:467); and Paton Yoder, "Tavern Regulation in Virginia: Rationale and Reality," *Virginia Magazine of History and Biography* 87 (1979): 259–278. For the continuing opposition to theater and other amusements see Burnett, *Letters*, 8:282; Joseph J. Ellis, *After the Revolution: Profiles of Early American Culture* (New York, 1979), 127–134; and Samuel Eliot Morison, *Harrison Gray Otis, 1765–1848: The Urbane Federalist* (Boston, 1969), 38–41, 53–54.

such limit the private property rights of unaffected individuals. On the other hand, to grant certain *exclusive* rights to the Bank of England, which was done on a large scale after the collapse of the South Sea Bubble, did infringe the property rights that individuals had previously enjoyed.[10] In colonial America the power to create monopolies was limited, of course, but it did exist and was regularly exercised with regard to such public utilities as mills, ferries, and bridges.

Much broader was regulation of the sort usually described under the general rubric of mercantilism—including a variety of bounties, drawbacks, protective or prohibitive duties, and regulations of quality and measure, together with the broad system of restrictions on imports and exports delineated by the Navigation Acts. Whatever the beneficent effects of such regulations upon the empire as a whole, all such restrictions limited the rights of property holders as individuals by depriving them of the full and free use of their possessions and labors. It is to be observed that while American colonial governments theoretically lacked this kind of power prior to 1776, since it was supposedly a parliamentary monopoly, in practice the colonies sometimes both regulated and taxed intercolonial trade. Furthermore, after independence the state legislatures enacted full-fledged mercantilistic systems, though sister states were exempted from restrictions against foreigners.[11]

[10] Vattel interprets the matter of monopolies and charters in just this way (*Law of Nations*, bk. 1, chap. 8, sec. 97, p. 42). Regarding the Bank of England, see chap. 4 below. For state constitutional prohibitions on monopolies see the Maryland Constitution of 1776, art. 39; the North Carolina Constitution of 1776, sec. 23; the Massachusetts Constitution of 1780 (Thorpe, *Constitutions*, 3:1690, 1890, 5:2788).

[11] The classic modern study of mercantilism remains that of Eli F. Heckscher, *Mercantilism*, 2d ed., 2 vols. (London and New York, 1962). The most thorough critique of mercantilism is, of course, Adam Smith's *The Wealth of Nations*. See also Oliver M. Dickerson, *The Navigation Acts and the American Revolution* (Philadelphia, 1951); George Louis Beer, *The Old Colonial System, 1660–1754*, 2 vols. (New York, 1912); and Lawrence A. Harper, *The English Navigation Laws: A Seventeenth-Century Experiment in Social Engineering* (New York, 1939). For examples of colonial regulation and taxation of intercolonial trade see Kammen, *New York*, 164; James, *Rhode Island*, 159; Weeden, *Economic and Social History*, 1:117–119, 187, 189, 261, 2:593–594. On state systems enacted between 1776 and 1789 see Forrest McDonald, *We the People: The Economic Origins of the Constitution* (Chicago, 1958), 409–411, which is derived from systematic study of all legislation enacted by all the states

One more form of regulation, inherent in the sovereign's disposition of parts of the public domain, was principally a matter of reserving. The reserving of property rights in the sovereign is not to be confused with such feudal conditions upon land grants as military or civil service; rather, it refers to reserved rights in things. In the common law, for instance, it was understood that, no matter how complete the grant of land and water to an individual, any swan found on the conveyed premises was royal property, as was any whale, except that its head belonged to the king and its tail to the queen. Similarly, though Vattel and other commentators on the law of nations maintained that the sovereign had power in its sole discretion to dispose of the public domain, there were always reservations or limitations even upon the sovereign, especially in regard to valuable minerals, since the property of a country belonged to the nation and was only held in trust by the sovereign. A complex system of reserved rights had long prevailed in regard to Cornwall, where copper, tin, and other minerals were abundant; and in colonial Virginia, North Carolina, and Pennsylvania, among other colonies, mineral rights had been divided among landholders, proprietors, and the Crown. Variations of such restrictions were carried over into the infant United States. In the land act of 1784 and in the Northwest Ordinance of 1787, Congress reserved to itself a one-third interest in all gold, silver, lead, and copper that might be found in or under lands that otherwise had been absolutely conveyed to individuals. In addition, one-thirty-sixth of all public lands was set aside for "public purposes" by the requirement that section sixteen of every township be reserved for purposes of public education.[12]

during that period. For comment upon state efforts see King, *Life of King,* 1:112-113, 115; Burnett, *Letters,* 4:516; 5:498; 8:189 n, 261, 262 n. The failure of state mercantile efforts led, in large measure, to the calling of the Convention of 1787 (see letters from Madison to Jefferson of Jan. 22, 1786, Mar. 18, 1786, in Boyd, *Papers of Jefferson,* 9:187-198, 334).

[12] Blackstone, *Commentaries,* 1:222, 290, 294-296; Vattel, *Law of Nations,* bk. 1, chap. 21, secs. 257-265, pp. 116-120; Thorpe, *Constitutions,* 5:2785, 3045, 7:3786, 3796. Rufus King wanted to include the reservation of salt to the national government in the land ordinances so as to prevent "the intolerable evil" of private salt monopolies (King, *Life of King,* 1:44).

As indicated, the restrictions imposed by regulation could sometimes amount to taking; a direct and outright form of taking was by forfeiture, which is to say as punishment for violating the law. More interesting than the intricate legal details surrounding the law of forfeiture was the theory on which it was based. Though English and Continental theorists had long maintained that property holding was an unalienable natural right that was morally and historically antecedent to government, this idea had undergone some important refinements in English law by the time of Blackstone. "The original of private property," Blackstone conceded, was "probably founded in nature," but he further declared that "certainly the modifications under which we at present find it, the method of conserving it in the present owner, and of transmitting it from man to man, are entirely derived from society." The right to property being therefore a civil right, conferred upon individuals in exchange for the natural freedom that a man sacrifices upon entering a political community, it was subject to forfeit if "a member of any national community violates the fundamental contract of his association, by transgressing the municipal law." In that event, "the state may very justly resume that portion of property, or any part of it, which the laws have before assigned him."[13]

English law governing forfeiture was blunt and harsh: broadly speaking, the real property of traitors and capital felons reverted to the Crown upon conviction and attainder, and the personal property reverted merely upon conviction. Attainder—by a court after conviction or by a parliamentary bill—was always accompanied by corruption of the blood. Since forfeiture was involved with sovereignty, it had only a limited and derivative applicability in the American colonies, but there remained the power of levying fines, which was a species of forfeiture. In some respects colonial law amounted to a relaxation and humanization of the severity of English law. For instance, Virginia

[13] Blackstone, *Commentaries*, 1:138, 299; see also 2:11 and the dissenting note by the editor. Vattel concurs, essentially, in the doctrine that private property is a civil right, not a natural right, though he is not unequivocal (*Law of Nations*, bk. 1, chap. 20, secs. 244–255, pp. 112–116).

substituted heavy fines for many of the offenses which in England were punishable by death; New Jersey effectively abolished corruption of the blood by permitting relatives of capital felons to redeem forfeited estates by paying a fee within two months of the execution; William Penn put a similar policy into effect in his colony, and also adopted the novel device of subjecting all land and goods of felons to seizure for compensating the wronged party in the amount of twice the damages.

On the other hand, during the eighteenth century, fines that amounted to total forfeiture were exacted of felons in all the American colonies, despite articles against excessive fines in Magna Carta, in the statute of 1 Westminster, c. 30, and in the 1689 English Bill of Rights. Too, in New England, fines ranging from a few shillings to virtual confiscation were still levied as punishment for a wide variety of proscribed social activities, including failure to attend church, being absent from court, entertaining strangers or even known guests without permission of the selectmen, overpaying workers, possessing playing cards, playing shuffleboard, or scolding a husband. Moreover, when the colonies became independent, they not only acquired the sovereign power to confiscate and declare forfeit; they also, as will be seen, revived a number of the harsher forms of the power, long since obsolete in England, and exercised them with a vengeance.[14]

[14]Blackstone, *Commentaries*, 1:300–302, 2:251ff., 267–286, 420–421, 4:378–388; Philip A. Bruce, *Institutional History of Virginia in the Seventeenth Century . . .* , 2 vols. (New York, 1910), 1:619–620; Thorpe, *Constitutions*, 5:2581, 3061–3062; Weeden, *Economic and Social History*, 1:73, 78, 80, 83, 104, 223, 225, 229, 2:549; Rutland, *Bill of Rights*, 6, 9; William E. Nelson, *Americanization of the Common Law: The Impact of Legal Change upon Massachusetts Society, 1760–1830* (Cambridge, Mass., 1975), 6, 36–47. For specific enunciations of the transfer of this sovereign power see the Constitution of Virginia, 1776, and the Pennsylvania Constitution of 1776, sec. 33 (Thorpe, *Constitutions*, 7:3818, 5:3089). In English law, *fine* was used in the sense employed here but also in quite another, referring to a legal action taken in regard to assurance of property by matter of record (see Blackstone, *Commentaries*, 2:348–357). It is ironic that while the newborn American states were indulging themselves in an orgy of confiscations, several were adopting declarations of rights or constitutions that prohibited excessive fines; these were Georgia, Maryland, Massachusetts, New Hampshire, North Carolina, Pennsylvania, and Virginia (Thorpe, *Constitutions*, 2:785, 3:1688, 1892, 4:2457, 5:2788, 3089, 7:3813).

A second direct form of taking was through the power of eminent domain. This power was claimed and exercised primarily for the building of public roads and secondarily for the erection of public buildings. The principle underlying it, in the words of Chancellor James Kent, is that it is better "that a private mischief is to be endured than a public inconvenience. On this ground rests the rights of public necessity." But this form of taking was restricted in the common law. It could be exercised only for bona-fide public purposes (hence government could not take property from one private party and give it to another private party), it could be exercised only in accordance with the law of the land, and it must be accompanied with just compensation. Moreover, under both English and American law, when land was taken for the purpose of building a highway, what was legally conveyed to the public was merely an easement, not the actual title; the owner retained all rights in the property, subject to the easement, including his rights to minerals beneath the surface. And in England it was not until the 1770s that property could be taken under eminent domain without a special act of Parliament; by the highway act of 13 George III, c. 78, property could be taken by the action of two justices, provided that reasonable compensation (with appeal to jury trial in the event of disagreement) be paid the owner.[15]

American legislatures had been less squeamish about invading private property rights. They began quite early to delegate eminent domain to local officials or units of government; for instance, in the road act of 1639, Massachusetts authorized towns to appoint juries to lay out the town roads, and other New England colonies generally followed that pattern. During the seventeenth century the Yankees, through a curious means, also avoided paying compensation. They provided that the owner of land over which a road passed not only retained title to the land but also retained the right to fence and erect gates across it;

15 Kent, *Commentaries*, 2:338–340; Blackstone, *Commentaries*, 1:138–139; Vattel, *Law of Nations*, bk. 1, chap. 20, secs. 244–246, pp. 112–113.

since the roads were thus not truly roads but only public rights of way, the legal position was that nothing had been taken from the owners and thus no compensation need be forthcoming. As a result, the network of roads that criss-crossed New England by 1700 was a maze in a wilderness—often only local residents could find the roads, although the owners were legally required to keep them clear of brush and obstructions, and town residents were required to labor on the roads for a certain number of days each year. Then, at the turn of the century, a royal decree required Massachusetts, Rhode Island, and Connecticut to maintain highways suitable for postal service between Boston and New York. To clear the through routes, the affected colonies narrowed existing roads and then gave to the adjacent landowners the land obtained from the narrowing as "compensation" for the land taken for highway use. In other words, New England colonial governments compensated landowners for taking part of their land by letting them keep the remainder of their land.[16]

In the South, the nature of road building was such that neither eminent domain nor compensation was especially relevant. Below the fall line in Virginia and South Carolina the main avenues of transportation and communication were rivers, and planters normally built private access roads to the rivers on their own plantations. Above the fall line, roads simply evolved, mainly through the wearing of Indian trails into larger trails by hog and cattle drives. The southern colonies did enact a great deal of legislation for the laying out of roads—Virginia passed such laws in 1632, 1658, 1662, and 1667—but almost nothing resulted. In one respect, Virginia was different from the rest: Anglican vestrymen there were required to see to it that bridle paths were clear enough to provide passage to the parish church, and they were empowered to (and did) seek redress in the county courts when planters obstructed those paths. Be-

[16] Weeden, *Economic and Social History*, 1:113–114, 206–211, 310–312, 408–410; James, *Rhode Island*, 165–167; Bushman, *Puritan to Yankee*, 33, 61–64. The actual nature of the bogus compensation in New England is inferred and pieced together from data supplied by Weeden and James, but it is not stated explicitly by them.

cause these and virtually all other public roads in the South ran along Indian trails, over which every person had the right of passage from immemorial usage, the question of taking did not arise. The only exception was in North Carolina. By a road act of 1764, twelve-man juries were appointed to lay out roads, ''as little as may be to the Prejudice of any Private Person or Persons inclosed Ground''; any damages done to private property were to be ascertained by the jury and paid to the landowner.[17]

In the Middle Colonies, eminent domain and just compensation were largely irrelevant concepts at first because roads were laid out by colonial proprietors over proprietary land. During the eighteenth century some fairly good roads were built in the area, especially in and around Philadelphia and New York; but almost all were built upon old Indian trails and drovers' trails, and only in New York did the principle of compensation become established.[18]

The form of taking that affected the widest spectrum of the population was taxation. In much of Europe, taxation was scarcely distinguishable from extortion by force: the crowns took because they had the power to take, the only limits being the ability (and ultimately the willingness) of subjects to pay. In England and in the colonies the situation was different. Though the Crown had revenues arising from the income on royal property and had, from immemorial usage, other revenues that amounted to taxation,

[17] Gray, *Southern Agriculture*, 1:129, 2:586; Bruce, *Institutional History of Virginia*, 1:114–115; Matthew P. Andrews, *Virginia: The Old Dominion* (Richmond, Va., 1949), 408–410; *The State Records of North Carolina*, vol. 23: *Laws, 1715–1776*, ed. Walter Clark (Goldsboro, N.C., 1904), 608; Hugh Talmage Lefler and Albert Ray Newsome, *North Carolina: The History of a Southern State* (Chapel Hill, N.C., 1963), 88–89, 95–97. In the Fundamental Constitutions of Carolina, 1669, the high steward's court was empowered to set out and improve roads, but compensation for damage to landowners was to be provided in ''such ways as the grand council shall appoint'' (Thorpe, *Constitutions*, 5:2778).

[18] Thorpe, *Constitutions*, 5:3049, 3056; Paul A. W. Wallace, *Pennsylvania: Seed of a Nation* (New York, 1962), 164–166; Wayland F. Dunaway, *A History of Pennsylvania* (New York, 1935), 292–295; Kammen, *New York*, 95, 152–153, 296–297; Kent, *Commentaries*, 2:338–340; *Laws of New York*, 1:514–515.

the greatest portion of the royal revenues came nominally in the form of *voluntary gifts or grants from the people to the sovereign.* This is to say, the people, through their representatives in the House of Commons, voted to assess themselves sums which they paid into the royal treasury. Moreover, since the late seventeenth century the Commons had determined how the Crown should spend the sums so granted. In each of the American colonies the same scheme prevailed, in miniature, with only insignificant variations: the lower house of assembly determined the amount and kind of this taxation in the form of a gift, and the sums thus raised were paid into the treasury of the royal, proprietary, or elected governor.[19]

Theoretically, then, in the English-speaking world taxation was a species, not of taking, but of voluntary giving. Whether the theory measured up to reality depended upon the meaning of two key terms: "the people" and "their representatives." Neither in England nor in America was it understood that "the people," for purposes of representation, included the entirety of the general population. Rather, "the people" included only those adult males who possessed certain amounts and kinds of property. The property qualifications for electors in England's boroughs varied; in its shires the requirement was a freehold estate the annual income from which was forty shillings—that being the amount, when the statute was passed in 1430, that would "furnish all the necessaries of life, and render

---

[19]Coke, *Institutes*, 2:528, 4:28; John Dickinson, "Letters from a Farmer in Pennsylvania," in *Empire and Nation*, ed. Forrest McDonald (Englewood Cliffs, N.J., 1962), letter 4, p. 21; Blackstone, *Commentaries*, 1:169–170. Since 1407 the Commons had had the sole right of initiating money bills; the Lords could only approve or disapprove. Sometimes the Lords attempted to assert a power to amend revenue measures, but they never succeeded (see Forrest McDonald and Michael Mendle, "The Historical Roots of the Originating Clause of the United States Constitution: Article I, Section 7," *Modern Age* 27 [1983]: 274–281). For provisions requiring initiation in the lower house and defining the role of the upper see the Massachusetts Constitution of 1780, pt. 2, art. 7; Delaware Constitution of 1776, art. 6; Maryland Constitution of 1776, body proper, arts. 10 and 22; New Hampshire Constitution of 1784, pt. 2; South Carolina Constitution of 1778, art. 16; Virginia Constitution of 1776 (Thorpe, *Constitutions*, 1:563, 3:1692, 1694, 1899, 4:2462, 6:3252, 7:3816).

the freeholder, if he pleased, an independent man." To be elected by such freeholders as a member of the House of Commons from the shires, a man had to have a clear estate of freehold or copyhold with an annual value of six hundred pounds; to represent the boroughs, an estate worth three hundred pounds per annum was sufficient. As to America, in New York and New England the requirement for voting for members of a colonial assembly was a freehold with a total value of £50 (or an annual income of 40 to 50 shillings, which was reckoned as about the same thing); in the colonies from Pennsylvania southward the requirement was a fifty-acre freehold, except in Virginia, where one hundred acres of unsettled land or twenty-five acres of improved land was required.[20]

Various theories were offered to justify property requirements for voters and their representatives. One was that of "the stake in society": only those with a property stake in the nation had the responsibility and permanence necessary for participation in its councils. The "true reason," however, according to Blackstone, was "to exclude such persons as are in so mean a situation that they are esteemed to have no will of their own"; were the propertyless to obtain the franchise, he pointed out, the artful or wealthy would gain a disproportionate share of influence. Additional reasons were that property owners wished to have control over the granting of their property in the form of taxes and that they feared the prospect of "leveling" legislation.[21]

To the extent that taxation and representation did reflect the will of those persons who bore the principal burden of

[20] Statutes of England, 8 Henry VI, c. 7, and 10 Henry VI, c. 2; J. R. Pole, *Political Representation in England and the Origins of the American Republic* (New York, 1966), 397–398; Blackstone, *Commentaries*, 1:172–173, 176; Chilton Williamson, *American Suffrage: From Property to Democracy, 1760–1860* (Princeton, N.J., 1960), 12–15.

[21] Pole, *Political Representation*, 25, 31; John Locke, *Second Treatise on Civil Government*, passim; Blackstone, *Commentaries*, 1:171. See the Virginia Bill of Rights, June 12, 1776, art. 6. See also the Address to the Convention, Massachusetts, 1780, in *The Popular Sources of Political Authority: Documents on the Massachusetts Constitution of 1780*, ed. Oscar Handlin and Mary Handlin (Cambridge, Mass., 1966), 437.

paying taxes, the English and American systems were, in truth, a matter of voluntary giving. But there were some catches in the system even in its purest form. When deciding whether to give away one's own property or somebody else's, humankind—being imperfect—has a disposition to give away somebody else's. Hence, for several centuries, the landed gentry in the House of Commons elected to have as much of the tax burden as possible fall either upon their tenants or upon gentlemen of trade. When the latter gained influence and power proportionate to their wealth, this trend was altered; but the cost of government rose astronomically during the eighteenth century, and country and city gentlemen tended to meet these costs by multiplying the kinds and amounts of taxes upon consumer necessities. They volunteered as many of the "gifts" as possible from the unrepresented poor.[22]

An opposite tendency prevailed in America. Because of the easy availability of land, quite a large proportion of the free adult male population—as high as eighty percent in some colonies—met the landed-property qualifications for voting. At the same time, the costs of government were extremely low except during wars, and the colonists habitually met the costs of war by resorting to a species of fraud: they issued unsecured bills of credit which rapidly depreciated. In these circumstances the American colonists developed an aversion to taxation for which they were to become celebrated. What was less celebrated, they tended to place the main burden of taxation, insofar as was possible, on merchants and on the well-to-do. The euphemism for this practice was requiring the most taxes from those who were best able to pay; again the reality was requiring somebody else to make the gift.[23]

[22] Blackstone, *Commentaries*, 1:307–333, 2:384–385; Pole, *Political Representation*, 456, 466, 478.

[23] Williamson, *American Suffrage*, passim; Pole, *Political Representation*, app. 2; Robert E. Brown, *Middle-Class Democracy and the Revolution in Massachusetts, 1691–1780* (Ithaca, N.Y., 1955); Robert E. Brown and B. Katherine Brown, *Virginia, 1705–1786: Democracy or Aristocracy?* (East Lansing, Mich., 1964). The observation regarding the placing of the tax load is based upon study of the legislation of each of the colonies/states during the eighteenth century. But see also Robert A. Becker, *Revolution, Reform, and the Politics of American Taxation, 1763–1783* (Baton Rouge, La., 1980).

The question of the representative nature of the gift is of crucial importance: after all, it was the pivotal point in bringing about the American Revolution, and was subsequently incorporated into every constitution in the United States. Americans responded to the Stamp Act by adopting, through the Stamp Act Congress, a series of resolutions of protest. Resolutions three through five enunciated the principle of "no taxation without representation," insisted that the colonies were not and could not be represented in Parliament, and contended that only the colonial legislatures could tax the colonists. The sixth resolution declared, "That ALL *supplies to the crown*, being free gifts of the people, it is *unreasonable, and inconsistent with the principles and spirit of the* British *Constitution*, for the people of *Great Britain* to grant to his Majesty *the property of the colonies*."[24] In 1767, in the most widely read tract of the Revolutionary period prior to Thomas Paine's *Common Sense* (1776), the Philadelphia lawyer John Dickinson (who would be an influential member of the Constitutional Convention) put the case clearly. Citing Coke's *Institutes*, Dickinson traced the evolution of "gifts and grants of their own property . . . made by the people [to the sovereign], under the several names of aids, tallages, tasks, taxes and subsidies, etc. . . . But whatever the name was, they were always considered as *gifts of the people to the crown, to be employed for public uses*."[25]

---

[24]Oct. 19, 1765, as quoted in McDonald, *Empire and Nation*, 23. See also "Petition to the House of Commons," in *The Revolution in America, 1754–1788*, ed. J. R. Pole (Stanford, Calif., 1970), 10–11; The Virginia Stamp Act Resolutions, May 30, 1765, in *Journals of the House of Burgesses of Virginia* (1761–1765), 360; Instructions of the Town of Braintree, Mass., on the Stamp Act, Oct. 14, 1765, in Adams, *Works of Adams*, 3:465ff.; James Lovell, "Oration," Apr. 2, 1771, in Niles, *Principles and Acts*, 18–19; Joseph Warren, "Oration," Mar. 5, 1772, ibid., 21, 26; Association of the Sons of Liberty, Dec. 15, 1773, ibid., 169; Citizens of Philadelphia in opposition to the importation of tea, Jan. 3, 1774, ibid., 201. Many colonial orators used the phraseology of William Pitt from his speech on the Declaratory Bill, *Bristol* (England) *Gazette*, Mar. 24, 1774: "'Taxation and representation are inseparable: this position is founded on the laws of nature; it is itself an eternal law of nature; for whatever is a man's own, is absolutely his own; . . . Taxation and representation are coeval with, and essential to, this constitution."

[25]Dickinson, "Letters from a Farmer in Pennsylvania," in McDonald, *Empire and Nation*, 21–23. For the practical immediacy of this principle on the state/colony level see, for example, the Essex County Convention Memorial, Apr. 25, 26, 1776,

Limitations upon the property holder's "sole and despotic dominion" imposed by government were not the only ones; there were also rights reserved to the public in its capacity as an aggregate of private individuals rather than in its corporate capacity. Among the reserved public rights of this description, the most important were grazing, wood gathering, hunting, passage, and the use of water. None of these rights was static: the tension between public and private property rights was continuous, ever subject to a gradual drift in favor of one at the expense of the other. Moreover, the drift could be simultaneously in different directions. For instance, in eighteenth-century England, private rights of property were on the increase in regard to grazing but on the decline in regard to the rights of passage.

The right of grazing, or of pasturage and pannage, offers abundant illustration of the complexity and the variations inherent in the subject. In England, before the enclosure movement—which unfolded in different places at different times—every subject (cottagers and servants partially excepted) had common grazing rights upon the "waste" lands of the manor of his residence, which nominally included only the woodlands and meadows but in practice extended to all lands not under cultivation. Grazing rights, however, were of two kinds, and these varied with the tenures of the owners of the animals. One kind, the right of common *appendant*, pertained only to holders of arable land; it permitted the owner to graze "commonable beasts upon the lord's waste, and upon the lands of other persons within the same manor," in proportion to his landholding. Commonable beasts were plow animals or those that manure the ground, such as horses, oxen, and cattle. The other kind, the right of common *appurtenant*, was a general right extending even to base or servile persons; it permitted owners of hogs, goats, and other noncommonable beasts to graze their stock on the lands of the manor.[26]

in Handlin and Handlin, *Documents on the Massachusetts Constitution*, 73–75, and its incorporation in the Massachusetts Constitution of 1780, arts. 10 and 23.

[26] Blackstone, *Commentaries*, 2:32–33. See also *The Agrarian History of England and Wales*, vol. 4, *1500–1640*, ed. Joan Thirsk (Cambridge, Eng., 1967); and J. A.

In America, common grazing rights followed two distinct patterns, each of which was a departure from the
English model. In New England and in much of New York
and New Jersey, common grazing was established at the
outset of settlement. The variation from the English system
was that during the crop-growing season, common pasture
was set off from other land and was fenced, and grazing
was supervised by herdsmen, employed by the towns; but
after fall harvest and until spring planting, animals roamed
at large on anyone's lands, in a form of open range. This
system had fallen into disuse in New England by the early
eighteenth century, and by the end of the century, common
grazing rights had virtually disappeared in New York and
New Jersey as well.[27]

But while private rights were thus gaining at the expense of public rights in the North, the opposite was the
trend in the southern colonies throughout the eighteenth
century and beyond. Partly because of the high ratio of
empty land to people in the area and partly because a large
proportion of the inhabitants originated in the western and
northern uplands of England and in the Celtic portions of
the British Isles, where open-range herding remained widespread until well into the eighteenth century, an open-
range system prevailed in the South from the early seventeenth century until the twentieth. The spirit of the system
of common pasturage, universally available to non-
landholders and landholders alike, was contained in the
Virginia fencing act of 1632, which provided that "every

Yelling, "Agriculture, 1500–1730," in *An Historical Geography of England and Wales,*
ed. R. A. Dodgshon and R. A. Butlin (London and New York, 1978), 151–172.

[27] Weeden, *Economic and Social History,* 1:58–67, 275–278, 404–405; Bidwell and
Falconer, *Northern Agriculture,* 21–25, 55–58; Kent, *Commentaries,* 3:403–408; David
Grayson Allen, *In English Ways: The Movement of Societies and the Transferal of
English Local Law and Custom to Massachusetts Bay in the Seventeenth Century* (Chapel
Hill, N.C., 1981), 46–47, 49–50. Hogs were partially an exception to the rule, for
they were difficult to keep penned, and despite the law, many farmers allowed
their swine to run free in the woods until they were brought in for fattening
preparatory to slaughter (see Bidwell and Falconer, *Northern Agriculture,* chap. 3).
The animals could be a nuisance, and many towns appointed "hogreeves" to
impound stray swine, but their efforts were often futile (see the Microfilm
Collection of Early Town Records, New Hampshire State Library, Concord).

man shall enclose his ground with sufficient fences or else to plant, uppon theire owne perill.'' Moreover, the fencing of any land except arable acreage actually under cultivation was prohibited by law in all southern colonies, and so accustomed were nonlandholding cattle and hog raisers to grazing their animals upon the lands of others that landowners who did build fences often found them burned to the ground. North Carolina attempted, by acts of 1715, 1729, and 1775, to restrict and regulate common grazing rights, but the laws were unenforceable. As late as the 1830s, planters in Virginia were still trying in vain to obtain legislation to permit the fencing of whole estates or even the pastures on their own land. And lest it be thought that the right of common pasturage and pannage was merely a nuisance and not a serious encroachment upon the property rights of landholders, one may consider this fact: among tobacco planters who attempted to protect their crops against the beasts of others, ''fencing costs alone required from one third to one half the income from landed property.''[28]

The common public right of wood gathering, or *estover*, was likewise general both in England in the American colonies. Every inhabitant of an area had the right to fell dead trees and to dig peat for building or heating dwellings for himself and his animals, and no landholder could prohibit outsiders from using his woodlands for those purposes. Indeed, in the South the right extended to the gathering of fruit. Several exceptions to *estover* rights in America should be noted, however. One was that in seventeenth-century New England, the towns adopted stringent restrictions on the cutting of live wood and prohibited its export, lest the supply be depleted through

[28] Gray, *Southern Agriculture*, 1:138–151, 2:843. For details on Southern grazing laws and practices see Forrest McDonald and Grady McWhiney, ''The Antebellum Southern Herdsman: A Reinterpretation,'' *Journal of Southern History* 41 (1975): 147–166, and ''The South from Self-Sufficiency to Peonage: An Interpretation,'' *American Historical Review* 85 (1980): 1105–1111; and J. Crawford King, ''The Closing of the Southern Range: An Exploratory Study,'' *Journal of Southern History* 48 (1982): 53–70. See also Terry G. Jordan, *Trails to Texas* (Lincoln, Nebr., 1981), 1–58.

wanton destruction. Another was that the eighteenth century witnessed the rise of a lumber and naval-stores industry and, with it, the development of exclusive rights of
felling and processing commercial timber on private lands.
Moreover, landowners in the Middle Colonies who developed a primitive iron industry came to enjoy exclusive
rights to the firewood on their property, though in Pennsylvania it was legally required that one-fifth of the woodland
remain uncut. On the other hand, certain kinds of trees
ceased to be susceptible to private ownership under any
circumstances; these came to be vested instead in "the
public" in its corporate capacity. The massive white pines
of upper New England were reserved in the eighteenth
century for the use of the royal navy. Agents of His
Majesty's Navy went through New Hampshire and Maine
and marked with the royal arrow all trees suitable for
masts, thus contributing to the strength of the maritime
forces of the British Empire but simultaneously undermin-
ing the loyalty of many landowning subjects. The principle
of reserving certain trees for public benefit, however, was
retained in the new United States: under acts of Congress,
beginning on March 1, 1817, the cutting of live oaks and red
cedars was prohibited by law, on the ground that they were
especially adaptable for ships' timbers. These trees were
therefore not subject to private ownership, being inherently
the property of the United States.[29]

Then there were hunting rights. According to eighteenth-century notions of natural law, wild animals that
were not subject to domestication, *ferae naturae*, were the
common possession of all, and hunting rights were thought
to have been universal in England before the Norman
Conquest. Since then, however, English law had evolved
toward depriving the general public of hunting rights and
placing them with the Crown, the nobility, and other

[29]Blackstone, *Commentaries*, 2:35; Gray, *Southern Agriculture*, 1:151–160; Kent,
Commentaries, 3:406–408; Weeden, *Economic and Social History*, 1:62–64 and passim;
James E. Defebaugh, *History of the Lumber Industry of America*, 2 vols. (Chicago,
1906, 1907), 2:138 and passim; Thorpe, *Constitutions*, 3:1886, 5:3046; John Ferdinand Dalziel Smyth, *A Tour in the United States of America*, 2 vols. (New York, 1968;
reprint of 1784 ed.), 1:69.

favored persons. Even Blackstone, who was willing to rationalize every quirk of English law, found it difficult to disguise his disapproval of this trend. In America, for the most part, nothing of the sort developed. Partly because of the abundance of game, partly because of the presence of such dangerous predators as bears and wolves—the killing of which was rewarded by bounties—the right to hunt on anyone's lands became such a well-established custom that no amount of legislation could have altered it. There was one notable exception: the colonies made repeated efforts to regulate the trapping and sale of valuable fur-bearing animals, especially beaver. While such restrictions sometimes created property rights in individuals, however, they did nothing to enhance the rights of landholders on whose property the animals might be found.[30]

Each of the three sets of public rights considered so far was theoretically limited by the law of trespass: if a stranger could not show that he had a legal right to be on the grounds of another, he had no rights of grazing, estover, and hunting. In practice, however, the laws of trespass, though designed to protect the individual landowner, contained so many exceptions as to be inconsequential except in regard to lands or buildings actively in use for agricultural or residential purposes. The right of passage was explicitly recognized in the theory of natural law, and it was a well-established principle in English law that the ownership or right to use a particular area of land implicitly carried with it a right of passage or way across such other lands as were necessary for access. Rights of way were

[30] Blackstone, *Commentaries*, 2:38–39, 415ff.; Weeden, *Economic and Social History*, 1:96, 102, 130–131, 136, 140, 277, 2:652, 880; Gray, *Southern Agriculture*, 1:202, 339–340, 441; Philip Alexander Bruce, *Social Life of Virginia in the Seventeenth Centu.*? (Williamstown, Mass., 1968), 211–217. The Massachusetts Body of Liberties guaranteed fowling as well as fishing rights, as did the 1683 Frame of Government of Pennsylvania; sec. 43 of the Pennsylvania Constitution of 1776 explicitly guaranteed hunting and fishing rights to all citizens, and this guarantee also appeared in sec. 39 of the proposed Vermont Constitution of 1777 (Thorpe, *Constitutions*, 5:3068, 6:3748; Morgan, *Puritan Political Ideas*, 182; and Theodore Thayer, *Pennsylvania Politics and the Growth of Democracy, 1740–1776* [Harrisburg, Pa., 1953], 225). Nelson, *Americanization of the Common Law*, 38, cites instances of prosecution "for killing the king's deer" in Massachusetts.

normally confined to designated and commonly used paths, but over the years such paths and roads had tended to proliferate; for if people made and used new pathways long enough, even without the consent of the landlord, the usage itself sanctified the right. For instance, cattle and hog thieves from the Scottish Highlands and Borders drove stolen animals along essentially the same routes through parts of England and Scotland for several centuries, and in time those trails were worn into public roads. In America the law was approximately the same as in England, except that rights of way were even more common; Indian trails automatically became public "roads," and colonial legislatures and town governments were lenient in allowing new rights of way. For example, in Connecticut and Rhode Island any owner of livestock had a right of way across the lands of others to harvest seaweed from Long Island Sound and Narragansett Bay, even if there were no common trail. In the South, the open range made a mockery of the very idea of trespass, for the herder could go wherever his animals went.[31]

A fifth category of limitations upon the private rights of property owners concerned the laws of water use. Theoretically the law of riparian rights was relatively simple. Under English common law, private title to land along navigable waters—which were defined as waters affected by the ebb and flow of the tides—extended to the high-water mark, and land below that mark belonged to the Crown. Navigable waterways were public highways and also public fisheries; the public had the right to use not only the water but also the banks, both for draft animals to pull barges or other craft and for drying, curing, or cleaning fish. Nonnavigable streams were quite another matter: the right to use them belonged exclusively to the owner of the land through which they flowed, and the owner could do

---

[31] Vattel, *Law of Nations*, bk. 1, chap. 9, sec. 104, p. 44; Blackstone, *Commentaries*, 2:35–36; Kent, *Commentaries*, 3:418–427; McDonald and McWhiney, "Antebellum Southern Herdsman," and the sources cited therein; Gray, *Southern Agriculture*, 1:129; Weeden, *Economic and Social History*, passim; Archibald R. B. Haldane, *The Drove Roads of Scotland* (London, 1952).

anything he pleased with the water so long as he did not interfere with the equal rights of landowners further downstream.[32]

In America, the law of riparian rights became more complicated than it was in England. For one thing, the common law of riparian rights was adopted only in New York, New Jersey, Virginia, Maryland, and the four New England colonies. For another, important variations were forthcoming in New England. By fiat of nature, there were precious few navigable streams in New England, under the common-law definition: except in Maine, the New England seashore is located mainly on or near the fall line, and only the Housatonic, Connecticut, and Piscataqua rivers were affected by the tides further than a few miles inland. More significant was the evolution in New England of the law regulating the building of dams on private streams. Owners of such streams could build weirs or weir dams for the entrapment of fish only if they had a license from the colonial assembly, and the license carried with it a fixed price for the sale of the fish. Mill dams were licensed and regulated in the same manner, as were private bridges or ferries. Thus the principle of governmental regulation of rates and standards of service in "public utility" enterprises was established early in New England. The other five colonies did not adopt the common law in regard to riparian rights; rather, the tendency there was to broaden the definition of navigable waterways until it extended to all fresh-water streams that were potentially navigable. The result was a considerable extension of public rights at the expense of private rights.[33]

[32] Blackstone, *Commentaries*, 2:18, 34, 39, 3:218, 219; Vattel, *Law of Nations*, bk. 1, chap. 22, secs. 266-278, pp. 124-125; Kent, *Commentaries*, 3:427-428; Sir Matthew Hale, *A Treatise De Jure Maris* (London, 1787), chaps. 4, 5; Anonymous, "The Law of Water Privilege," *American Jurist and Law Magazine* 2 (1829): 25-38; Joseph K. Angell, *A Treatise on the Law of Watercourses* (Boston, 1854); Charles Molloy, *De Jure Maritimo et Navali* . . . (London, 1676). In 1779, when the long and complicated debate over fishing rights in international context began, Henry Laurens laid, as an underlying principle, that the inhabitants of the several states "had enjoyed such right from their earliest settlement" (in Burnett, *Letters*, 4:113).

[33] Kent, *Commentaries*, 3:427-432; Weeden, *Economic and Social History*, 1:102-103, 110, 134; Nelson, *Americanization of the Common Law*, 122, 160. The extension

A recitation of the rights reserved to the general public in the private property holdings of individuals could go on and on. One could consider, for instance, the doctrine of nuisance, which restricts the rights of individual property owners without conveying positive property rights either to the general public or to the government. Under this doctrine, owners of a stream could not pollute it so as to endanger wildlife or human life; householders could not erect fences or set out plants that would obstruct the view of neighbors; property owners could not burn, cook, or process anything that fouled the air; and so on.[34]

We have been concerned here principally with limitations upon the rights of real property or, more accurately, with restrictions upon corporeal herediments imposed by the existence of incorporeal herediments. In regard to real property, as indicated, American law was considerably more advanced—meaning less encumbered—than was English law. In regard to personal property, however, and particularly to commercial activity, English law was fully half a century more advanced than American law. That subject will be considered in a later chapter.

Americans' thinking about liberty, until the Revolution popularized alternative formulations, generally rested upon the same kinds of historical and legal foundations as their thinking about property. Liberty, like property, was not a right but a congeries of rights—liberties, not liberty—that were derived from civil society and ultimately from the

of public rights regarding waterways is illustrated by the experience of Pennsylvania. In that colony's 1681 Concessions, landholders were given sole and exclusive rights over rivers and other waterways that crossed their land, but the legislature subsequently whittled away at those rights; by an act of 1771, for instance, the Delaware and Lehigh rivers and parts of the Susquehanna and Juniata rivers were made public highways (Thorpe, *Constitutions*, 5:3045; Dunaway, *History of Pennsylvania*, 292–295). Similarly, the Northwest Ordinance of 1787 specified that "the navigable waters leading into the Mississippi and Saint Lawrence, . . . shall be common highways and forever free."

[34]Blackstone, *Commentaries*, 3:216–222.

sovereign. Common sense taught that man needed the
protection that the sovereign provided against one's fellow
man; history taught that man needed protection from the
sovereign as well. Liberties, in this sense, consisted in
limitations upon the powers of the sovereign and in a
sharing, enjoyed by freemen, in the exercise of those
powers.[35]

In England, liberties had been granted by the Crown
(usually under duress) to the Lords, the Commons, or the
Parliament, or had simply been declared by the Parliament
whether the Crown approved or not. Magna Carta is the
most obvious example of the extraction of liberties from the
Crown by force—though it is couched as a statement of
custom and principle—but the constitutional struggles of
the seventeenth century better illustrate the processes by
which English liberties were won. Clause 39 of Magna
Carta, for instance, had declared that "no freeman shall be
. . . arrested, or detained in prison, . . . unless by the
lawful judgment of his peers [and] by the law of the land."
The appropriate legal remedy in cases of arbitrary violations
of this clause was a writ of habeas corpus ad subjiciendum,
whereby the prisoner was ordered to be brought before a
judge, who could cause the prisoner to be released if he was
being unlawfully held. The writ had functional defects,
however, and was ineffectual against a determined mon-
arch. The matter surfaced as a major political issue upon the
accession of the Stuarts. In 1610 Sergeant Hedley delivered
a speech in Parliament brilliantly expounding the common-
law principle that the law was above the Crown, but that
scarcely stopped James I (1603–1625) from making arbitrary
arrests. Charles I (1625–1649) flagrantly violated clause 39,
and Parliament, in the 1628 Petition of Right, protested the
practice, but again to no lasting avail. A greatly strengthened habeas corpus procedure was enacted in 1641, but the

[35] Americans could derive their English constitutional history from a variety of
sources, but the most common were two: Hume's *History of England* and
Blackstone's *Commentaries*. Hume's *History* was unfashionable among ideologue
republicans because it failed to depict the Stuart monarchs as unmitigated
scoundrels and the Commonwealth Whigs as unalloyed men of virtue. For that
reason, Blackstone's version was the more generally accepted in America.

Long Parliament and the Protectorate subsequently employed arbitrary imprisonments on a larger scale than any
kings had done. Only upon the passage of the Habeas
Corpus Act of 1679—which Charles II was not strong
enough to prevent—did security against arbitrary detain-
ment become a reality.[36]

Some protections of English liberties were granted without duress. Prior to the reign of Mary I (1553–1558), for
example, persons accused of capital crimes were not allowed to have counsel, to testify in their own behalf, or to
have witnesses in their favor. Mary ("whose early sentiments, till her marriage with Philip of Spain, seem to have
been humane and generous") was appalled by this in-
justice, so she ordered her chief justice to admit witnesses
and counsel for the accused. This concession was partly
confirmed by parliamentary enactment during Elizabeth's
reign, but witnesses for defendants were not allowed to
testify under oath, which meant that their testimony had
less credence than that of witnesses for the Crown. Finally,
under Queen Anne (1702–1714), a statute was passed
allowing witnesses for the accused, in every case of treason
or felony, to be examined under oath, just as were witnesses against him.[37]

Other rights and liberties evolved in various ways. One
important set of protections for English liberties rested
upon shaky ground. Blackstone and others deplored what
the Romans called *privilegia*, or private law, such as ex post
facto laws or bills of attainder and bills of pains and
penalties; but the fact was that Parliament retained the
power to enact such "unreasonable" legislation. And yet,
however evolved and however solid or tenuous their
footing, a formidable array of liberties of the subject vis-à-
vis the sovereign had become established in England and
America by the late eighteenth century. In addition to those

---

[36] Blackstone, *Commentaries*, 3:130–137; Kent, *Commentaries*, 2:22–32. See also
William F. Duker, *A Constitutional History of Habeas Corpus* (Westport, Conn.,
1980), 12–63, 225. I am indebted to J. H. Hexter for some of the data in this
paragraph.
[37] Blackstone, *Commentaries*, 4:359–360.

mentioned, a check list of such liberties would include the rights to face one's accuser, to be secure against unwarranted searches and seizures, and to be exempt from being tried twice for the same offense.[38]

These civil and essentially passive rights were complemented by political or active rights in the form of grants to the people—or more properly, to freemen—of a measure of participation in government. That such participation was a concession from the sovereign is indicated by the legal terminology for the right to vote, the suffrage franchise. Suffrage derives from the medieval Latin *suffragium*, meaning support, assistance, intercessory prayer; franchise derives from the French *franchir*, meaning to set free; thus the sovereign grants his subjects the freedom to support, assist, or pray for him. But for some centuries before the Revolution of 1688 this "freedom" took the form of a contest for power in which the people, as embodied in the House of Commons, ultimately emerged triumphant. Moreover, though the revolutionary settlement inaugurated an era of government by Crown-in-Parliament, the tendency from that time on was for the powers of the Commons to swallow up those of the other two branches.

Thus the Bill of Rights that was enacted in 1689 and related acts that soon followed, though they guaranteed some individual rights such as freedom of petition and assembly, were aimed mainly at securing the rights of the House of Commons and secondarily at making the Commons more responsible to the electorate. The Bill of Rights confirmed free speech, frequent meetings of Parliament, and free elections (the Triennial Act of 1694 provided for parliamentary elections every three years). It also prohibited the keeping of standing armies without the approval of Parliament and confirmed Parliament's exclusive power to levy taxes. This last feature ensured the supremacy of the Commons, for it had long since been established that the Commons had the exclusive right to originate money bills, and the Lords would become virtually powerless to amend them.

[38] Ibid., 1:46, 3:369, 4:359, 440–442.

Having a voice, through representatives, in the law-making process was not the only right of Englishmen in regard to government, nor was it even the most important: the genuinely crucial right was that of trial by jury. For in the absence of bureaucratic administrative machinery, juries were the dispensers of justice, both civil and criminal. It was widely believed, though it was not historically true, that trial by jury had existed in Britain "time out of mind," as Blackstone put it, and that it was "certain . . . that they were in use among the earliest Saxon colonies." For a long period, however, juries were subordinate to judges, who had the power to punish and imprison jurors for handing down verdicts contrary to law or to the judges' reading of the evidence. The Bushell case, in 1670, effectively terminated that power, and for the better part of ninety years English juries ruled with impunity both as to law and as to fact. Then, after William Murray, the earl of Mansfield, became lord chief justice in 1756, the English courts began to employ an assortment of devices—special pleading, special verdicts, compulsory nonsuits, instructions in law and evidence to juries, and the setting aside of verdicts for improper procedures or decisions that were contrary to law or to the evidence—to curtail the powers of juries.[39]

In America such devices were largely unused or ineffective, and juries exercised all but absolute power on a case-by-case basis. In an everyday sense, juries were the government, and it was upon them that the safety of all rights to liberty and to property depended. *Juris dictio:* they spoke the law, finding its source in nature and in principles of natural justice and disregarding, if they saw fit to do so, the instructions of the judges as to what the law was and, for that matter, even the plain language of an act of Parliament or of a colonial or state legislative enactment. Moreover,

[39] Ibid., 3:349; Baker, *English Legal History,* 10–11, 88–91; *Bushell's Case,* Vaughan 135. In that landmark case, a jury had found a verdict of not guilty in a case involving William Penn, despite both the evidence and the law; Bushell, as foreman of the jury, was summarily jailed by the judge, whereupon he sued for and obtained his freedom. Some judges, notoriously Jeffreys, continued to deal with juries in a high-handed manner. Regarding Mansfield's innovations see chap. 4 below.

after 1776 Americans repeatedly denounced "the new-fangled doctrine of lord Mansfield," whose "habit of controuling juries does not accord with the free institutions of this country."[40]

But the coming of independence created tensions and contradictions among the rights that Americans claimed. As colonists, Americans had cherished both kinds of liberties, passive and active, and had claimed the right to them by virtue of being Englishmen as well as by direct grants from the Crown in their royal charters. Except in Connecticut and Rhode Island, where the governments continued to operate under royal charters, independence dissolved those claims. Where rights would come from thereafter was a knotty question, one that will be considered in later chapters; but for now it can be said that there was general agreement that sovereignty devolved in 1776 upon the people, in one capacity or another, and that grants of fundamental rights could thenceforth originate only in compacts among the people. That being so, the rationale for the institution of trial by jury was somewhat undermined. It was one thing for juries to disregard legislative enactments under the empire, for then they could plausibly assert that they did not merely represent the people but in fact were the people. It was quite another to do so afterward, for now the legislatures acted—or claimed to act— under authority of grants of power from majorities of the people in whole political societies. To the extent that those claims were legitimate, the case for the absolute authority of the juries was questionable.

Not only were American liberties now on uncertain ground; they also were less broad in scope than might

[40]Morton J. Horwitz, *The Transformation of American Law, 1780–1860* (Cambridge, Mass., 1977), 142, 316 n. 13; Nelson, *Americanization of the Common Law,* 22–30, and "The Eighteenth-Century Background of John Marshall's Constitutional Jurisprudence," *Michigan Law Review* 76 (1978): 904–917. See also Jefferson to Philip Mazzei, Nov. 28, 1785, in Boyd, *Papers of Jefferson,* 9:70–71. In Georgia, grand juries were permitted to and often did make presentments chastising the state legislature (Nathan Dane to Samuel Phillips, Jan. 20, 1786, in Burnett, *Letters,* 8:287 and n. 4).

appear from the resounding language in which they were proclaimed. Their conceptually limited nature is abundantly illustrated by the idea of freedom of conscience and of religion. As for the English heritage, Blackstone could write that the "religious liberties of the nation" were "established (we trust) on an eternal basis" simply by the accession of Elizabeth I in 1558. But Blackstone clearly meant the religious liberty of the country from papal domination, not religious liberty for individuals; and despite the Toleration Act of 1696 (which permitted all persons except Catholics, Jews, and Unitarians to worship as they pleased), severe restrictions remained even upon Protestants. For example, apostasy was a crime: any person who was educated in or who professed Christianity but subsequently renounced the faith was thereby rendered incapable of holding public office; for a second offense, he was denied most of his legal rights, including the right to own land, and was subject to three years of imprisonment. As for the colonies, all except Rhode Island—which provided complete religious freedom for all Christians and toleration for others—imposed limitations upon various sects; no colony gave full rights to Catholics or Jews; and most colonies had tax-supported denominational establishments. Penalties for dissenters, apostates, blasphemers, and idolators were numerous and severe.[41]

Some of the state constitutions adopted during the Revolution relaxed religious restraints, but so habituated were Americans to thinking in Protestant terms that few could conceive of a civil order in any other way. For example, Pennsylvania, which had been one of the more liberal colonies in matters of religion, nonetheless restricted civil rights to people "who acknowledge the being of a God" and required that officeholders take an oath declaring belief in the divine inspiration of the whole of the Bible. Maryland, though it partially disestablished the Anglican Church and readmitted Catholics to political rights, nonetheless required oaths of belief in the Holy Trinity as

[41] Blackstone, *Commentaries*, 4:43–44, 432; Joseph Story, *Commentaries on the Constitution of the United States*, 3 vols. (New York, 1970), 1:84–85.

prerequisites for both voting and officeholding. Most revealing of habits of mind was the Virginia Declaration of
Rights. After declaring that "all men are equally entitled to
the free exercise of religion, according to the dictates of
conscience," article 16 of the document went on to say
"that it is the mutual duty of all to practice Christian
forbearance, love, and charity towards each other." And
five states (New Hampshire, Massachusetts, Connecticut,
South Carolina, and, partially, Maryland) continued to
have tax-supported established churches.[42]

Indeed, during the postwar period two states that had
previously liberalized their religious laws experienced
movements based on a belief that liberalization had been
carried too far. One of these movements appears to have
originated at least in part as a cover for fraud. Samuel
Chase, Luther Martin, and other political operators in
Maryland had speculated deeply in confiscated Loyalist
property; and with the connivance of the intendant of the
revenues, Daniel of St. Thomas Jenifer, they acquired the
property at prices far below its value. Proving unable to
meet his installment payments, Chase took on a prospec-
tively lucrative commission to prosecute the claims of the

---

[42] Sanford H. Cobb, in *The Rise of Religious Liberty in America: A History* (New
York, 1902), 499–507, summarizes the constitutional and statutory provisions
concerning religion during the Revolutionary period. Maryland's 1776 Bill of
Rights provided that no one could be compelled to attend or support any
particular form of worship, but it also authorized taxation to support the Christian
religion.

In their efforts to encourage religion and religious teaching, several states
effectively provided for the separation of church and state. In South Carolina, for
example, ministers of the gospel were excluded from holding public office during
their ministry and "for two years after," so as "not to be diverted from the great
duties of their function" (Thorpe, *Constitutions*, 6:3253). Similar provisions were
made in the Delaware Constitution of 1776, the Georgia Constitution of 1777, the
New York Constitution of 1777, and the North Carolina Constitution of 1776
(ibid., 1:567, 2:785, 5:2637, 2793).

In the 1790s, several of the new state constitutions liberalized religious
qualifications for officeholding. In the Pennsylvania Constitution of 1790, art. 9,
sec. 4, a new section implicitly allowed Jews political rights (ibid., 5:3100). But the
phraseology was such as to exclude atheists, pantheists, and animists: the
religious doctrines of the French Enlightenment had little effect upon American
constitution making. For the perdurance of such features see the Maryland
Constitution of 1851 (ibid., 3:1715).

heir to an estate that had been confiscated. To do so would require discharging the anti-Tory atmosphere, which Chase and his friends had previously stirred up. The means they chose was to charge the air with a new emotional issue. At Chase's instigation, the House of Delegates resolved to have printed, for public discussion, a bill levying taxes for the support of the Christian religion. It accomplished its purpose: in 1785 more space in newspapers and pamphlets was devoted to argument about this issue than had been given to any subject in Maryland's history. The bill never became law, but it had generated a great deal of support.[43]

The other movement was more sober in its origins. The Virginia Declaration of Rights had effectively disestablished the Anglican Church, though Baptists and other dissenters were not thereby accorded full rights. Whether because of disestablishment, the war, or other reasons, the 1780s witnessed a decline in religiosity in Virginia; and a number of the state's political leaders, otherwise ardent in their defense of liberty, became alarmed. As Richard Henry Lee wrote to James Madison, "Refiners may weave as fine a web of reason as they please, but the experience of all times shows Religion to be the guardian of morals." Accordingly, at the urging of Patrick Henry, a bill was introduced in 1784 to incorporate the Protestant Episcopal Church, which would have made the old Anglican vestries self-supporting by giving them various landed property. Another bill, introduced in the same session, would have levied a "General Assessment" whose proceeds were to be used to support teachers of Christianity without regard to denomination. Episcopalians and Presbyterians supported the bill; the other dissenters did not. At the suggestion of George Mason, Madison drafted a "Memorial and Remonstrance against Religious Assessments," to be circu-

[43] Commissioners' Ledger and Journal, 186–190, and Sale-Book of Confiscated British Property, 1781–1785, pp. 30–32, in Maryland Hall of Records, Annapolis; Baltimore *Maryland Journal*, Jan. 18, 25, 28, Feb. 8, Mar.–Apr., 1785; Annapolis *Maryland Gazette*, Jan. 20, Sept. 29, Dec. 1, 8, 15, 1785, Nov. 2, 1786; Philip Crowl, *Maryland during and after the Revolution: A Political and Economic Study* (Baltimore, Md., 1943), passim; *Votes and Proceedings of the House of Delegates*, Jan. 8, 1785.

lated for signatures and presented as a petition to the legislature. It attracted 1,552 signatures, and other petitions based upon different premises attracted 9,377 more; and the bill was defeated. Such were feelings on the subject, however, that Madison found it prudent to keep his authorship a guarded secret.[44]

The "Memorial and Remonstrance" contained fifteen overlapping arguments against levying taxes for the support of religion, but the central message was contained in the first. Sounding much like Locke, Madison argued: "It is the duty of every man to render to the Creator such homage and such only as he believes to be acceptable to him. This duty is precedent, both in order of time and in degree of obligation, to the claims of Civil Society. . . . And if a member of Civil Society, who enters into any subordinate Association, must always do it with a reservation of his duty to the General Authority; much more must every man who becomes a member of any particular Civil Society, do it with a saving of his allegiance to the Universal Sovereign." Religion, therefore, was "wholly exempt" from the "cognizance" of government.[45] However, Madison's view was not generally shared.

The existence of restraints and limitations upon freedom can also be seen in regard to those other most precious of liberties, freedom of speech and freedom of the press. The Continental Congress included a ringing endorsement of a free press in its Quebec declaration of 1774, and nine of the eleven Revolutionary state constitutions guaranteed liberty of the press in one way or another. And yet, in 1776, Congress urged the states to pass laws to prevent people from being "deceived and drawn into erroneous opinion." By 1778 every state had done so, clamping harsh restrictions upon the utterance or publication of opinions that

[44] Lee to Madison, Nov. 26, 1784, and Editorial Notes, in *The Papers of James Madison*, ed. Robert A. Rutland et al., multiple vols. (Chicago, 1962-), 8:149, 195-197, 295-298, 9:430-431.
[45] Ibid., 8:298-304.

were contrary to the cause of independence or were critical of Congress, the state governments, or public officials. A Virginia act passed in the same year as the adoption of the state's Declaration of Rights, for example, provided a fine of up to £20,000 and imprisonment up to five years "if any person residing or being within this commonwealth shall . . . by any word, or open deed, or act, advisedly and willingly maintain and defend the authority, jurisdiction, or power, of the king or parliament of Great Britain, heretofore claimed and exercised within this colony, or shall attribute any such authority, jurisdiction, or power, to the king or parliament of Great Britain."[46]

No hypocrisy was involved in this seemingly contradictory behavior; rather, operative words had meanings different from those they later took on. Twelve of the states provided, by statute or constitution, for the continuation of the common law as it had been received before 1776; and under the common law both "freedom of speech" and "liberty of the press" had specific and restricted meanings. Freedom of speech, for the most part, referred not to a civil right but to a parliamentary privilege. Beginning during the reign of Queen Elizabeth, the House of Commons had claimed for its members the right to speak without fear of retaliation from the Crown, and that right was confirmed by the English Bill of Rights. The same right was claimed by the American colonial legislatures throughout the eighteenth century. In the Massachusetts Bill of Rights of 1780 this freedom is covered in article 21, which reads: "The freedom of deliberation, speech, and debate, in either house of the legislature, is so essential to the rights of the people, that it cannot be the foundation of any accusation or prosecution, action or complaint, in any other court or place whatsoever." But neither Parliament nor the colonial

[46] Leonard W. Levy, *Legacy of Suppression: Freedom of Speech and Press in Early American History* (Cambridge, Mass., 1960), 181; Hening, *Laws of Virginia,* 9:170. Claude H. Van Tyne, *The Loyalists in the American Revolution* (New York, 1902), 327–329, includes several of the revolutionary enactments restricting freedom of speech; see also Richard Buel, Jr., "Freedom of the Press in Revolutionary America: The Evolution of Libertarianism, 1760–1820," in *The Press & the American Revolution,* ed. Bernard Bailyn and John B. Hench (Worcester, Mass., 1980), 59–97.

assemblies extended the privilege to nonmembers: criticism of the legislative bodies or of royal officials, along with dissenting religious opinions, was rigorously suppressed.[47]

To be sure, there had been occasional early references to freedom of speech as a civil right, but these were so rare prior to the 1720s that the idea can almost be said not to have existed. John Milton, writing in 1644 and again in 1673, cried out for freedom of speech in matters of religion, but he made it clear that he sought the privilege only for himself and like-minded souls, not for Catholics, advocates of different forms of Protestantism, or non-Christians. The English Levellers John Lilburne and Richard Overton held similar views. An anonymous "Tory Author" (probably Joseph Addison), writing in 1712, likewise advocated free speech as a civil right; but he saw the right as being limited to "whatever is not against law" and also limited by "Morals or Good Manners," truthfulness, innocence of malice, and due submission to constituted authority. It was John Trenchard and Thomas Gordon, in *Cato's Letters*, who first gave unreserved endorsement to free speech as being indispensable to "Liberty, Property, true Religion, Arts, Sciences, Learning, Knowledge" and who were willing to extend the privilege to all, including those who disagreed with them. Bolingbroke echoed the message, and both Cato and Bolingbroke were widely read by American Patriots. Nonetheless, precious few Patriots thought for a moment that the right to freedom of speech extended to Loyalists.[48]

Liberty of the press had a different history and a more precise meaning. The art of printing, when introduced during the fifteenth century, had been regarded as "a matter of state." From the outset, in England as elsewhere

---

[47] J. E. Neale, "The Commons' Privilege of Free Speech in Parliament," in *Tudor Studies*, ed. R. W. Seton-Watson (London, 1924), 257–286; Harold Hulme, "The Winning of Freedom of Speech by the House of Commons," *American Historical Review* 61 (1956): 825–853; Levy, *Legacy of Suppression*, 113–114; Massachusetts Bill of Rights, in Commager, *Documents*, 109. The Pennsylvania Constitution of 1776 is the only one to state the right *of the people* to free speech; other state constitutions list freedom of speech as a right of the members of the legislature (Thorpe, *Constitutions*, 5:3083, 3:1687, 1892, 4:2457).

[48] Levy, *Legacy of Suppression*, 91–92, 95–96, 114–115, 118.

in Europe, it was subject to regulation and licensing. The various regulations were codified by a Star Chamber decree of 1637, which required the obtaining of a license before any book could be legally published. Star Chamber was abolished in 1641, but the Long Parliament reenacted the licensing requirement in 1643, 1647, 1649, and 1652, and the Restoration Parliament renewed those enactments in 1662. Renewals continued to be enacted until 1694, at which time "the press became properly free": prior restraint was no longer the law except in respect to reporting parliamentary proceedings. In both England and America, throughout the eighteenth century, liberty of the press meant that and nothing more. "The liberty of the press," as Blackstone put it, "consists in laying no *previous* restraints upon publications."[49] It did not, however, exempt people "from censure for criminal matter when published. Every freeman has an undoubted right to lay what sentiments he pleases before the public: to forbid this, is to destroy the freedom of the press: but if he publishes what is improper, mischievous, or illegal, he must take the consequences."[50]

The consequences were to be inflicted by the law of libels, of which there were four major descriptions: private, blasphemous, obscene or immoral, and seditious. Libels, according to Blackstone, were "malicious defamations of any person, and especially a magistrate, made public . . . in order to provoke him to wrath, or expose him to public hatred, contempt, and ridicule." In private libels, truth could be a defense, but it was not a defense in criminal libels. In Chancellor Kent's explanation, "the truth of the libel could not be shown by way of justification, because, whether true or false, it was equally dangerous to the public peace." Under the common law, the jury could therefore rule only as to whether the accused had printed the material in question and as to whether the material were criminal. The measure of criminality was the "bad tendency" test: the "tendency which all libels have to create

---

[49] Blackstone, *Commentaries*, 4:151.
[50] Ibid., 4:151–152.

animosities, and to disturb the public peace." The theory underlying the most repressive form of libel law, that of seditious libel, was (in the words of Lord Chief Justice Sir John Holt) that "if people should not be called to account for possessing the people with an ill opinion of the government, no government can subsist. For it is very necessary for all governments that the people should have a good opinion of it." This was especially true in a popular government. The Pennsylvanian Alexander Addison phrased it thus: "To mislead the judgment of the people, when they have no power, may produce no mischief. To mislead the judgment of the people, where they have *all* power, must produce the greatest possible mischief."[51]

A careful modern student of the subject has reported that no public figure in America during the 1780s expressed a view of freedom of the press that differed in any substantial way from the views of Blackstone and Holt. Benjamin Franklin, one of the most ardent defenders of liberty of the press, endorsed "the Liberty of discussing the Propriety of Public Measures and Political opinions," but that was as far as he would go. He declared that a publisher should regard himself as a "Guardian of his Country's Reputation, and refuse to insert such Writings as may hurt it"; and in his autobiography he wrote that newspapers which printed scurrilous or defamatory remarks on government were an "infamous disgrace."[52]

---

[51] Ibid., 4:150–151; Levy, *Legacy of Suppression*, 10; Kent, *Commentaries*, 2:15; Buel, "Freedom of the Press," in Bailyn and Hench, *Press & the Revolution*, 85–86. The first American constitutional provision for admitting truth as a defense in cases of seditious libel was in the Pennsylvania Constitution of 1790; the second, in the Delaware Constitution of 1792 (Thorpe, *Constitutions*, 1:569, 5:3100). Fredrick Seaton Siebert, in *Freedom of the Press in England, 1476–1776* (Urbana, Ill., 1952), 5, says that after 1735 "it was almost impossible to get a London jury to find a defendent guilty" of seditious libel, but that prosecutions became "extremely effective" again later.

[52] Levy, *Legacy of Suppression*, 186–187 and passim. Lawrence H. Leder, in "The Role of Newspapers in Early America 'In Defense of their Own Liberty,'" *Huntington Library Quarterly* 30 (1966): 1–16, corrects Levy in some particulars and shows that several colonial newspapers during the 1740s and 1750s had moved toward a liberalized view of the subject. Especially, "by defining the object of loyalty more precisely, the press had blunted the weapon of seditious libel."

If the Founding Fathers' utterances about freedom of speech and press seem to be divorced from substantive reality, the same is even more true in regard to their talk of equality and their practice of keeping slaves. The language of the Declaration of Independence would appear to be unequivocal: "All men are created equal," and all men are endowed by their Creator with unalienable rights to "life, liberty, and the pursuit of happiness." And yet, of the 3.9 million Americans counted in the First Census in 1790, no fewer than 697,000 were bound in perpetual, hereditary, chattel slavery.

Some Americans expressed concern about the matter. No small number of Virginia slaveholders, including Jefferson, Madison, and George Mason, agonized over it, though few made serious efforts to free their own slaves. Too, the language with which different Virginians denounced slavery was so similar that it sounded more like a mandatory litany than like a heartfelt sentiment. (Mason's remarks in the Constitutional Convention were almost repetitive of Jefferson's observations in his *Notes on Virginia*. Slaves, Mason said, "produce the most pernicious effect on manners. Every master of slaves is born a petty tyrant. They bring the judgment of heaven on a Country. As nations can not be rewarded or punished in the next world they must be in this . . . providence punishes national sins, by national calamities.")[53] In the North, to be sure, some positive efforts were forthcoming. Slavery was prohibited in New Hampshire, and by the time of the Constitutional Convention, Massachusetts had abolished it and Connecticut had made provision for some abolition. Quakers in Pennsylvania and New Jersey were seeking abolition there, and an antislavery society, of which Hamilton was an active member, had been formed in New York. Oliver Ellsworth's reply to Mason's remarks thus seems more sincere than Mason's, since Ellsworth prefaced it with the statement

---

[53]Farrand, *Records*, Aug. 22, 2:370. Madison's difficulties in reconciling theory with the reality of slavery were clearly heartfelt. See his June 19 statement, ibid., 1:318, "Where slavery exists, the Republican Theory becomes still more fallacious."

that "he had never owned a slave." "Considered in a moral light," he said, Americans "ought to go farther and free those already in the Country." But even Ellsworth could not perceive the problem as anything other than a practical one: in time, he thought, "poor laborers will be so plenty as to render slaves useless. Slavery in time will not be a speck in our Country."[54]

Most Americans, however, seem to have been indifferent with regard to slavery and, indeed, to have felt no embarrassment about the apparent contradiction between the Declaration and the existence of slavery. They could be so for various reasons, the most obvious being that slavery was a widely accepted social norm. As Charles Pinckney pointed out in the convention, the ancient Greek and Roman republics had been based upon slavery, and the institution had been sanctioned by the modern nations of western Europe. "If slavery be wrong," Pinckney said, "it is justified by the example of all the world. . . . In all ages one half of mankind have been slaves."[55] Moreover, slavery had been sanctioned, under certain conditions, by most of the great writers on natural law and natural rights, including Locke.[56] Two additional facts of life made it easy for Americans to accept slavery. First, from Pennsylvania southward, many Americans or their forebears had themselves experienced a form of temporary slavery, having immigrated as indentured servants.[57] Second, very little active enslavement had taken place in America since the 1760s; and as of 1787 the vast majority of American slaves had been born into slavery in America, and thus neither slaves nor masters had known any other system. (The

[54] Ibid., Aug. 22, 2:370–371.

[55] Ibid., Aug. 22, 2:371.

[56] Locke, *Two Treatises* (2d tr., par. 23–24), 85, 172. Vattel allowed enslavement of prisoners captured in war. Burlamaqui was the only exception I have noted.

[57] Abbot Emerson Smith, *Colonists in Bondage: White Servitude and Convict Labor in America, 1607–1776* (Chapel Hill, N.C., 1947), passim; David Galenson, *White Servitude in Colonial America* (New York, 1981); R. J. Dickson, *Ulster Emigration to Colonial America, 1718–1775* (Belfast, 1966), 82, 87–97; Peter Wilson Coldham, *Bonded Passengers to America*, 3 vols. (Baltimore, Md., 1983); David Noel Doyle, *Ireland, Irishmen and Revolutionary America, 1760–1820* (Dublin, 1981).

social inertia that led to the acceptance of slavery as an existing institution, it should be added, did not extend to encouraging the expansion of slavery: slavery was acceptable; enslavement was not. Every state except South Carolina had prohibited the importation of slaves constitutionally or by statute, and even South Carolina did so on a temporary basis; and the prohibition of slavery in the Northwest Territory, which was incorporated into article 6 of the Northwest Ordinance, met with virtually no resistance.)

A related reason for the acceptance of American Negro slavery was that it was a comparatively mild institution. Travelers to colonial Virginia from the North and from Europe, expecting to see horrors, repeatedly reported that they saw none and that slaves appeared to live easy and easygoing lives. Americans who had traveled in Europe knew that "free" European peasants suffered considerably greater oppression and misery than did American bondsmen. Modern scholarship has shown that the exploitation rate—the percentage of the worker's production that was taken from him by his owners—was lower among slaves than among European peasants, that work loads were light, and that slaves actually experienced a considerable measure of personal freedom. On rice plantations in South Carolina and Georgia, for example, slaves worked under the task system, whereby a day's labor was defined as the performance of particular standardized tasks. Normally these were light enough so that a worker could complete them in three or four hours. His time was his own when his task was done, and it was not uncommon for slaves, in their free time, to work the acres that were uniformly allotted to them by their masters and thereby to accumulate personal property. It was more common for slaves to double up on their work—to do two or even three tasks in a day—and then to take several days off, during which they might travel many miles by horse or boat to visit friends, family, or lovers on other plantations. In an age in which the great mass of mankind almost everywhere groaned under unspeakable wretchedness, it was difficult for Americans to be much concerned about the lot of their slaves.[58]

One must also consider that the words *equal* and *equality*, as used in the eighteenth century, did not necessarily imply a conflict with the institution of slavery. Broadly speaking, five general usages of these terms (apart from those referring to nations under natural law) were current in American political discourse during the late eighteenth century. Two were derived from Locke. The first was that all men are equal in the sense that none has a natural or God-given right to rule over another. The idea could be extended logically to discredit slavery, but ordinarily it was not. The usual understanding was that the doctrine applied only to the supposed divine right of kings; and upon that understanding, almost every American agreed that all men are created equal.

The other Lockean conception of equality lay in his epistemological proposition that humans were born with a tabula rasa, and that what they become as adults—wise or foolish, good or evil—was a function of time and circumstance, of what they experienced and of what they were taught and learned. An obvious inference from this premise was that mankind could be greatly (if not infinitely) improved by education and by the conscious reorganization of society. In one way and another, a number of the founders accepted this precursor of the Idea of Progress. Alexander Hamilton, however, was one of the few Americans who were willing to tie Locke's epistemology to the question of slavery: Hamilton was convinced that the supposed inferiority of American blacks was a result of conditions under which they lived and that under equal circumstances

[58] Gray, *Southern Agriculture*, 1:518; McDonald and McWhiney, "South from Self-Sufficiency to Peonage," 1096–1104; Eugene D. Genovese, *Roll, Jordan, Roll: The World the Slaves Made* (New York, 1974), 61–64; Robert W. Fogel and Stanley L. Engerman, *Time on the Cross: The Economics of American Negro Slavery* (Boston, 1974); Philip D. Morgan, "Work and Culture: The Task System and the World of Lowcountry Blacks, 1700 to 1880," *William and Mary Quarterly* 39 (1982): 563–599; Thomas R. Statom, "Negro Slavery in Eighteenth-Century Georgia" (Ph.D. diss., University of Alabama, 1982).

blacks would prove to be intellectually and socially equal to whites.[59]

Another conception of equality concerned morality. John Taylor of Caroline was expressing a widely held view when he maintained that all men were equally bound by moral duties and that they had the moral right to perform those duties.[60] Slavery was not necessarily condemned by this definition, for in an ultimate sense moral accountability was to God: blacks and whites were equal in His eyes, and that should be enough for any man. In a society in which almost everyone believed in a future state of eternal rewards and punishments (and in which reminders of one's own mortality were almost continuous), that was no trivial abstraction.

Nor was slavery incompatible with the view of equality which held that it meant equality before the law. Slaves did not have standing in law equal to that of freemen, but neither did women or children. And as will be seen, limiting the rights of citizenship to "freemen" was entirely consistent with republican principles; indeed, in most versions of republican theory such a limitation was not only acceptable but also indispensable.

There remains one further conception of equality that had gained some currency, and it alone negated the possibility of slavery as a morally acceptable institution. This was the Scottish Common Sense school of philosophy, which held that all adult human beings are endowed with a moral sense—an innate knowledge of what is right and what is wrong, of what is good and what is evil—and with a disposition to do good. "In this respect," wrote Francis Hutcheson, "all men are originally equal," and they have equal capacities for judging whether their rulers are good or bad. From that position it is but a short step to radical democracy, and no distance at all to the conclusion (again in

[59] On the Framers' attitudes toward education see chap. 6 below. For Hamilton's view of blacks see Hamilton to Jay, Mar. 14, 1779, in Syrett, *Papers of Hamilton*, 2:17–19.

[60] Leslie Wharton, *Polity and the Public Good: Conflicting Theories of Republican Government in the New Nation* (Ann Arbor, Mich., 1980), 15–16.

Hutcheson's words) that "Nature makes none masters, none slaves." Thomas Jefferson, among others, was powerfully influenced by Hutcheson and the Common Sense school. It is scarcely a wonder, then, that Jefferson could write, apropos slavery, "I tremble for my country when I reflect that God is just."[61]

But few of his countrymen trembled with him.

[61] See Garry Wills, *Inventing America: Jefferson's Declaration of Independence* (Garden City, N.Y., 1978), 228 and passim. Wills's book has been challenged by Kenneth S. Lynn ("Falsifying Jefferson," *Commentary* 66 [1978]: 66–71) and all but demolished by Ronald Hamowy ("Jefferson and the Scottish Enlightenment: A Critique of Garry Wills's *Inventing America: Jefferson's Declaration of Independence*," *William and Mary Quarterly* 36 [1979]: 503–523). Yet it is possible that they have been as guilty of overkill as Wills was of overstatement. The influences of the Scottish Common Sense school are obvious, though perhaps not definitive. See also Harry V. Jaffa, "Inventing the Past: Garry Wills's *Inventing America* and the Pathology of Ideological Scholarship," *St. John Review* 33 (1981): 3–19. See also Thomas Jefferson, *Notes on the State of Virginia*, ed. William Peden (Chapel Hill, N.C., 1955), 162–163.

III

SYSTEMS OF POLITICAL THEORY

AMERICANS LIKED TO BELIEVE that their rights —whether to life, liberty, property, or anything else—were founded, not on mere will or caprice, but upon some broader legitimating principle. Accordingly, when the First Continental Congress had convened in September of 1774 and had appointed a committee to draft a statement of "rights, grievances, and means of redress," the committee immediately entered into an extended preliminary discussion of the sources of American rights. Richard Henry Lee of Virginia led off by asserting that "the rights are built on a fourfold foundation," namely, natural law, the British constitution, the charters of the several colonies, and "immemorial usage."[1] Those, together with Scripture, were in fact the grounds on which spokesmen for colonial rights had argued for more than a decade; but it quickly developed that there were tensions among the several theories of rights and that their implications tended in different directions.

James Duane of New York and Joseph Galloway of Pennsylvania, who were possibly the ablest students of natural law in the Congress, contended strongly against an appeal to natural law. Duane's stated reason was that the law of nature would be "a feeble support." A sounder case,

[1] Burnett, *Letters*, 1:20.

he insisted, would be made by looking to history and "grounding our rights on the laws and constitution of the country from whence we sprung," and upon charters, which, being "compacts between the Crown and the people," were therefore inviolable.[2] There was, however, another consideration: to claim rights on the basis of natural law was to go outside the forms and norms of English law and to squint toward independence—which, at that time, both Duane and Galloway opposed.

Natural law had, to be sure, been developed since the seventeenth century into a large, systematic, and respectable body of legal theory that had gained some standing even in the courts of England. But its applicability had been limited, so far, to matters concerning sovereign entities, on the ground that sovereigns, lacking a common sovereign over them, were in a "state of nature" with one another. Thus it could be brought to bear in prize cases, for instance, because those fell under the "law of war," an important branch of the law of nature and one to which, by and large, Western nations adhered during the eighteenth century. But it was entirely alien to matters of concern within a single kingdom, empire, or commonwealth. For American colonies to appeal to natural law in September of 1774 was therefore to imply that they were in a state of nature, government having been dissolved, or that they had the status of independent states, or both at once. Indeed, that was precisely why Richard Henry Lee and other radicals embraced it.

When the decision for independence was made, all claims to rights that were based upon royal grants, the common law, and the British constitution became theoretically irrelevant. Independence—the very existence of the United States—was unequivocally justified in the Declaration itself by an appeal to "the Laws of Nature and of

[2] Ibid., 1:21, 22–25, 40, 52, 88. Regarding Duane's learning in natural law see also his decision in *Rutgers* v. *Waddington*, in *The Law Practice of Alexander Hamilton: Documents and Commentary*, ed. Julius Goebel, Jr., 2 vols. (New York, 1964, 1969), 1:401.

Nature's God." Quite as clearly, it was declared that the rights of Americans arose from the same source.

That opened a can of worms. As indicated, in fact and in law, Americans already enjoyed a complex and interrelated variety of property rights, derived from the disavowed British sources, and the same was true of their liberties. Yet, according to one reading of the version of natural-rights theory that was most applicable to their circumstances—that associated with John Locke—declaring independence threw them temporarily into a state of nature wherein all previously existing law (except the law of nature itself) was nullified.[3] Blackstone had solemnly intoned that "no human laws will . . . suppose a case, which at once must destroy all law, and compel men to build afresh upon a new foundation; nor will they make provision for so desperate an event, as must render all legal provisions ineffectual."[4] And yet that is the "case" and "event" that the Continental Congress brought into being.

Nor was natural-rights theory the only set of principles inherent in the decision for independence that brought into question the legitimacy of existing relationships. The decision itself jeopardized, and soon entirely undermined, both the liberty and the property rights of those who remained loyal to the Crown. More subtly, independence implied republicanism, and republicanism ineluctably implied a set of attitudes toward liberty and property that were foreign to those to which most Americans were accustomed. More subtly yet, independence brought with it the triumph, at least temporarily, of the anticapitalistic, "country-party" ideology that had been coined earlier by leaders of the English Opposition, most notably by the Whigs John Trenchard and Thomas Gordon and by Bolingbroke and his radical Tory circle.

Now, the Framers of 1787 have been justly acclaimed as a hard-headed, practical band of men who disdained

[3] See the statement of Patrick Henry in Burnett, *Letters*, 1:12: "we were reduced to a State of Nature." The question, however, was an ambiguous one; see pp. 144–152, 279–281, below.

[4] Blackstone, *Commentaries*, 1:161–162.

chimerical theory, but they could not entirely disregard these various bodies of theory. The theories had already produced consequences that amounted to prior commitments, and these could not easily be undone, if they could be undone at all. Moreover, as was suggested earlier, the theories permeated the thinking of the Framers far more deeply than they cared to admit—and perhaps more deeply than they knew.

The Patriots had turned to Locke rather than to the other great natural-law theorists—Hugo Grotius, Samuel von Pufendorf, Thomas Rutherforth, Burlamaqui, Vattel—for the reason that none of the others was so well adapted to their purposes. Vattel, the most respected of the lot, went so far as to say that rights were "nothing else but the power of doing what is morally possible," that is to say, what is proper and consistent with duty; and none of the theorists except Locke furnished a clear-cut rationale for independence.[5]

Locke's *Two Treatises of Government*, written mainly in 1679–1680 and first published in 1690, is among the most widely read works of political theory ever penned. It has been through perhaps a hundred printings in at least fourteen languages and in a variety of versions. It was the subject as well as the source of a large amount of polemical writing during the eighteenth century, and it has stimulated an enormous corpus of scholarly literature in the twentieth. And given the simplicity of its ideas, it has been astonishingly misinterpreted.[6]

[5] Vattel, *Law of Nations*, xli, xlii. Morton White, in *The Philosophy of the American Revolution* (New York, 1978), makes a convincing argument that Burlamaqui's work was also drawn upon. White is especially valuable on the relations between rights and duties (ibid., 185–228). Harvey, in his *Burlamaqui in American Constitutionalism*, presents more evidence than White does but is less convincing, for he claims far too much. That Burlamaqui was respected for his natural-law theories but not considered as a justifier of revolution (and therefore not dangerous *after* 1776) is suggested by the fact that Burlamaqui was reprinted in six American editions before the Civil War, whereas there were no new American printings of Locke during that period.

[6] The authoritative edition is Peter Laslett, 2d ed. (Cambridge, Eng., 1967). All citations to the *Two Treatises* which follow are to the Laslett edition, but for the

To Locke, natural law was based upon three fundamental principles, from which many subsidiary rights and obligations can be rationally inferred. One, the duty of every man to "praise, honour, and glory" God, does not enter directly into man's social relations except as the fount of the others.[7] The second is that mankind ought to be preserved, the word *ought* having, at the time, the quality of a command. That this principle flows from the first is evident: man "has not Liberty to destroy himself. . . . For Men being all the Workmanship of one Omnipotent, and infinitely wise Maker; All the Servants of one Sovereign Master, sent into the World by his order and about his

convenience of readers who have different editions, I have also cited treatise and paragraph number. Laslett's 118-page Introduction is indispensable to the Locke scholar; and his lengthy bibliography, together with his critical footnotes, form a useful guide. It should be noted that ordinary people probably got their ideas about a "Lockean" state of nature not from Locke but from Defoe's *Robinson Crusoe* (first published in 1719), the underlying political philosophy of which—though Defoe counted himself a Lockean—differs in subtle but important ways from that of Locke. On Defoe as Lockean see Richard Ashcraft and M. M. Goldsmith, "Locke, Revolution Principles, and the Formation of Whig Ideology," *Historical Journal* 26 (1983): 773–800. Jay Fliegelman, in *Prodigals and Pilgrims: The American Revolution against Patriarchical Authority, 1750–1800* (Cambridge, Eng., 1982), 67–81, develops the thesis that Defoe was the popular American source of a different set of Lockean ideas, those concerned with education. *Robinson Crusoe,* Fliegelman contends, "offered the American reading public a theologically and hence politically acceptable model for successful filial disobedience, a justifiable assertion of independence." Inasmuch as Crusoe does "rebel" against his parents and, as a result of divine providence, survives his tribulations and makes out quite handsomely on his own, and inasmuch as the first American edition of the novel was published (in abridged form) in 1774 and was followed by a staggering 125 additional American editions during the next half century, the argument has a great deal of appeal. Fliegelman does not deal with the role of *Robinson Crusoe,* if any, in popularizing the idea of the state of nature; and Defoe's God is by no means the "Nature's God" of the Declaration of Independence. Also omitted from consideration, regarding the possible implications for Americans, is the fact that Crusoe ultimately becomes a "king" to the "subjects" on his island; Fliegelman mentions the fact but does not consider its incompatibility with American republicanism. Finally, one wonders how Fliegelman would accommodate the extremely complex parent-child relationships in *Moll Flanders.*

[7] The quotation is from James Tully, *A Discourse on Property: John Locke and His Adversaries* (Cambridge, Eng., 1980), 50. I find Tully's work to be far the most persuasive study of the subject, and my summary here generally accords with his analysis. Tully sees the duty to glorify God, however, as the third principle, not the first, and sees it as playing no important role "in determining man's rights." My reason for rearranging the order should be clear from the text.

business, they are his Property, whose Workmanship they
are, made to last during his, not one anothers Pleasure."[8]

The third principle, in turn, arises from the second: it is
that man, being obliged by nature to live in society, without
which he cannot survive, is obliged to preserve society in
order to preserve himself. Locke penned that thought in at
least three places, expressing it in a slightly different way
each time. In his "Essays on the Laws of Nature" (written
ca. 1663) he said that "God . . . [has] designed Man for a
sociable Creature," and that man feels himself "urged to
enter into society by a certain propensity of nature."[9] In
1678 he wrote in his journal that since "God has made . . .
men in a state wherein they cannot subsist without society
and has given them judgment to discern what is capable of
preserving that society, can he but conclude that he is
obliged and that God requires him to follow those rules
which conduce to the preserving of society?"[10] And in the
Second Treatise he wrote, "God having made Man such a
Creature, that, in his own Judgment, it was not good for
him to be alone, put him under strong Obligations of
Necessity, Convenience, and Inclination to drive him into
Society, as well as fitted him with Understanding and
Language to continue and enjoy it."[11]

Central to the development of Locke's political theories
is the idea of the state of nature. In light of the passages just
quoted, it should be obvious that this did not mean a
situation in which autonomous individuals live outside of
society, as critics have misrepresented Locke as saying, for
that were contrary to the laws of nature: naturally impossible. Rather, it meant the absence of organized *political*
society and of government. That such a circumstance
existed in all societies of men at some early time Locke did
not doubt. He indicated, as proof, tribes of American
Indians and Africans, and he also pointed out the common
proposition in natural-law thinking that sovereigns were

[8] Locke, *Two Treatises*, 289 (2d tr., par. 6).
[9] Ibid., 337 n; Tully, *Discourse on Property*, 49.
[10] Tully, *Discourse on Property*, 48.
[11] Locke, *Two Treatises*, 336–337 (2d tr., par. 77).

mutually in a state of nature.[12] (Had Locke been more historically minded, he could have cited an example closer to home, that of Celtic Britain and Ireland.)

In a state of nature, Locke maintained, all men are free and equal. They are free, that is, "to order their Actions, and dispose of their Possessions, and Persons as they think fit, within the bounds of the Law of Nature, without asking leave, or depending upon the Will of any other Man." They are equal only in a negative sense: "All the Power and Jurisdiction is reciprocal, no one having more than another."[13] (Locke's insistence upon the natural equality of man had a specific context and a specific point: he wrote his treatises in refutation of Sir Robert Filmer's *Patriarcha*, an influential and, from Locke's point of view, dangerous attempt to demonstrate the natural and divine inequality of mankind, a proposition that led Filmer to assert an especially biting, because naturalistic, version of the divine right of kings.)[14]

In this natural state, the earth and the things of the earth are given to mankind in common, yet legitimate individual ownership does arise. Every man has a property, says Locke, in his own person, which "no Body has any Right to but himself. The *Labour* of his Body, and the *Work* of his Hands" are likewise properly his. "Whatsoever then he removes out of the State that Nature hath provided, and left it in, he hath mixed his *Labour* with, and joyned to it something that is his own, and thereby makes it his *Property*." The same principle applies to property in land: "*As much Land* as a Man Tills, Plants, Improves, Cultivates, and can use the Product of, so much is his *Property*. He by his Labour does, as it were, inclose it from the Common."[15]

But natural law, according to Locke, places strict limits upon the amount of property that may justly be accumulated. "*God has given us all things richly,*" Locke says, drawing upon Paul's First Epistle to Timothy, "But how far

---

[12] Ibid., 294–296 (2d tr., par. 14–15).
[13] Ibid., 287 (2d tr., par. 4).
[14] Ibid., Introduction, passim; Tully, *Discourse on Property*, 53–61 and passim.
[15] Locke, *Two Treatises*, 305–306, 308 (2d tr., par. 27, 32).

has he given it us? *To enjoy*. As much as any one can make use of to any advantage of life before it spoils; so much he may by his labour fix a Property in. Whatever is beyond this, is more than his share, and belongs to others. Nothing was made by God for Man to spoil or destroy."[16] The limiting factors, then, are two: how much a man can use, and how much he can improve with his labor.

Those limits, it might be supposed, would prevent men from producing more than they could consume; but Locke reasons otherwise. The creation of surpluses is to the advantage of all, so long as the surpluses are not allowed to go to waste, and man is stimulated to raise surpluses by the invention of money. "The greatest part of *things really useful* to the Life of Man . . . *are* generally things *of short duration;* such as, if they are not consumed by use, will decay and perish of themselves." But other things derive their value from opinion: "Gold, Silver, and Diamonds, are things, that Fancy or Agreement hath put the Value on." If a man should acquire a quantity of nuts and exchange them for "a piece of Metal, pleased with its colour; or exchange his Sheep for Shells, or Wool for a sparkling Pebble or a Diamond, and keep those by him all his Life, he invaded not the Right of others, he might heap up as much of these durable things as he pleased; the *exceeding of the bounds of his just Property* not lying in the largeness of his Possession, but the perishing of any thing uselessly in it."[17]

The introduction of money, though legitimate, is a corrupting influence. Earlier, there was "little matter for Covetousness or Ambition," but both of these "unnatural" passions were brought into play by the acceptance of the idea of money. These evil desires—"the Root of all Evil"— replace a desire to act for the general good, and men come to be motivated by "the fantastical *uneasiness,* (as itch after *Honour, Power,* or *Riches,* etc.) which acquir'd habits by

16 Ibid., 308 (2d tr., par. 31).

17 Ibid., 317–318 (2d tr., par. 46). It is to be noted that this argument constitutes a modification of Locke's well-known labor theory of property rights. It is an "opinion theory of value," though not quite a market theory, for Locke believed in the "just price" (see John Dunn, "Justice and the Interpretation of Locke's Political Theory," *Political Studies* 16 [1968]: 68–87).

Fashion, Example, and Education have settled in us, and a thousand other irregular desires, which custom has made natural to us."[18]

This corruption is what leads man to surrender his natural freedom and equality by entering into a political society and agreeing to submit to its authority: the enjoyment of his rights has become "very uncertain, and constantly exposed to the Invasion of others."[19] Otherwise, "were it not for the corruption, and vitiousness of degenerate Men, there would be no need" for government. The purpose of uniting under governments is to preserve all men in their "Lives, Liberties, and Estates," which Locke calls "by the general Name, *Property.*" To accomplish this goal, government must establish "settled, known *Law,*" which must accord with the law of nature; provide a *"known and indifferent Judge,* with Authority to determine all differences according to the established Law"; and provide power to give such decisions "due *Execution.*"[20] Thus constituted, government can have no powers except such as are compatible with the end for which it is established; and it cannot act arbitrarily, depart from its own laws, take from any man his property without his consent, or delegate the law-making power to other hands.[21] If government violates these strictures, it ceases to be legitimate and can, under certain conditions, be legitimately overthrown.

Thenceforth, all specific property rights derive from the laws of the political society, not from nature; but this does not mean either that civil laws can permit any individual to appropriate endless amounts of property to himself, as has sometimes been argued, or that civil laws can permit the emergence of a propertyless proletariat, as has also been argued.[22] For no civil law can be valid unless it "be

---

[18] Locke, *Two Treatises,* 356 (2d tr., par. 107); Tully, *Discourse on Property,* 150.

[19] Locke, *Two Treatises,* 368 (2d tr., par. 123).

[20] Ibid., 368–370 (2d tr., par. 123–128).

[21] Ibid., 368–381 (2d tr., par. 123–142).

[22] The leading work that espouses this mistaken interpretation is C. B. Macpherson, *The Political Theory of Possessive Individualism: Hobbes to Locke* (Oxford, Eng., 1962). For critiques of Macpherson see Locke, *Second Treatise,* Introduction, 105; Tully, *Discourse on Property,* passim; Alan Ryan, "Locke and the Dictatorship

conformable to the Law of Nature," and the law of nature decrees that no man can have such a "Portion of the things of this World" as to deprive "his needy Brother a Right to the Surplusage of his Goods. . . . As *Justice* gives every Man a Title to the product of his honest Industry, and the fair Acquisitions of his Ancestors descended to him; so *Charity* gives every Man a Title to so much out of another's Plenty, as will keep him from extream want."[23]

Such, in brief, was Locke's theory of the origin and nature of rights. It accorded with the goals of the Patriots of 1776; it did not accord with the desires of the society of acquisitive individualists that emerged afterward. Perhaps that helps to explain why, after the only edition published in America during the colonial period (1773), there was no new American printing of the *Two Treatises* for 164 years.

Independence also brought with it a commitment to republicanism, at first only as a by-product of a general reaction against the supposed excesses of George III. A good many Americans, to be sure, had become attracted to and reasonably well versed in republican principles of political theory even before the break with the mother country. College graduates had studied the history of the ancient republics, with a particular view toward the causes of their declines. Montesquieu's analysis of republican principles reached a wider audience, and David Hume had opined, in a much-read essay, that the government of England was actually closer to a republic than to an absolute monarchy, though he thought the pendulum was swinging back toward monarchy. Educated persons in New England had studied the works of seventeenth-century English commonwealthmen; the writings of Algernon Sidney, John Milton, and James Harrington had helped to

of the Bourgeoisie," *Political Studies* 13 (1965): 219–230; and John Dunn, *The Political Thought of John Locke: An Historical Account of the Argument of the 'Two Treatises of Government'* (London, 1969), passim.

[23] Locke, *Two Treatises*, 375, 188 (2d tr., par. 135, 1st tr., par. 42).

shape the republicanism of John and Samuel Adams and many another Yankee Patriot.[24]

Most Patriots, however, came to republicanism as the nation did, which is to say late and willy-nilly, with neither a historical nor a philosophical understanding of what they were embracing. Republicanism, to most, meant government of the sort to which they were accustomed, but without royal or proprietary officials; or it meant the kind they thought existed in England, except that all branches were elective; or it was simply a negative concept, meaning the absence of hereditary status; or most commonly, it meant representative democracy. Then, between 1776 and 1787, increasing numbers of public men took the trouble to learn about the history of republics and to study the writings of theorists of republicanism; and many who did so displayed their erudition in orations and in political tracts published in the newspapers.[25]

Some Americans took their republicanism neat, directly from the ancient sources. Among the more widely read Romans were Cicero, Livy, and Tacitus; among the Greeks, Demosthenes, Aristotle, and Polybius. Doubtless the most widely read ancient work, however, was Plutarch's *Lives*.

[24] Hume, "Whether the British Government Inclines more to Absolute Monarchy, or to a Republic," in *David Hume: Philosophical Works*, ed. Thomas Hill Green and Thomas Hodge Grose, 4 vols. (London, 1886), 3:122–126; Caroline Robbins, "Algernon Sidney's *Discourses Concerning Government*: Textbook of Revolution," *William and Mary Quarterly* 4 (1947): 267–296; Caroline Robbins, *The Eighteenth-Century Commonwealthman: Studies in the Transmission, Development, and Circumstance of English Liberal Thought from the Restoration of Charles II until the War with the Thirteen Colonies* (Cambridge, Mass., 1959). See also Zera S. Fink, *The Classical Republicans: An Essay in the Recovery of a Pattern of Thought in Seventeenth Century England* (Evanston, Ill., 1949); Richard M. Gummere, *The American Colonial Mind and the Classical Tradition* (Cambridge, Mass., 1963), 55–75, 173–190; and Gilbert Chinard, "Polybius and the American Constitution," *Journal of the History of Ideas* 1 (1940): 38–58. Republicanism was so fashionable in the eighteenth century that even Catherine the Great could regard herself as a republican, and not without reason (see David Griffith, "Catherine II: The Republican Empress," *Jahrbücher für Geschichte Osteuropas* 21 [1973]: 323–344).

[25] The bibliography on this subject is large. Possibly the most nearly exhaustive study is Gordon S. Wood's *The Creation of the American Republic, 1776–1787* (Chapel Hill, N.C., 1969). I disagree in many ways with Wood's analysis, however, and have based this work on my own research—which includes, among other things, having read virtually every line of virtually every extant American newspaper for the period and a large body of personal correspondence.

Writers of political tracts for the newspapers conventionally signed their articles with pseudonyms, often taken from Plutarch, and they could assume that their readers would understand something of their message from their choice of pen name. For example, in the debates over the Constitution, two anti-Federalists used the pseudonym Cato; one used Cato Uticensis (Cato of Utica, that is, Cato the Younger); two, Brutus; one, Brutus, Jr.; and one, Cassius. All of these were thereby identifying themselves with defenders of the late Roman republic and thus suggesting that the Constitution was antirepublican. Another used the name Agrippa, after the Greek skeptic, and another, Cincinnatus. Still another used a Latinism—Vox Populi (voice of the people)—to identify his cause with the common man, thus suggesting that the Constitution was the work of an aristocratic conspiracy. By contrast, Hamilton, Madison, and Jay signed the *Federalist Essays* Publius, after the Roman who, following Lucius Brutus's overthrow of the last king of Rome, established "the republican foundation of the government." Earlier, in essays opposing the highly popular postwar practice of persecuting Loyalists, Hamilton had used the name Phocion, after the Athenian general who was celebrated for his magnanimity toward defeated enemies and his efforts to protect prisoners of war from demagogues seeking to persuade "the people in their anger into committing some act of cruelty." (As Hume put it, Phocion "always suspected himself of some blunder when he was attended with the applauses of the populace.")[26]

Far more Americans got their republicanism, both classical and modern, second hand or through filters. The most popular means were plays, newspapers, orations, and

[26] Adair, "A Note on Certain of Hamilton's Pseudonyms," in Colbourn, *Fame and the Founding Fathers,* 272–285, is the pioneering study of the use of classical pseudonyms. Adair's article, however, contains some erroneous statements about Hamilton which are corrected in Thomas P. Govan, "Alexander Hamilton and Julius Caesar: A Note on the Use of Historical Evidence," *William and Mary Quarterly* 32 (1975): 475–480. The anti-Federalist pseudonyms are taken from the table of contents in *The Complete Anti-Federalist,* ed. Herbert J. Storing, 7 vols. (Chicago, 1981). Interestingly, one anti-Federalist in New England wrote as Hampden, and two in New York wrote as Sidney/Sydney. The Hume quotation is from Dugald Stewart's introduction to Smith's *Theory of Moral Sentiments,* xxxix.

charges to grand juries. During the late colonial and early national periods theatrical productions of Addison's *Cato*, Shakespeare's *Julius Caesar*, Nathaniel Lee's *Alexander the Great*, Thomas Otway's *Venice Preserved*, and Henry Brooke's *Gustavus Vasa, the Deliverer of His Country*, among many others, familiarized American audiences with classical lore and republican ideals. (Ironically, the Continental Congress in 1774 and 1778 adopted resolutions condemning plays and peremptorily prohibiting all persons "holding an office under the United States" to perform in or attend them. Despite the ban, General Washington had *Cato* performed at Valley Forge to boost the morale of his troops.) Meanwhile, since the 1720s American printers had been reprinting (usually without crediting their sources) essays, articles, plays, and poems from the *Tattler*, the *Guardian*, the *Craftsman*, the *Spectator*, and other British publications. In this way, thousands of Americans who perhaps never read any book except the Bible could share the classical revival that had begun to flourish in Britain during the seventeenth century and continued to do so during the eighteenth, and could thereby absorb republican sentiments and values without being aware of where they came from. The message was cast wider in public orations, which were among the limited number of forms of popular entertainment. (In an oration in Boston on March 5, 1781, commemorating the Boston Massacre, Thomas Dawes, Jr., harangued the crowd with a learned history of republics, quoting, among others, Marcus Aurelius, the *Spectator*, Ovid, Pope, Seneca, Newton, Blair, Juvenal, Addison's *Cato*, Blackstone, and the Bible.) Grand-jury charges, such as those delivered by John Jay, were likewise popular forums for the spreading of republican values.[27]

[27] George O. Seilhamer, *History of the American Theatre*, 2 vols. (reprint of 1888, 1889 vols.; New York, 1968), 1:16, 94, 114, 118, 130, 197, 236, 237, 242, 332, 333, 2:51–52; Elizabeth Christine Cook, *Literary Influences in Colonial Newspapers, 1704–1750* (New York, 1912), passim; Niles, *Principles and Acts*, 67–71, 182. On the influence and popularity of grand jury charges see Richard D. Younger, *The People's Panel: The Grand Jury in the United States, 1634–1941* (Providence, R.I., 1963), 27–55.

The more important second-hand sources of republican thought imbibed by Americans were the works of six-teenth-century Italians, most notably Machiavelli, and an assortment of eighteenth-century thinkers—Trenchard and Gordon, Bolingbroke, Montesquieu, and Hume. As for the filters, these were the local traditions, prejudices, and circumstances that predisposed people in the various parts of the country to choose selectively among the sources of their ideas.

Speaking broadly, even grossly, one may characterize American schools of republican thought as being in two categories: those which reduced their principles into systems or ideologies, and those which did not. Those which did—again speaking broadly, for there were shades and overlappings, and the substantive differences are clearly visible only at the extremes—may likewise be characterized in two categories. One, the more nearly classical, may be described as puritan; the other, the more modern, may be described as agrarian.

The two versions of ideological republicanism held a number of attitudes in common, the most crucial being preoccupation with the mortality of republics ("Half our learning," said Dawes, "is their epitaph.") The vital—that is life-giving—principle of republics was *public virtue*. It is important to understand just what these two words signified. Like their Greek counterparts, *polis* and *arete*, they did not connote what is suggested by the idea of Christian virtue, with its emphasis upon meekness, passivity, and charity; quite the opposite, for the Christian concept of virtue was originally formulated as the central ethic in a counterculture that arose as a conscious protest against the classical cult of manliness. Nor did the public (or the *polis*) include everybody. Not coincidentally, *public*, like *virtue*, derives from Latin roots signifying manhood: "the public" included only independent adult males. Public virtue en-tailed firmness, courage, endurance, industry, frugal living, strength, and above all, unremitting devotion to the weal of the public's corporate self, the community of virtuous men. It was at once individualistic and communal: individualistic in that no member of the public could be dependent upon any other and still be reckoned a member of the public; communal in that every man gave himself totally to the good of the public as a whole. If public virtue declined, the republic declined, and if it declined too far, the republic died. Philosophical historians had worked out a regular life cycle, or more properly death cycle, of republics. Manhood gave way to effeminacy, republican liberty to licentiousness. Licentiousness, in turn, degenerated into anarchy, and anarchy inevitably led to tyranny.[28]

What distinguished puritanical republicanism from the agrarian variety was that the former sought a moral solution to the problem of the mortality of republics (make better people), whereas the latter believed in a socio-economic-political solution (make better arrangements). Almost nothing was outside the purview of a puritanical republican government, for every matter that might in any way contribute to strengthening or weakening the virtue of the public was a thing of concern to the public—a *res publica*—and was subject to regulation by the public. Republican liberty was totalitarian: one was free to do that, and only that, which was in the interest of the public, the liberty of the individual being subsumed in the freedom or independence of his political community.[29]

Lest this seem an overstatement, consider what John Adams had to say about republics. Republican principles, he wrote to Mercy Warren, were "productive of every Thing, which is great and excellent among Men," but those principles were "as easily destroyed as human Nature is corrupted." Republican governments could be supported only "by pure Religion or Austere Morals. Public Virtue

---

[28]See J. G. A. Pocock, *The Machiavellian Moment: Florentine Political Thought and the Atlantic Republican Tradition* (Princeton, N.J., 1975). The concept of cyclical decay owes most, of course, to Polybius. See also the provocative article by Paul A. Rahe, "The Primacy of Politics in Classical Greece," *American Historical Review* 89 (1984): 265–293. Fliegelman, in *Prodigals and Pilgrims*, 42, says that the Frenchman Charles Rollin, whose *Ancient History* was a "bestseller" in America on the eve of the Revolution, "saw in the rise and fall" of ancient empires the "revolutionary alternation of national virtue and corruption."

[29]Pocock, *Machiavellian Moment*; see, particularly, index entries under "corruption" and "virtue."

cannot exist in a Nation without private, and public Virtue is the only Foundation of Republics. There must be a positive Passion for the public good, the public Interest, Honour, Power and Glory, established in the Minds of the People, or there can be no Republican Government, *nor any real liberty.*'' The public passion, he emphasized, ''must be Superiour to all private Passions. Men must . . . be happy to sacrifice . . . their private Friendships and dearest Connections, when they stand in Competition with the Rights of Society.'' To his wife Abigail, Adams wrote that their children might suppose that he should have labored more for their benefit, but ''I will not bear the Reproaches of my Children. I will tell them that I studied and laboured to procure a free Constitution of Government for them to solace themselves under, and if they do not prefer this to ample Fortune, to Ease and Elegance, they are not my Children, and I care not what becomes of them.'' He planned a Spartan existence for them: ''They shall live upon thin Diet, wear mean Cloaths, and work hard, with Chearfull Hearts and free Spirits.'' His sons must ''revere nothing but Religion, Morality, and Liberty''—the liberty to be good republicans.[30]

And, lest one think that Adams was alone in these sentiments, consider a proclamation issued by the Massachusetts legislature a few months before independence: ''That Piety and Virtue, which, alone can Secure the Freedom of any People, may be encouraged, and Vice and Immorality suppressed, the great and general Court have thought fit to issue this Proclamation, commanding and enjoining it upon the good People of this Colony, that they lead Sober, Religious, and peaceable Lives, avoiding all Blasphemies, contempt of the holy Scriptures, and of the Lord's day and all other Crimes and Misdemeanors, all Debauchery, Prophaneness, Corruption, Venality, all riotous and tumultuous Proceedings, and all Immoralities.

[30]Quoted in Philip Greven, *The Protestant Temperament: Patterns of Child-Rearing, Religious Experience, and the Self in Early America* (New York, 1977), 346. For a study of the role of women see Linda K. Kerber, *Women of the Republic: Intellect & Ideology in Revolutionary America* (Chapel Hill, N.C., 1980).

. . . And all . . . civil officers, within this Colony, are hereby Strictly enjoined and commanded that they . . . bring to condign Punishment, every Person who . . . shall be guilty of any Immoralities whatsoever."[31]

One thinks of the remark of the Athenian Alcibiades about Sparta, the ancient republic that American republicans professed to admire most: "No wonder the Spartans cheerfully encounter death; it is a welcome relief to them from such a life as they are obliged to lead."[32]

Until the winter of 1786–1787, when Shays' Rebellion gave their faith a devastating jolt, New Englanders were generally and accurately known as the "most republican" of Americans. That is scarcely surprising, given the Yankees' heritage: in many respects John Adams's republicanism seems little more than John Winthrop's puritanism revisited. Puritanical republicanism was not, however, confined to New England. The Lees of Virginia were quite as militant in their republicanism as were the Adamses of Massachusetts, and so were many other denizens of the tobacco-growing region. Extreme republicanism was common in those parts of Virginia in which the Great Awakening (especially in its Baptist phase) had had its strongest impact. Quite possibly, as Philip Greven has suggested, there was a psychological affinity between republicanism and "the evangelical temperament," which was inherent in both seventeenth-century puritanism and eighteenth-century revivalism.[33]

But puritanical republicanism was considerably less pervasive outside of New England than was the agrarian

[31] *American Archives*, ed. Peter Force, 9 vols. (Washington, D.C., 1837–1853), 4:833–835. That these injunctions were enforced by numerous prosecutions is abundantly documented in Nelson, *Americanization of the Common Law*, 36–41, 110–112, though prosecutions declined sharply after 1786.

[32] Quoted by Fisher Ames in *Works of Fisher Ames: As Published by Seth Ames*, ed. W. B. Allen, 2 vols. (Indianapolis, Ind., 1983), 1:97.

[33] See Edmund S. Morgan, "The Puritan Ethic and the American Revolution," *William and Mary Quarterly* 24 (1967): 3–43; but compare the quotations from Adams, above, with John Winthrop's "Little Speech on Liberty" (1645), in *Old South Leaflets*, 9 vols. (Boston, 1896–1922), 3:8–10; Rhys Isaac, *The Transformation of Virginia, 1740–1790* (Chapel Hill, N.C., 1982), passim; Greven, *Protestant Temperament*, 336–338; William Gribbin, "Republican Religion and the American

species of republican ideology. This variety was densely concentrated in tobacco-plantation country, and for another reason of temperament. In marked contrast to the industry, frugality, and work ethic that were socially instilled into New Englanders, southern society taught its members indolence, prodigality, and a leisure ethic. Despite their easygoing ways, however, southern republicans could believe that their society produced a sufficient supply of virtue, for there was an alternate and more recently formulated body of republican theory available to them. Virtue meant manliness, and manliness meant independence. James Harrington, in his *Oceana* (1656), had advanced the proposition that the necessary independence could be had only if a man owned enough land, unencumbered by debts or other obligations, to provide himself and his family with all their material needs; and this independence, in the words of J. G. A. Pocock, was "in the last analysis measured by his ability to bear arms and use them in his own quarrels." Trenchard and Gordon, in *Cato's Letters* (1720), and Bolingbroke, in various writings, reiterated and embellished the idea. In this scheme of thought, virtue, independence, liberty, and the ownership of unencumbered real property were inextricably bound together. "To live securely, happily, and independently," Cato wrote, "is the End and Effect of Liberty . . . and real or fancied Necessity alone makes Men the Servants, Followers, and Creatures of one another. And therefore . . . Property is the best Support of the Independency so passionately desired by all Men."[34] In sum, ownership of the land begat

Churches in the Early National Period," *Historian* 35 (1972): 61–74. For a careful analysis of the evolution of religious doctrine in lock step with political thought see Nathan O. Hatch, *The Sacred Cause of Liberty: Republican Thought and the Millennium in Revolutionary New England* (New Haven, Conn., 1977). A. G. Roeber, in *Faithful Magistrates and Republican Lawyers: Creators of Virginia Legal Culture, 1680–1810* (Chapel Hill, N.C., 1981), 171–202, points out that Virginia grand juries frequently brought indictments for immorality out of professed concern for republican virtue, but that county justices almost invariably threw the indictments out.

[34] *The English Libertarian Heritage from the Writings of John Trenchard and Thomas Gordon in* The Independent Whig *and Cato's Letters,* ed. David L. Jacobson (Indianapolis, Ind., 1965), 177–178. The Pocock quotation is in his *Politics, Language, and Time: Essays on Political Thought and History* (New York, 1971), 110.

independence, independence begat virtue, and virtue begat republican liberty. The New Englanders as well as the southern republicans embraced the dogma that landowner- ship was a natural preservative of virtue; but the southern- ers, unlike the New Englanders, believed that a wide distribution of landownership, together with an extreme jealousy of power and careful attention to its allocation, would preserve an adequate stock of public virtue, inde- pendent of the store of private virtue. Indeed, in the southern scheme of things, private virtue, in the rigorous sense in which it was defined by the Yankees, was unneces- sary to the maintenance of republican liberty. The arch agrarian John Taylor of Caroline put it succinctly: "The more a nation depends for its liberty on the qualities of individuals, the less likely it is to retain it. By expecting publick good from private virtue, we expose ourselves to publick evils from private vices." Taylor went on to deal at length with the importance that the structure of political institutions had for republican liberty.[35]

Elsewhere Pocock says of that work that in it he had attempted to show the "messianic and apocalyptic overtones" in eighteenth-century classical republi- canism "and that it possessed important affinities with the image of the Puritan saint" (see "Virtue and Commerce in the Eighteenth Century," *Journal of Interdisciplinary History* 3 [1972]: 134).

[35] In regard to the preference of southerners for the leisure ethic, rather than the work ethic, see, among others, Andrew Burnaby, *Travels through the Middle Settlements in North-America in the years 1759 and 1760* (Ithaca, N.Y., 1960), 22, 27; *The Carolina Backcountry on the Eve of the Revolution: The Journal and Other Writings of Charles Woodmason, Anglican Itinerent*, ed. Richard J. Hooker (Chapel Hill, N.C., 1953), 52; *A Mirror for Americans: Life and Manners in the United States, 1790–1870, as Recorded by American Travelers*, ed. Warren S. Tyron, 3 vols. (Chicago, 1952), 1:20; Johann David Schöpf, *Travels in the Confederation*, (1783–1784), trans. Alfred J. Morrison, 2 vols. (Philadelphia, 1911), 2:40, 89, 93–95; Smyth, *Tour in the United States*, 1:23, 41–43, 65–67; and McDonald and McWhiney, "The South from Self- Sufficiency to Peonage."

Students of southern republicanism have, in my judgment, been somewhat misled by excessive attention to the writings of Jefferson and Madison, who were more idosyncratic than typical. One can, however, pick one's way through a considerable body of literature on the subject, some of which is excellent: see, for example, Norman K. Risjord, *The Old Republicans: Southern Conservatism in the Age of Jefferson* (New York, 1965); Richard Buel, *Securing the Revolution: Ideology in American Politics, 1789–1815* (Ithaca, N.Y., 1972); Stuart Gerry Brown, *The First Republicans: Political Philosophy and Public Policy in the Party of Jefferson and Madison* (Syracuse, N.Y., 1954); Dice Robins Anderson, *William Branch Giles: A Study in the*

Agrarian republicanism was therefore essentially negative in the focus of its militance: it demanded vigilance only
in regard to certain kinds of men and institutions which, as
its adherents viewed history, had proved inimical or fatal to
liberty. The version of history that was involved was what
has been described as the Anglo-Saxon myth. Free institutions, according to this myth, had originated among the
ancient Teutonic tribes, who planted them in Britain during
the sixth and seventh centuries. From then until the Norman Conquest, England was an agrarian paradise. Society
and the minimal government that was necessary were
organized around farmers, great and small, whose landholdings were absolutely free and around powerful heads
of families, either nuclear or extended. No coercion was
necessary in such a society, relations were governed by
tradition and consent, and every man was free to worship
God as he saw fit. Any dispute that might arise was settled
by established custom and the common law, which all men
understood and revered. When foreign invaders threat-
ened, the heads of families mustered in militia companies
and repulsed the intruder.[36]

The trouble was that the world always contained a few
wicked and designing men who were perpetually conspir-
ing to destroy this Eden, and it was against them that one
must be vigilant. The Anglo-Saxons, the myth went on,
had relaxed their vigil during the eleventh century, and the

Politics of Virginia and the Nation from 1790 to 1830 (Gloucester, Mass., 1965);
Robert E. Shalhope, *John Taylor of Caroline: Pastoral Republican* (Columbia, S.C.,
1980), from which, at p. 160, the quotation is taken; Harry Ammon, *James Monroe:
The Quest for National Identity* (New York, 1971); Wharton, *Polity and the Public
Good*, 13–31; Lance Banning, *The Jeffersonian Persuasion: Evolution of a Party Ideology*
(Ithaca, N.Y., 1978). That southern republicans imbibed their agrarianism mainly
from *Cato's Letters* and Bolingbroke, rather than directly from Harrington, seems
clear. Madison, Jefferson, and Mason apparently studied Harrington, but I have
seen little evidence to suggest that many others did. For readers who seek an
introduction to Harrington's thought without wading through his turgid prose, I
recommend Fink's *Classical Republicans*, 52–89. Pocock's many writings on Harrington are powerful, but their prose is often as murky as Harrington's own.
[36] Harold Trevor Colbourn, *The Lamp of Experience: Whig History and the
Intellectual Origins of the American Revolution* (Chapel Hill, N.C., 1965); Rodger D.
Parker, "The Gospel of Opposition: A Study in Eighteenth-Century Anglo-
American Ideology" (Ph.D. diss., Wayne State University, 1975).

Norman Yoke was the result. They had won back their liberties in Magna Carta in 1215, and in the ensuing centuries they had repeatedly lost and regained them. During the seventeenth century it was the Stuart kings who attempted to destroy liberty, until they were ousted in the Glorious Revolution of 1688. And then, just when it seemed that liberty had finally triumphed, new enemies appeared in the form of prime ministers and their trains of placemen and their aristocratic and stock-jobbing allies.

Republican ideologues of both descriptions kept in their heads a checklist of indicators of corruption, and they thought, spoke, and wrote in code words that designated symptoms of decay. Standing armies, priests, bishops, aristocrats, luxury, excises, speculators, jobbers, paper shufflers, monopolists, bloodsuckers, and monocrats were among the staples in their demonological vocabulary. And there was another thing: republican ideologues could scarcely utter a thought concerning public affairs that was not related, one way or another, to the eighteenth-century English Opposition.[37]

The ideology of the English "country party" Opposition was the third body of ideas inherent in the American decision for independence. Its roots went back to the writings of seventeenth-century commonwealthmen, especially Harrington and Sidney, and ultimately to Virgil, if not further back in time; but the version that was received by most Americans had begun to take shape during the "standing army controversy" of the late 1690s, with the polemics of Charles Davenant and others who feared that the expectations attendant upon the Glorious Revolution were being betrayed.[38] It ripened considerably during the controversy surrounding the South Sea Bubble, most influentially in *Cato's Letters*. It reached full fruition in the writings of Bolingbroke and his Tory friends, in the pages

[37] The best account of the demonological vocabulary used in England is Parker, "Gospel of Opposition." For many examples of uses in America see Storing, *Complete Anti-Federalist*, passim.

[38] Pocock, *Machiavellian Moment*, 427, 436ff.

of *The Craftsman*, and in a host of books, pamphlets, and plays. The message was recapitulated in 1774 in James Burgh's *Political Disquisitions*. All of this Oppositionist literature was widely known in America, and by 1776 it had been thoroughly absorbed into the American political vocabulary.[39]

As it related to liberty, the most striking attribute of the ideology was its belief that there were conspiracies against freedom. Bolingbroke and the others repeatedly charged that "wicked and designing" ministers, "money men," and "placemen" were engaged in a monstrous and never-ending conspiracy to subvert the liberty of the people; and as the sixties and seventies unfolded, American Patriots became convinced that such a conspiracy was now aimed at them. The Loyalist Samuel Seabury said in 1774 that the idea that the British government "have laid a regular plan to enslave America" had been repeated "over, and over, and over again"; and he was right. George Washington believed "beyond the smallest doubt" that the British were "endeavoring by every piece of art and despotism to fix the shackles of slavery upon us." Jefferson wrote that there was "a deliberate and systematical plan of reducing us to slavery." John Adams said that "somebody or other in Great Britain" had "meditated for us . . . a direct and formal design . . . to enslave all America." Richard Henry Lee, John Dickinson, George Mason, and hundreds more echoed the charge.[40]

The habit of believing in conspiracies against American liberties did not end with the Revolution. The formation in

[39] The body of literature on the Opposition is large. Among the more important works are Pocock's *Machiavellian Moment*; Isaac Kramnick, *Bolingbroke and His Circle: the Politics of Nostalgia in the Age of Walpole* (Cambridge, Mass., 1968); Robbins, *Eighteenth-Century Commonwealthman*; Colbourn, *Lamp of Experience*; Jacobson, *English Libertarian Heritage*; Bernard Bailyn, *The Ideological Origins of the American Revolution* (Cambridge, Mass., 1967). None of these, however, is nearly so sound or thorough as Parker, "Gospel of Opposition," on which I have relied heavily. James Burgh's *Political Disquisitions* (New York, 1971; reprint of 1774 London ed.) differs from the others in being both more libertarian and more democratic.

[40] Bailyn, *Ideological Origins*, 119-125; John M. Head, *A Time to Rend: An Essay on the Decision for American Independence* (Madison, Wis., 1968), 99; Gordon S. Wood, "Conspiracy and the Paranoid Style: Causality and Deceit in the Eight-

1783 of the Society of the Cincinnati, a fraternal order of former officers of the Continental Line, was denounced and feared as an aristocratic conspiracy.[41] Shays' Rebellion was accompanied by a fairly widespread belief that it was a counterrevolutionary conspiracy backed by Sir Guy Carleton, Lord Dorchester.[42] Virginians devoutly believed that the world-wide collapse of tobacco prices in the mid eighties had been the conspiratorial doing of the Philadelphia merchant and erstwhile superintendent of finance, Robert Morris.[43] In the summer of 1787 a rumor circulated, and was doubtless believed by many, that the Constitutional Convention was negotiating with a nephew of George III, with a view toward making him king.[44] And any effort by the convention to provide for the Revolutionary War debts in a way that smacked of the English system was sure to be greeted as a monocratic conspiracy hatched in London. (The very mention of the debts in the convention inspired a Bolingbrokean tirade by Pierce Butler against "bloodsuckers" and "money men.")[45]

eenth Century," *William and Mary Quarterly* 39 (1982): 401–441. The Pennsylvania constitution incorporated the charge that George III had "the avowed purpose of reducing them to a total and abject submission to the despotic domination of the British Parliament" (Thorpe, *Constitutions*, 5:3081). Michael Kammen suggests (in a letter to the author, Nov. 29, 1984) that the use of the slavery metaphor may be rooted in the internalization of Locke's *Second Treatise*, chap. 4.

[41] See, for example, Elbridge Gerry to Samuel Adams, Sept. 5, 1785, to John Adams, Nov. 8, 1785, and Stephen Mix Mitchell to Jeremiah Wadsworth, May 3, 1786, in Burnett, *Letters*, 8:211, 251, 350; Washington to Hamilton, Dec. 11, 1785, in Syrett, *Papers of Hamilton*, 3:639; Aedanus Burke, *Considerations on the Society or Order of the Cincinnati* . . . (Philadelphia, 1783); Jefferson to Washington, Apr. 6, 1784, in *The Best Letters of Thomas Jefferson*, ed. J. G. deRoulhoc Hamilton (Boston, 1926), 4–9; Jefferson to Washington, Nov. 14, 1786, in Boyd, *Papers of Jefferson*, 10:532; and virtually every American newspaper, 1783–1785.

[42] See, for example, Henry Lee to Washington, Nov. 11, 1786, and Edward Carrington to Edmund Randolph, Dec. 8, 1786, in Burnett, *Letters*, 8:506, 516.

[43] The origin of the idea of the Morris conspiracy is apparently Jefferson's letter to Jay, from Paris, May 27, 1786, published in *The Diplomatic Correspondence of the United States*, ed. Jared Sparks, 5 vols. (Washington, D.C., 1832–1833), 3:57–63. See also Jefferson to John Adams, July 9, 1786, in Boyd, *Papers of Jefferson*, 10:106, and to Montmorin, July 23, 1787, ibid, 11:614–615; Forrest McDonald, *E Pluribus Unum: The Formation of the American Republic, 1776–1790* (Indianapolis, Ind., 1979 ed.), 134–135 and nn. 21, 22.

[44] Hamilton to Jeremiah Wadsworth, Aug. 20, 1787, and David Humphreys to Hamilton, Sept. 1, 1787, in Syrett, *Papers of Hamilton*, 4:236 and n. 1, pp. 241–242.

[45] Farrand, *Records*, Aug. 23, 2:392.

There might appear to be one glaring exception to the assertion that virtually all the thinking of republican ideologues came from, could be derived from, or was related to the English Opposition, for American republicans regarded selected doctrines of Montesquieu's as being virtually on a par with Holy Writ; but the appearance is deceptive. Montesquieu was profoundly influenced by Bolingbroke, and book 11, chapter 6, of *The Spirit of the Laws*, in which Montesquieu sets forth his theory of the separation of powers, was derived directly from Bolingbroke's (misleading) description of the English constitution.[46]

To appreciate Montesquieu's influence in America, it is useful to begin with the observation that in thinking of government, Americans followed a practice that was deepseated in the Western world, namely, the almost mystical habit of thinking in threes. In part that habit may have stemmed from the concept of the Holy Trinity; in part it doubtless stemmed from Aristotle's division of forms of government into monarchy, aristocracy, and polity or constitutional democracy (with their counterpart evils—tyranny, oligarchy, and ochlocracy, or the mob rule of lawless democracy—each of which arose when rulers became excessively and successfully ambitious for power). Yet another source was the practice, which was apparently common to all Indo-European societies, of dividing men into three classes: those who fight, those who pray, and those who work. In medieval Europe these classes translated into estates; in England, the corresponding estates of the realm had been the Lords Temporal, the Lords Spiritual, and the Commons.[47]

But the English system was asymmetrical, or rather it had been until the seventeenth century. The three estates

---

[46]Robert Shackleton, "Montesquieu, Bolingbroke, and the Separation of Powers," *French Studies* 3 (1949): 25–38; Kramnick, *Bolingbroke and His Circle*, 144–152.

[47]The pioneer work on this subject was done by Georges Dumézil; for versions in English and applications to European history see C. Scott Littleton, *The New Comparative Mythology: An Anthropological Assessment of the Theories of Georges Dumézil* (Berkeley, Calif., 1982), and Georges Duby, *The Three Orders: Feudal Society Imagined*, trans. Arthur Goldhamner (Chicago, 1980).

were conventionally regarded as comprehending everyone in the kingdom, under the Crown, yet they were arranged in only two houses of Parliament, the theoretical embodiment of the whole people. Moreover, predominant lay opinion had it that the bishops, or Lords Spiritual, sat in the upper house by a civil, rather than a religious, right: their offices amounted to a peerage. The lack of symmetry was rectified in the pronouncement issued by Charles I in 1642, the *Answer to the xix propositions,* in which Charles declared that the three estates were the King, the Lords Spiritual and Temporal, and the Commons. The three together constituted Parliament; and as in the Trinity, each was separate and distinct yet all were one.[48]

This arrangement, sometimes referred to as government by Crown-in-Parliament, but more commonly described as mixed government or a mixed form of government—which some Americans had studied in the works of Polybius—became the norm in both England and America after 1688. From it arose the idea or ideal of checks and balances: each of the parts of the mixed constitution was supposed to restrain the power of the others in the interest of a harmonious whole.[49]

Montesquieu taught Americans a different trinitarian taxonomy. At the outset, he divided the three forms of government in a thoroughly unorthodox fashion. They were, he declared, republics, which could be either aristocratic or democratic; monarchies, "in which a single person governs by fixed and established laws"; and despotisms, "in which a single person directs everything by his own will and caprice."[50] More importantly, Montesquieu developed at length the doctrine of the separation of powers. American republican ideologues could recite the central points of Montesquieu's doctrine as if it had been a catechism.

[48] The evolution and permutations of the concept of the three estates in England are traced in Michael Mendle, *Dangerous Positions: Mixed Government, the Estates of the Realm, and the Making of the* Answer to the xix propositions (Tuscaloosa, Ala., 1985).

[49] Blackstone, *Commentaries,* 1:51.

[50] Montesquieu, *The Spirit of the Laws,* trans. Thomas Nugent (New York, 1949), 8–18 (bk. 2).

First, Montesquieu defines political liberty as "a tranquillity of mind arising from the opinion each person has of his safety," and then he recites a series of propositions about how government must be constituted so as to bring about such liberty. "When the legislative and executive powers are united in the same person, or in the same body of magistrates," he says, "there can be no liberty. . . . Again, there is no liberty, if the judiciary power be not separated from the legislative and executive." The legislative itself must be divided into two houses, one representing "persons distinguished by their birth, riches, or honors" and the other representing the common people. The executive must have no part in legislation, though it must have the veto power. The legislature must have no share in the executive power, though it must have the power to impeach. The power of the purse must reside exclusively in the legislature, but appropriations must not be made in perpetuity or for long periods. Command of the army is the province of the executive, but the legislature must have the power to disband the army at will. Finally, the judiciary should not be a permanent body, but should be one whose personnel are frequently changed, and the judges should be "no more than the mouth that pronounces the words of the law."[51]

It is important to notice that Montesquieu's theory of the separation of powers is not only different from but is also nearly irreconcilable with the English idea of checks and balances. In the English scheme of things judicial power was exercised mainly by the king's courts, but for certain purposes both the Lords and the Commons had judicial authority; and several traditionally executive powers, including control of the military and the currency, had for practical purposes devolved upon the Commons. In principle, the British constitution provided for separation of personnel, rather than for division of function, and even that principle had come to be largely disregarded in practice. The Crown, no longer daring to use the veto that

[51] Ibid., 151–162 (bk. 11, chap. 6).

theoretically gave it a direct role in the legislative process, maintained the balance of the system through patronage. That is to say, it influenced or directed affairs in Parliament by bribing members or their followers with appointments to positions of preferment and profit. The lines separating the three estates thus became interpenetrated by "placemen" who frequently held more than one office. Had things been otherwise, checks and balances would have been impossible.[52]

Many American Patriots became disillusioned with the idea of checks and balances by reading a single, grand polemical tract, Thomas Paine's *Common Sense*. To say that the English constitution was a "*union* of three powers, reciprocally *checking* each other," Paine wrote, is "farcical." The contention that the Commons provided a necessary check upon the king presupposed that he had "a thirst for absolute power" which made him untrustworthy, and that the Commons was wiser and more deserving of trust. Yet the constitution also gave the Crown the power to check the Commons, which "supposes that the king is wiser than those whom it has already supposed to be wiser than him." It was only the republican part of the constitution, Paine argued, that "Englishmen glory in, viz. the liberty of choosing an house of commons from out of their own body." Charging that the English system of government was "so exceedingly complex, that the nation may suffer for years together without being able to discover in which part the fault lies," Paine prescribed a "form of government from a principle in nature which no art can overturn, viz. that the more simple any thing is, the less liable it is to be disordered, and the easier repaired when disordered."[53]

---

[52] J. H. Plumb, *England in the Eighteenth Century* (Harmondsworth, Middlesex, Eng., 1950) and *The Origins of Political Stability, England 1675–1725* (Boston, 1967); Lewis Namier, *Monarchy and the Party System* . . . (Oxford, Eng., 1952); Harvey C. Mansfield, Jr., *Statesmanship and Party Government: A Study of Burke and Bolingbroke* (Chicago, 1965). See also Hume's essay "Of the Independency of Parliament," in Green and Grose, *Hume's Philosophical Works*, 3:120–121.

[53] The quotations are from *Selections from the Works of Thomas Paine: The American Crisis, The Age of Reason, Common Sense*, ed. Arthur Wallace Peach (New York, 1928), 6, 7, 16.

After Paine's onslaught, Americans tended, by and large, to embrace the doctrine of separation of powers rather than the idea of checks and balances. It has been argued, persuasively, that Americans would have favored separation of powers as a result of their colonial experience even if Montesquieu had never written his book.[54] As Carl Becker suggested, men are generally influenced by those books which clarify their own thought, express their own notions well, or suggest to them ideas they are predisposed to accept. So it was with Montesquieu and the early American constitution makers: he transformed the familiar into a respectable body of doctrine. Accordingly, the doctrine was reflected in all the Revolutionary state constitutions and explicitly endorsed in six of them.[55] The most fulsome endorsement was that of the Massachusetts constitution: "The legislative department shall never exercise the executive and judicial powers, or either of them: the executive shall never exercise the legislative and judicial powers, or either of them: the judicial shall never exercise the legislative and executive powers, or either of them: to the end it may be a government of laws and not of men."[56]

But there was less to this than met the eye. For one thing, not every state departed from the English model. The framers of the Maryland constitution devised an elaborate system of elections—some officials were chosen directly by the voters, others were chosen by electors who were chosen by the voters, and a graduated scale of property qualifications delimited the eligible voters and officeholders at various levels—the whole being designed to provide substitutes, based upon property holdings, for the hereditary English estates. New York's framers provided even more ornate artificial checks and balances. New Jersey's constitution provided for a traditional tripartite division of powers, but vested them in the executive and a two-

[54] Benjamin F. Wright, Jr., "The Origins of the Separation of Powers in America," *Economica* 13 (1933): 169–185.

[55] The six that expressly endorsed the doctrine were Georgia, Maryland, Massachusetts, New Hampshire, North Carolina, and Virginia (Thorpe, *Constitutions*, 2:778, 3:1687, 1893, 4:2457, 5:2787, 7:3813, 3815).

[56] Ibid., 3:1893.

part legislature; a court system was provided for, but the governor and the upper house constituted the ultimate court of appeals, in imitation of English practice to the extent that the House of Lords was the supreme appellate court of England.[57]

The last of these was symptomatic of something fundamental: few Americans except lawyers trusted a truly independent judiciary. To be sure, Montesquieu contended that the judicial power should be separate from and independent of the executive and legislative powers. But in Montesquieu's schema the judges were to be temporary officeholders, periodically drawn from and returned to the ranks of ordinary citizens; clearly, what Montesquieu had in mind were the juries, which at the time of the publication of L'Esprit des lois (1748) had not yet begun to be curtailed by Mansfield's "usurpations." Judges were what Americans distrusted, and Mansfield was one of the reasons for this distrust. Most states provided long terms for judges, but the notion that the judges should be so independent as to have power to overrule juries or to pass upon the constitutionality of laws enacted by legislative bodies was alien to American theory and practice. As James Duane said in his decision in the case of Rutgers v. Waddington, supposedly a precedent for the doctrine of "judicial review" of legislative enactments, the judiciary could never overrule a statute, "for this were to set the judicial above the legislative," which derived its powers directly from the sovereign people. Besides, judgment of matters of constitutionality in New York was vested in the state's unique Council of Revision, whose personnel were drawn partly from the executive and partly from the judicial branch. As to whether juries could disregard statute law, that question, as indicated earlier, was a vexing one.[58]

[57] Ibid., passim.
[58] Montesquieu, Spirit of the Laws, 153 (bk. 11, chap. 6); Goebel, Law Practice of Hamilton, 1:415. For the New York "council to revise all bills" see Thorpe, Constitutions, 5:2628–2629. The Maryland Court of Appeals (ibid., 3:1700) was also an attempt to define and delimit the power of judicial review. Similarly, the Delaware Constitution of 1776 (ibid., 1:565) had an appeal mechanism from the supreme court which was an admixture of legislative, executive, and judicial

Americans were even less trustful of executive power. American constitution makers, stunned and embittered by what they regarded as betrayal by George III, were loath to lodge executive authority in any single person. Part of it, that having to do with the conduct of war and of relations with other nations, was vested in Congress, which was all but powerless to carry out its assigned duties. At the state level, only three states had governors who served more than one-year terms, and no state endowed its governor with real power. Only one state (Massachusetts) gave its governor a conditional veto over legislation. Most of the traditional executive power was vested in state legislatures, and the actual enforcement of the laws was commonly entrusted to county sheriffs, to justices of the peace, and above all, to juries. For good measure, most of the new constitutions provided against a British-style growth of executive power by forbidding or restricting the holding of more than one office, and several called for rotation in office.[59]

That left, by way of either checks and balances or separation of powers, such separation and restraint as was afforded by having two branches of a legislature. Pennsylvania's legislature was unicameral, and so, for practical purposes, was that of Georgia. Of the remaining nine constitutions, four (those of South Carolina, Maryland, New Jersey, and Virginia) severely limited the checking power of their senates by denying to the upper house the authority to amend money bills. Four others (Massachusetts, New Hampshire, North Carolina, and Delaware) did

officers. The constitutions of New Jersey and Pennsylvania set seven-year terms for supreme court judges (ibid., 5:2596, 3088).

[59] For provisions regarding rotation in office see ibid., 3:1689, 1890–1891, 5:3083, 6:3752, 7:3813; for limitations on multiple officeholding see ibid., 1:565, 2:780, 781, 3:1689, 1909, 4:2469, 5:2598, 2792, 2793, 3087, 6:3244, 3253, 3758, 7:3815. The Delaware Constitution of 1776 (ibid., 1:565) provided that "the members of the legislative and privy councils shall be justices of the peace for the whole state," just as the Pennsylvania Constitution of 1776 provided (ibid., 5:3087) that "every member of the [supreme executive] council shall be a justice of the peace for the whole commonwealth, by virtue of his office." For the direct responsibility of justices of the peace and sheriffs and their frequent election see ibid., 1:565, 2:784, 3:1698, 5:2597, 2634, 3089, 6:3246.

vest the upper house with powers equal to those of the "democratic" branch, and New York established its Council of Revision. But the primary checks upon the legislatures in most states were annual elections of one or both houses and the destabilizing reserved right in the people of the states, severally, to alter or abolish their governments.[60] Unless and until additional restraints should be developed, the claims of juries would stand as the sole barriers to the majoritarian tyranny of legislative bodies.

Both republican theory and Oppositionist ideology entailed special attitudes toward property. Classical republicanism and avidity in the pursuit of wealth were, in a word, incompatible, at least in most versions of republican theory. Lycurgus, the designer of "the most perfect model of government that was ever framed," that of Sparta, forbade trade entirely and instituted equality of landholding among those who participated in public affairs. And Montesquieu taught that the virtue that was indispensable to sustaining a republic could be preserved only through frugality, simplicity, and a "mediocrity" of "abilities and fortunes." Indeed, Montesquieu wrote, if equality should break down, "the republic will be utterly undone." Thus it was "absolutely necessary there should be some regulation in respect

[60] For frequency of elections see ibid., 1:562, 2:778, 3:1687, 1895, 1898, 1900, 5:2596, 2790, 3084, 7:3813; similarly, a mandate for the frequency of legislative sessions is seen ibid., 1:562, 3:1687, 1892, 4:2457, 7:3815. Georgia, Maryland, Massachusetts, New Hampshire, and Pennsylvania had articles demanding that legislative and executive officers be accountable to the people, though without specifying how this was to be achieved (ibid., 2:784, 3:1687, 1890, 1892, 4:2454, 5:3082). A guarantee of the right of "frequent recurrence to fundamental principles" and the right to alter forms of government are contained in the constitutions of Maryland, Massachusetts, New Hampshire, North Carolina, Pennsylvania, Virginia, and in the Vermont one of 1786 (ibid., 3:1687, 1890, 4:2455, 5:2788, 3083, 7:3813; 6:3752, 3754). Closely allied was the right of the people to petition the legislature (ibid., 1:570, 3:1687, 1892, 4:2457, 5:2788, 3084, 6:3754). The theoretical underpinnings of these provisions are expounded by most political writers of the period, and maxims such as "Where annual elections end, there slavery begins" were commonplace. Also oft quoted was the Pope couplet "Like bubbles on the sea of matter borne, / They rise, they break, and to that sea return." For just one example see John Adams, "Thoughts on Government," in Adams, *Works of Adams*, 4:189–202.

to . . . all . . . forms of contracting. For were we once allowed to dispose of our property to whom and how we pleased, the will of each individual would disturb the order of the fundamental law.'' (There was available as a model a commercial republic, the ''Most Serene Republic'' of Venice, and among the seventeenth-century classical republicans in England that model had been highly appealing. During the eighteenth century, however, the attractiveness of Venice had largely vanished, at least among Americans, partly because of the city's decline and partly because Otway's popular play *Venice Preserved* depicted the republic as a wretched, corrupt oligarchy, ''Where all agree to spoil the public good, / And villains fatten with the brave man's labours.'')[61]

Carter Braxton, a Virginia signer of the Declaration, penned a telling description of the ideologue republicans whom he saw around him. To them, he wrote, ''*Public* virtue . . . means a disinterested attachment to the public good, exclusive and independent of all private and selfish interest. . . . A man, therefore, to qualify himself for a member of such a community, . . . must not, through ambition, desire to be great, because it would destroy that equality on which the security of the government depends; nor ought he to be rich, lest he be tempted to indulge himself in those luxuries, which, though lawful, are not expedient, and might occasion envy and emulation.'' Braxton, who thought such a system an especially pernicious form of tyranny, added: ''To this species of government every thing that looks like elegance and refinement is inimical. . . . Hence, in some ancient republics, flowed those numberless sumptuary laws, which restrained men to plainness and similarity in dress and diet, and all the mischiefs which attend Agrarian laws, and unjust attempts

[61]Montesquieu, *Spirit of the Laws*, 40–46, 94 (bk. 5, chaps. 1–5, bk. 7, chap. 1); Pocock, *Machiavellian Moment*, 387–390, 443, 534, and passim; Fink, *Classical Republicans*, 144–146; Adams, *Works of Adams*, 4:347–356. For a succinct statement of the incompatibility see Dickinson's remark on July 26, in Farrand, *Records*, 2:123, that he ''doubted the policy of interweaving into a Republican constitution a veneration for wealth. He had always understood that a veneration for poverty & virtue, were the objects of republican encouragement.''

to maintain their idol equality by an equal division of property."[62]

For every Braxton who decried such republicanism, there were ten public men who endorsed it, at least as long as the Spirit of Seventy-six prevailed. At the beginning of the Revolution, John Adams strongly recommended sumptuary laws so as to prevent excessive accumulation and consumption. "Whether our countrymen have wisdom and virtue enough to submit to them," he added, "I know not; but the happiness of the people might be greatly promoted by them. . . . Frugality is a great revenue, besides curing us of vanities, levities, and fopperies, which are real antidotes to all great, manly, and warlike virtues."[63] At the end of the war an anonymous pamphleteer in Charleston, South Carolina, quoted *Cato's Letters* approvingly: "Men in moderate circumstances, are most virtuous. An equality of estate, will give an equality of power; and equality of power is a natural commonwealth. . . . The first seeds of anarchy are produced from hence, that some are ungovernably rich, and many more are miserably poor; that is, some are masters of all means of oppression and others want all the means of self-defence."[64] In between these two, writers and orators and political leaders rang endless changes on these sentiments.[65]

[62] Carter Braxton, "An Address to the Convention . . ." (*Virginia Gazette*, June 8, 15, 1776), in *American Political Writing during the Founding Era, 1760–1805*, ed. Charles S. Hyneman and Donald S. Lutz, 2 vols. (Indianapolis, Ind., 1983), 1:334. By agrarian laws, Braxton means laws that redistribute landholdings.

[63] Adams, "Thoughts on Government," ibid., 1:403, 407, 408.

[64] "Rudiments of Law and Government Deduced from the Law of Nature" (1783), ibid., 1:577–578. On the matter of equality of property see Jefferson to Madison, Oct. 28, 1785, in Boyd, *Papers of Jefferson*, 8:681–682; and on its implications for republican political economy, Madison to Jefferson, June 19, 1786, ibid., 9:659–660.

[65] See for example, Hyneman and Lutz, *American Political Writing*, 1:499–526, 528, 577–578, 595, 659, 661, 663; Morgan, *Puritan Political Ideas*, 358–359, 365; Niles, *Principles and Acts*, 28, 57, 62–66, 385–386; Burnett, *Letters*, 3:84, 451–452, 482–484, 500, 4:163, 255, 260. For examples of Patriots' bemoaning the loss of virtue through love of luxury see Niles, *Principles and Acts*, 20, 39, 47, 52, 69, 74–75, 337. The idea was expressed often in the Constitutional Convention; see, for one example, Farrand, *Records*, Aug. 13, 2:268.

Moreover, the precepts were acted upon. The two principal methods for doing so, as Braxton indicated, were sumptuary laws and agrarian laws. As for sumptuary laws, Congress itself repeatedly adopted resolutions limiting or prohibiting a wide range of activities, from spending on luxuries to theatergoing, but Congress had no power to enforce its resolutions. The states did have power, and they exercised it. Most of the state constitutions directly or indirectly enjoined the passage of such restrictive legislation. The Massachusetts Bill of Rights, for instance, declared that a "constant adherence" to principles of "piety, justice, moderation, temperance, industry and frugality, are absolutely necessary to preserve the advantages of liberty"; and that the people had "a right to require of their lawgivers and magistrates an exact and constant observance" of those principles "in the formation and execution of the laws."[66] Pennsylvania's constitution said that "laws for the encouragement of virtue, and prevention of vice and immorality, shall be made and constantly kept in force."[67] Authorized by such constitutional mandates, the state legislatures deluged their constituents with laws proscribing "every thing that looks like elegance and refinement."[68]

As for agrarian laws, it is true that no proposals for redistribution of the land owned by Patriots had been seriously considered, but what had been done in that direction was enough to inspire uneasiness in the bosom of every substantial landholder. Wholesale wartime expropri-

[66] Commager, *Documents*, 109.

[67] Thorpe, *Constitutions*, 5:3091.

[68] See chap. 2, n. 9, above. The Pennsylvania Constitution of 1776, sec. 45, gave a specific mandate for the passage of sumptuary laws (Thayer, *Pennsylvania Politics*, 226, and Thorpe, *Constitutions*, 5:3091). For fundamental law upon which specific sumptuary laws could be erected see the Massachusetts Constitution of 1780, chap. 5, sec. 2, also pt. 1, sec. 3; the Virginia Bill of Rights, art. 15; the New Hampshire Constitution of 1784, pt. 2; the proposed Vermont Constitution of 1777. Certain state taxation policies had the effect of sumptuary legislation: see Madison to Jefferson, Mar. 18, 1786, in Boyd, *Papers of Jefferson*, 9:335. In the Constitutional Convention, Mason was the strongest supporter of "sumptuary regulations" (Farrand, *Records*, 2:606); but his proposal to enable Congress to enact such legislation was defeated on Aug. 20 by a vote of 8 to 3 (ibid., 2:344).

ation of the holdings of Loyalists and British subjects was still fresh in mind when the 1787 Convention met; indeed, sale of the property was still going on. And though a variety of motives—avarice not least among them—entered into the confiscations and divestments, state after state specifically directed that the larger confiscated estates be sold in small parcels, so as to break up "dangerous monopolies of land."[69]

In this connection it should be observed that while the more strident republicans were on the whole entirely sincere in their protestations about "simplicity" and "mediocrity of property"—John Adams listed laws that occasioned "frequent division of landed property" as one of five main sources of liberty in New England—there were among them some who played at demagoguery and exploited the politics of envy for personal gain.[70] Thus, in practice, sales of confiscated property had often been colossal boondoggles, carried out to enrich political insiders. Indeed, it is impossible to be precise about the amount of Loyalist property that was confiscated, because so much fraud was involved. For instance, bands of speculators in Maryland, all the while uttering republican pieties, were able, through chicanery, to acquire confiscated estates at about a tenth of their prewar market value. Apparently the total value of all confiscated property in the state was about $1.3 million, though far less was realized in the sale of it. In New York, sales in the Southern District alone brought in about $1.25 million, and sales in the state as a whole totaled nearly $4 million; most of the purchases were made by large-scale speculators. Property confiscated in Georgia was worth an estimated $1 million, though much less was paid for it; purchasers in North Carolina paid about $1.5 million for confiscated estates. All told, it seems safe to estimate that the value of property confiscated by bills of

[69]The state confiscatory legislation is summarized in detail in Van Tyne, *Loyalists*, 327–341, which covers all states except Maryland. Regarding Maryland see the Annapolis *Maryland Gazette*, Mar. 3, 10, Apr. 21, 28, 1780, and Laws of Maryland, Oct. sess., 1780, chap. 45.

[70]The quotation is from John Adams to Abigail Adams, Oct. 29, 1775, in Adams, *Familiar Letters of Adams*, 120–121.

attainder—without either due process or compensation of any kind—amounted to more than $20 million, or close to a tenth of the value of all improved real estate in the country.[71] In addition, the estates of absentee proprietors that were taken by divestment acts—from the Penns in Pennsylvania, the Calvert heirs in Maryland, the Granville proprietors in North Carolina, and the Fairfaxes in Virginia—were, according to the claims of the dispossessed owners, worth well over $8 million.[72]

This orgy of breaking up "dangerous monopolies of land" had abated by 1787, but large property holders had no reason to be cocksure that it would never be resumed: if one turn of the wheel of politics had brought such a fate to Loyalists and English proprietors, another turn could bring the same fate to men of wealth who had been Patriots. The republican "levelling spirit," as Elbridge Gerry called it at the Constitutional Convention, remained alive and well even in respectable circles, as a well-known tract published by Noah Webster during that year abundantly attested.[73] Most frightening of all was the prospect that the *demos*

[71] Commissioners' Ledger and Journal, and Sale-Book of Confiscated British Property, 1781–1785, both manuscripts in Maryland Hall of Records, Annapolis; Harry B. Yoshpe, *The Disposition of Loyalist Estates in the Southern District of the State of New York* (New York, 1939); Sale-Book of Confiscated Estates, 1782, 1785, manuscript in the Georgia Department of Archives and History, Atlanta; Robert O. DeMond, *The Loyalists in North Carolina during the Revolution* (Hamden, Conn., 1964), 171–174; Van Tyne, *Loyalists.* Charles A. Beard, in *An Economic Interpretation of the Constitution of the United States* (New York, 1913), 37, made some ingenious calculations and emerged with an estimate that the value of all taxable land in 1787 was about $400 million. I believe that estimate a bit high; but in any event, because the quantity of privately held land had increased so greatly through the acquisition of western lands, it seems safe to estimate the improved real property during the Revolution at about half that figure. For a British summary of the state of Loyalist property in 1783 see *Documents of the American Revolution, 1770–1783,* ed. K. G. Davies, 21 vols. (Dublin, 1972–1981), 21:200–201. It is to be observed that bills of attainder were prohibited by several state constitutions.

[72] Divestments and the claims of former proprietors are conveniently summarized in DeMond, *Loyalists in North Carolina,* 210–211. Regarding the Pennsylvania proprietors see also Robert L. Brunhouse, *The Counter-Revolution in Pennsylvania, 1776–1790* (Harrisburg, Pa., 1942), 79–80.

[73] Farrand, *Records,* May 31, 1:48; Noah Webster, "An Examination into the Leading Principles of the Federal Constitution . . . ," in *Pamphlets on the Constitution of the United States,* ed. Paul L. Ford (New York, 1968; republication of 1888 ed.), 34–35.

might rise and, in the name of republican virtue, redistribute all property by force. In truth, there was no ground for such a fear, for the vast majority of American families held a comfortable amount of land, and poverty of the depth that was common in Europe was all but unknown;[74] yet the reality could not entirely dissolve the specter.

The Oppositionist tradition also delimited property relationships in America, for it had at its core an almost hysterical fear of and hostility toward monetized paper credit, complementing its glorification of ownership of the land. In the 1720s and 1730s Bolingbroke, echoing the thoughts and language employed earlier in *Cato's Letters*, excoriated the "kind of false wealth, called paper credit" and charged that it had undermined the gentry, corrupted the body politic, and poisoned English society. Stockjobbers and moneymen and figure jugglers—who lived and grew rich, not by honest labor or trade or by "any other business of use or advantage to mankind"—were "cankers" who "preyed on the vitals of their country till they had reduced it to the most declining condition."[75] John Adams, who always admired Bolingbroke, was one of innumerable Americans who parroted these sentiments. "Credit has been the Inlet to most of the Luxury & Folly which has yet infected our People," he wrote. "He who could devise a method to abolish it forever, would deserve

[74] For documentation of this in two states see Brown and Brown, *Virginia: Democracy or Aristocracy?* passim, and Brown, *Middle-Class Democracy,* passim. For those who are not persuaded by the Browns' studies, I recommend travel accounts: virtually every traveler in British North America and the United States during the eighteenth century commented on the general level of property holding and the absence of poverty. See, for example, François Barbé-Marbois, *Our Revolutionary Forefathers* (Letters of 1779–1785), trans. Eugene P. Chase (Freeport, N.Y., 1969). See also, for example, Franklin to Jefferson, Mar. 20, 1786, in Boyd, *Papers of Jefferson,* 9:349, and Charles Thomson to Jefferson, Apr. 6, 1786, ibid., 9:380. For comparisons with France see Jefferson to Eliza House Trist, Aug. 18, 1785, ibid., 8:404; and Ames, "No Revolutionist," in Allen, *Works of Ames,* 1:10.

[75] Kramnick, *Bolingbroke and His Circle,* 70–71 and passim.

a Statue to his Memory."[76] As vigorously, Bolingbroke glorified the gentry; Thomas Jefferson's oft-quoted assertion that "those who labor in the earth are the chosen people of God if ever He had a chosen people, in whose breasts He has made His peculiar deposit for substantial and genuine virtue" might have been taken directly from Bolingbroke's *Craftsman*.[77]

This mystique of the land could be used to justify agrarian laws, but it could also be made to justify getting rich by speculating in land. That is, if one obtained a few thousand or a few score thousand acres of land from the public domain, if one recruited settlers, and if one retailed the land in, say, hundred-acre parcels to them, then one was contributing to the public weal both by helping to retire the public debt and by increasing the number of independent (and therefore virtuous) citizens. The profits therefrom, being mere useless gold, were even compatible with Lockean principles of natural law. Thus could republicans legitimize the amassing of great wealth through land jobbing, all the while espousing the equality of wealth and denouncing paper speculators as sores on the body politic.[78]

One more point needs making. The hostility that agrarian republicans who speculated in the public lands expressed toward people who trafficked in public securities was powerfully underscored by a conflict of interests between the two. The states and the Congress were, in 1787,

[76] John Adams to King, June 14, 1786, in King, *Life of King*, 1:182. Jefferson to Alexander Donald, July 28, 1787, in Boyd, *Papers of Jefferson*, 11:633: "The maxim of buying nothing without money in our pocket to pay for it, would make of our country one of the happiest upon earth. . . . I look forward to the abolition of all credit."

[77] Jefferson, *Notes on Virginia*, Query 19; also Jefferson to Jay, Aug. 23, 1785, in Boyd, *Papers of Jefferson*, 8:426: "Cultivators of the earth are the most valuable citizens. They are the most vigorous, the most independent, the most virtuous, and they are tied to their country and wedded to it's liberty. . . . I consider the class of artificers as the panders of vice and the instruments by which the liberties of a country are generally overturned."

[78] See, for example, David Ramsay, "Oration," July 4, 1778, in Niles, *Principles and Acts*, 380–381; William Grayson to Washington, Apr. 15, 1785, in Burnett, *Letters*, 8:96. Grayson, a staunch republican, owned 8,500 acres of western land; Washington eventually owned upwards of 500,000 acres.

crushed under a burden of public debts amounting to about $100 million. Supporting these debts was far beyond the means of government under existing political arrangements, and certificates of public debt accordingly circulated at one-quarter to one-tenth of their nominal value. But governments had a huge asset as well, in the form of vacant lands. Congress had the Northwest Territory; Massachusetts had the largely unoccupied province of Maine, as well as its claims in New York; only one-third of New York, Pennsylvania, and New Hampshire was occupied; and three of the four states south of the Potomac had solid claims to lands extending to the Mississippi River. Speculators could contract with governments to purchase vacant lands at a dollar or so an acre and to pay for them in several annual installments in depreciated public securities at their face value, or ten to twenty-five cents an acre. The prospective profits were irresistible, and hordes of speculators—literally thousands—were busily negotiating purchases.

Only one thing could go wrong. If genuine and successful efforts to restore public credit were forthcoming, the market value of public securities would rise, and overextended land speculators would have to make cash payments of many times what they had bargained for. This had, in fact, already happened on a small scale in New York: in 1786 the state had put its public debt (and its share of the national debt) on an improved footing, prices of securities had risen, and a number of speculators in confiscated Loyalist estates had been bankrupted.[79]

[79] McDonald, *E Pluribus Unum*, 112–113 and n. 57. It should be added that some men speculated both in land and in securities; sometimes they were aware of the conflict, and sometimes they were not. Sometimes, indeed, there was no conflict, since some bought land for cash, not in securities, though among large-scale speculators that was unusual. One land speculator who understood the conflict of interests was Senator William Maclay of Pennsylvania, who grumbled, after the assumption of state debts by Congress in 1790, that "we have ruined our land-office by the assumption. The state certificates were the materials to buy the lands with" (*Journal of William Maclay . . .* , ed. Edgar S. Maclay [New York, 1890], 336). Maclay's colleague Robert Morris was speculating in both land and securities, was aware of the conflict, and supported Hamilton's funding system, even though doing so led ultimately to Morris's bankruptcy. See also pp. 220–222 below.

On the opposite hand, the collapse of public credit was
among the main reasons for the meeting of the Constitutional Convention. (Congress had not approved the Annapolis Convention's recommendation for calling the
Philadelphia Convention until February of 1787, when it
became clear that its hopes of obtaining an independent
source of revenue, through amendments to the Articles of
Confederation proposed in 1783, had been shattered.) And
if the convention took strong measures to restore public
credit, the ensuing rise in the market value of public
securities would—in addition to a wholesale wiping out of
land speculators—engender the creation of an enormous
amount of liquid property, of a sort that most Americans
had been conditioned to fear.

IV

SYSTEMS OF POLITICAL ECONOMY

THERE WAS YET ANOTHER DIMENSION TO THE question of relations between society and government, and that had to do with the body of thought that was coming to be called "political economy"—ideas about the policies governments should or should not pursue regarding property relations to promote the general welfare. The very concept of an economy had only recently emerged, and the common signification of the word "economist" (or "oeconomist," from the Greek for household manager) continued to be a private one, referring to a person who "economized" or lived frugally.[1] By the late 1780s, however, preoccupation with systems of political economy—triggered by postwar dislocations as well as by the powerful works of Sir James Steuart and Adam Smith—had become pandemic in western Europe and the United

[1]For example, in describing the qualities that he wanted in a wife, young Alexander Hamilton said he wanted her to be good natured and generous, that "she must neither love money nor scolding, for I dislike equally a termagent and an oeconomist" (Hamilton to John Laurens, Apr. 1779, in Syrett, *Papers of Hamilton,* 2:37). The word "oeconomy" was used on three recorded occasions during the Constitutional Convention—once each by Hamilton, Gerry, and Mason—and each time it was used to mean frugality (Farrand, *Records,* 1:57, 287, 2:606). In the popular literature the word, when used at all, was used in this manner; see, for example, Henry Fielding, *The History of Tom Jones, A Foundling* (1749), bk. 2, chap. 2, last paragraph. Samuel Johnson defined economy as household management, distribution of expense, frugality, disposition of things, and so on; he had no entry for "economist." As late as 1828, Noah Webster was defining economy the same way; he does define "economist" as one who manages frugally or writes about doing so.

States. Indeed, to judge from the debates in the state legislatures, from the output of legislation, and from the tracts published in newspapers, working out a felicitous relationship between government and economy would appear to have ranked among the primary public concerns on the eve of the Constitutional Convention. And after all, the express purpose of calling the predecessor Annapolis Convention had been to draft a uniform plan of commercial regulations.

Attitudes on the matter depended upon two considerations: beliefs as to what was possible and perceptions of what was desirable. The most common belief was that the wealth of the world was more or less fixed and therefore that a person or a nation could grow wealthier only at the expense of another. Generally accompanying this view was some variant of mercantilism, which held that a nation's share of the fixed store of wealth (commonly reckoned in gold) could and should be increased by trade and that governmental policy should be designed to help bring this about. An opposing body of theory, that of the French physiocrats, defined wealth more broadly and held that the amount of it could be increased, but only through agricultural labor minimally encumbered by restrictions and burdens. Two others, the Scots Steuart and Smith, contended that wealth could be increased enormously through capital investment and through an increase in the supply and efficiency of labor; but they took diametrically opposed stands regarding governmental interference in private economic activity. Each of these various positions, together with composites of them, had its advocates in America, and a few choice spirits were thinking along more sophisticated lines. Not everyone, however, agreed that increasing the wealth of the nation was entirely desirable, even if it were possible. Many believed that wealth would corrode public virtue by giving the people a taste for luxuries, by spreading a fever for gambling and speculation, and by bringing with it the rise of the "mobs of great cities."

These and other ideas about systems of political economy pervaded the public councils as the Constitutional

Convention approached: almost everyone had an opinion. The whole subject was a new one; indeed, the whole mode of thought was a new one. And thus, in this respect, experience could not be the Framers' only guide.

Moderns know that wealth and property have increased enormously since the late eighteenth century, but it must be admitted that history, until that time, appeared to be on the side of those who maintained or believed or felt that economic activity was a zero-sum game, one in which if any player gained, another lost in proportion. The twentieth-century economist Sumner Slichter has calculated mathematically that throughout human history the annual production of wealth could not, in fact, have increased a great deal from the days of Adam and Eve until approximately the year 1750.[2] It is therefore easy to understand John Adams and the puritanical view for which he spoke and also to understand the many other Americans who shared a somewhat pessimistic attitude toward the future of mankind, despite the optimism of the influential Locke and despite the abundance that was all around them. By the grace of God or by a turn of the wheel of fortune, Adams was not present at the framing, but his ideas were; and because he gave coherent expression to a widely held set of views, it is instructive to survey those portions of his theories which pertained to political economy.

Adams (who was to become a warm admirer of the work of Thomas Malthus) was convinced that there could be no net per capita economic growth, even through an increase in population and the settlement and cultivation of vacant lands. Indeed, Adams wrote that "the multiplication of the population so far transcends the multiplication of the means of subsistence, that the constant labor of nine-tenths of our species will forever be necessary to prevent all of them from starving with hunger, cold, and pestilence." And yet some people and some nations did grow wealthy.

[2] Sumner H. Slichter, *Economic Growth in the United States: Its History, Problems, and Prospects* (New York, 1966), 54–55.

There was only one legitimate way by which they could, and that was by practicing republican and/or puritanical virtues: frugality, temperance, prudence, and industry. Consequently, there was a "great and perpetual distinction in civilized societies" between the virtuous and wealthy few and the nonvirtuous and impoverished many.[3]

Two political implications were to be drawn from this view of the human condition. One was that the rich and virtuous should be given exclusive control of one branch of the legislative, the senate, so that they might not be corrupted by association with the vulgar. (Curiously, during the Constitutional Convention, Hamilton, Gouverneur Morris, and Franklin supported just such an arrangement, but for precisely the opposite reason. Morris put it thus: "The Rich will strive to establish their dominion & enslave the rest. They always did. They always will. The proper security agst them is to form them into a separate interest," whereby they could be checked by the democratic branch and the executive.) The other political implication of Adams's view was that government should continuously intervene in private economic activity, regulating it in all its aspects to ensure that fair value was always exchanged for fair value, and thus that no man should grow wealthy except by virtuous means.[4]

Adams's economic pessimism was reinforced by reflection upon the grinding poverty he saw in France and, to a lesser extent, in England during his years of diplomatic service. Fear of the consequences of such poverty, combined with the notion of economic activity as a zero-sum game, had led earlier to the development of mercantile systems in England and elsewhere. It was calculated in the late seventeenth century that out of a total English popula-

---

[3] Adams, *Works of Adams*, 6:560; Wharton, *Polity and the Public Good*, 48–49. See also Zoltan Haraszti, *John Adams & the Prophets of Progress* (Cambridge, Mass., 1952), 34–37. Haraszti maintains that most of Adams's ideas on the subject were derived from Harrington, though one would scarcely think so from the quotations cited here. Adams, it should be pointed out, was far from consistent in his political economy; at different times, for example, he damned all credit, praised Sir James Steuart, applauded Bolingbroke, and admired Malthus.

[4] Wharton, *Polity and the Public Good*, 87–88; Farrand, *Records*, July 2, 1:512.

tion of five and a half million people, more than a million and a quarter were "cottagers, paupers, vagrants, gypsies, thieves, beggars"; the country was plagued with an army of rootless workers who in times of depression or famine might, as an early mercantile writer put it, cause "dangerous uproars."[5]

In medieval times, rulers had sought to secure plenty by prohibiting exports and by facilitating imports. Mercantilists turned that policy around: they argued that exports, shipped to foreign markets where they were scarce and dear and exchanged for goods that were plentiful and cheap there but expensive at home, resulted in creating abundance at home. One of the pioneer English mercantilists, Thomas Mun, captured the spirit of the system in writing (ca. 1625) against a law prohibiting the exportation of bullion: "For if we behold the actions of the husbandman in the seed-time, when he casteth away much good corn into the ground, we will rather accompt him to be a mad man than a husbandman; but when we consider his labours in the harvest, we find the worth and plentiful encrease of his actions." What was essential was to obtain a favorable balance of trade. The hard core of mercantilist thought— and it must be remembered that mercantilism, though having a number of articulate spokesmen, was less a body of theory or a "school" of political economy than a corpus of flexible policy prescriptions—was that certain activities promoted and others defeated this end, and that it was the duty of the state to adopt those measures which promoted it.[6]

Americans had learned their mercantilism through the operation of the English Navigation Acts, and Patriots everywhere (except in South Carolina and Georgia, which

[5] Charles Wilson, "Social Mercantilism," in *Mercantilism: System or Expediency?* ed. Walter Minchinton (Lexington, Mass., 1969), 88. This little volume presents an excellent introduction to the subject from a wide range of interpretive points of view. Wilson's article was originally published as "The Other Face of Mercantilism," in *Transactions of the Royal Historical Society* 9 (1959): 81–101.

[6] Wilson, "Social Mercantilism," 88–89 and passim, and Thomas Mun, "The Means to Enrich this Kingdom, and to Increase Our Treasure," 7–10, both in Minchinton, *Mercantilism.*

had profited handsomely from a bounty on indigo) had joined in denouncing the acts; but after independence every state began to develop a mercantilist system of its own. The specific content of the several systems varied, of course, with the nature of the state's economy. Massachusetts, for instance, had no agricultural staples of consequence and nothing significant to export except lumber, fish, and the potash and pearlash that were by-products of the clearing of land. Accordingly, its mercantilistic program was a complex one, involving bounties on exports, protective duties on imports, inspection laws, and, above all, the promotion of manufactures through a combination of what might be styled state capitalism and a partnership between governmental and private economic endeavor. In 1786, for example, on the recommendation of Governor James Bowdoin, the state required the several towns to establish potash and pearlash works and to produce certain amounts annually for export by the state government. At various times it also authorized lotteries to raise capital for the building of privately owned woolen mills, paper mills, glass works, and loaf-sugar mills; granted Simon Willard a five-year monopoly on the making and selling of clock jacks; and granted John Noyes and Paul Revere a fifteen-year monopoly on the manufacture of iron with the use of steam power. Such measures, combined with a new spirit of enterprise in some quarters, bore fruit. Exclusive of spermacetti oil works, distilleries, and shipbuilding—the state's main prewar manufacturing activities—there were 2,397 factory establishments in Massachusetts by 1786. These were small operations, to be sure, but the value of goods they were producing annually for export by the late 1780s was three times as large as the total annual production of all New England before the war.[7]

[7] Messages of Bowdoin to the legislature, June 2, Oct. 25, 1785, Feb. 8, 21, 1786, statutes of Mar. 6, May 7, 1782, Feb. 26, Mar. 1, 1783, June 2, 1784, Nov. 28, 30, 1785, Feb. 8, Mar. 6, 1786—all in *Acts and Laws of the Commonwealth of Massachusetts,* 13 vols. (Boston, 1781–1789); "Evaluations and Taxes," vol. 163, in Massachusetts Archives, Boston. Data on the value of prewar manufactures that were produced for export are derived from *United States Commercial and Statistical Register,* ed. Samuel Hazard, vol. 1, no. 1 (Philadelphia, 1839), 4–5. The value of

In New York, which produced a large quantity of wheat and flour as well as manufactured goods for export, the emphasis was placed upon the regulation and inspection of local commodities so as to maintain a reputation for quality products in international markets. The legislature rechartered the Chamber of Commerce, enacted a uniform system of weights and measures, and passed acts for the regulation and inspection of, to list a few, pearlash and potash, sole leather, flour, flaxseed, lumber, butter, lard, beef, pork, and bread. The energetic state government headed by Governor George Clinton did not, however, neglect promotional and developmental activities. In addition to passing protective tariffs, it established a bounty to encourage the growth of hemp, promoted an iron-manufacturing works, and granted a monopoly to John Fitch for the navigation of state waterways with steamboats. Moreover, it authorized a survey that would ultimately lead to the construction of the Erie Canal by the state government.[8]

The tobacco-growing states faced a special situation. Planters had long been convinced that the enormous debts they owed to English and Scottish merchants had been a function of the Navigation Acts, and they expected to prosper in the postwar era by avoiding British middlemen and by exporting directly to the European Continent. When the golden age failed to materialize—tobacco prices reached a high in the mid eighties, but then they broke, rarely again to rise to truly profitable levels—the planters blamed everyone but themselves. Most particularly, as was indicated

exported postwar manufactures is calculated from "Account of the Exports and Clearances of the Port of Boston for the Years 1787 and 1788," in the Massachusetts Miscellaneous Collection in the Manuscripts Division of the Library of Congress; "Abstract of Imports [sic] Previous to 1792," in the Customs Office Records, Port of Salem, in the Fiscal Section of the National Archives; Beverly Customs Office Records, in Beverly (Mass.) Historical Society; and various newspapers. See also Oscar Handlin and Mary F. Handlin, *Commonwealth: A Study of the Role of Government in the American Economy: Massachusetts, 1774–1861* (New York, 1947).

[8] *Laws of the State of New York Passed at the Sessions of the Legislature*, vols. 1–3 (Albany, 1886–1887), 1:599, 625, 630, 665, 680, 2:295, 298, 472, 714, 718. See also Alfred F. Young, *The Democratic Republicans of New York: The Origins, 1763–1797* (Chapel Hill, N.C., 1967), 236–237, 245, 248–250.

earlier, they blamed Robert Morris, who had negotiated a three-year monopoly contract for the shipment of American tobacco to France. (Thomas Jefferson spent much of his official energy while minister to France in efforts to undo that contract, even as John Adams labored in England mainly to secure advantages for the New England fishing and whaling industries.)[9]

But in Virginia and Maryland the legislatures also tried, through their own variants of mercantilist systems, to strike at what they regarded as the root cause of the depression in tobacco prices. The difference between prices in America and those in Europe was enormous, and planters were convinced that the reason for this was that Virginia and Maryland were dependent upon foreign shippers to carry their tobacco to market. People in these states were unwilling to change their ways and go into trading, but they believed that if enough local vessels were built to carry about a third of the tobacco, competition would drive freight costs down, and profits would rise proportionately. In accordance with such thinking and with inducements provided by the legislatures, Marylanders and Virginians constructed a sizable fleet during the four years after the peace. The potential advantages to planters in the selling and buying of their goods were large.[10]

[9] Prices can be traced in the various newspapers. For example, in Alexandria the price fell from over 40 shillings a hundred in mid 1784 to 30 shillings late in Feb. 1785, then steadily downward to 22 in Dec. and 21 in Jan. 1786 (Alexandria *Virginia Journal*, Feb. 24, Apr. 14, June 30, Aug. 4, Sept. 29, Dec. 1, 1785, Jan. 12, 1786). See also Simeon Deane to Barnabas Deane, Nov. 13, 1784, in *Correspondence between Silas Deane, His Brothers, and Their Business and Political Associates, 1771–1795, Collections* of the Connecticut Historical Society, vol. 23 (1930), 205. A similar course may be seen in William Hemsley to Tench Tilghman and Company, Mar. 21, 29, Apr. 1, 4, May 3, 31, July 19, 1785, in William Hemsley Papers, Library of Congress; compare the curve of wheat prices in New York, steadily downward from 9s. 6d. per hundredweight in Dec. 1784, to 7s. 6d. a year later, in *New York Packet*, Dec. 13, 1784, Mar. 7, June 11, Oct. 3, Dec. 8, 1785. Historians (see, e.g., Merrill Jensen, *The New Nation: A History of the United States, 1781–1789* [New York, 1950], 203; and Frederick L. Nussbaum, "American Tobacco and French Politics, 1783–1789," *Political Science Quarterly* 40 [1925]: 497–516) have generally tended to attribute the decline to Morris. I did so myself in an earlier work: *We the People*, 55, 267–268. See also n. 43 of chap. 3 above.

[10] For details and discussion of this idea see Caroline County's instructions, in Richmond *Virginia Gazette*, Oct. 25, 1783; "To Lord North," ibid., Nov. 1, 1783;

Two additional aspects of legislative activism in regard to economic enterprise want notice. One is that in adopting mercantile systems, the states were not entirely reversing the positions that Patriots had taken earlier against the Navigation Acts. Rather, in considerable measure their programs were enacted to overcome or retaliate for new restrictions that had been imposed by Parliament after the peace. Britain had closed its ports to the products of American fisheries, had enacted a prohibitive duty on whale oil, and had banned American shipping from the British West Indies. Moreover, British ships continued to carry a large share of American goods. By 1786, cries for counteraction to remedy the situation were common in American ports, and committees of merchants and trades-men were being organized to promote a united national policy by giving the Confederation Congress the power to regulate international commerce.

The other aspect of the matter, one that posed vexing problems for members of the Constitutional Convention, was that the whole subject was plagued by interstate jealousies. The states did not become involved in tariff wars with one another, as had once been expected: each state expressly exempted from its tariffs goods imported from sister states. Even so, New York and Pennsylvania, through which neighboring states did most of their importing, collected sizable revenues from import duties that were ultimately paid by consumers in New Jersey, Delaware, and Connecticut. Those states were as eager to share such revenues as the New Yorkers and Pennsylvanians were to keep them. More troublesome was that large numbers of southerners feared that if Congress were given power to pass navigation acts, northerners would combine to give themselves a monopoly of American shipping and to

"Mentor's Reply," ibid., Apr. 10, 17, 1784; Nansemond's instructions, ibid., Nov. 12, 1784; "A," ibid., Nov. 19, 1785; John Marshall to Charles Simms, June 16, 1784, in Charles Simms Papers, Library of Congress; "Columbus," in Phila-delphia *Freeman's Journal*, July 11–25, 1787; Madison to Jefferson, Aug. 20, 1784, in Rutland, *Papers of Madison*, 8:102–110. The expansion of the fleets of the two states has been observed in the Naval Officer Returns, Virginia State Library, Richmond, and in the Baltimore Import and Export Books, National Archives.

promote northern manufactures through protective tariffs at southern expense.

A radically different set of ideas about political economy was that worked out between the 1750s and the 1770s by the French physiocrats, the first group to refer to themselves as "economists" in the modern sense of the term. François Quesnay, the leading thinker in the group, built upon the idea of a circular flow of goods and services which had been conceived by Richard Cantillon—whose book also influenced Sir James Steuart and Adam Smith and, through them and others, but apparently not directly, found its way into American thinking—to develop the first graphic and quantitative "model" of how a national economy actually works, namely, Quesnay's *tableau oeconomique*. Quesnay postulated that the land and the land alone could produce a surplus, which is to say a product of greater value than that of the labor invested in it: because of nature's bounty, the labor of twenty-five adults could yield a sustenance for a hundred adults. From this proposition he divided people into two classes, "productive" and "sterile." The productive were the cultivators or, more properly, the *fermiers*, who owned no land but owned their tools and animals and who constituted a sort of agricultural entrepreneurial class. The sterile were landowners and merchants, who produced nothing but consumed much through their rents and profits, and urban artisans, who produced an amount equal to but never exceeding the value of their labor, which provided them a bare subsistence. The *tableau oeconomique* would be regarded by later economists as a significant advance in economic thought, though it was too complicated and abstract to be understood by many people in a world in which thinking quantitatively was not a common habit. For that and other reasons—most importantly that physiocratic theory ran into irreconcilable tensions in its efforts at "adapting free market economics and possessive individualism to the specifically French experience"—

Quesnay and his followers failed to gain many adherents among their countrymen.[11]

Considerable numbers of Americans, however, did find physiocratic theory appealing. Among those who had embraced the agrarian ideal, the theory gave what appeared to be scientific confirmation of their bias by its insistence upon the absoluteness of property rights, the uniqueness of land as the source of wealth, and the superiority of agriculture as a way of life. There was another source of appeal as well. The physiocrats had coined the slogan *laissez faire:* they taught that there were natural laws governing economic activity and that if those laws were followed, the result would be increased productivity and maximum benefits for society as a whole. This did not necessarily imply a liberal political regime; indeed, Quesnay held that in France absolute monarchy would be required in order to force people to behave "economically" and "naturally." The compatibility (though by no means the identity) of such thinking with Bolingbroke's idea of a patriot king is striking.

No American of John Adams's turn of mind could swallow the physiocrats' message; but many, including Benjamin Franklin and Thomas Jefferson, were signifi-

[11]On the physiocrats in general see Ronald L. Meek, *The Economics of Physiocracy: Essays and Translations* (Cambridge, Mass., 1963), and Elizabeth Fox-Genovese, *The Origins of Physiocracy: Economic Revolution and Social Order in Eighteenth-Century France* (Ithaca, N.Y., 1976); the quotation is from the latter, 16. For a brief summary see Overton H. Taylor, *A History of Economic Thought: Social Ideals and Economic Theories from Quesnay to Keynes* (New York, 1960), 12–27. For a great economist's appraisal of the *tableau* see Joseph Schumpeter, *A History of Economic Analysis* (New York, 1954), 223–243. Regarding the matter of learning to think numerically see Patricia Cline Cohen, *A Calculating People: The Spread of Numeracy in Early America* (Chicago, 1982), passim.

I am indebted to Elizabeth Fox-Genovese for calling Cantillon to my attention. An Irishman who went to France as a part of John Law's entourage, Cantillon made a fortune in speculations before writing his *Essai sur la Nature du Commerce* during the 1730s. The work circulated in manuscript form for more than twenty years, most of that time in the hands of Mirabeau, and then was published in 1755. I have found no American references to it, but it was borrowed from and quoted extensively by Postlethwayt, Hume, Steuart, and Smith, all of whom were studied by Americans. For a brief summary of Cantillon's thinking and his influence see Guy Routh, *The Origin of Economic Ideas* (White Plains, N.Y., 1975), 62–68.

cantly influenced by Quesnay. Franklin had come directly under the influence of physiocratic thinkers during his service as a colonial agent during the 1760s. Like Adams, Franklin was appalled by the poverty of Europe, but he was led thereby to cherish the primarily agricultural society of his homeland. Of Americans who wanted to forsake that way of life for the riches of manufacturing and trade, he wrote bitterly: "I can put them in a way to obtain a Share of it. Let them with three fourths of the People of Ireland, live the Year round on Potatoes and Butter milk, without Shirts, then may their Merchants export Beef, Butter, and Linnen. Let them, with the Generality of the Common People of Scotland go Barefoot, then may they make large Exports in Shoes and Stockings: And if they will be content to wear Rags like the Spinners and Weavers of England, they may make Cloths and Stuffs for all Parts of the World."[12]

And in 1769 Franklin had written to his friend Henry Home, Lord Kames, the Scottish jurist and philospher: "There seem to be but three ways for a nation to acquire wealth. The first is by *war*, as the Romans did, in plundering their conquered neighbours. This is *robbery*. The second by *commerce*, which is generally *cheating*. The third by *agriculture*, the only *honest way* . . . wrought by the hand of God in his favour, as a reward for his innocent life and his virtuous industry."[13] Some historians who have looked closely at the record would be surprised to discover that Franklin was ever engaged in any activity that was both entirely innocent and entirely virtuous; but a lot of Americans, then and later, shared the sentiments he expressed.

The doctrine of *laissez faire* found its way into American thinking, not primarily through the works of the phys-

[12] Drew R. McCoy, *The Elusive Republic: Political Economy in Jeffersonian America* (Chapel Hill, N.C., 1980), 52, 57–58, and "Benjamin Franklin's Vision of a Republican Political Economy for America," *William and Mary Quarterly* 35 (1978): 605–628; Alfred Owen Aldridge, *Franklin and His French Contemporaries* (New York, 1957), 23–30.

[13] *The Political Thought of Benjamin Franklin*, ed. Ralph L. Ketcham (Indianapolis, Ind., 1965), 229.

iocrats, but through Adam Smith's epoch-making book entitled *An Inquiry into the Nature and Causes of the Wealth of Nations*. Yet Smith's book owed a great deal to the earlier thought of the Dutch-born British subject Bernard Mandeville, whose writings conveyed a message that was at once unwelcome and irresistibly attractive.

Mandeville was both noted and notorious for a doggerel poem, first published in 1705 and republished with a lengthy commentary in 1714 as a book called *The Fable of the Bees*, subtitled *Private Vices, Publick Benefits*. The poem is an allegory of a beehive in which everyone is motivated by vicious drives and yet, because of the unfathomable workings of the complex social mechanism, prosperity comes to the whole.

> Millions endeavouring to supply
> Each other's Lust and Vanity . . .
> Thus every Part was full of Vice,
> Yet the whole Mass a Paradise.

But the bees, hypocritically feigning discontent at having their prosperity depend upon their vices, pray to be made virtuous. Unexpectedly, their prayers are granted, with catastrophic results. Avarice, luxury, debauchery, waste, intemperance, and gluttony suddenly disappear; and as suddenly, millions are unemployed. Prosperity, in sum, depends neither upon the designs of the state nor upon the benevolence of individuals, but upon having individuals act freely in their own self-interest.[14]

Mandeville was the spokesman for a radical new age, just then aborning but more than a century from its full fruition, in which both the Christian heritage and the republican tradition of civic humanism—both of which

[14] The definitive edition, containing all of Mandeville's works, is that edited by F. B. Kaye, 2 vols. (Oxford, Eng., 1924); the quoted passage is at 1:18, 24. Kaye's introduction, "Critical, Historical, and Explanatory," is a masterpiece of intellectual history, indispensable to any who would understand Mandeville and his influence. See also J. A. W. Gunn, *Beyond Liberty and Property: The Process of Self-Recognition in Eighteenth-Century Political Thought* (Kingston and Montreal, 1983), 96–119.

were fundamentally communitarian—would be over-
whelmed by naked materialism and acquisitive individualism. Two parallel institutional developments, one in the
field of commercial law and the other in the field of public
finance, would during the next few decades transform life
in the English-speaking world, with profound implications
for the American founding.

The common-law proscriptions of "offenses against the
public trade," mentioned in chapter 2, had been based
upon the ancient and medieval idea of the *justum pretium,*
or just price, which held that every commodity had a fair
value, corresponding approximately to the amount and
quality of labor required to produce it. In a world of villages
and manors and of designated once-a-week market towns,
that concept and its attendant prohibitions made a certain
amount of sense. In the realm of international trade they
made no sense whatever. Accordingly, international merchants had evolved their own body of customs, known as
the *lex mercatoria,* or law merchant, which applied only to
themselves and operated outside the framework of local
law but more or less had standing in the courts.[15]

Four major areas in which *lex mercatoria* differed from
the common law will illustrate the whole: usury, price,
negotiability, and contract. As for usury, in mid-eighteenth-
century England the legal interest rate was five percent; in
the southern American colonies it was eight to ten percent.
For local transactions, such rates were normally adequate,
given the supply of and demand for money and given the
ready availability of collateral security to minimize the risk
of making a loan. In regard to transoceanic commerce,
however, the risk of losing a ship and its cargo made fixed
interest rates unfeasible. Thus, merchants developed the
practice of insuring their cargoes, and lenders added the
insurance charge to the cost of their loans. If, for instance, a
London merchant borrowed £1,000 to finance a cargo of

---

[15] The standard eighteenth-century treatise on the subject was Wyndham
Beawes's *Lex Mercatoria Rediviva, or the Merchant's Directory* (London, 1758). See
also Leon E. Trakman, *The Law-Merchant: The Evolution of Commercial Law*
(Boulder, Colo., 1983).

woolen cloth to be shipped to Philadelphia and if the estimated likelihood of the loss of the ship was one chance in ten, he would pay fifteen percent rather than the legal five percent. In law, however, the transaction was viewed as two—one involving a five percent interest charge and another involving a ten percent insurance charge—and the lender was prohibited from acting as insurer, a third party being required for that purpose.[16]

The problem of price can be seen in the marketing of tobacco. During the seventeenth century, Virginia repealed its acts against engrossing and forestalling insofar as tobacco was concerned, for such restrictions were irrelevant in regard to a product to be consumed in Europe.[17] Nor was the principle of the just price applicable to sale in England, for the cost of getting the tobacco there bore little relation to the cost of producing it in America, and none at all to the market for it on the Continent, to which half or more was reexported. As a rule, tobacco and other American staples were exchanged internationally on the basis of the "laws" (though they were not yet so described) of supply and demand, except as these were restricted by the Navigation Acts. There had been two significant recent changes in the scheme of things: the Revolution had placed Americans outside the constraints and benefits of the Navigation Acts, and all southern states had reenacted their laws against engrossing and forestalling.[18]

The matter of negotiable instruments was rather more involved. The common law distinguished between two kinds of personal property, a *chose* (from the French for thing) *in possession* and a *chose in action*. The meaning of the first is self-evident; a *chose in action* was something due but not in possession, into which category fell all forms of promises to pay. It was a firmly established feature of the

---

[16] Gray, *Southern Agriculture*, 1:410; Blackstone, *Commentaries*, 2:459; Adam Smith, *An Inquiry into the Nature and Causes of the Wealth of Nations*, 2 vols. (Indianapolis, Ind., 1981), 1:109. This is the Glasgow Edition, edited by R. H. Campbell, A. S. Skinner, and W. B. Todd and published in the Liberty Classics series.

[17] Gray, *Southern Agriculture*, 1:419–420.

[18] Ibid., 2:588–589.

common law that no *chose in action* was assignable. Hence, if party A borrowed a sum from party B and gave as security a note promising to repay the sum, together with lawful interest, in one year, and if during that period party B fell into difficulty and needed funds, he could not sell the note to party C. Yet paper credit was the life's blood of international trade, and under the *lex mercatoria*, merchants worked out their own devices.[19]

The most important such device was the bill of exchange, a draft similar to a modern bank check except that it was drawn by a merchant upon his credit with another merchant. Suppose a London merchant wishes to buy a cargo of wheat in Philadelphia; he does not want to ship gold or silver and has no favorable balances with mercantile correspondents in Philadelphia, but does have a favorable balance with a merchant in Jamaica. He draws a bill of exchange upon the merchant in Jamaica and uses it to pay for the wheat in Philadelphia. The Philadelphia seller might trade regularly with Jamaica, in which case he would present the bill of exchange for payment there, or he might endorse it and use it to buy goods elsewhere in the Atlantic trading community. Bills might thus remain in circulation for a considerable time; they might also be postdated. Regular procedures were worked out to govern circumstances in which payment was refused by the house or merchant on whom it was drawn.[20]

Bills of exchange had come into being as early as the thirteenth century, and somewhere along the line foreign bills of exchange attained legal status in England. It was

[19] This and the two paragraphs that follow are derived from Blackstone, *Commentaries*, 2:442, 464–470. See also Horwitz, *Transformation of American Law*, 212–215.

[20] Sir James Steuart says that properly there are four parties to a bill of exchange: (1) the drawer, who has a balance in a distant place; (2) the buyer of the bill, to whose order it is to be paid; (3) the person on whom it is drawn in the distant place; and (4) the person to whom it is to be paid. Two of these (1 and 4) are creditors; the other two are debtors. By means of the bill, a London debtor of a Paris merchant repays his debt by paying a creditor London merchant, and a Paris debtor of a London merchant pays the Paris creditor merchant; hence, no money has to go from one place to the other (see *An Inquiry into the Principles of Political Oeconomy*, ed. Andrew S. Skinner, 2 vols. [Chicago, 1966], 2:568).

not, however, until the reigns of William III and Anne that inland bills of exchange were put on the same footing. The act of 3 and 4 Anne, c. 9, giving domestic bills that sanction, also made promissory notes assignable and endorsable, just as bills of exchange were.

The common law regarding contracts was still less congruent with the needs of trade. The definition of a contract was plain enough—according to Blackstone, it was "an agreement upon sufficient consideration, to do or not to do a particular thing"—and it was both morally and legally binding.[21] But the common law could become arcane in defining what was or was not an "agreement" or a "sufficient consideration," and there was the restriction against assignability if the contract was to do, deliver, or exchange something in future, for it was then a *chose in action*. Again, a statute of 29 Charles II, c. 3, provided that no contract for the sale of goods worth more than £10 could be valid unless the buyer received part of the goods at the time of the contract—an obvious impossibility if buyer and seller were in different countries. More importantly, there were complexities arising from the concept of the just price and fair value. As Blackstone said, "If I take up wares from a tradesman, without any agreement of price, the law concludes that I contracted to pay the fair value," which assumes that there is a "fair" value. When goods or services were exchanged or sold, the contract could be negated if either party could show that the consideration was unfair. If, for instance, a good that had been sold should prove to have a defect unknown to buyer and seller, the contract could be set aside, even though bargaining had been in good faith. As Patrick Henry put it, "there are thousands and thousands of contracts, whereof equity forbids an exact literal performance." A new contract theory, in which the market was the sole determinant of value, had recently emerged in England—"it is the consent of the parties alone, that fixes the just price of any thing, without reference to the nature of things themselves, or to

21 Blackstone, *Commentaries*, 2:442–443, 448.

their intrinsic value"—but in 1787 that innovation was yet to be adopted by any American state.[22]

Strains within the law of personal property became strong during the eighteenth century. For one thing, the sheer volume of trade increased enormously; that between Britain and its American colonies multiplied tenfold between 1697 and 1774, and more expansion was soon to come. For another, Britain was swept by a widespread "phrenzy" for gambling which produced many abuses of conventional commercial practices, particularly as related to insurance. In response, wholesale reform of the law began about the time of the accession of George III. In part, reform was a matter of parliamentary legislation, such as the statute 14 George III, c. 48, which prohibited the insurance of lives or events wherein the insured party had no interest and also prevented the recovery of damages in a greater amount than the interest of the insured. Much more, however, came through a succession of decisions rendered by the Court of the King's Bench during the chief justiceship of Lord Mansfield (1756–1788). Mansfield reshaped the law of bills of exchange, promissory notes, bank checks, and contracts to make them flexible and viable, and he also established the new field of marine insurance. By the time he was done, the *lex mercatoria* had been systematized and made an integral part of the law of the land in Britain.[23]

The United States lagged far behind.[24] There were, to be sure, a few American innovations in the direction of

[22] Jackson Turner Main, *The Antifederalists: Critics of the Constitution, 1781–1788* (Chapel Hill, N.C., 1961), 166; Horwitz, *Transformation of American Law*, 160–181. The English quotation is from John Powell's *Essay upon the Laws of Contracts and Agreements* (London, 1790), as cited by Horwitz, 160. For an example of the disarray of the American legal system because of the lack of uniformity see William Samuel Johnson to Matthew Griswold, Aug. 18, 1785, in Burnett, *Letters*, 8:190–191.

[23] Cecil H. S. Fifoot, *Lord Mansfield* (Oxford, Eng., 1936); Sir William S. Holdsworth, *A History of English Law*, 7th ed., revised vols. 6–8 (London, 1966); John C. Campbell, *The Lives of the Chief Justices of England . . .* , vol. 3 (London, 1857); John Holliday, *The Life of William, Late Earl of Mansfield* (London, 1797).

[24] Excellent accounts of the backwardness of American law in these areas are in Horwitz, *Transformation of American Law*, 161ff., and Nelson, *Americanization of the Common Law*, 51–52, 54–63. Regarding the Virginia system see Gray, *Southern Agriculture*, 1:228–230.

commercialization. One was the tobacco warehouse system, as regularized by a Virginia act of 1748, which became the prototype for acts in other tobacco-growing colonies/states. Under the Virginia statute, planters deposited their tobacco in public warehouses and received in exchange notes that were not only freely negotiable but also legal tender. Another innovation, a strange one, was that in the southern colonies/states slaves were by statute declared to be real property, not personal—which facilitated the seizure of slaves when slaveholders failed to pay their debts.[25]

Otherwise, Americans made do with the limited acceptance of the *lex mercatoria* which had prevailed in England before Mansfield, and it appeared unlikely in 1787 that a Mansfield-style transformation of American law was in the offing. As indicated, Mansfield's very name was anathema among many Americans because of what he had done to the jury system; moreover, many Southern agrarian republicans cherished the unchecked jury system precisely because of its usefulness in preventing the commercialization of the law.[26] There were, however, in the Constitutional Convention at least a few delegates—including Hamilton, Wilson, and Gouverneur and Robert Morris—who fully understood the implications of what Mansfield had done in England and were hopeful, even determined, that a similar transformation could be made to happen in America.

The same was true of a species of property that was newly evolved in England but did not yet exist in America, namely, a monetized public debt. The process by which

[25] Gray, *Southern Agriculture*, 1:416.
[26] Horwitz, *Transformation of American Law*, 142. Regarding the connection between debts, the law, and the court system see Roeber, *Faithful Magistrates*, 128–137, and *The Debates in the Several State Conventions on the Adoption of the Federal Constitution*, ed. Jonathan Elliot, 5 vols. (Washington, D.C., 1830–1836), 3:530–531, 542, 545–547, 578–579. The most recent in a long succession of studies of the Virginia debts is Charles F. Hobson, "The Recovery of British Debts in the Federal Circuit Court of Virginia, 1790 to 1797," *Virginia Magazine of History and Biography* 92 (1984): 176–200.

that revolutionary form of property came into being is of central importance, partly because of what it did to property law, partly because the American founders were acutely conscious of the new order, and partly because it provided one course that the United States might (and, in fact, did) follow in 1787 and afterward.

The proximate beginning of the Financial Revolution, as it has been called, lay in the wars in which England became involved directly upon (and largely as a result of) the accession of William and Mary. The wars lasted almost a quarter of a century, with but a four-year interlude along the way, and were the most expensive that England had ever fought. So expensive were they that the traditional sources of deficit financing were exhausted within the first five years.

Financing of government on credit had always been limited. On the one hand it was limited by the lack of a concept of the state, over and beyond the concept of the person of the Crown: the king could borrow, but so long as the source of revenue, the Commons, was a separate entity, his credit was restricted and inflexible, amounting at most to a few hundred thousand pounds. The revolutionary settlement radically changed that: thenceforth the three estates of the realm were embodied in a single state, whose resources and thus whose credit potentially comprehended the whole kingdom. On the other hand, the traditional borrowing power had also been limited by the readily accessible lenders: goldsmiths, scriveners, and tax farmers. Goldsmiths—craftsmen and traders in the precious metal—had customarily been moneylenders as well; and scriveners —literally scribes, or people who could write—had customarily been brokers as well. Both had had a tenuous legal standing, but both had been able to perform a service that no one else could do and therefore were tolerated, law or no law. Tax farmers, who received handsome commissions for the collection of taxes on real estate (and earlier, the customs), were often in a position to make somewhat more substantial loans to the Crown, but the sums available from that source were still fairly small. What was wanted, in the context of the 1690s, was an institutionalized source of loans, a financial counterpart to the newly emerged state.[27]

The institution was established in 1694, in the form of the Bank of England. The idea underlying the bank, the brainchild of a Scotsman named William Paterson, was that an association of individuals, chartered as an artificial person (a corporation), would raise a loan to the government that, instead of being repayable at a fixed future date, would return perpetual interest. The corporation would also be entitled to purchase any additional government debt, currently outstanding or to be created in future, and to issue circulating notes, to buy and sell bullion, and to trade in bills of exchange. The original capital of the bank, all of which was invested in certificates of government obligations called annuities, was £1,200,000. The departure of the new form of the public debt from older forms of property in England is illustrated by two circumstances. One is that the annuities themselves and the notes and bills of the bank were expressly exempted from all common-law restrictions upon the exchange of personal property. The other is that jointly the king and queen personally subscribed £10,000 to the initial loan.[28]

The debt grew astronomically during the next few years, and so did the bank and two sister institutions. By 1714 the total debt was £36 million, more than half of which was owned by the bank, the East India Company, and the South Sea Company. The East India Company, formed by a merger of older companies in 1709, was given a monopoly of trade with Asia in exchange for the purchase of a large sum of annuities. The South Sea Company, formed in 1711, purchased £9 million in annuities in exchange for a monop-

---

[27] P. G. M. Dickson, *The Financial Revolution in England: A Study in the Development of Public Credit, 1688–1756* (London, 1967), 5, 39–45, 341–343; Kramnick, *Bolingbroke and His Circle*, 40; see also Robert Ashton, *The Crown and the Money Market: 1603–1640* (Oxford, Eng., 1960), passim. Four of Samuel Johnson's seventeen definitions of the noun *state* relate in some way to government. Definition 5 is "Mode of government"; 6 is "The community; the publick; the commonwealth"; 8 is "Civil power, not ecclesiastical"; and 9, most interestingly, is "A republick; a government not monarchical."

[28] Kramnick, *Bolingbroke and His Circle*, 41–42; Dickson, *Financial Revolution*, 51–57.

oly of trade in commodities and slaves with Africa. By 1719 the public debt was more than £50 million. That meant a perpetual tax burden for interest payments, but it also meant that £50 million in absolutely liquid property had been brought into existence.[29]

The property had yet to become stabilized. In 1720 an orgy of speculation produced a sensational rise in the prices of annuities, of the stock of the three great corporations, and of the stock of newly proliferated joint-stock companies (organizations similar to corporations but lacking the legal status of a person); and then came an even more sensational collapse. This South Sea Bubble, as it was called, ruined many wealthy families and almost ruined the government of England into the bargain.[30]

That the public credit was saved was largely due to the efforts of Sir Robert Walpole, who served as chancellor of the exchequer and principal minister of the Crown from 1721 to 1742. Parliament had adopted the practice of making new issues of public debt redeemable after a long period instead of being perpetual, and in 1716 it had created a "sinking fund," a treasury reserve built up by setting aside the revenues from certain fixed taxes. Ostensibly the purpose of the sinking fund was to reduce and utimately to retire the public debt; under Walpole's administration its function instead turned out to be to convince people that the debt would be paid. By ostentatiously increasing the fund, Walpole restored public faith in the government's solvency, which in turn raised the market price of annuities and accordingly reduced interest rates. As this was happening, a complementary illusion was being created by the Bank of England: to facilitate an effort to refinance the entire debt at lower interest, the bank developed the practice of buying and selling annuities on the London stock exchange. This had the expected effect of making the market high and steady, but it also had the unexpected advantage of convincing the public that annuities and money would always be perfectly interchangeable. That

[29] Dickson, *Financial Revolution*, 39–75.
[30] Ibid., 90–156.

belief made the annuities into money, as well as a basis for money in the form of bank notes.[31]

Not everyone welcomed the Financial Revolution. To those who did, it appeared to be the philosopher's stone; and in truth, no economic development in England's history, not even the enclosure movement, long under way, or the Industrial Revolution, yet to come, would be so creative of the wealth of the nation. On the other hand, no economic development was half so disruptive. The entire institutional structure of society and politics in England had traditionally been based upon landholding: power had flowed from the holding of real property and, with minor exceptions, from real property alone. And now, of a sudden, personal property came to be quantitatively as important as real property and qualitatively far more so, for it was infinitely more mobile and therefore infinitely more dynamic.[32]

Americans tended to be among those who deplored the development; as was indicated earlier, vast numbers of them embraced the Opposition ideology that was worked out by Walpole's enemies. Not least among the reasons was that Walpole's regime ushered in, on a grand scale, one final form of property, that in public office. Such property was nothing new—it had existed as serjeantry during the Middle Ages and in other forms as well—but the huge sums paid out to "placemen" were unprecedented, and so was the artful "corruption" by which Walpole and his successors used patronage to control the flow of politics.

The new order in the mother country was based squarely, albeit not professedly, on Mandevillian principles, but it was a Scotsman, Sir James Steuart, who formulated the whole into a cogent system of principles. In a 1767 treatise called *An Inquiry into the Principles of Political Oeconomy*—a work often neglected by historians but one that was

[31] Ibid., 157-215; E. James Ferguson, "Political Economy, Public Liberty, and the Formation of the Constitution," *William and Mary Quarterly* 40 (1983): 390-398.

[32] Kramnick, *Bolingbroke and His Circle*, passim.

apparently read and admired by many Americans, including Hamilton, Madison, and Adams—Steuart set out to explain the emergence of what he called the "exchange economy."[33] He begins by examining the relationship between agricultural abundance and population increase— a matter of special concern to the physiocrats, whom he had thoroughly studied. Abundance will not of itself stimulate an increase, Steuart says, for farmers without markets have no incentive to produce any more than is required for their subsistence. If, however, a considerable segment of the population is composed of "free hands," which is to say they are not engaged in agriculture, and if the free hands have the means with which to buy, farmers will produce surpluses. The free hands, in turn, earn their wherewithal by producing commodities for the rich, who obtain their riches from rents on the land. Then, "as the ingenuity of workmen begets a taste in the rich" for attractive nonessentials, "so the allurement of riches kindles an ambition, and encourages an application to works of ingenuity, in the poor."[34]

This cycle is set in motion by the introduction of luxury and money. Unlike Mandeville, Steuart treats luxury in morally neutral terms: "By LUXURY," he says, "I understand *the consumption of any thing produced by the labour or ingenuity of man, which flatters our senses or taste of living, and which is neither necessary for our being well fed, well clothed, well defended.*" To money he gives a definition more sophisticated than that of many modern economists: "By MONEY,

[33] Joseph Dorfman, in *The Economic Mind in American Civilization, 1606-1865*, 2 vols. (New York, 1946), 1:243, wrote that all Americans "seemed to know Sir James Steuart." Michael Perelman, in *Classical Political Economy: Primitive Accumulation and the Social Division of Labor* (Totowa, N.J., 1984), 145-148, says that Steuart was far more influential in America than was Adam Smith during the eighteenth century. Perelman points specifically to Adams, Madison, and Hamilton. It must be noted, however, that Perelman's work is careless: I observed at least seven errors of fact, dates, or citation in those four pages. On the relative influence of Smith and Steuart see also Salim Rashid, "Adam Smith's Rise to Fame: A Reexamination of the Evidence," *Eighteenth Century: Theory and Interpretation* 23 (1982): 64-85. In the introduction to Hamilton's "Report on the Establishment of a Mint," Jan. 28, 1791, the editors note Hamilton's reliance upon Steuart (Syrett, *Papers of Hamilton*, 7:462ff).

[34] Steuart, *Principles of Political Oeconomy*, 1:40-42, 45-46.

I understand *any commodity, which purely in itself is of no material use to man for the purposes above-mentioned, but which acquires such an estimation from his opinion of it, as to become the universal measure of what is called value, and an adequate equivalent for any thing alienable.*" Whenever such "imaginary wealth" becomes well introduced into a country, "luxury will very naturally follow; and when money becomes the object of our wants, mankind become industrious, in turning their labour towards every object which may engage the rich to part with it." Money, in sum, creates a demand for luxury, which creates a demand for labor, which creates a demand for food; and each demand creates supply.[35]

Four fundamental premises underlie Steuart's thinking throughout the rest of the work. The first is that though there are "natural" economic "laws," or, rather, what he calls "principles" that govern economic activity, disasters can result if things are not carefully managed. Therefore "in treating every question of political oeconomy," Steuart emphasizes, "I constantly suppose a statesman at the head of government, systematically conducting every part of it, so as to prevent the vicissitudes of manners, and innovations, by their natural and immediate effects or consequences, from hurting any interest within the community."[36] If that statement is taken too literally, as contemporaries were wont to take it, Steuart's meaning is lost. Steuart's "statesman . . . conducting every part" of the economy is not one who attempts to direct the economy in detail, which is best left to individual bargainers, but a minister who attends to general trends and takes measures to prevent violent disruptions in the course of trade. (He mentions as statesmen of "great genius" Jean Baptiste Colbert, John Law, and Sir Robert Walpole.) Moreover, Steuart not only rejects the physiocrats' endorsement of absolute monarchy; he insists that an exchange economy is incompatible with

35 Ibid., 1:43–45, 137.
36 Ibid., 1:122.

arbitrary government and is most suited to a regime of liberty, law, and republicanism.[37]

Steuart's second basic premise is that different policies are appropriate at different phases in the growth of an exchange economy. In the "infant" phase, industries are to be encouraged through protective tariffs, bounties, and the whole range of mercantilist devices. Once industries are well established, however, all such encouragements must be withdrawn, because they are impediments to growth in the next phase—the "foreign" phase, or the period of international trade, when it is in the interest of the nation to seek freedom of trade. During the "foreign" phase, rulers are to "banish luxury," which was encouraged during the infant phase; "to encourage frugality; [and] to fix the lowest standard of prices possible." Luxury during the foreign phase "still tends as much as ever to the advancement of industry; the statesman's business only is, to remove the seat of it from his own country." When the country becomes rich enough from international trade, it can turn inward to the mature phase, that of "inland" trade, and once again domestic luxury and consumption are to be encouraged.[38]

Steuart's third underlying principle is that coin is an inadequate money supply and that provision must therefore be made for the paper monetization of all alienable things, goods, and services. This is to be done by developing institutionalized forms of credit, whereby "solid property" is made liquid. The use of "symbolic money" in the form of bonds, notes, mortgages, accounts, and other instruments "enable those who have effects, which by their nature cannot circulate (and which, by-the-bye, are the principle cause of inequality), to give, to the full extent of all their worth, an adequate circulating equivalent for the services they demand. In other words, it is a method of melting down, as it were, the very causes of inequality, and of rendering fortunes equal." He adds, in another place,

[37] Ibid., 1:74, 206–217; see also the account of the duke of Orleans's arbitrary and destructive behavior in the matter of John Law's scheme, 2:532–563.
[38] Ibid., 1:228, 260–265.

the Mandevillian note that advocates of "Agrarian laws and of universal equality, instead of crying down luxury and superfluous consumption," ought rather to be encouraging "this charming leveller *dissipation*, the nurse of industry."[39]

The fourth premise is that the most efficacious way of monetizing the whole economy is by establishing a monetized public debt, which will create a huge fund of "symbolic money" that can supply the means with which banks and other institutions can "melt down" all the rest. Steuart insists that no new property is created by doing this. If a nation collects £5 million a year in revenues and spends it, or if it borrows £100 million at five percent to pay perpetual interest, it has not created any new wealth, but has only allocated the same resources differently. Yet it has increased the circulating medium greatly by "melting down" the taxing power. Steuart illustrates his observations on the monetization of public debt, first by a lengthy account of what went wrong with John Law's scheme in France, and then by a longer and more detailed account of how the British system had evolved.[40]

As a treatise in economic theory, Steuart's work is neither complete nor flawless. He had no model of circular flow like Quesnay's *tableau*, though he was attempting to describe the same thing, and he did not pay much attention to the importance of capital in industrial development or, for that matter, distinguish between wages and profits. But to any American statesman seeking to remake his country in the image of England—and to set it on a sustained course of great economic growth—*An Inquiry into the Principles of Political Oeconomy* was an invaluable guide.

Adam Smith deliberately avoided mentioning Steuart or his work in the *Wealth of Nations*, though Smith wrote at least in part to rebut his fellow countryman. One of the most quoted passages in Smith's book, for example, was obviously aimed directly at Steuart's ever-meddling states-

[39] Ibid., 1:316–317, 2:437–442.
[40] Ibid., 2:532–563, 599–669.

man: "The statesman, who should attempt to direct people in what manner they ought to employ their capitals, would not only load himself with a most unnecessary attention, but assume an authority which could safely be trusted, not only to no single person, but to no council or senate whatever, and which would nowhere be so dangerous as in the hands of a man who had folly and presumption enough to fancy himself fit to exercise it."[41]

Smith did mention Mandeville in another connection, but went to considerable lengths to dissociate himself from *The Fable of the Bees*. He did so in a way that is not entirely convincing: he declared that Mandeville grossly exaggerated by labeling as vices what were, when exercised with propriety and restraint, normal and entirely moral appetites and needs. That was unfair, for Smith knew that Mandeville had deliberately written in caricature, for comic effect and for shock value, and did not intend always to be taken literally; and besides, Mandeville was attacking the "rigorists," the political ideologues and puritanical fanatics of his day who insisted that even the slightest deviation from absolute moral purity constituted vice. Nonetheless, so scandalous was Mandeville's work that Smith found it prudent to disclaim any kinship.[42]

Having registered that disclaimer in his *Theory of Moral Sentiments*, Smith could maintain in the *Wealth of Nations* that the proper actuating spring of economic activity was in fact what Mandeville would have called vice. "It is not from the benevolence of the butcher, the brewer, or the baker, that we expect our dinner," Smith wrote, "but from their regard to their own interest. We address ourselves, not to their humanity but to their self-love, and never talk to them of our own necessities but of their own advantages." Again, the self-interested individual, "led by an invisible hand to promote an end which was no part of his intention, . . . frequently promotes [the interest] of the society more effectually than when he really intends to promote it."[43]

---

[41] Smith, *Wealth of Nations*, 1:456 (bk. 4, chap. 2).
[42] Smith, *Theory of Moral Sentiments*, 487–494 (pt. 7, sec. 2, chap. 4).
[43] Smith, *Wealth of Nations*, 1:26–27 (bk. 1, chap. 2), 1:456 (bk. 4, chap. 2).

That line of thinking posed a dilemma for the American Framers. On the one horn, almost all believed that men were motivated by their baser "passions"—drives for self-gratification—and most shared Mandeville's and Smith's analysis of the self-interested sources of prosperity; and if they had read neither, they could absorb the same message from Steuart, from Alexander Pope's *Essay on Man*, and from a variety of other sources. But on the other horn, they were thoroughly committed to the republican experiment and to the seemingly inescapable part of the commitment, that the actuating principle of republics was virtue in the citizenry.[44]

In several important and interrelated ways—in addition to the depth and range of his observations on a variety of economic matters that neither Mandeville nor Steuart touched upon—Smith differed from one or both of those men in his economic thought. The first difference reflected a disagreement with both in regard to mercantilism. Mandeville was a thoroughgoing mercantilist, and Steuart advocated mercantilistic measures during the infant phase of growth, whereas Smith devoted almost all of book 4 of the *Wealth of Nations* to a massive repudiation—some have argued overkill, and others that Smith was setting up and knocking down straw men—of the mercantile system and all its works.[45]

[44] Mandeville, *Fable of the Bees*, Kaye's Introduction at cxviii and note. The role of the theory of the passions among the Framers is treated in some detail below, pp. 163–164 and 188–191. Michael Kammen, in "A Different 'Fable of the Bees': The Problem of Public and Private Sectors in Colonial America," in *The American Revolution: A Heritage of Change*, ed. John Parker and Carol Urness (Minneapolis, Minn., 1975), 53–68, has treated this problem from a different perspective, as his subtitle implies. He argues persuasively that Americans attempted to transform the Mandevillean formula of private vices, public benefits, into one in which private virtue would be encouraged and public vices would be controlled. The tensions inherent in that attempt are developed in larger scope in Kammen's *People of Paradox: An Inquiry Concerning the Origins of American Civilization* (New York, 1973).

[45] Eli Heckscher, "Mercantilism—A Theory of Society," in Minchinton, *Mercantilism*, 39; Smith, *Wealth of Nations*, 1:429–543, 2:545–662 (bk. 4, chaps. 1–8). It has been argued that Mandeville was not at all a mercantilist (see Norman

On a second important point, Smith differed only from Mandeville. Mandeville believed, or appears to have believed, in the zero-sum theory; and Smith went (as Steuart did, though in an entirely different way) to great lengths not only to demonstrate that wealth could in fact be increased but also to analyze how this could be done. Mandeville contended that even if poverty could be overcome, it should not be: there was always, he wrote, an "abundance of hard and dirty Labour" to be done, and poverty was the only way to get people to do it. Men "have nothing to stir them up to be serviceable but their Wants, which it is Prudence to relieve, but Folly to cure."[46]

It was precisely because wealth was essentially a fixed quantity in Mandeville's system, and not in Smith's, that the pursuit of gain was a vice in the one and not in the other. If there is not enough to go around and one man takes as his share more than he needs, he is behaving immorally. But if by investing his capital, by organizing and dividing the burdens of labor, or by devising improved techniques of production or distribution a man actually adds to the available total of useful goods or services, he is benefiting his fellow man and is therefore behaving morally, and it does not matter that he does so for the sake of profit. In this very different sense from that prescribed by John Adams, virtue and riches can go together: the virtuous man creates wealth which is shared by society as a whole.

It was in regard to capital and capital formation that Mandeville, Smith, and Steuart differed most in their economic theories. Mandeville was almost totally lacking in a sense of capital formation. Indeed, as mercantilism can in some ways be seen as a forerunner of the welfare state and the "planned" economy, Mandeville may in a sense be regarded as a precursor of Keynesian or post-Keynesian "demand side" economics. "The *Fire* of London," he

Rosenberry, "Mandeville and Laissez-Faire," *Journal of the History of Ideas* 24 [1963]: 183–196). I consider the mercantilist argument to be more convincing. See also Jacob Viner, *The Long View and the Short: Studies in Economic Theory and Policy* (Glencoe, Ill., 1958), 341.

[46] Mandeville, *Fable of the Bees*, 1:lxix.

wrote, "was a Great Calamity, but if all the Carpenters, Bricklayers, Smiths," and all others who profited by rebuilding and replacing what was destroyed "were to Vote against those who lost by the Fire; the Rejoicings would equal if not exceed the Complaint."[47] Smith, by contrast, understood that capital formation and investment, which alone made the division of labor feasible, were indispensable to the increase of the world's wealth.

Advanced as his ideas were in many respects, however, Smith lacked Steuart's grasp of the principles of public finance. Accordingly, Smith thought capital could be accumulated only by frugality and failed to comprehend that by far the most potent source of capital formation was the public debt. The oversight, to be sure, is understandable. He had seen the public debt grow to outsized proportions (it had reached £129 million by 1775)[48] and had seen taxes grow correspondingly. He was convinced that the public debt would ultimately bankrupt the nation if drastic means were not soon adopted to reduce it, or at least to check its expansion.[49] Too, he had observed that many of the great holders of the public funds dissipated their earnings in gambling, corrupt political activity, and luxurious consumption. For example, in seventy years Englishmen invested as much money in developing the resorts at Bath as they invested in cotton-textile-manufacturing activity during the entire eighteenth century.[50] Moreover, even Steuart, for all his sophistication, thought of monetized public debt only in terms of facilitating exchange. Nonetheless, the capacity for generating productive capital from the public debt was enormous, and in fact that was the source of capital for the great industrial expansion that was just beginning in England. And yet the "Father of Capitalism" declared flatly that "the practice of funding [public debts]

[47] Ibid., lxvii.

[48] Smith, Wealth of Nations, 2:923 (bk. 5, chap. 3).

[49] Ibid., 2:907–947 (bk. 5, chap. 3); see also David Hume, "Of Public Credit," in Green and Grose, Hume's Philosophical Works, 3:360ff.

[50] R. S. Neale, " 'The Bourgeoisie, Historically, has played a Most Revolutionary Part,' " in Feudalism, Capitalism, and Beyond, ed. Eugene Kamenka and R. S. Neale (New York, 1975), 93.

has gradually enfeebled every state which has adopted it."[51]

Smith, who had already established a great reputation with his *Theory of Moral Sentiments*, created a sensation with the *Wealth of Nations*.[52] Most public men in America acquired at least a passing acquaintance with the work, almost all praised it, and many gave it thorough study. Hamilton worked arguments derived from it into various of his public papers.[53] Madison was said to have quoted from it almost unconsciously, without attribution, in his speeches, and some in his audiences recognized the words.[54]

But there is this to be said about the reception of the *Wealth of Nations* in America: almost everyone who responded to it blended the parts they approved of with ideas or biases they had previously entertained, and thus ended up with something different from the original. Hamilton, as was his wont, used Smith's ideas as a springboard for going beyond where Smith had been able to go. Madison, as was his, borrowed from Smith, mixed Smith's ideas with those of others, and emerged with a composite that seemed entirely original.

The one group that came closest to accepting Smith's doctrines in their entirety was the agrarian republicans, most notably tobacco planters. Smith's work furnished them with a body of thought whereby their circumstances, mores, prejudices, and attraction to Bolingbrokean ideology could be fashioned into a symmetrical and satisfactory whole. As of 1787, they had not yet found a spokesman to

[51] Smith, *Wealth of Nations*, 2:928 (bk. 5, chap. 3).

[52] Rashid, in "Adam Smith's Rise to Fame" (see n. 33 above), demonstrates that Smith's doctrines by no means became prevailing doctrine overnight, but he does not question the fact that *The Wealth of Nations* was an immediate and sensational best seller.

[53] See, for example, the Introductory Note to Hamilton's "Report on Manufactures," in Syrett, *Papers of Hamilton*, 10:1–14, and the report itself, passim. See also Edward G. Bourne, "Alexander Hamilton and Adam Smith," *Quarterly Journal of Economics* 8 (1894): 328–344.

[54] Ames to George Richards Minot, May 29, 1789, in Allen, *Works of Ames*, 1:635–639.

formulate that philosophy, but that was only because, until the adoption of the Constitution and the implementation of Hamilton's system of political economy, there was neither occasion nor need for such a formulation. The ideas were there, and they were shared by the planters as a group; and when John Taylor of Caroline, the deepest American theorist of agrarianism, put them together, he was only expressing what most already knew in their bones.

The obvious source of Smith's appeal to the plantation gentry was his seemingly authoritative demonstration that agriculture was by far the most fruitful form of investment and activity. Smith gently but effectively picked apart the physiocrats' rather silly proposition that city dwellers could add no net value by their labors, but that made his praise of agriculture all the more persuasive. Taylor, in his *Enquiry into the Principles and Tendency of Certain Public Measures* (1794), was willing to allow artisans and craftsmen, though not merchants, a productive role. In all his subsequent writings on political economy, however, he treated commerce as legitimately productive on the ground that it involved mental labor. Otherwise, Taylor was in perfect agreement with Smith's doctrine that there was a natural order of productive and socially desirable capital investment, in which agriculture came first, commerce second, and manufacturing a poor third. In the absence of governmental interference, capital would naturally flow into those channels in the most beneficial sequence.[55]

Almost as obvious a source of affinity was Smith's attack upon the mercantile system. As indicated, the Virginia planters were convinced that their great indebtedness to British merchants had come about because the Navigation Acts had made planters captives and thereby made it possible for merchants to swindle them. But there was more to the affinity than that. One of the many criticisms Smith levied against mercantilism was that it had artificially promoted manufacturing in England on an inadequate

[55] Smith, *Wealth of Nations*, 2:663–679 (bk. 4, chap. 9); Wharton, *Polity and the Public Good*, 19; McCoy, *Elusive Republic*, 43–44; Shalhope, *John Taylor of Caroline*, 176–177.

agricultural base. Dreadful poverty had resulted, and so in the most civilized country of all, "the people who cloathe the whole world are in rags themselves." The planters feared that a similar fate awaited them or their posterity if ever America should adopt a national system of mercantilism. Thus, apart from the efforts made between 1784 and 1787 to promote a local shipping industry, the planters embraced free trade ardently and rarely deviated from it. (Later, when Madison and Jefferson attempted, out of Francophilia and sympathy for the French Revolution, to use navigation acts to force trade away from Britain and toward France, they could not hold their southern followers together. Indeed, for more than a century southerners would regard the doctrine of free trade as sacrosanct.)[56]

Smith's ideas appealed to Taylor and the plantation gentry in more subtle ways as well. Taylor shared Smith's view (a novel one at the time, though it could be inferred from Mandeville) that the true measure of a nation's wealth was neither gold nor the amount of goods it could accumulate, but the level of consumption. He agreed with Smith that money was a useful commodity in facilitating trade, though it had no inherent value, and that there were two measures of value—the intrinsic value arising from the quantity and quality of the labor invested in producing an object and the subjective value created by consumers through the laws of supply and demand. Finally, Taylor and other planters could be titillated by Smith's suspicions of the honor of merchants and could positively revel in his devastating, if not entirely sound, attack upon the evils of the public debt.[57]

In only one significant respect did Taylor's views differ markedly from Smith's. Smith held that banking in general, if managed as carefully as the Bank of England was usually managed, was a wholesome lubricant to trade; only when banks engendered speculation or overexpanded credit or were otherwise mismanaged did he regard them

[56] Shalhope, *John Taylor of Caroline*, 178–179; McCoy, *Elusive Republic*, 47.
[57] Wharton, *Polity and the Public Good*, 16–22.

as pernicious. The very mention of banks was enough to incite Taylor to a tirade of denunciation. He developed the fanciful notion that banking was a form of theft, or taxation, "whereby labour suffers the imposition of paying an interest on the circulating medium." He insisted that bank notes did not represent "real" money but only (or mainly) credit, issued to several times the amount of a bank's resources—on all of which the stockholders collected interest at the expense of the public.[58] Strange as Taylor's conception of banking was, however, it should be added, in fairness, that few people then or later were privy to the mysteries of banking and that in the worldly wise city of Philadelphia, not long before the Constitutional Convention, intelligent and articulate enemies of the Bank of North America had advanced similar analyses.[59]

For some agrarian republicans, however, Smith's "natural" formulae were inadequate, for some perceived that to let nature take its course was to doom the republic in the long run. In part this gloomy outlook was inspired by tangible considerations. Soon or late, as capital worked its way through the succession of natural channels, agriculture and commerce would become fully developed, and factory production would begin. Such production was a mixed benefit, greatly increasing the nation's wealth, but at a high social cost. Smith's well-known example of the benefits of the division of labor in a pin factory—whereby ten workers produced thousands of times as many pins in a day as they would have been able to make if they worked separately—is counterbalanced by what was once an equally well known description of what happens to those workers. Unlike

[58] Ibid., 23–24.
[59] See the running debate on the charter of the Bank of North America in 1785 and 1786, as recorded in the Philadelphia *Evening Herald*, the Philadelphia *Freeman's Journal*, the Philadelphia *Pennsylvania Journal*, and the Philadelphia *Pennsylvania Packet*. In a letter of Jan. 2, 1782, Oliver Wolcott wrote: "But the Principles upon which Banks are established is so little understood that I suppose many will object against it" (Burnett, *Letters*, 6:285). "Understanding" would have generated even greater objection.

farmers, whose diversified activities require a variety of knowledge and superior understanding, "the man whose whole life is spent in performing a few simple operations, of which the effects too are, perhaps, always the same . . . generally becomes as stupid and ignorant as it is possible for a human creature to become . . . , not only incapable of relishing or bearing a part in any rational conversation, but of conceiving any generous, noble, or tender sentiment." He is the worst of citizens, and yet "in every improved and civilized society this is the state into which the labouring poor, that is, the great body of the people, must necessarily fall, unless government takes some pains to prevent it."[60]

That prospect was disturbing enough, but there was another that, to those of an abstract and speculative turn of mind, was even more so. Quesnay, as well as Smith and several other writers of the Scottish Enlightenment—including David Hume, Adam Ferguson, John Millar, and Lord Kames—had developed the idea that there were "stages of progress" through which societies naturally and inevitably evolve. There were several versions of this "philosophical history," in which the number of stages varied from three to five, but the general outlines of all were the same. In Smith's own version there were five stages: hunting and gathering, herding, tillage agriculture, commerce, and manufacturing. Being disposed to think that occupation was the principle determinant of character and having seen their own country transformed in less than a century, the Scots believed that each stage bred progressively more refined manners and morals among the people.[61]

Perhaps the most succinct statement of this view was that of David Hume. Hume insisted—contrary to the ten-

[60] Smith, *Wealth of Nations*, 1:14–16, 2:782 (bk. 1, chap. 1; bk. 5, chap. 1).

[61] The stages of progress theory is discussed and analyzed at length in Ronald L. Meek, *Social Science and the Ignoble Savage* (Cambridge, Eng., and New York, 1976). Good general works on the Scottish Enlightenment abound; see, for example, Jane Rendall, *The Origins of the Scottish Enlightenment* (New York, 1978); Gladys Bryson, *Man and Society: The Scottish Inquiry of the Eighteenth Century* (Princeton, N.J., 1945); Anand C. Chitnis, *The Scottish Enlightenment: A Social History* (London, 1976), 91–118.

dency of many eighteenth-century thinkers who roman-
ticized the noble savage—that in hunting-and-gathering
societies life was crude, brutish, precarious, and short. As
for the next, the herding stage, "one may safely affirm, that
the TARTARS are oftener guilty of beastly gluttony, when
they feast on their dead horses, than EUROPEAN courtiers
with all their refinements of cookery." And he added, "I
believe every man would think his life or fortune much less
secure in the hands of a MOOR or TARTAR, than in those of a
FRENCH or ENGLISH gentleman."[62]

As society evolved toward tillage agriculture, things got
better—though not much. In rude unpolished nations,
"where all labour is bestowed on the cultivation of the
ground," society is divided into two classes, proprietors of
the land and their "vassals and tenants." The proprietors
are petty tyrants who either engage in endless feuds or
submit to an absolute master for the sake of peace and
order. The vassals and tenants "are necessarily dependent,
and fitted for slavery and subjection." Lacking trade and
markets for any surpluses they may produce, they are
habitually indolent and will cultivate only such land as will
provide them a bare subsistence, and they can have no
incentive to exercise or expand their minds.[63]

Then comes commerce, and refinement truly begins.
Interchanges of ideas as well as of goods take place, and the
taste for finer things stimulates industriousness and in-
ventiveness. Moreover, "refinements in the mechanical
arts" breed refinements in the liberal arts. "We cannot
reasonably expect, that a piece of woollen cloth will be
brought to perfection in a nation, which is ignorant of
astronomy, or where ethics are neglected. The spirit of the
age affects all the arts; and the minds of men, being once
roused from their lethargy, and put into a fermentation,
turn themselves on all sides, and carry improvements into
every art and science." The increase of industry, knowledge, and humanity in private life also infuses the public

62 "Of Refinement in the Arts," in Green and Grose, *Hume's Philosophical Works*, 3:302, 307; see also "Of Commerce," ibid., 3:287–299.
63 Ibid., 3:293, 306.

councils, and these "render the government as great and flourishing as they make individuals happy and prosperous."[64]

From the perspective of many Americans, there were serious flaws in this rosy picture. One was that the evolution of society did not end there. According to Smith and most of the Scots, ultimately all the land was taken, the dispossessed drifted from the country into the cities, and the drudgery of factory life began for the masses. What was worse was that beyond the earliest and simplest period of the commercial stage, economic activity rapidly led to a love of luxury. Hume, in the essay just quoted, insisted that despite a widespread belief (inspired, he thought, by a misperception of the example of ancient Rome), luxury did not necessarily lead to vice, corruption, and decay. The puritan, agrarian, and republican traditions all taught otherwise: luxury, vice, and corruption were the same thing, and from them no future but further decay was possible.

Here, then, was yet another dilemma. The vital principle of republics was virtue, but progress through the various stages was automatic and inevitable if men were free. Republics therefore, or so it would seem, were inherently self-defeating, self-destructive. James Madison, more than any other American, addressed himself to this problem, and by the time of the Constitutional Convention he thought he had found a way around it, one that appealed to a goodly number of Americans for a variety of reasons. The essence of it was that government should intervene to arrest the evolution of the stages of progress at the commercial agricultural stage, so that America might enjoy the refinements but not be subject to the corruption. This would involve commercial regulations that would secure markets for American agricultural production, promote the household manufacture of simple objects, and keep America dependent upon Europe for finer manufactures; and

[64] Ibid., 3:301–302. Oliver Goldsmith developed a similar argument ("to luxury we owe not only the greatest part of our knowledge but even of our virtues") in the comical series *The Citizen of the World*, letter 11 (*Collected Works of Oliver Goldsmith*, ed. Arthur Friedman, 5 vols. [Oxford, Eng., 1966], 2:50–53).

crucially, it would involve a policy of territorial expansion to ensure that there would be land enough to keep most of the people on farms and thus to prevent the growth of the "superfluity" of population which was thought to be necessary for the development of large-scale manufacturing industries.[65]

As was usual with Madison, he had thought the matter through, thoroughly and systematically, and he knew precisely what it required. First, a national government with adequate powers must be created. Next, that government must encourage American shipping and enact a schedule of tariffs that would discriminate against British ships and goods. Madison was convinced that the British economy was on a precarious footing and that the reduction of American importation of British fineries would quickly force Parliament to abolish its commercial restrictions. The United States would then cancel its own restrictions, having abundant markets for its agricultural output and having a source of manufactured goods without being required to produce them. Meanwhile, as a first step toward territorial expansion, the United States should exert whatever pressure was necessary to induce Spain to open the Mississippi for navigation, so that settlers would be attracted to the interior.

This was pie-in-the-sky political economy, based upon abstract theory and a lack of understanding of the British economy, international trade, and the requisites of credit, both public and private. Nonetheless, it gained many adherents. Pie-in-the-sky economic theories often do.

The principal architect of the first national system of political economy was, of course, Alexander Hamilton, whose views on the subject were as far removed from Madison's as Smith's and Bolingbroke's were from Walpole's. There is a mystery here: despite their close collab-

[65]Madison's political economy is brilliantly analyzed in McCoy, *Elusive Republic*, 129–132 and passim; for an aspect of it see Roy Branson, "James Madison and the Scottish Enlightenment," *Journal of the History of Ideas* 40 (1979): 235–250.

oration in 1787–1788 and the many conversations on public matters they had engaged in during that period, Hamilton and Madison apparently never discussed at any length their thoughts on political economy. When, in the period 1789–1791, the differences between them became overwhelmingly obvious, both men were genuinely surprised.

Hamilton, who was thirty years old when the convention met, had read and studied the works of all the political economists mentioned so far, with the possible exception of Cantillon and Mandeville, and he knew both of them through other authors if not directly. He had also studied Malachy Postlethwayt's *Universal Dictionary of Trade and Commerce*, Montesquieu, Vattel, and the memoirs of the erstwhile minister of the finances of France, Jacques Necker. In addition, he had acquired, mainly but not exclusively from Steuart, a thorough familiarity with the policies of Sir Robert Walpole and with the dreams and schemes of the brilliant but calamitously erratic Scots financial genius John Law. Hamilton, however, went beyond his bookish mentors. Perhaps the easiest way to describe his program is to indicate how it differed from theirs.[66]

One key departure from Smith had to do with what was "natural" economic behavior. Smith posited that profit maximization was natural and universal: "Every individual is continually exerting himself to find out the most advantageous employment for whatever capital he can command," and every individual "necessarily endeavours" to direct his industry so "that its produce may be of the greatest possible value." Hamilton perceived that this

[66] The following summary is drawn from the more fully developed analysis in Forrest McDonald, *Alexander Hamilton: A Biography* (New York, 1979). In that work, I overlooked the extent of the influence of Steuart upon Hamilton's thinking. I knew that Hamilton had drawn upon Steuart in writing his "Report on the Mint," and I read the appropriate parts of Steuart's *Principles of Political Oeconomy*, but I did not read the whole work until 1984; when I did so, Hamilton's debt to Steuart became obvious to me. However, that does not in any way alter my understanding of Hamilton's program; and it is to be observed that Hamilton went far beyond Steuart, particularly in understanding banking and in realizing that the public debt could be turned into a great pool of liquid capital. Too, Hamilton's desiderata were quite different from Steuart's.

thinking was flawed; he recognized that social values and habits normally dictate economic activity, not the other way around. "Experience teaches," he wrote, "that men are often so much governed by what they are accustomed to see and practice, that the simplest and most obvious improvements, in the [most] ordinary occupations, are adopted with hesitation, reluctance and by slow gradations." Men would resist changes that would improve their lots so long as even "a bare support could be ensured by an adherence to ancient courses," and possibly even longer.[67]

The policy to be inferred from this perception was that government, when skillfully applied, could and should redirect man's habits toward self-improvement and thus for the improvement of the society as a whole. This was not to be done by force; to Hamilton, that was the least desirable path for government to follow, and one that should be taken only as a last resort.[68] Nor was it, despite the historical cliché, a matter of tying the interests of the wealthy to the interests of the national government. Hamilton flirted with that idea in his youth but expressly rejected it in maturity, partly on principle and partly because experience had taught him—what his historical critics never learned—that state governments were far better equipped to manipulate interests to win supporters than was the national government.[69] Rather, Hamilton's method was, in the language of modern economists, to structure market alternatives—that is, to make it convenient and advantageous for all people to conduct their economic activity in ways that would lend strength and stability to the national government and to make it difficult, if not impossible, to conduct their affairs in detrimental ways.

Closely related was Hamilton's sophisticated understanding of what constituted wealth. He saw that beyond

---

[67] Smith, *Wealth of Nations*, 1:454, 455 (bk. 4, chap. 2); Hamilton, "Report on Manufactures," in Syrett, *Papers of Hamilton*, 10:266–267.

[68] Hamilton to Washington, Sept. 1, 9, 1792, Aug. 2, 21 (first letter), 1794, "Tully" nos. 2 and 3, ibid., 12:312, 345, 17:17–18, 123–124, 148, 160.

[69] Hamilton's youthful advocacy of such an approach is in Hamilton to ———, Dec. 1779, ibid., 2:248; his mature rejection of it is in "The Defense of the Funding System," July 1795, ibid., 19:40–41.

money, land, tools, machines, goods, and consumption,
wealth is also the industriousness of a people, channeled
through institutions. And there was more. Locke and many
other writers had recognized that an "imaginary" or "fantastical" element was involved in placing value upon
things—indeed, that imagination gave value to things that
were not "real." Most of them found the thought disturbing.[70] Hamilton accepted the fact, and even more than
Steuart did, he appreciated its implications. A mere promise, hope, or expectation could constitute wealth if the
necessary honor, faith, and belief were present. After all, a
bill of exchange had value that derived from nothing more
than belief in the honor of the issuing merchant or in the
expectation that he could and would redeem it at a designated time.

The imaginary or fantastical ingredient in property and
wealth was most important in regard to credit, especially
public credit (in Latin *credere* means "to believe"). Public
credit, Hamilton pointed out, was normally a function of
"character," meaning "good reputation," and was earned
"by good faith, by a punctual performance of contracts.
States, like individuals, who observe their engagements,
are respected and trusted: while the reverse is the fate of
those, who pursue an opposite conduct." The Congress
and the several states, by following that opposite course,
had virtually destroyed their credit. Nevertheless, one dim
ray of hope remained. During the eighteenth century the
Dutch were bankers to the world: if a government had
credit with Dutch bankers, it could have a workable system
of public finance, and if not, not. Should the Constitutional
Convention produce a plan for a viable government—or, in
a pinch, even if the old Congress were vested with taxing
power—the Dutch would be disposed to give the Americans a second chance. The Dutch would be so disposed
because, as Hamilton put it, "in nothing are appearances of
greater moment, than in whatever regards credit. Opinion
is the soul of it, and this is affected by appearances, as well

[70]Pocock, *Machiavellian Moment*, chap. 13.

as realities." The act of establishing a government would, temporarily, create the appearance—not necessarily justified—that the United States now could make and intended to make adequate provision for its public debts. Dutch investors would buy American securities (which, in fact, they began to do when news of the calling of the convention reached Europe), and prices would automatically rise, creating wealth as they did so. If the market prices rose to the par value of the securities, the American investing public would be convinced that public credit had been restored, and the conviction itself would mean that credit was restored.[71]

But only temporarily: that sequence of events would both necessitate and make possible what Hamilton perceived as the next step. Contrary to the advice of virtually everyone whom he had read on the subject except Steuart, Hamilton believed the debts should be "funded" in the British manner. Adequate public revenues should be inviolably pledged to make regular payments of interest, redemption of the principal should be left to the discretion of the government, and a sinking fund should be established. In only two major respects did the system that Hamilton envisaged depart significantly from the British model. One was designed to overcome what Smith and Hume regarded as a fatal flaw in the British system, namely, the inherent tendency to expand the debt endlessly. To prevent that, Hamilton proposed that in taking on any long-term obligations, the government should establish, at the time of floating the loan, revenues that would be irrevocably committed to payment of the interest and retirement of the principal. The other departure was fundamental. The British system was designed as a means of financing government, and though its political, economic, and social byproducts were profound, they were incidental to this main purpose. Hamilton's system was designed to use financial means for achieving political, economic, and social ends.[72]

---

[71] McDonald, *Hamilton*, 154–165; "Report Relative to a Provision for the Support of Public Credit," Jan. 9, 1790, in Syrett, *Papers of Hamilton*, 6:68, 97.
[72] Ibid., 6:51–110: "Report on a Plan for the Further Support of Public Credit," Jan. 16, 1795, ibid., 18:46–148 and especially at 104–109. See also Donald F.

Though in Hamilton's eyes the establishment of public credit was necessary for the nation's honor and useful in creating a strong and stable government, it was but a step toward erecting his system of political economy. The next step was to create a national bank, most of whose capital would be in the form of certificates of the public debt. (It would be safe to base most of the capital on government debt, for expectations that the bank would be immensely profitable made government paper as "good as gold," since it could be used to buy bank stock.) A bank was central to Hamilton's plans partly because of its convenience as a source of short-term loans to the government, but it also had a broader purpose. Money and liquid capital had always been in short supply in America, and it would take forever to accumulate by frugality what Hamilton considered to be an adequate store. But the very essence of banking currency is that it is money created in the present, not out of past savings but out of the expectation of future earnings or profits. The magnitude of the operation can be expressed simply. Certificates of public debt that had a market value of x (about one-sixth of their face value) in 1787 would rise in value to $6x$ through a funding system, and then, since banks could safely issue notes of four or five times the amount of their capital, the public debt which formed that capital would be worth $24x$ to $30x$.[73]

There were dangers in such an undertaking, but Hamilton anticipated them. One was the possibility of a speculative bubble of the kind that had destroyed John Law's grand scheme and had almost destroyed the British system. Making the national bank a privately owned institution (though one in which government would be a shareholder) would be a restraining factor, for the interests of the stockholders and directors in safety as well as in profits would make them cautious. There was also a backup source of restraint: the sinking fund could be used to stabilize

Swanson, *The Origins of Hamilton's Fiscal Policies* (Gainesville, Fla., 1963), 67–72, and McDonald, *Hamilton*, passim.

[73] The themes in this and the following paragraph are developed at length in McDonald, *Hamilton*, 138–236.

security prices by means of open market operations. Another potential source of danger was more insidious. This was that the newly created wealth would either be used "to pamper the dissipation of idle and dissolute individuals," as had happened in England, or would be sunk into the development of western lands that would not become productive for many years. To channel it properly would be the last step in Hamilton's overall system, a comprehensive program of inducements and deterrents designed to expand the manufacturing that the country was already engaged in and to promote the development of other industries that it needed or for which it was well adapted.

As for the evils that other people saw in manufacturing, Hamilton dismissed them. Much of the manufacturing could be done in farm households, and virtually every kind that lent itself to the division of labor in a factory system was extremely light work. No great impoverished labor force would therefore be necessary: farmers living near towns could supplement their incomes by working in factories during the off-seasons, and their wives and children, "who would otherwise be idle," could augment the family's earnings and be "rendered more useful" by working for most of the year. By bringing them into the money economy and by giving them a taste for what money could buy, such manufacturing would increase both supply and demand.[74]

The greatest benefits of a government-stimulated and government-channeled system of free private enterprise for profit, as Hamilton visualized things, were spiritual, not economic—the enlargement of the range of human freedom and the diversification of the possibilities for human endeavor. "Minds of the strongest and most active powers," he wrote, echoing Hume's sentiments, "fall below mediocrity and labour without effect, if confined to uncongenial pursuits. And it is thence to be inferred, that the results of

[74]"Report on Manufactures," in Syrett, *Papers of Hamilton,* 10:249–255. Hamilton foresaw that for a long time there would be a shortage of labor in America, not an excess, and he wanted to expand the labor force by inducing women and children to enter it and by encouraging immigration.

human exertion may be immensely increased by diversifying its objects." In its own right, "to cherish and stimulate the activity of the human mind" was a distinct good. Too, "even things in themselves not positively advantageous, sometimes become so, by their tendency to provoke exertion. Every new scene, which is opened to the busy nature of man to rouse and to exert itself, is the addition of a new energy to the general stock of effort. The spirit of enterprise, useful and prolific as it is, must necessarily be contracted or expanded in proportion to the simplicity or variety of the occupations and productions, which are to be found in a Society. It must be less in a nation of mere cultivators, than in a nation of cultivators and merchants; less in a nation of cultivators and merchants, than in a nation of cultivators, artificers and merchants."[75]

[75] Ibid., 10:255–256.

V

THE LESSONS OF EXPERIENCE:
1776–1787

VARIOUS OF THE IDEAS AND IDEALS that we have been considering served as guides to the Patriots of Seventy-six, and during the eleven years after the Declaration of Independence they also served as prisms through which public events were perceived. That gave those events colorations and meanings that were not entirely the same as what would appear from study of the objective record.

Objectively, the first decade of the history of the United States was a whopping success. The greatest achievement, of course, was the winning of independence, but there was more. Despite certain postwar economic dislocations, most Americans were prospering. It is true that the country had no national government and that after 1783 the Confederation Congress all but dissolved, there rarely being enough members in attendance to constitute a quorum. The vast majority of the people, however, would probably have agreed that they had no need for a stronger union. To be sure, there were assorted complaints, but not enough to shake most people from the conviction that the states were adequate to perform all the necessary functions of government except national defense, and that problem appeared to be solved by the perpetual treaties of friendship and alliance that had been signed with France in 1778. Furthermore, if anyone questioned the attractiveness of American freedom and opportunity, he needed only to go to the port cities of Scotland, Wales, and Ireland, where he could see tens of thousands of emigrants setting sail for the new nation.

But none of that mattered to the many Americans who were concerned about the nation's honor, or were concerned that the nation be great, or were concerned lest the experiment in republicanism should fail. From those perspectives, by the winter of 1786–1787, the American republic was in peril, and the institutional safeguards for liberty and property that had been erected had proved inadequate. This is not to suggest that the principal supplements to colonial experience upon which Patriots had drawn—natural-law and natural-rights theory, republican ideology of both the classical-cum-puritanical and the Harringtonian-cum-Bolingbrokean variety, Montesquieu, the English legal tradition, the Scottish Enlightenment—were suddenly and totally rejected. Those systems of ideas continued to pervade the thinking of most of the Framers of 1787, albeit sometimes in modified ways. But a few of them, mainly young and practical-minded men, idealistic but non-ideological, had been driven by the experience of the years since 1776 to reexamine the subject of government, and to plunge into the deep and murky philosophical waters of the nature of man and society. They had learned what many writers on politics had taught but the Patriots had disregarded—namely, that republican forms of government were not synonymous with security for liberty and property. They had learned, indeed, that there were threats to liberty and property that were peculiar to republics, if the people did not have an adequate measure of virtue; and they had become convinced that the American people did not have it. They had become convinced, finally, that if American government were not radically and immediately reconstructed, anarchy and then tyranny were soon to come.

No small number of the problems that plagued the public councils arose from the Lockean justification for the

Revolution. Locke had concluded his second treatise with a chapter entitled "Of the Dissolution of Government." As an analysis of the conditions under which government may be legitimately overthrown, the chapter could scarcely be more clear; and its principles and much of its phraseology were incorporated into the Declaration of Independence. As to what legitimately follows the dissolution of government, however, the chapter is ambiguous. Locke begins it by admonishing his readers to distinguish between a political society and a government, the implication being that dissolving a government does not dissolve the political society and return people to a state of nature.[1] Yet, in the preceding chapter he had said that when a sovereign puts himself "into a State of War with his People" (compare the Declaration: "He has abdicated Government here, by . . . waging War against us"), the people are left "to that defence, which belongs to every one in the State of Nature."[2] Moreover, he subsequently says that under those circumstances "the People become a confused Multitude, without Order or Connexion."[3]

In the United States this ambiguity was doubly vexing. If dissolving the political bands which had connected the colonies with the mother country *did not* throw Americans into a state of nature, then thirteen political societies continued to exist, and there was no United States. If dissolving the political bands *did* bring a reversion to a state of nature, the question was open whether the people of, say, Virginia were in a state of nature with those of Massachusetts, or only among themselves. Either way, property rights were placed on a slippery footing. Locke had been clear in asserting that when men left a state of nature, they took their previously acquired property rights with them into the political society; but it did not necessarily follow that property rights obtained from a civil government continued to exist after the dissolution of that government. When men returned to a state of nature, did

---

[1] Locke, *Two Treatises*, 424 (2d tr., par. 211).
[2] Ibid., 420 (2d tr., par. 205).
[3] Ibid., 429 (2d tr., par. 219).

they take their acquired property rights with them, and if they did, what protection was there for those rights?

Superficially the point might appear to be trivial, even nit-picking, but closer scrutiny reveals that it had many practical implications, as a survey of but one set of them will make evident. In the First Continental Congress, Patrick Henry, anticipating independence, flamboyantly declared that "all Government was dissolved, and that we were reduced to a State of Nature. That there were no longer any such distinction as colonies, that he conceived himself not a Virginian but an American."[4] By 1777, however, Marylanders were contending on just those grounds that the Revolution had vacated the Virginia charter of 1609, that the vast tract of ungranted western lands in Virginia thereby reverted to the Crown, and that with independence, the lands passed to the "common Stock"—that is, to Americans collectively.[5] Five years later a number of inhabitants of "a tract of Country called Kentuckey," reasoning on the same principles, petitioned Congress to be separated from Virginia and admitted to the Union as a state. On that occasion, James Madison insisted that "the dissolution of the Charter did not break the social Compact among the people" or, in other words, that dissolving the government had not dissolved the Virginia political society or returned any Virginian to a state of nature. "The Charter was an agreement between the King, the proprietors, and the people. Though the King, by the dissolution of the Charter, might succeed to the rights of the proprietors, the rights of the people remained entire,

[4]Burnett, *Letters*, 1:12.
[5]Richard Henry Lee to Jefferson, Aug. 25, 1777, ibid., 2:468. The question of jurisdictional conflicts arising from independence is treated at length in Peter S. Onuf, *The Origins of the Federal Republic: Jurisdictional Controversies in the United States, 1775–1787* (Philadelphia, 1983). Onuf does not, however, take into account the theoretical sources of those conflicts. James H. Kettner, in *The Development of American Citizenship, 1608–1870* (Chapel Hill, N.C., 1978), 173–247, explores skillfully and at length the implications that independence had for the concepts of allegiance and citizenship. He also calls attention, at p. 176, to the fact that the Declaration of Independence asserts the independence of *colonies*, not of colonists or people.

and the king had no right to cut them into separate Governments without their consent."[6]

At stake in that one issue were more than 25 million acres of land; and similar disputes, all turning upon interpretations of what happened after a Lockean justification for independence was embraced, involved even more. Inhabitants of northeastern New York, declaring themselves to be in a state of nature, successfuly seceded and governed themselves as the independent republic of Vermont. Inhabitants of western North Carolina formed themselves, on the same ground, into the independent state of Frankland, though after a minor civil war that state collapsed. Massachusetts claimed western New York and ended up getting title to (though not political jurisdiction over) nearly a third of it. And title to unoccupied lands was only one of many claims to property whose validity depended on this trivial, nit-picking point.

On the question—which may be rephrased as, Where did sovereignty go when George III "abdicated" it?— Americans were divided in myriad ways, but in general terms these may be classified in four groups. Each separate answer affected previously existing rights in its own way.

Rhode Island and Connecticut followed the simplest and least disruptive course. Both operated under seventeenth-century colonial charters that had made them essentially self-governing and that had recognized their right to their domains as having derived from conquest, purchase, and labor. Their governments continued to function as before, and Locke had unambiguously indicated what happened only in such cases: "The *Power that every individual gave the Society*, when he entered into it, can never revert to the Individuals again, as long as the Society lasts" and as long as the legislative continues to function.[7] Ergo, nothing was changed for the residents of Rhode Island and Connecticut except that they no longer professed allegiance to the Crown of Great Britain.[8] There was a complication in

6 Debates of Aug. 27, 28, 1782, in Burnett, *Letters*, 6:456–457.
7 Locke, *Two Treatises*, 445–446 (2d tr., par. 243).
8 Willi Paul Adams, *The First American Constitutions: Republican Ideology and the Making of the State Constitutions in the Revolutionary Era*, trans. Rita Kimber and

regard to Connecticut: its charter, which presumably was still valid, extended the state's boundaries from sea to sea, thus giving Connecticut a claim to a portion of New York and the northern third of Pennsylvania. The issue was still pending when the Constitutional Convention met.[9]

Patriot leaders in Massachusetts and New Hampshire attempted to do what their sister colonies in New England had done, but they ran into insurmountable difficulties. One of these was that they had been royal colonies in which the governor and council, constitutionally part of the "legislative," were appointees of the Crown. Separation from Britain had terminated those portions of the legislature, even though the colonial assemblies continued to operate. The rump legislatures of these two newborn states drafted constitutions—providing for governments much like the old ones except that all offices were popularly elected—and proclaimed them to be in effect. In large parts of the interior, however, the inhabitants refused to recognize the "governments" so constituted. Armed bands closed the county courts and announced that no debts could be collected. Those in Pittsfield, Massachusetts, were the most outspoken: they declared "that since the Dissolution of the power of Great Britain over these colonies they have fallen into a state of Nature," and that no lawful authority could exist until the people (not their representatives under a previous condition of government) had drawn up a new

Robert Kimber (Chapel Hill, N.C., 1980), 66–67. It is unfortunate that Adams did not compare the new state constitutions with the previous charters and terms of governance.

[9] Primary sources on Connecticut's land operators and their efforts to obtain lands are abundant; see particularly *The Susquehanna Company Papers, 1750–1772,* ed. Julian P. Boyd, 4 vols. (Wilkes-Barre, Pa., 1930–1933); *The Records of the Original Proceedings of the Ohio Company,* ed. Archer B. Hulbert, 2 vols. (Marietta, Ohio, 1917); the Pickering Papers in the Massachusetts Historical Society; the various Connecticut and Philadelphia newspapers, 1785–1786, especially the articles in the *Connecticut Courant,* beginning Jan. 4, 1785, and the issues of Mar. 6, Apr. 3, and Sept. 18, 1786. See also Boyd's articles "The Susquehanna Company," in *Connecticut Tercentenary Commission Publications* (New Haven, Conn., 1935), and "Connecticut's Experiment in Expansion: The Susquehanna Company, 1753–1803," *Journal of Economic and Business History* 4 (1931–1932): 38–69, and "Attempts to Form New States in New York and Pennsylvania, 1786–1796," *Quarterly Journal of the New York State Historical Association* 12 (1931): 258–263.

"fundamental Constitution."[10] Those who so insisted ultimately prevailed, as the renegade Vermonters were doing with the same argument. Not until Massachusetts called a popularly elected convention for the special purpose of drafting a constitution and not until the document had been ratified in town meetings—which can be read as implying that sovereignty had reverted to the towns—did the state get its first constitution. That took until 1780; the same procedure in New Hampshire took until 1784. Meanwhile, taxes, debts, and property relations in general were in limbo. Farmers held their farms by right of occupancy, use, and labor, in accordance with Lockean principles.[11]

A third position, one that had attracted little support at first but had gained some favor by 1787, was that sovereignty had passed directly to the Continental Congress, even though in 1776 that body existed only de facto, not de jure. Its support derived from two main sources. The first was people (especially prospective land speculators) in the states that had no charter claims to western lands, who therefore wanted the lands to be held in common.[12] The second was a small group of ardent nationalists, most notably James Wilson and Alexander Hamilton, who had begun to develop the doctrine of inherent powers—that is, that certain powers logically derive from responsibilities—

[10] Handlin and Handlin, *Documents on the Massachusetts Constitution*, 90–91. See also Robert J. Taylor, *Western Massachusetts in the Revolution* (Providence, R.I., 1954), passim.

[11] The process by which Massachusetts established its constitution of 1780 is abundantly documented in Handlin and Handlin, *Documents on the Massachusetts Constitution*; for a brief summary see Adams, *First American Constitutions*, 86–93. I have traced the evolution of the New Hampshire constitution in the running summaries of the activities of the convention in the Portsmouth *New Hampshire Gazette*, 1781–1784; the issues of Feb. 3 and June 28, 1783, are especially useful. For a secondary account see Richard F. Upton, *Revolutionary New Hampshire . . .* (Hanover, N.H., 1936), chap. 13.

[12] William Franklin to Lord George Germain, Nov. 12, 1778, in Davies, *Documents of the American Revolution*, 15:249–250; Jonathan Trumbull to William Tryon, Apr. 23, 1778, ibid., 15:104–105; Thomas Paine, "Public Good: Being an Examination into the Claim of Virginia to the Vacant Western Territory, and of the Right of the United States to the Same: to which is Added Proposals for Laying off a New State, to be Applied as a Fund for Carrying on the War, or Redeeming the National Debt" (1780), in *The Complete Writings of Thomas Paine*, ed. Philip S. Foner, 2 vols. (New York, 1945), 303–333.

to justify an expansion of the authority of Congress. Wilson first took this position in an effort to protect the corporate status of the Bank of North America, which existed under dubious congressional authorization as well as under a corporate charter from Pennsylvania which that state's legislature had canceled in 1785.[13] Hamilton's motives were purely nationalistic.[14]

The polar-opposite position was more logical, and at first it was the common one, though in the 1787 Convention only one delegate, Luther Martin of Maryland, still openly espoused it. This was that the several states, as previously existing political societies, continued to exist—or, alternatively, that the people of each state returned to a state of nature only among themselves, and subsequently reconstituted themselves as political societies—and that as sovereign entities, they were in a state of nature with one another.[15] The Declaration of Independence had been ambiguous in that regard: it referred to Americans as "one people" and used the term *United* States, but it also declared that the colonies were now "free and independent states," using plural verbs to describe their rights and powers. The Articles of Confederation (proposed in 1777, ratified in 1781) seemed to settle the matter. The first substantive article declared that "each state retains its sovereignty, freedom, and independence," and the states could scarcely have retained their sovereignty if they did not have it to retain. That interpretation was confirmed in the document that gave the United States legal status, the 1783 treaty of peace. Article 1 of that document reads, "His Britannic Majesty acknowledges the said United States, viz. New Hampshire, Massachusetts Bay, Rhode Island and Providence Plantations, Connecticut, New York, New Jersey, Pennsylvania, Delaware, Maryland, Virginia, North Carolina, South Carolina, and Georgia, to be free, sovereign and independent states."

[13] Charles Page Smith, *James Wilson: Founding Father, 1742-1798* (Chapel Hill, N.C., 1956), 152.

[14] McDonald, *Hamilton*, 42-43, 61, 205.

[15] Farrand, *Records*, June 27, 1:437-438, 440.

Virginia and Maryland, though fiercely at odds in many respects, shared a large tangible stake in this aspect of the question. At the onset of the Revolution, tobacco planters in those states owed British merchants upwards of £2 million sterling, or nearly $10 million—more than four times the value of all the tobacco produced in America annually. It has often been asserted that a primary motive of firebrand advocates of independence in the tobacco colonies was to escape those debts; in any event, many of them did take advantage of the opportunity. In October of 1777 the Commonwealth of Virginia exerted its newly proclaimed sovereignty to sequester all debts due to British subjects by citizens of the state, and it provided that Virginia debtors could pay what they owed to the state and thereby be relieved of all further liability. The crucial feature of the act was a provision that payments could be made in paper money at face value, even though the paper was then circulating at the depreciated rate of approximately five to one. A goodly number of debtors escaped their obligations in that manner during the first year of the act; the less scrupulous, who were more numerous, waited until the second and third years, when paper money had depreciated to forty for one and then to sixty for one. All told, under the Sequestration Act, Virginians wiped out £273,554 (about $1.2 million) in personal debts by making payments in paper that had a sterling value of £15,044 (about $67,000). Thus did about five hundred members of the First Families of Virginia—including Thomas Jefferson, Patrick Henry, and various Lees, Balls, Flemings, and others—retain the wherewithal to remain First Families.[16]

Such doings were of questionable validity under natural law. Vattel had opined that sequestration of the property of

[16]Richard B. Sheridan, "The British Credit Crisis of 1772 and the American Colonies," *Journal of Economic History* 20 (1960): 161–186; Isaac S. Harrell, *Loyalism in Virginia: Chapters in the Economic History of the Revolution* (Durham, N.C., 1926), 27–28, 80–83, and passim; DeMond, *Loyalists in North Carolina*, 174. Sequestration was an old and complex action, applicable mainly to church property in England; essentially it involved separation of the property holder from the yield of his property, the sovereign taking that yield unto itself until permanent disposition of the property was effected.

enemy aliens could technically be justified but that it was not good practice and was contrary to modern European custom.[17] Locke had not addressed the subject directly, but the tenor of his chapter on conquest indicates that he would have considered the sequestration impermissible.[18] Twice after the war, in 1784 and in 1787, the Virginia House of Delegates entertained motions to open Virginia courts to suits by British creditors, but the motions were rejected both times. Thus, as long as Virginia remained in a state of nature with outsiders—that is, subject to no common authority with them—its debtors were safe.[19]

Whatever the methods by which they constituted their governments, the several states attempted to secure property rights in accordance with the self-proclaimed Lockean justification for their existence. They employed three principal means to that end. The first was to affirm man's natural rights to property, either in declarations of rights or in the body of their constitutions. Seven states followed that course, four of them explicitly (Pennsylvania, Virginia, Massachusetts, and New Hampshire) and three only implicitly but nonetheless unmistakably (New York, North Carolina, and Georgia). The language used in Virginia was characteristic: all men have "certain inherent rights, . . . namely, the enjoyment of life and liberty, with the means of acquiring and possessing property, and pursuing and obtaining happiness and safety."[20]

The second method was to attempt to avoid the complications and embarrassments of discontinuity by expressly declaring previous law to be still in force. New Hampshire's 1784 constitution extended this provision only to colonial and state statutes, but it also provided additionally for continuity by keeping all existing officials in

---

[17] Vattel, *Law of Nations*, 323 (bk. 3, chap. 5, sec. 77).
[18] Locke, *Two Treatises*, 402–415 (2d tr., par. 175–196).
[19] *Journal of the House of Delegates of the Commonwealth of Virginia* (Richmond, 1828), 1784, Oct. sess. 1787.
[20] Thorpe, *Constitutions*, 7:3813.

office until new elections could be held. Four states—
Delaware, Maryland, New Jersey, and New York—declared
the common law of England to be part of their constitutions, together with all statutes of Parliament that had been
found applicable by colonial courts and with all colonial
enactments that had not expired. (This would lead to
complications after the war, for there was more in the
common law than the Revolutionary constitution makers
realized.) In addition, there were two special cases, involving the erstwhile corporate colonies: property rights in
Connecticut and Rhode Island were, by their charters, fixed
in accordance with English law as of the 1660s.[21]

The third method was to incorporate specific legal
protections of property rights into the constitutions. The
most common form of protection was the requirement of
property qualifications for voters and officeholders. Requirements for voters ranged from merely being a "tax-
payer" in Pennsylvania to having a small freehold in most
places; those for officeholders ranged as high as £10,000
"clear of debts," the requirement for the governor of South
Carolina.[22] South Carolina apportioned representation by
parish partly on the basis of property values and partly on
the basis of population. Restrictions on the taxing power,
prohibitions against monopolies, and provisions for jury
trials in cases involving property were common, the third of
these being the only protection of rights to be found in all
thirteen of the states. To ensure a wide distribution of
property, North Carolina authorized the legislature to regulate entails, and Georgia abolished primogeniture and
entail. (The latter was a rather extravagant precaution, in
light of the fact that the state of Georgia contained about
thirteen thousand unoccupied acres of land for every white
family.) Five states—Massachusetts, Maryland, New Hampshire, North Carolina, and Pennsylvania—declared that no

[21] Ibid., 5:2787; see also Zachariah Chafee, Jr., "Colonial Courts and the
Common Law," *Proceedings of the Massachusetts Historical Society* 68 (1952):
132-159.

[22] Adams, *First American Constitutions*, 295-307, contains a convenient summary of property qualifications for electors and officeholders in all the states.

person could be deprived of his life, liberty, or property except "by the judgment of his peers, or the law of the land."[23]

These precautions did not prove effective: quite apart from the matter of persons who remained loyal to the Crown, Americans were not as secure in their property rights between 1776 and 1787 as they had been during the colonial period. The reason, in the eyes of many Americans, was that governments were now committing unprecedented excesses, even though—or precisely because—governments now derived their powers from compacts amongst the people.

On the general level the Continental Congress, despite a lack of formal powers, engineered a massive expropriation of private property through a calculated policy of inflation. Financing wars by issuing unsecured paper money, called bills of credit, had long been practiced on a relatively small scale by colonial legislatures; normally the money depreciated to such a low rate of exchange that it could be painlessly taxed out of existence. The Continental Congress issued its first $6 million in bills of credit in 1775 and another $32 million during the next two years. By October of 1777 the bills had depreciated to a ratio of three for one. In 1778 another $63.4 million was issued, and by the end of the year the ratio had fallen to eight for one. Still another $124.8 million was printed in 1779, and despite legal-tender laws and price-control legislation, the specie value of the bills dropped to more than forty for one. In desperation, Congress devalued all the outstanding bills on a forty-for-one basis, cutting a $200 million obligation to $5 million. Even so, the bills continued to depreciate, reaching 167 for one in April, 1781, and thereafter going to nothing. Not all of the inflation and devaluation amounted to expropriation, of course. Since much of the paper was already depreciated upon issue, Americans parted with only about $45 million in goods and services for the $226 million in bills that was paid to them. But the $45 million depreciated to zero, and

[23] See the various constitutions in Thorpe, *Constitutions*.

was therefore a loss to those who had accepted the bills in payment. Benjamin Franklin defended the inflationary policy on the ground that since the bills depreciated slightly in the hands of every holder and since the wealthy handled them (along with other money) more than did the poor, inflation had worked as an equitable form of taxation. John Adams defended devaluation with the flat statement that "the public has its rights as well as individuals."[24]

The states likewise adopted inflationary policies and otherwise violated property rights during the war, but their greatest abuses came after the peace. Many, for example, treated former Loyalists as second-class citizens, despite the provisions of the treaty of peace. New York, whose lower regions, including the city, had been occupied throughout the war and whose citizens were bitterly anti-Tory, was understandably the worst offender. After the British had evacuated the city, the state government began vigorously enforcing three major anti-Tory statutes that had been enacted earlier. One was the Confiscation Act of 1779, whose substance is evident in its title; another was the Citation Act of 1782, which stayed executions on debts that Patriots owed to Loyalists and permitted the debtors to pay their obligations in depreciated paper currency; and the third was the Trespass Act of 1783, which offered relief for Patriots who had fled the city by permitting them to recover damages from persons who had occupied or used their premises during the war.[25]

The Trespass Act dramatically illustrated—what almost no Patriots had foreseen in 1776—the inherent tension between government by established law and government by unbridled democracy. It was an immensely popular act,

[24] E. James Ferguson, *The Power of the Purse: A History of American Public Finance, 1776-1790* (Chapel Hill, N.C., 1961), 3-24, 30, 32; *The Writings of Benjamin Franklin,* ed. Albert H. Smyth, 10 vols. (New York, 1907), 9:231-232. Vattel declared that the sovereign could resort to inflation (through debasement of the coin) in cases of dire necessity, but that if this unjust expedient be employed, the sovereign was obliged, after the emergency, to make good all losses that had been suffered as a result (*Law of Nations,* 45 [bk. 1, chap. 10, sec. 106]). The bills of credit that Congress issued were never redeemed.

[25] This and the next two paragraphs are drawn from the fuller account in McDonald, *Hamilton,* 64-69.

having the almost unanimous approval of the citizenry, yet it flouted fundamental principles of law. The common law—incorporated into New York's constitution—required that actions for trespass must be tried where the property was located, but the act allowed Patriots to sue in any court where the defendant could be found. Contrary to the laws of war—a division of natural law, which Americans had proclaimed sacred to them—the act prohibited defendants from pleading that they had acted under orders of the occupying British army. Contrary to established Anglo-American legal tradition, the act denied to defendants the right to appeal decisions to a higher court. It violated the law of nations, the treaty of peace, and a mandate from Congress to the states.

In 1784 the constitutionality of the act was challenged in *Rutgers* v. *Waddington*. The outcome of the suit was unsatisfactory to all. The court expressly refused to declare the act unconstitutional, but it did rule partially for the defendant on the ground that it assumed that the legislature could not have intended to violate the law of nations. The aftermath demonstrated the inability of judges to check the will of popular majorities. The decision was condemned in public gatherings and in petitions to the legislature, and the legislature itself adopted a resolution denouncing the decision, though it stopped short of removing the judges. Thereafter the legislature did as it pleased, and judges dared not interfere.

During the next three years the legislatures of every state repeatedly violated individual property rights. To be sure, the paper-money movement of that period was not as much a matter of defrauding creditors as was once believed; for the most part, the paper issues were designed to help the states to service their public debts, and only the currency that was issued in North Carolina and Rhode Island depreciated significantly. Nonetheless, the rights of creditors were trampled in those two states—when Rhode Island's supreme court ruled in behalf of a creditor who refused to accept the depreciated paper, the legislature censured the court and replaced the judges. Other states also enacted laws staying executions for debts and making worthless land legal tender.[26] Meanwhile the government of Pennsylvania, having declared that what one session of the legislature of the sovereign people could give or do, another session could take back or undo, revoked the charter of the Bank of North America.[27] By the time of the 1787 Convention, popular agitation had mounted in a number of states for more radical legislative interference in property relations.

These attacks upon property rights were, in the eyes of many, symptomatic of the excesses that were inherent in democracy. For most persons who so believed, that judgment represented a rethinking of attitudes that they had held earlier—specifically, the tendency, shared by most Americans who embraced the revolutionary cause, to confuse popular power with popular liberty.

Advocacy of democracy had not, to be sure, been the most extreme position that had gained adherents, for there were some who espoused a virtual elimination of all government. Supporters of radical libertarianism were especially numerous among the Scotch-Irish frontiersmen who populated most of the back country from Pennsylvania to Georgia. The Old World heritage of these people predisposed them to regard all government with suspicion, if not with outright hostility, and their circumstances and recent history reinforced that disposition. The late colonial and the early state governments, in these people's view, provided little in the way of services or protection and were commonly visible only in the shape of the tax collector.

[26] Ibid., 146–148, 248–249; McDonald, *We the People*, 123, 126, 132, 153–155, 166–167, 210–212, 242, 263–267, 293–295, 328–337; James R. Morrill, *The Practice and Politics of Fiat Finance: North Carolina in the Confederation, 1783–1789* (Chapel Hill, N.C., 1969), 57–99.

[27] The position that the legislature was not bound by acts of preceding legislatures is set forth in the MS Journal of the Council of Censors, Aug. 27, 1784, vol. 2, pp. 520–526. The opinion given there concerned the charter of the University of Pennsylvania, but the same logic was applied in the repeal of the bank charter. The debates over the latter are reported in the Philadelphia *Evening Herald*, Sept. 7, 8, 1785.

Crèvecoeur described the frontiersmen as being marked by "idleness, frequent want of oeconomy, ancient debts, . . . The few magistrates they have, are in general little better than the rest; they are often in a perfect state of war." They were, he said, "no better than carnivorous animals of a superior rank." The portrait may be overdrawn, but it is clear that the frontiersmen were all but ungovernable.[28]

Nor was every advocate of radical libertarianism a lawless bumpkin. In a 1777 oration delivered in Boston, Benjamin Hichborn defined "civil liberty to be, not 'a government by laws,' made agreeable to charters, bills of rights or compacts, but a power existing in the people at large, at any time, for any cause, or for no cause, but their own sovereign pleasure, to alter or annihilate both the mode and essence of any former government, and adopt a new one in its stead."[29]

The most articulate spokesman for a radical libertarian position was one of the most cultivated of all Americans, Thomas Jefferson. As was typical of him, Jefferson arrived at his theories of liberty largely by mixing an eclectic sampling of the ideas of others with a few conceits that were peculiar to himself. He borrowed his ideas regarding equality from the Scottish Common Sense school and took his epistemology from Locke. From Quesnay and the Scottish Enlightenment he absorbed the "stages of progress" model of social development, and from his study of Indians he concluded that the primitive stages produced happier and more virtuous men. To all this he added his

[28] Quotations from (J. Hector St. John) Crèvecoeur, *Letters from an American Farmer* (Garden City, N.Y.; reprint of 1782 ed.), 52. The bibliography on the Scotch-Irish frontiersmen is large, but much of it, being somewhat filiopietistic, ignores or downplays their virtual ungovernability. In the Scottish Highlands, the Hebrides, and Ulster, social order had traditionally been preserved by the blood-feud system, and the inhabitants had, for practical purposes, been out of the reach of the governments in Edinburgh, London, or Dublin. For an excellent description of the system see Jennifer M. Brown, *Scottish Society in the Fifteenth Century* (New York, 1977), and Jenny Wormald, *Court, Kirk, and Community: Scotland, 1470–1625* (Toronto, 1981). Regarding the lawlessness on the frontier see Richard Maxwell Brown, *The South Carolina Regulators* (Cambridge, Mass., 1963), passim; Rachel N. Klein, "Ordering the Backcountry: The South Carolina Regulation," *William and Mary Quarterly* 38 (1981): 661–680; Hooker, *The Carolina Backcountry.*

[29] Niles, *Principles and Acts,* 47.

own notion that generations lacked the right to bind their successors (he proposed an abolition and rewriting of all constitutions and laws, as well as a cancellation of all debts, every nineteen years) and his abstract cherishing of bloodshed ("the tree of liberty must be refreshed from time to time, with the blood of patriots and tyrants"). Stirring the mix, what he came up with was, in theory at least, very near to a stateless society under the benevolent leadership of what he called the natural aristocracy.[30] It was a theory that could have been used to justify the traditional societies of the Scottish Highland and Island clans and the Irish tuaths as well as the Virginia society in which Jefferson lived. ("At the southward," observed the Massachusetts Federalist Fisher Ames, "a few gentlemen govern; the law is their coat of mail.")[31]

At the northward, most people preferred a position that was considerably further removed from natural liberty. "It is an unguarded expression," Ames observed, "to say, that we part with a portion of our natural liberty, to secure the remainder—for what is the liberty of nature? Exposed to the danger of being knocked on the head for a handful of acorns, or of being devoured by wild beasts, the melancholy savage is the *slave* of his wants and his fears." This attitude came far closer than that of radical libertarians to being an American norm. Indeed, most Americans saw, not tension, but interdependence between liberty and law and order. "There is no other liberty than civil liberty," Ames

---

[30] The best account I have seen of Jefferson's radical libertarianism is Richard K. Matthews, *The Radical Politics of Thomas Jefferson: A Revisionist View* (Lawrence, Kans., 1984), which I have followed here. This interpretation of Jefferson's political philosophy would seem to be totally contrary to the interpretation of "Jeffersonian Republicanism" in my earlier work, *The Presidency of Thomas Jefferson* (Lawrence, Kans., 1976), ix and passim, as being derived mainly from Bolingbroke and others in the agrarian tradition. I was concerned there, however, with the "ism," not with the man. Jefferson did embrace radical libertarianism and Bolingbrokean agrarianism as well. Like John Adams, he held different opinions at different times. Besides, Jefferson puts one in mind of Walt Whitman's lines: "Do I contradict myself? / Very well then I contradict myself, / (I am large, I contain multitudes)." Jefferson was large; he contained multitudes. See also Joyce Appleby, "What Is Still American in the Political Philosophy of Thomas Jefferson?" *William and Mary Quarterly* 39 (1982): 287-309.

[31] Allen, *Works of Ames*, 2:879.

added; "we cannot live without government." The reason
is implicit in John Dickinson's statement (strikingly reminiscent of Montesquieu's) that liberty is best described "in
the Holy Scriptures . . . in these expressions—'When every
man shall sit under his vine, and under his fig-tree, and
none shall make him afraid.' " The function of government, in
bringing about such a condition, was to protect the people
against themselves.[32]

The conception of the nature of man that underlay this
point of view was the reverse of that from the libertarian
viewpoint. Jefferson thought that man, as an individual,
was moral; but he distrusted men in large aggregates and
men acting in a corporate capacity. The more general view
was that men acting privately were not to be trusted and
that they needed to be protected from one another by
governments which were based upon popular consent.
Thus it was that the Revolutionary state constitutions,
though genuflecting in the direction of separation of
powers and bills of rights, in practice vested virtually
unlimited powers in popularly elected legislatures. The
principle was expressed in a pamphlet that Hamilton
published in 1774. "The only distinction between freedom
and slavery," he wrote, "consists in this: In the former
state, a man is governed by the laws to which he has given
his consent, either in person, or by his representative: In
the latter, he is governed by the will of another." To this
way of thinking, which was especially common in New
England, the only necessary check upon the legislatures
was frequent elections by the people. The slogan "Where
annual elections end, slavery begins" was on thousands of
lips. (By contrast, Jefferson, apropos of the need for restraints upon the powers of the Virginia legislature, warned
that "173 despots would surely be as oppressive as one.")[33]

In part the faith in the people that had been held by the
early advocates of representative democracy derived from
naïve enthusiasm, but it had other foundations as well.

[32] Ibid., 1:64; Dickinson, "The Letters of Fabius," letter 3, in Ford, *Pamphlets*,
14. See also White, *Philosophy of the American Revolution*, 186–195.
[33] Syrett, *Papers of Hamilton*, 1:47; Jefferson, *Notes on Virginia*, 120.

Both theory (Hume's, among others) and observation taught the stabilizing effects of extragovernmental institutions and forces—church, family, community—and taught appreciation of the force of inertia in human affairs. Hamilton's remarks on human inertia were quoted earlier, and John Adams would lecture the Senate on it repeatedly when he became vice-president; but one need look no further than the Declaration of Independence, for even Jefferson was aware of the force of human inertia, though he deplored it: "All Experience hath shewn, that Mankind are more disposed to suffer, while Evils are sufferable, than to right themselves by abolishing the Forms to which they are accustomed."[34]

Another cause for faith in the people was that "the people" was narrowly defined. John Adams penned an elaborate analysis of the reasons for such a definition. "It is certain, in theory," he wrote, "that the only moral foundation of government is, the consent of the people." But that did not mean that everyone in the community, "old and young, male and female, as well as rich and poor, must consent, expressly, to every act of legislation." Women were excluded because "nature has made them fittest for domestic cares" and unfitted them for "the great businessess of life, and the hardy enterprises of war, as well as the arduous cares of state." Children, servants, and the propertyless were excluded because they were "too little acquainted with public affairs to form a right judgment, and too dependent upon other men to have a will of their own."[35] All told, though widespread ownership of land

34 The principle of cultural conservatism, which describes a far-greater stabilizing force than government, is familiar to anthropologists; but historians commonly overlook it, concentrating upon politics and government. Partly the neglect arises from the relative unavailability of sources, and doubtless it arises in part from the tradition of civic humanism—the idea that, in Isaac Kramnick's words, man is "a political being whose realization of self occurs only through participation in public life, through active citizenship in a republic" ("Republican Revisionism Revisited," *American Historical Review* 87 [1982]: 629–664). But a number of the founders were acutely aware of the force of cultural conservatism, and the writings of some of the people whom they read—Hume and Montesquieu, for example—are suffused with it.

35 Adams to James Sullivan, May 26, 1776, in Adams, *Works of Adams*, 9:375–378.

resulted in the broadest-based electorate in the world, only
about one American in six was eligible to participate in the
political process, and far fewer were eligible to hold public
office.[36]

And yet, by 1787 a number of Americans had come to
believe that even that modicum of democracy was incompatible with security for liberty and property. In thinking
the subject through, James Madison and various others
focused upon a feature of republics that had always been
troublesome, namely, the tendency of men to divide into
factions or parties and to put the interests of the parties
ahead of those of the public. David Hume, whose rumina-
tions on the subject were most influential upon the Framers, held that the tendency was universally operative, even
under despotism; but it was generally agreed that factions
occurred more frequently and were more dangerous in
republics and, indeed, that factionalism was the most
common proximate cause of their downfall.[37] Factions were
not, it is true, entirely inevitable. In those miniature republics, the towns of New England, unanimity often prevailed:
town meeting after town meeting, in choosing selectmen,
settling local issues, electing representatives, and even
voting for governor, repeatedly turned in unanimous
votes—187 to 0, 243 to 0, 121 to 0.[38] Moreover, thoughout
the United States, juries of the county courts, which may
also be regarded as miniature republics, disposed of astonishing numbers of civil and criminal cases rapidly and,
of course, unanimously. But that kind of public harmony
was rare in the larger history with which Americans were
familiar.

In Hume's taxonomy, there were two kinds of factions,
personal and real. Personal factions—those of rival families

[36] Williamson, *American Suffrage.*

[37] "Of Parties in General," in Green and Grose, *Hume's Philosophical Works,*
3:127–133.

[38] See, for example, MS Votes for Governor and Lieutenant Governor, 1787, in
the Massachusetts Archives: Worcester County, votes by the towns of Millford
(114 to 0), Ashburnham (84 to 0), Northboro' (50 to 0), Menden (124 to 0);
Middlesex County, Townshend (44 to 0), Dracut (44 to 0), Tewksbury (100 to 0);
Plymouth County, Plympton (113 to 0), Halifax (51 to 0); and so on.

and their connections—he saw as arising most readily in small republics, where "every domestic quarrel . . . becomes an affair of state." The "real" factions he divided into those based upon interest, those based upon principle, and those based upon affection. Hume considered that factions based on interest were "the most reasonable, and the most excusable," and, for that matter, the least pernicious. Parties arising "from *principle*, especially abstract speculative principle"—including religious disputation—were "known only to modern times" and were destructive to the point of "madness." The third kind were those "which are founded on the different attachments of men towards particular families and persons, whom they desire to rule over them."[39] All three forms were potential threats in America; the extent to which each was perceived as being seriously dangerous varied with the angle of perception. The more ideological the viewer, the more likely was he to see the danger as arising from unsound principles; and thus it was with puritanical republicans. Among the great body of agrarian republicans (and with Madison, too, though Madison was by no means philosophically at one with them), factions based upon interest seemed more likely to arise and more likely to be inimical to liberty as they understood it. Ardent nationalists among the Framers feared most the rise of factions based upon personal attachment.

The last of these fears had both philosophical and experiential foundations. The philosophical base was grounded in the theory of the passions. Men, according to this model of human behavior, were driven by direct passions, such as "desire and aversion, grief and joy, hope and fear," and by indirect passions, such as pride or humility and love or hatred. Reason was never a motive force; it was simply a morally neutral instrument for satisfying the passions. The idea was generally held that every person had one "ruling" passion that tended to override the rest, and it was a cliché that in public affairs the

---

[39] For Hume, see Green and Grose, *Hume's Philosophical Works*, 3:128, 130–133.

ruling passions of most men were avarice and ambition, the love of money and the love of power or popular applause. Notice the term "popular," which, unlike "public," comprehended everybody, or at least all adult males, including the propertyless rabble. A passion for seeking the approbation of the public was good for a republic; a passion for popular favor was entirely to the contrary. Cicero designated the parties of the late Roman republic as *Populares*, who were willing to destroy the republic in their quest for popular acclaim, and as *Optimates*, who, in all public conduct, "regulated themselves by the sentiments of the best and worthiest of the ROMANS." A popular preacher in seventeenth-century England was a radical and a rabble-rouser; a popular politician in eighteenth-century America was a demagogue. Given their ruling passion, demagogues posed endless dangers to the life of a republic because, by definition, their actions were not restrained by any nobler passion.[40]

Fear of demagogues also had a foundation in observation. During the four years between the Peace of Paris and the meeting of the Constitutional Convention, demagogues had risen to power in state after state and, in the eyes of American *Optimates*, had caused needless turmoil and had disgraced the new nation. George Clinton and his cronies in New York, John Hancock and his in Massachusetts, Samuel Chase and his cohorts in Maryland, Patrick Henry and his minions in Virginia, the entire constitutionalist party in Pennsylvania, and the hordes of petty leaders in Rhode Island all fit the description. None, to be sure, had so cynically flouted the Constitution and destroyed public

[40] For the Framers' sources of the theory of the passions see, among others, Hobbes's *Leviathan*; Hume's *Treatise of Human Nature*, bk. 2, in Green and Grose, *Hume's Philosophical Works*, 2:75–228; Smith's *Theory of Moral Sentiments*, 75–101; and what was the most popular source, Pope's "Essay on Man," epistle 2, in *Alexander Pope: Selected Poetry*, ed. Martin Price (New York and Toronto, 1970), 135–142. See also Arthur O. Lovejoy, *Reflections on Human Nature* (Baltimore, Md., 1961), 87–117. Regarding Cicero see Green and Grose, *Hume's Philosophical Works*, 3:134 n. See also the etymology of *popular* in the *Oxford English Dictionary*. *Optimates* is commonly translated as "aristocracy," to correspond with the Greek *aristoi*, but that has misleading connotations. Its closest kin in Latin is *optimus*, the superlative form of *bonus*, meaning "good": "the best."

tranquility as, according to Plutarch, the likes of Caius Marius and Lucius Cornelius Sulla had done during the late Roman republic; but the tumults in Massachusetts in 1786–1787 seemed to portend something of the sort.[41]

Madison devised a two-part plan to overcome these dangers. The first part would be to create a national government that would have the power to veto state legislation. It was crucial, Madison wrote, echoing a theme that had been central to the thinking of Harrington, that the officers in this government be chosen by a process which would ensure the selection of what Harrington characterized as the "natural aristocracy" and what Madison described as "men who possess the most attractive merit and the most diffusive and established characters." Ideas about how to do this varied considerably among those who shared Madison's position, but there was no disagreement as to the intent. In Madison's words, it was "to refine and enlarge the public views," not by attempting to increase the virtue of the populace, but by filtering popular views "through the medium of a chosen body of citizens, whose wisdom may best discern the true interest of their country, and whose patriotism and love of justice will be least likely to sacrifice it to temporary or partial considerations."[42]

The second part of Madison's plan, which was formulated from materials supplied by Hume, was one that he believed would be efficacious even if the other failed. This was his analysis of factions, which he gave in the form of speeches during the convention and developed at length in *Federalist* number 10. It was not possible to remove factions entirely, Madison said, except by tyrannical means, but it was possible to minimize the mischiefs that they did. The key was to "extend the sphere," to spread the republic over a large and diverse territory, and thereby to "make it

[41] See McDonald, *E Pluribus Unum*, 71–257.

[42] *Federalist* number 10, p. 59; Adams, *First American Constitutions*, 106–117; William R. Everdell, *The End of Kings: A History of Republics and Republicans* (New York, 1983), 2–6; Fink, *Classical Republicans*, 55–62; Gordon S. Wood, "Democracy and the Constitution," in *How Democratic Is the Constitution?* ed. Robert A. Goldwin and William A. Schambra (Washington, D.C., and London, 1980), 10–12; Ann Stuart Diamond, "Decent, Even Though Democratic," ibid., 26–30.

less probable that a majority of the whole will have a common motive to invade the rights of other citizens; or if such a common motive exists, it will be more difficult for all who feel it to discover their own strength, and to act in unison with each other."[43]

This idea, like Madison's theory of political economy, was tinged with wishful thinking. As Hamilton noted, there was truth in Madison's principles, "but they do not conclude so strongly as he supposes—the Assembly when chosen will meet in one room if they are drawn from half the globe—& will be liable to all the passions of popular assemblies."[44] Nonetheless, the theory was important. It overcame two formidable theoretical stumbling blocks to republican nationhood, Montesquieu's dicta that republican forms were adaptable only to small territories such as cities and towns and that only monarchies could govern large areas. It also provided a persuasive argument that it would be safe to entrust power to a national government.

Arguments to that end had, so far, been to no avail. The forces of history, habit, and interest combined to make most men loyal to the familiar, tangible state governments rather than to an abstraction called the United States. One might suppose that the merchants in the larger port cities, accustomed as they were to regular intercourse with one another and the outside world, might, from experience as well as from self-interest, have learned to think nationally. By and large they had; but mutual mistrust had prevented them from cooperating frequently or effectively in the national interest, as the many covert violations of the various commercial boycotts against Britain had shown in the 1760s and 1770s and as the rancor between merchants in Philadelphia and New York in the mid eighties was reconfirming. Similarly, public creditors constituted a potentially strong pressure group favoring a strengthened national authority, and indeed in 1782–1783 Superintendent of Fi-

---

[43] *Federalist* number 10, p. 61; Farrand, *Records*, June 5, 1:134–136.
[44] Farrand, *Records*, June 6, 1:146.

nance Robert Morris and several of his nationalist friends attempted to organize the public creditors as a lobbying force. That effort had failed, however, and thereafter the influence of the creditors was dissipated. Many of them, creditors of the states, objected to giving Congress a source of revenue lest the states be thereby rendered unable to pay; and the most nearly cohesive groups of Continental creditors, those in New York and Pennsylvania, were taken care of when those two states assumed responsibility for servicing much of the Continental debt held by their citizens.[45]

In the absence of effectual cooperation among merchants and public creditors, only three significant nationalizing influences were operative in the young nation. One was pure love of country, which was most commonly found among those who had been born abroad and thus had not developed provincial loyalties (Hamilton, Robert Morris, James Wilson), among those who were educated abroad and thus had outgrown much of their provincialism (John Rutledge, John Dickinson), and among those who were inspired by the grandness of the opportunity to gain immortal fame by securing the blessings of liberty for posterity (Washington, Madison). The second and third main sources of nationalist sentiments derived from wartime experience. Those parts of the country which had been proven to be militarily most vulnerable—particularly the seaboard portions of the Middle States and the tidewater portions of the lower South—were seedbeds of national feeling; and veterans of lengthy service in the Continental Army were, for the most part, intensely nationalistic.

Nationalists of all three descriptions, though influential, were in a decided minority. Their weight in public affairs after 1783 was overbalanced by that of ideologue republicans, who were extremely distrustful of congressional power, and by the even greater weight of politicians who were state-oriented by reason of self-interested motives. The relative impotence of nationalists prior to 1787 is

[45] These matters are analyzed at length in McDonald, *E Pluribus Unum*, chap. 2.

abundantly illustrated by a brief review of the efforts of Congress to manage its affairs after the war.

Congress addressed itself mainly to problems in regard to the public lands, relations with other nations, and the public debts. Quibbling over title to the lands west of the Appalachians was frequent from 1776 onward. The states that had claims to such lands by virtue of their colonial charters were determined to retain them; the states that held no such claims were eager for the lands to become the possession of Congress so that they might share in them. The issue held up ratification of the Articles of Confederation for more than three years, after which, through a complex series of negotiations, Congress acquired title to the lands north of the Ohio. Virginia, North Carolina, and Georgia retained their interior lands westward to the Mississippi. Many in the landless states remained uneasy about the security of Congress's hold on the "national domain," however, even though Congress did pass ordinances providing for the survey and governance of the territory. Connecticut was particularly anxious to have a piece of the territory, a "western reserve," conferred upon itself. As for the South, its politicians and adventurers indulged themselves in a veritable orgy of speculation in the state-owned western lands.[46]

Land speculation became involved in one of the principal efforts of Congress to work out American relations with foreign powers. During the war Spain, allied with France against Britain but not a party to the Franco-American alliance, was nonetheless reasonably friendly toward the United States, and it opened its West Indies colonies to American shipping. Afterward, perceiving the United States to be a threat to its empire, Spain not only reclosed its colonies but also denied western Americans the privilege of depositing their products for transshipment at New

---

[46]Merrill Jensen, "The Creation of the National Domain, 1781–1784," *Mississippi Valley Historical Review* 26 (1939): 323–342, and *The Articles of Confederation: An Interpretation of the Social-Constitutional History of the American Revolution, 1774–1781* (Madison, Wis., 1940), 198ff.; McDonald, *E Pluribus Unum*, 188–189, 192–194, and the sources cited therein.

Orleans, which effectively closed off the navigation of the Mississippi River. That was of no special consequence to most settlers in the West, for what they produced for market was cattle and swine which they drove overland to the East; but it did anger land speculators, for their prospective profits depended on the transformation of the West into a producer of agricultural staples for international markets.[47]

It was against this background that controversy over the Jay-Gardoqui negotiations took place. Diego Gardoqui, the minister from Spain to America, offered a trade-off to Secretary for Foreign Affairs John Jay: if the United States would renounce its claim to a right to navigate the Mississippi for twenty-five years, Spain would open its empire to American commerce. Jay had been specifically instructed by Congress not to forgo the right to navigate the Mississippi, but he found the proffered commercial concession attractive, and he responded to Gardoqui's proposal by asking Congress to change his instructions. Southern reaction to the request was bitterly hostile; many people, in both North and South, began to talk seriously about dividing the Confederation in two.[48]

Other congressional efforts to improve America's commercial relations were frustrated by a combination of provincialism and ideological rigidity. Adams and Jefferson were not atypical in laboring more diligently on behalf of regional interests than national interests during their service abroad. And when Congress considered asking the

[47] Samuel Flagg Bemis, *Pinckney's Treaty: A Study of America's Advantage from Europe's Distress, 1783-1800* (Baltimore, Md., 1926), chap. 1; Arthur P. Whitaker, *The Spanish-American Frontier, 1783-1795* . . . (Boston, 1927). Regarding the wartime opening of Cuba to American trade see the Philadelphia *Evening Herald,* Sept. 8, 1785, and the Philadelphia *Pennsylvania Packet,* Mar. 29, 1785. Most historians of the subject take at face value the cries of land speculators that closing the Mississippi injured the hardy pioneers of Kentucky and Tennessee, without realizing that at that time, livestock raising was almost the only commercial activity in those places.

[48] The Jay-Gardoqui affair is summarized in the works of Bemis and Whitaker cited in n. 47; in Burnett's *Continental Congress,* 478, 655-659; and in Jensen, *New Nation,* 170-174. The vehemence of the southern reaction and the talk of splitting the Confederation can be traced in many letters in vol. 8 of Burnett, *Letters;* see, for example, Theodore Sedgwick to Caleb Strong, Aug. 6, 1786, ibid., 8:415-416.

states to amend the Articles of Confederation by granting Congress power to regulate interstate and foreign commerce, ideological restraints were clearly revealed. On one such occasion in 1785, Virginia congressmen James Monroe and William Grayson (both being republican ideologues who had learned a measure of nationalism through military service) favored the enlarged power; the opposition was successfully led by their fellow Virginian Richard Henry Lee, an archrepublican who insisted that "the Spirit of Commerce thro'out the world is a Spirit of Avarice."[49] About the same time, the legislature of Massachusetts instructed its congressional delegates—Rufus King, Elbridge Gerry, and Samuel Holten—to present Congress with a resolution calling for a general convention to enlarge the powers of Congress. They refused to do so, giving their reasons to Governor James Bowdoin in a letter that was a perfect gem of republican fears of conspiracies. "The great object of the Revolution," they wrote, "was the Establishment of good Government, and each of the States, in forming their own, as well as the federal Constitution, have adopted republican principles." Those arrangements were in danger, they went on, for "plans have been artfully laid, and vigorously pursued," to change "our republican Governments, into baleful Aristocracies." Any proposal to increase the powers of Congress, in regard to commerce or any other matter, should therefore be considered with the utmost caution.[50]

As for the other main area of national concern—the Revolutionary War debts—the record was abysmal. Congress's only sources of revenue, the requisitions it levied upon the states and whatever it could borrow abroad, all but dried up after 1783. In 1781 and again in 1783 Congress proposed amendments to the Articles of Confederation that would have empowered it to collect duties on imports. Amendments required the consent of the legislatures of all

[49] Burnett, *Continental Congress*, 635. Richard Henry Lee to Madison, Aug. 11, 1785, in Rutland, *Papers of Madison*, 8:340, is also a clear statement of the fears of a northern monopoly designed to destroy the South; see, in addition, ibid., 8:336 n. 2.

[50] Sept. 3, 1785, in Burnett, *Letters*, 8:206–210.

thirteen states, however, and each of the two proposals was killed by one state—the first by Rhode Island, the second by New York. James Madison proposed that Congress be authorized to collect requisitions from delinquent states by force and even argued that the Articles gave it an implied power to do so, but he gained little support. Congress did appoint commissioners who undertook the arduous and complicated task of auditing the tens of thousands of claims for goods and services that had been rendered in the Revolutionary cause, and by 1787 that work had nearly been completed. It also tried to keep up with back interest payments by issuing new public securities called indents. Neither of these positive steps counted for much, and King wrote to Gerry in the summer of 1786, "the Treasury now is literally without a penny."[51]

Not only were state particularists and archrepublicans unconcerned by the national bankruptcy, many of them regarded it as advantageous. Their reasoning is evident in a letter that Richard Henry Lee wrote to John Adams in 1785, after Congress had adopted its resolution for the survey and sale of the land in the Northwest Territory. "The soil and climate of that country is incomparably fine," Lee wrote, "and I have no doubt will be greedily purchased with the public securities. If this plan succeeds, our debt will soon be removed." Lee did not need to add that liquidation of the debt in that manner would save the republic by preventing a Walpolizing of America. As Samuel Osgood had written to Adams earlier, "I am apprehensive that if you were here, you would find it very difficult to establish Funds that would not have a Tendency to destroy the Liberties of this Country. . . . Our Danger lies in this— That if permanent Funds are given to Congress, the aristocratical Influence, which predominates in more than a Major Part of the United States will finally establish an arbitrary Government in the United States."[52]

[51] Regarding Madison see Burnett, *Continental Congress*, 504. The quotation is from King to Gerry, June 18, 1786, in Burnett, *Letters*, 8:392. On the subject of congressional finance in general see Ferguson, *Power of the Purse*, passim.

[52] Lee to Adams, Aug. 1, 1785, and Osgood to Adams, Jan. 14, 1784, in Burnett, *Letters*, 8:174 and 7:414.

Nationalists, chagrined by the impotence of Congress, the recalcitrance of state particularists and republican ideologues, and the seeming indifference of the population at large, were powerless to do anything about the decay of the Union. Some were determined to try, as their efforts at the Mount Vernon Conference and the Annapolis Convention attest. In the meantime, no small number of them began to study the history of other confederations, both republican and nonrepublican, in an effort to find guides for restructuring the American confederation. Montesquieu had warmly endorsed confederations as a means for preserving small republics, but his observations were too general to be of use. There were better sources, however, including Plutarch on the ancient Greek confederations, Pfeffel on the Germanic, Sir William Temple on the Netherlands, and the Abbe Millot and the Abbe Mably on those and several more.[53]

The most thorough student of the subject was Madison, though Hamilton, Wilson, and others were well versed in it. They concluded, not surprisingly, that confederations were successful to the extent that the central authority was given power over the whole and that when the central authority was as weak as the American Congress, the confederation ended in calamity. As Madison would write in *The Federalist*, the Germanic empire, like the American Union, was "a community of sovereigns," and the Diet, like the Congress, was "a representation of sovereigns." Moreover, "the history of Germany is a history of wars between the Emperor and the Princes of States; of wars among the Princes and States themselves; of the licenciousness of the strong, and the oppression of the weak; of

[53] These several authorities are cited in *Federalist* numbers 9 and 18–20, the first by Hamilton, the other three by Madison with Hamilton's collaboration. For the works referred to, see the notes to numbers 18–20 in Syrett, *Papers of Hamilton*, 4:377–395. For Madison's "Notes on Ancient and Modern Confederacies," Apr.–June, 1786, see Rutland, *Papers of Madison*, 9:3–24. The first volume of John Adams's "A Defence of the Constitutions of Government of the United States of America," containing a detailed survey of republics, was published in 1787 and "was much circulated in the convention" (Adams, *Works of Adams*, 4:276, 303–373). See also the casual lesson in history in King to Jonathan Jackson, Sept. 3, 1786, in Burnett, *Letters*, 8:459.

foreign intrusions, and foreign intrigues; of requisitions of men and money, disregarded, or partially complied with; of attempts to enforce them, altogether abortive, or attended with slaughter and desolation, involving the innocent with the guilty; of general imbecility, confusion and misery." Hamilton went a step further, at least metaphorically: "the separate governments in a confederacy," he wrote, "may aptly be compared with the feudal baronies."[54]

The shortcomings of the American systems of government were most dramatically demonstrated—and the opportunity nationalists were seeking was provided—by the course of events in New England. One might have supposed the Yankees to have been abundantly endowed with republican virtue: they were devoutly religious, they spoke endlessly of treasuring industry and frugality and plain living, their statute books were teeming with sumptuary laws, and landholding was more widely distributed among them than among denizens of any other part of the country. Massachusetts and New Hampshire had the most carefully crafted and balanced of all the new constitutions, and Rhode Island and Connecticut had successfully governed themselves under their charters for well over a century. Nevertheless, it was New England that came closest to degenerating into licentiousness.

Connecticut was the most nearly stable of the New England states during the postwar years, but its government had insoluble problems. The most pressing were fiscal: the state had emerged from the war with a large public debt which, given the absence of good ports and therefore significant revenues from import duties, was beyond the capacity of the government to service. The state attempted to collect taxes on land, but the effort was vain and provoked some rebellious grumbling during the winter of 1786–1787. Moreover, many public creditors suffered the absurd experience of having their farms sold for nonpay-

---

[54] *Federalist* numbers 19 and 17, in Syrett, *Papers of Hamilton*, 4:386–387 and 374.

ment of taxes that had been levied to pay them interest on
their public securities. Under existing arrangements there
was little the state could do to manage its financial problems, and what it did do only compounded them. The
government of Connecticut, though highly democratic in
form, was in practice under the control of a tight oligarchy
of old landed families. They repeatedly returned to the
office of state treasurer one of their number, John Lawrence, though he was old, enfeebled, and nearly blind. In
1787 the General Assembly, not having had a report from
Lawrence in nearly a decade and meanwhile having levied
taxes and made appropriations without knowing the condition of the treasury, finally asked for an accounting. He
resigned in protest, and it took a legislative committee two
full years to figure out what had been happening.[55]

New Hampshire was nearly in a state of nature. Its
rugged, heavily wooded terrain and severe winters isolated
most of its citizens from one another and bred an intense
localism—loyalty to a town or a village or a valley rather
than to the state and the nation. In the southeastern part of
the state, where the Piscataqua and other streams made
movement less difficult, many of the farmers neglected
their planting in the spring so as to work in lumbering for
cash wages, and then they led idle, drunken, disorderly,
and sometimes riotous lives during the rest of the year.
Thus, anyway, were they described by the contemporary
minister and historian Jeremy Belknap. In any event, the
New Hampshire Yankees as a whole were almost as lawless
and ungovernable as the Scotch-Irish frontiersmen in the
South.[56]

---

[55] This paragraph is drawn from the Hartford *Connecticut Courant*, the *Middlesex
Gazette*, the New Haven *Connecticut Journal*, and the New London *Connecticut
Gazette* for the appropriate period; see especially the letters by Erastus Wolcott in
the *Connecticut Courant* for Feb. 9, 23, 1787; see also the manuscript volume
Finance and Currency, vol. 5, pp. 284-287, in the Connecticut Archives, Hartford.

[56] Jeremy Belknap, *The History of New Hampshire*, 3 vols. (Boston, 1791–1792),
vol. 3, especially at 210ff. and 261; *New Hampshire Spy* (especially the issue of Oct.
24, 1786); and the Portsmouth *New Hampshire Gazette*, *Fowle's New-Hampshire
Gazette*, and the *New-Hampshire Mercury and General Advertiser*. The general
description given here is also drawn from town records in the Microfilm
Collection of Early Town Records in the New Hampshire State Library, Concord.

But it was Rhode Islanders who shocked the nation the most, or at least they were the focus of anxiety until Massachusetts erupted in rebellion. Rhode Islanders had won the animus of many in their sister states during the war, when they profiteered blatantly in supplying French and American armies, and again in 1782, when (as a part of some crass speculations) they killed the amendment to the Articles of Confederation that would have given Congress a source of revenue from import duties. They did nothing to enhance their reputation by their unorthodox views toward government, which held that government existed to facilitate (by fraudulent means if necessary) the business activities of its citizens, or by their business ethics, in which the only limits upon trickery, deception, and sharp trading were those required by a regard for future trading.[57]

All these doings earned the state the opprobrious sobriquet of Rogue's Island, but it was the paper-money scheme of 1786 that provoked the greatest hostility, shame, and alarm. The state legislature, burdened with more public debts than it could support by ordinary means, issued a large amount of unsecured paper currency, lending the money to its citizens against mortgages on real estate. The interest that was due to the state equaled the interest that it owed on its public debt; the plan was that as the individual borrowers repaid their loans, the state would repay its own creditors with the paper money, then tax that currency out of existence. For a variety of reasons the scheme went awry, and the currency depreciated until it was worth no more than seven or eight cents on the dollar.[58]

[57] This general description is pieced together from study of the Maritime Papers in the Rhode Island Archives; the *Providence Gazette*, Jan., 1782, to Feb., 1783; the Frederick S. Peck Collection, the Moses Brown Papers, and the Rhode Island Historical Society Manuscripts—all in the Rhode Island Historical Society; and the Brown and Arnold Papers in the John Carter Brown Library. See also James B. Hedges, *The Browns of Providence Plantations: Colonial Years* (Cambridge, Mass., 1952), 329–332 and passim; David Howell to Welcome Arnold, Nov. 17, 1782, in Burnett, *Letters*, 6:542–543; and Mr. Otto to the Comte de Montmorin, Apr. 10, 1787, in Farrand, *Records*, 3:15.

[58] For fuller accounts of the Rhode Island paper-money scheme described in this and the following paragraph see McDonald, *We the People*, 324–338, and *E Pluribus Unum*, 209–217.

The legislature had declared the paper to be legal tender, had disfranchised anyone who refused to accept it at par, and had provided that debtors whose creditors refused the paper could cancel their debts by depositing the paper with certain courts and also publishing a notice in the newspapers. In actuality, not much fraud was involved—only 156 men paid their debts in paper against the refusals of their creditors—and the amount of disruption of ordinary economic activity was minimal, but these facts went unnoticed outside the state. Rhode Island was widely castigated for its corruption and venality; a New York newspaper, for instance, ran a column entitled "The Quintessence of Villainy; or, Proceedings of the Legislature of the State of Rhode Island."[59] What was happening, in other words, was not so important as what outsiders thought was happening, namely, that democracy in Rhode Island had run amok and that wild-eyed levelers had taken over.

Something similar occurred in regard to the tumults in Massachusetts. That state's excellent constitution had produced a demagogic governor in the person of John Hancock—who, after his appetite for money had been sated, proved willing to go to great lengths to win the plaudits of the multitude. Toward the goal of pleasing everyone, he induced the legislature to make provision for an outlandishly generous funding of the state's war debts; and then, having thus won the fancy of the public creditors, he won that of the taxpayers by declining to collect any taxes. In 1785 the wages of sin fell due, so to speak, and Hancock saw fit to retire, on the professed ground that attacks of gout had temporarily rendered him incapable of devoting further service to the public. His successor, James Bowdoin, was a humorless man who believed that public obligations were sacred; and Bowdoin set out to collect the taxes that the Hancock-inspired legislators had cheerfully levied.[60]

[59] New York *Daily Advertiser*, Apr. 6, 1787. For three of many such comments see Gorham's characterization of Rhode Island in Farrand, *Records*, July 18, 2:42; Washington's letter to David Stuart, July 1, 1787, ibid., 3:51; and Madison to Randolph, Apr. 2, 1787, in Burnett, *Letters*, 8:570.

[60] *Massachusetts Centinel*, 1784, 1785, passim; Acts and Resolves of Massachusetts, 1784, chap. 25, and acts of Mar. 18 and July 2, 1785; Journal of the House of

A taxpayers' revolt, which came to be called Shays' Rebellion, ensued. In September of 1786 armed bands gathered to prevent the sitting of the county courts in several interior counties, and conventions of malcontents gathered to draw up statements of grievances—protesting, among other things, the level of taxation, the cost of government, efforts to pay off the state debt at par, the cost of court proceedings, and the location of the state capital in Boston. Subsequently, about two to three thousand rebels were organized into military companies and began to drill. Just what they intended to do remains a mystery; whatever they intended, they never did it, for in late January, 1787, the rebellion was crushed by a volunteer army recruited in Boston and its environs.[61]

The general impression of what Shays' Rebellion had been about was fabricated by Henry Knox, the former artillery general who was then serving as superintendent of war under the Confederation. Knox wrote Washington that the Shaysites had between twelve and fifteen thousand disciplined men under arms and that they intended to march on Boston, loot the Bank of Massachusetts, recruit additional rebels in New Hampshire and Rhode Island, and then march southward with the intention of redistributing all property. The letter, in one version or another, found its way into the newspapers and was copied and spread through private correspondence.[62]

Representatives, Feb. 20, June 8, 1784, and Bowdoin's message to the legislature, June 2, 1786; Ferguson, *Power of the Purse*, 245-246, 273-275. See also the extended account of Massachusetts' difficulties during the period in McDonald, *E Pluribus Unum*, 217-226, 231-250.

[61]McDonald, *E Pluribus Unum*, 244-256. The most recent study of Shays' Rebellion, David P. Szatmary's *Shays' Rebellion: The Making of an Agrarian Insurrection* (Amherst, Mass., 1980), contends that the uprising reflected a deep cultural split between areas that were committed to commercialism and acquisitive individualism, on the one side, and those which held more traditional values, on the other. The thesis is not without merit, though it is difficult to reconcile with the fact that the rebellious areas subsequently became, and long remained, strongholds of Federalism.

[62]Knox to Joseph Williams, Oct. 16, 1786, to Congress, Oct. 18, 1786, to Washington, Oct. 23, 1786, James Swan to Knox, Oct. 26, 1786, Major North to Knox, Oct. 29, 1786—all in Knox Papers, Massachusetts Historical Society; Burnett, *Continental Congress*, 671-672; *Journals of Congress*, Oct. 21, 1786. For an example of the spreading of Knox's version see Charles Pettit to Franklin, Oct. 18,

The impact of this understanding—or, rather, misunder-standing—of the rebellion can scarcely be overrated. In immediate terms it stimulated Congress to approve, and it stimulated several states to name delegates to, the general meeting in Philadelphia that had been proposed by the handful of men who had attended the abortive commercial convention in Annapolis the preceding September. Thus it helped to make the Constitutional Convention a reality. More fundamentally, it shocked a large number of Ameri-cans into reconsidering their ideas about republican forms of government and about safeguards to liberty and prop-erty. New Englanders in droves abandoned the Harring-tonian notion that the ownership of land automatically created republican virtue, and many ended their flirtation with classical republicanism altogether, returning to a pris-tine puritanism whose central concern was the imposition of the authority of the righteous over the lawless and the sinful. In the circumstances, such authority could come only from a greatly strengthened national government. (Thus ended the unnatural alliance between puritanical republicans and agrarian republicans, between Yankees and tobacco planters, that had dominated national politics off and on since 1776.)

A bitter lesson emerged from the disruptions in New England, one that was reinforced elsewhere by corruption, demagoguery, and the refusal or inability of Congress and the several states to honor their obligations. The lesson, as

1786, in Burnett, *Letters*, 8:487. Abigail Adams, in London, wrote to Jefferson mentioning the cry of some Shaysites for "an equal distribution of property," but she saw "Luxery and extravagance" as the causes of "these commotions" (Boyd, *Papers of Jefferson*, 11:86). Madison also wrote to his father that "an abolition of debts public & private, and a new division of property are strongly suspected to be in contemplation" (Rutland, *Papers of Madison*, 9:154). That Washington believed Knox and accepted the agrarian-law implications is evident in his letters (see, for example, Washington to Madison, Nov. 5, 1786, ibid., 9:161). For the continuing concern and discussion among the various correspondents see Henry Lee to Washington, Nov. 11, 1786, in Burnett, *Letters*, 8:505–506. For accounts of the rebellion which stress the need for order and law to protect liberty and to prevent tumults see, for example, Isaac Backus, *An Address to the Inhabitants of New-England, Concerning the Present Bloody Controversy Therein* (Boston, 1787), and George Richards Minot, *The History of the Insurrections, in Massachusetts* (Worces-ter, Mass., 1788).

some were candid enough to put it, was that the American public did not possess a sufficient stock of virtue to sustain a republic, as republics had traditionally been conceived. Man did not have such virtue naturally, nor did he obtain it by laboring in the earth, nor did many men acquire it through religious instruction.

The practical inferences to be drawn from the lesson were varied. One could give up on republicanism and restore a more authoritarian form of government, monarchical or otherwise. Or one could attempt to create a more virtuous public by means of education, by setting good examples, or by making it to the interest of individuals to strive for the public good. Or one could try to establish republican government upon principles other than virtue, upon the assumption that most men, most of the time, would act out of motives of self-interest rather than of the public interest. Advocates of each position would be present in the Constitutional Convention.

Despite the vehemence with which Patriots had rejected monarchy, the monarchical habit died hard, for thorough conditioning had left its mark. Manifestations of the habit were evident in postwar America in a number of ways. One telling sign of a lingering taste for monarchy was the ritual exchange of greetings and congratulations between governors and legislatures that took place, in solemn imitation of colonial and British practice, upon the annual convening of every legislature except that of Pennsylvania, which had no chief executive. More revealing is that Americans ritually celebrated the birthday of Louis XVI as they had once celebrated the birthday of George III; they named counties Bourbon; Congress requested and ultimately received a portrait of Louis and Marie Antoinette to hang in its meeting hall; and when the dauphin was born, the event occasioned festivities and congratulations all over America. Perhaps most revealing is the adulation with which almost all Americans regarded Washington, and the not infrequent overtures that were made to enthrone him—which, for better or for worse, he invariably and indignantly declined.[63]

After Shays' Rebellion began, considerable numbers of Americans, especially among the far-from-lowly orders of men in New England, began to talk of constitutional monarchy as a safer guardian of liberty and property than republicanism could ever be, at least in a country as large as the United States. George Richards Minot, clerk of the Massachusetts House of Representatives and the first historian of the rebellion, wrote that "persons respectable for their literature and their wealth" formed the "seeds of a party" favoring monarchy, thus inspiring "very serious apprehensions" among those who continued to favor republicanism. Crèvecoeur reported to a friend that "in the 4 Provinces of New England they Are So weary of the Govt . . . that they Sigh for Monarchy." Somewhat ambiguously, Knox wrote to Washington that about "three-sevenths" of the people in Massachusetts favored the establishment of a national government "analogous to the British Constitution."[64]

That many New Englanders could change their positions so violently was seen by contemporaries as a normal shift from excess in one direction to excess in another. New England had been too republican, the common explanation

[63] Regarding the monarchical habit see Robert Dennis Fiala, "George III in the Pennsylvania Press: A Study in Changing Opinions, 1760–1776" (Ph.D. diss., Wayne State University, 1967); William David Liddle, "A Patriot King, or None: American Public Attitudes Toward George III and the British Monarchy, 1754–1776" (Ph.D. diss., Claremont Graduate School, 1970), and " 'A Patriot King, or None': Lord Bolingbroke and the American Renunciation of George III," *Journal of American History* 65 (1979): 951–970. John Adams commented on the "natural disposition to respect" kings in his "Discourses on Davila," no. 8, in Adams, *Works of Adams,* 6:258. I have observed the continuation of monarchical rituals in the records of the several legislatures (the rituals were continued nationally under Washington and Adams but abandoned by Jefferson). The celebrations of events in the lives of the French royal family were routinely reported in newspapers. Regarding the overtures to Washington and the subject in general see Louise Burnham Dunbar, *A Study of "Monarchical" Tendencies in the United States from 1776 to 1801* (New York and London, 1970). For graphic depictions of attitudes toward Washington and their perdurance see *Promoted to Glory: The Apotheosis of George Washington,* ed. Patricia A. Anderson (Northampton, Mass., 1980).

[64] Dunbar, *Monarchical Tendencies,* 55, 71, 72; Minot, *History of the Insurrections,* 61–62; Madison to Edmund Randolph, Feb. 25, 1787, in Rutland, *Papers of Madison,* 9:299.

went, and now it had been shocked into veering too far toward the opposite extreme.[65] Perhaps this was a sound judgment, but there may have been more to it than that. Puritanical republicans felt comfortable in a state of crisis or with a sense of impending doom: only when the world seemed or could be made to seem to be coming to an end was their militance necessary or desirable. Success, well-being, happiness, *otium*, were not only alien to them, they were a threat to them. Thus when a genuine crisis, or the appearance of one, was thrust upon them, they agonized verbally, but they inwardly rejoiced: they and their militance were justified and in demand. That they might have to reverse their previously declared positions disconcerted them not at all. For the sole change of mind of which an ideologue is incapable is that of ceasing to be an ideologue.

As for members of the Constitutional Convention, the evidence is inconclusive. Many years afterward James Monroe, who had been a member of Congress in 1786, asserted that Nathaniel Gorham, then president of Congress, wrote to Prince Henry of Prussia about "his fears that America could not sustain her independence, and asked the prince if he could be induced to accept regal power on the failure of our free institutions." By the time Monroe's assertion was made, Gorham had long been dead. In the convention, Gorham had made no suggestions favoring monarchy, but he was outspokenly pessimistic about the future of republican institutions in America, and he supported a strong executive. Nicholas Gilman, a late-coming delegate from New Hampshire, wrote to his brother shortly after arriving in Philadelphia that men of "vigorous minds and warm Constitutions" in the convention were advocating a "high toned Monarchy." George Mason wrote afterward that Gouverneur Morris had said to him privately that "we must have a Monarchy sooner or later . . . and the sooner we take him, while we are able to make a Bargain with him, the better." That kind of language was characteristic of Morris, but what he is recorded

---

[65] See, for example, George Mason to George Mason, Jr., May 20, 1787, in Farrand, *Records*, 3:22; or Madison to Edmund Pendleton, Feb. 24, 1787, in Burnett, *Letters*, 8:547.

as having said openly on the subject is ambiguous. John Dickinson expressed warm admiration for the British constitution and said that "a firm Executive could only exist in a limited monarchy," that limited monarchy was among the best forms of government, and that "it was certain that equal blessings had never yet been derived from any of the republican form"; but he made no recorded monarchical proposals in the convention. Afterward, James McHenry claimed to have seen a list, drawn up by his fellow delegate from Maryland John Francis Mercer, which identified upwards of twenty monarchists in the convention; but the circumstances of the claim are confused. At one point, four of the ten states that were present voted for a lifetime chief executive, but Madison said that the vote was merely tactical and that no more than three or four delegates actually favored the proposal.[66]

The closest recorded approximation to a proposal of monarchy came from Hamilton. He declared that he was "as zealous an advocate for liberty as any man whatever, and trusted he should be as willing a martyr to it," but he had grave doubts as to whether republican forms were adequate to protect it. He was candid in his admiration for the British government, and "doubted much whether any thing short of it would do in America." He recognized, however, that it would be impracticable to propose a monarchy, for the simple reason that most Americans would not yet accept one. Accordingly, he said, "we ought to go as far in order to attain stability and permanency, as republican principles will admit." To that end he proposed that the executive and members of one branch of the legislature be elected for life terms and that members of the other branch be elected for three-year terms.[67]

The most common attitude among the delegates was doubtless close to the one that Washington expressed. No person had resisted monarchy more firmly than Washington had, but by early 1787 he was willing to admit that "the

[66] Farrand, Records, June 1, 2, July 6, 17, Aug. 6, 1:66, 86–87, 545, 2:34–36, 191–192, and appendixes on 3:66, 319–324. See also Dunbar, Monarchical Tendencies, 60, 91; Burnett, Letters, 8:459 n.
[67] Farrand, Records, June 18, 26, 1:282–311, 424.

utility;—nay necessity of the form" might become evident in time. He was convinced, however, "that the period is not arrived for adopting the change without shaking the Peace of this Country to its foundation." He shared with many a belief that monarchy might be staved off for a while—and, with God's blessing, forever—if the convention would act promptly to create a strong and stable national government in which a powerful executive could check the excesses of the legislative. Madison also expressed this view, adding that "if no effectual check be devised" to restrain the excesses of the state legislatures, "a revolution of some kind or other would be inevitable." Gouverneur Morris echoed the sentiment: "the way to keep out monarchical Govt. was to establish such a Repub. Govt. as wd. make the people happy and prevent a desire of change."[68]

The sense of urgency was pervasive. Jay expressed a widespread feeling when he wrote to Jefferson that if republicanism were to fail in America, it would not be likely to be tried again anywhere else. Perhaps Mason best captured the prevailing mood as the convention opened. "The eyes of the United States are turned upon this assembly," he wrote to his son, "and their expectations raised to a very anxious degree." The break from Britain and the formation of the state constitutions, he went on, "were nothing compared to the great business now before us. . . . to view, through the calm, sedate medium of reason the influence which the establishment now proposed may have upon the happiness or misery of millions yet unborn, is an object of such magnitude, as absorbs, and in a manner suspends the operations of the human understanding."[69]

[68] Ibid., June 26, July 17, 1:424, 2:35–36; Madison to Washington, Feb. 21, 1787, and to Edmund Pendleton, Feb. 24, 1787, in Burnett, *Letters*, 8:545–548; Dunbar, *Monarchical Tendencies*, 58; Washington to Madison, Mar. 31, 1787, in Rutland, *Papers of Madison*, 9:342–343.

[69] Jay to Jefferson, Oct. 27, 1786, in Boyd, *Papers of Jefferson*, 10:488–489; Mason to Mason, Jr., June 1, 1787, quoted from Niles, *Principles and Acts*, 306, and from Farrand, *Records*, 3:32–33 (the two versions vary slightly). For additional perceptions of the crisis for the republican form see Amicus Republicae, 1786, in Hyneman and Lutz, *American Political Writing*, 1:641.

VI

THE FRAMERS:
PRINCIPLES AND INTERESTS

ALMOST ALL THE DELEGATES WHO ATtended the Constitutional
Convention were nationalists in the narrow sense that they
believed it necessary to reorganize and strengthen the
central authority. A vote on that question was taken at the
outset of the deliberations, and only three individuals are
known to have voted in the negative.[1] Few delegates,
however, thought of themselves as representing America
or the American people. The others thought of themselves
as representing the people of the several states severally—
or to put it differently, they were there as representatives of
separate political societies—and the rules of the debates,
including the rule that each state's delegation had but one
vote, no matter what the number of its delegates, reflected
that distinction.[2]

Most of the delegates also attached reservations or
conditions to their willingness to strengthen the central
authority. Some of the reservations were ideological,
though doctrinaire ideologues by no means constituted a
majority of those in attendance. (Fortunately for the nation,
John Adams was in London and Jefferson was in Paris, and

[1]Farrand, *Records*, May 30, 1:35. The three were Yates, Ellsworth, and
Sherman. The last two, after the agreement that the states would have equal
representation in the Senate had been reached, supported a strengthening of the
central government. Yates left the convention after about six weeks and opposed
ratification of the Constitution.

[2]For the rules see ibid., 1:8–10.

Sam Adams, Richard Henry Lee, Patrick Henry, and most of the other archrepublican Patriot leaders of Seventy-six were either not chosen as delegates by their legislatures or declined to attend.) Other reservations arose from personal or group prejudices or interests, such as those of public-security holders, land speculators, merchants, and slave owners. The strongest reservations arose from the perceived interests, political or economic, of the individual political societies that the delegates represented. Thus, one absolutely central issue—perhaps the absolutely central issue—before the convention was the role, if any, that the states would play in the reorganized and strengthened common authority.

To understand the motives and the actions of the Framers, it is necessary to ascertain, in regard to as many of them as possible, where they stood on this issue and also where they stood in respect to the various and conflicting interests and ideological and philosophical positions that we have been considering.

Possibly the most important group of delegates consisted of those whose nationalism was undiluted or nearly so. Heading the list was Washington, who was crucial to the successful outcome of the convention even though he contributed little to the debates. Two in this group were from Massachusetts, Nathaniel Gorham and Rufus King; King had overcome the fear of an "aristocratical conspiracy" that he had so shrilly expressed in 1785, his perspective having been shifted by Shays' Rebellion, by his marriage to the daughter of a wealthy New York merchant, and by more than a year of intimate association with Alexander Hamilton. Seven were from the Middle States: Hamilton, Gouverneur Morris, Robert Morris, James Wilson, George Clymer, Thomas Fitzsimons, and George Read. Franklin should probably be added to the list, along with William R. Davie of North Carolina and perhaps William Pierce of Georgia. In several respects, Madison and Charles Pinckney can also be counted as being in this group, for they were in agreement with the nationalists on many points; but the two differed from them in certain fundamental ways, and therefore must properly be considered as being in categories by themselves.[3]

All of these men, who might loosely be described as "court-party" nationalists, shared a complex of experiences and attitudes. In the backgrounds of all except the convert King were one or more of the following elements: they had been born or educated abroad or had traveled extensively abroad; they had served for a considerable time as officers in the Continental Line; or they had held important civilian positions in the Confederation during the climactic years 1781 to 1783. All or nearly all of them admired the British system, were somewhat elitist in their leanings (or at least wanted to create a national government that would be high-toned as well as powerful), and were concerned with national honor and glory in addition to the protection of liberty and property. They were hard-nosed and tough-minded, but they were also idealistic, some to the point of romanticism. They were practical men of experience and talent who were scornful of ideology and abstract specula-

[3]This classification of delegates is based upon study of the records of the convention and of such biographical data as are available. The principal external sources on which I have drawn concerning the court-party nationalists are *The Writings of George Washington*, ed. John C. Fitzpatrick, 39 vols. (Washington, D.C., 1931–1944); James T. Flexner, *George Washington*, 4 vols. (Boston, 1965–1972); Douglas Southall Freeman, *George Washington: A Biography*, 7 vols. (New York, 1948–1957); King, *Life of King;* Robert Ernst, *Rufus King: American Federalist* (Chapel Hill, N.C., 1968); for Gorham see Timothy Thompson Sawyer, *Old Charlestown: Historical, Biographical, Reminiscent* (Boston, 1902), 189ff., and the scattered correspondence in Burnett, *Letters*, vol. 8; Syrett, *Papers of Hamilton*, and the sources cited in McDonald, *Hamilton;* Howard Swiggett, *The Extraordinary Mr. Morris* (Garden City, N.Y., 1952), and the Morris-Hamilton correspondence; *The Papers of Robert Morris, 1781–1784*, ed. E. James Ferguson and John Catanzariti et al., 6 vols. (Pittsburgh, Pa., 1973–1984); Ferguson, *Power of the Purse;* Clarence L. Ver Steeg, *Robert Morris: Revolutionary Financier* (New York, 1976); Smith, *Wilson;* for Read see the sketch in *Biographies of the Signers to the Declaration of Independence*, ed. John Sanderson, 5 vols. (Philadelphia, 1831), 3:351ff.; Smyth, *Writings of Franklin; Biographical History of North Carolina from Colonial Times to the Present*, ed. Samuel A. Ashe et al., 6 vols. (Greensboro, N.C., 1907), 5:458ff.; *William Richardson Davie: A Memoir . . .* , ed. J. G. deRoulhoc Hamilton (Chapel Hill, N.C., 1907); and M. E. Bradford, *A Worthy Company: Brief Lives of the Framers of the United States Constitution* (Marlborough, N.H., 1982). Madison and Pinckney are discussed below.

tion, but some of them were extremely learned in history and political thought. The intellectual influences upon them were varied. For example, Gouverneur Morris, Wilson, and Hamilton were thoroughly versed in ancient history and in English legal and constitutional history, and all three expressed ideas derived from Hume and Smith; but in other respects, Morris seems to have been most influenced by Blackstone, Wilson by Burlamaqui and Francis Hutcheson, and Hamilton by Steuart, Vattel, and Necker.[4]

The court-party nationalists were in agreement that in framing a constitution, it was prudent to act on the assumption that most men in government would put their own interests ahead of the public interest much of the time. This way of thinking, together with the key to the problem that it posed to republican constitution makers, was familiar to them from, among other sources, Hume's essay "On the Independency of Parliament." It was a maxim, Hume wrote, "that, in contriving any system of government, and fixing the several checks and controuls of the constitution, every man ought to be supposed a *knave*, and to have no other end, in all his actions, than private interest. By this interest we must govern him, and, by means of it, make him, notwithstanding his insatiable avarice and ambition, co-operate to public good."[5] Hume was proposing a modified Mandevillean scheme: modified in the sense that the "vice-ridden" hive was to be deliberately constructed by men who were themselves dedicated to the public good.

Several of the court-party men spoke in the convention as if they had committed Hume's essay to memory. Franklin declared that men were governed by ambition and avarice, as if he had coined the thought. Hamilton paraphrased Hume at length: "Take mankind as they are, and what are they governed by? Their passions. There may be

---

[4] The observations about Morris are inferred from remarks that he made in the convention; regarding Wilson see White, *Philosophy of the American Revolution*, 132–136, and Harvey, *Burlamaqui in American Constitutionalism*, 114–116 and passim; regarding Hamilton see McDonald, *Hamilton*, passim, but see also n. 66 of chap. 4 above.

[5] Green and Grose, *Hume's Philosophical Works*, 3:117–118.

in every government a few choice spirits, who may act from more worthy motives. One great error [however] is that we suppose mankind more honest than they are. Our prevailing passions are ambition and interest; and it will ever be the duty of a wise government to avail itself of those passions, in order to make them subservient to the public good.''[6]

It is a grave mistake, however, to assume from this that the Framers (or even the court-party nationalists or even Hamilton) cynically abandoned the whole notion of virtue in the republic and opted to substitute crass self-interest in its stead. Several historians have made that assumption, and at least one has gone so far as to pronounce the judgment that the very tradition of civic humanism, of men finding their highest fulfillment in service to the public, thereby was brought to an end. To commit that mistake is to fail to understand two subtle but crucial aspects of the concept that men are driven by their passions.[7]

The first is the simpler of the two. Men are driven by their passions, and in devising governments, it is wise to assume that ambition and avarice are the ruling passions of all. Hume himself, however, in the very passage just cited, indicated that the assumption was "false in *fact*." To prepare for the worst was to err on the side of prudence, but the court-party nationalists actually expected something better, for men are driven by a variety of passions, and many of these—love of fame, of glory, of country, for example—are noble. When any such passion becomes a man's ruling passion, he must necessarily live his life in virtuous service to the public; and it was such men whom the nationalists counted on to govern others through their baser passions. Sir James Steuart put the matter succinctly. Self-interest, he wrote, is the "only motive which a statesman should make use of, to engage a free people to concur in the plans which he lays down for their government." But he adds, immediately: "I beg I may not here be understood

---

[6]Farrand, *Records*, June 2, 1:82; ibid., Yates's Notes, June 22, 1:381.

[7]Pocock, *Machiavellian Moment*, 519–534; Wood, *Creation of the American Republic*, 606–618; Pole, *Political Representation*, 531–532.

to mean, that self-interest should conduct the statesman: by no means. Self-interest, when considered with regard to him, is public spirit."[8]

It was generally agreed that the love of fame—the desire for secular immortality in the grateful remembrance of posterity—is the noblest of the passions. Fame is bestowed upon men for a variety of achievements which writers from Plutarch to Machiavelli to Sir Francis Bacon to Hume had ranked on hierarchical scales. On Bacon's scale (from the bottom upwards), those who won fame were fathers of their country, who "reign justly, and make the times good wherein they live"; champions of empire, who in honorable wars "enlarge their territories or make noble defence against invaders"; saviors of empire, who deliver their country from civil war or from tyrants; lawgivers, who provide constitutions by which they govern wisely and well after they are gone; and at the pinnacle, "FOUNDERS OF STATES AND COMMONWEALTHS." Clearly, quite a number of delegates to the convention were driven, to lesser and greater degrees, by a passion for fame, and so were many others of the founding generation. Moreover, they were convinced that—during their generation, at least—enough men were driven by the love of fame and other noble passions to permit the establishment of government on solid foundations.[9]

As for the future, they did not propose to leave it to chance, for they had a plan, dear to Washington's heart, for training a class of *Optimates*. Concern with reforming the American public to ensure that it would contain an ample supply of virtuous men in the future had, of course, occupied the Patriot constitution makers, who had provided for educational and religious institutions that were designed to inculcate virtue. But these, by and large, aimed at the grandiose goal of remaking the whole people; in the

[8] These themes run through Hume's political essays and through Smith's *Theory of Moral Sentiments*. The Steuart quotation is from *Principles of Political Oeconomy*, 1:142. See also Pope's "Essay on Man," epistle 2; and Colbourn, *Fame and the Founding Fathers*, 4–26.

[9] Colbourn, *Fame and the Founding Fathers*, 9–15.

words of Benjamin Rush, the desideratum was "to conform the principles, morals and manners of our citizens to our republican forms of government." What several of the Framers—including Madison, Washington, Wilson, and Pinckney—had in mind was more modest and seemingly more practical. They proposed to make the government conform to the existing morals and manners of the citizens, but to provide leaders for it by establishing a national university, which would select the cream of American youth, overcome the provincialism of the young men, and instill in them a love of the nation and a desire to serve it.[10]

The other relevant aspect of the theory of the passions is more complex: it discarded, as being virtually impossible, all hope of attaining or maintaining the kind of public virtue required by classical and puritanical republicanism, yet it provided a means by which people with ordinary human faults and failings could comport themselves virtuously. The model of human behavior that was involved can be best explained by reference to the example of George Washington.

[10] Rush, "Address to the People of the United States," 1787, in Niles, *Principles and Acts*, 234; Farrand, *Records*, Sept. 14, 2:616. Note the emphasis on education in the Northwest Ordinance of 1787 and in the state constitutions, as seen in Thorpe, *Constitutions*, 2:784, 3:1906–1907, 4:2467, 5:2794, 3091, 6:3760. Jefferson's insistence upon education as the best preservative of freedom is well known—see, for one example, Jefferson to George Wythe, Aug. 13, 1786, in Boyd, *Papers of Jefferson*, 10:244–245—but his programs were more elaborate and state-oriented than were those of the Framers. John Adams later amended his thinking to arrive at the position that "knowledge will forever be a natural cause of aristocracy" (Adams to John Taylor, Apr. 15, 1814, written in response to Taylor's commentary on Adams's "Defence of the Constitutions"). But most republicans tied general education and the dissemination of knowledge to the success of a republic, as is seen in the rules and regulations of various of the private societies such as the Society for Political Inquiries and the Constitutional Society of Virginia (Foner, *Paine*, 41–42; Rutland, *Papers of Madison*, 8:71–72). In the convention, the matter of education and a national university was pressed by several delegates, but unsuccessfully (Farrand, *Records*, 2:322, 325, 620). Washington proposed the establishment of a national university in his first annual address to Congress and again in his Farewell Address (see Syrett, *Papers of Hamilton*, 20:311–314, 316–320, 381, 384–385).

The matter of Washington's being unreservedly trusted
—and trustworthy—repays close scrutiny. In part, trust in
Washington derived from the fact that he had repeatedly
proved that he was worthy of it, both by the diffidence with
which he always accepted the mantle of power and by the
alacrity with which he always voluntarily surrendered
power upon the completion of the undertaking for which it
was granted. Partly, too, his physical appearance and de-
meanor gave him an aura that inspired men to follow him.
Tall and powerfully built, "the best horseman of his age, and
the most graceful figure that could be seen on horseback," as
Jefferson put it, Washington was readily recognized as the
commander in chief by soldiers who had never seen him
before; and it is striking how often monarchical imagery was
used in contemporary physical descriptions of him. An
Englishman said that there was "not a king in Europe but
would look like a valet de chambre by his side." And when
Abigail Adams, by then a veteran of receptions at St.
James's, finally met him in 1789, she was almost moon-
struck, gushing that he moved "with a grace, dignity, and
ease that leaves Royal George far behind him."[11]

It is obvious why Washington was trusted, however;
the more elusive question is how a man could become so
utterly trustworthy. Admittedly, he was far from being an
ordinary man, but he was a long way from being a saint. As
a soldier he had been capable of blundering, rashness, and
poor judgment. He was addicted to gambling, apparently
indulged in a good deal of wenching, was avid in the
pursuit of wealth, and was a "most horrid swearer and
blasphemer." He was vain, pompous, pretentious, and
hot-tempered in the extreme; and though he was normally
a perfect gentleman in his public behavior, he could be a
perfect alley cat in his private behavior. Even in public his
conduct was not always free of blemish. During the war he
had been willing to hang an innocent British prisoner,

[11] Paul Leicester Ford, *Washington and the Theatre* (New York, 1899), 50; Flexner,
Washington, 2:40, 372; Forrest McDonald, *The Presidency of George Washington*
(Lawrence, Kans., 1974), 26; Anderson, *Promoted to Glory*.

Capt. Charles Asgill, in retaliation against the unauthorized behavior of some hooligan New York Loyalists; and Washington was not sufficiently magnanimous to grant the request of the unfortunate Maj. John André to be shot as a soldier rather than to be hanged as a spy. And yet a whole nation could entrust him with its liberty and, indeed, its fate, in revolutionary circumstances which almost invariably breed Caesars and Cromwells, and could know that it was safe to do so.[12]

To understand Washington and to understand the species of republican virtue provided for a few by the theory of the passions, one must begin with the recognition that Washington was ever concerned, almost obsessively, with creating and then living up to what he called his "character"—what in the twentieth century would be called his reputation or public image. Quite revealing was the way in which he had accepted the command of the Continental Army, which repeated a pattern he had followed in accepting command of the expedition to the forks of the Ohio in 1753. Obviously, he wanted to be commander in chief: he attended the sessions of the Continental Congress dressed in a resplendent military uniform which he himself had designed. Yet, when the position was offered to him, he declared solemnly that "lest some unlucky event should happen, unfavorable to my reputation, I beg it to be remembered, by every gentleman in the room, that I, this day, declare with utmost sincerity, I do not think myself equal to the command I am honored with." To his brother-in-law, Washington wrote that if a firm belief in the cause, close attention to prosecuting it, and integrity "cannot supply the place of ability and experience, the cause will suffer, and more than probable my character along with it."[13]

---

[12] Flexner's four-volume biography catalogs Washington's shortcomings in a balanced way; see also his one-volume version, *Washington: The Indispensable Man* (Boston, 1974).

[13] Flexner, *Washington*, 2:16; John Adams to Mrs. Adams, May 29, 1775, One of the Virginia Delegates to _____, June 14, 1775, Eliphalet Dyer to Joseph Trumbull, June 17, 1775, John Adams to Mrs. Adams, June 17, 1775—all in Burnett, *Letters*, 1:102, 124, 128, 130; Ford, *Journals of Congress*, 2:92; Washington to Burwell Basset, June, 1775, in Fitzpatrick, *Writings of Washington*, 3:297.

After his "character" had been firmly established in the hearts of his countrymen, Washington guarded it carefully and was loath to risk it by further participation in public life. It was with something bordering on dread that he consented to attend the Constitutional Convention. Afterward, he was reluctant to accept the presidency, lest he be regarded as having broken the promise, made in 1783, that he was unalterably retiring to private life. Indeed, he dared not discuss the matter with anyone without fearing that he would be thought to be betraying "an impropriety of conduct, or without feeling an apprehension that a premature display of anxiety, might be construed into a vainglorious desire of pushing myself into notice as a Candidate." What was arguably the most important decision on domestic policy he made during his presidency, and certainly the most important constitutional decision—to sign the bill chartering the Bank of the United States—stemmed, not from considerations either of policy or of constitutionality, but from concern with his "character."[14]

Because Washington was self-consciously playing a role—living his life in such a way as to establish and maintain a certain public image—it is crucial to examine the possible models for that role. An Adams or a Jefferson could find role models in books, but Washington was not a bookish man. There was also the military ideal, with its

[14]Washington to Jefferson, May 30, 1787, to La Fayette, June 6, 1787, Madison to Edward Everett, June 3, 1827, in Farrand, *Records*, 3:31, 34, 476; Flexner, *Washington*, 3:85-111. Edward Carrington in a letter to Jefferson, June 9, 1787, pointed out one of the difficulties facing Washington: "In every public act he hazards, without a possibility of gaining, reputation. He already possesses everything to be derived from the love or confidence of a free people, yet it seems that it remained for himself to add a lustre to his character, by this patriotic adventure of all, for his countries good alone" (Boyd, *Papers of Jefferson*, 11:407-408). The later concern for proprieties can be seen in Hamilton to Washington, Aug. 13, Sept., Nov. 18, 1788, Washington to Hamilton, Aug. 28, Oct. 3, Nov. 6, 1788, in Syrett, *Papers of Hamilton*, 5:201-202, 206-208, 220, 222, 222-224, 230, 233. See also Flexner, *Washington*, 3:195-196; Fitzpatrick, *Writings of Washington*, 30:319-321; McDonald, *Presidency of Washington*, 25-26, 29-30. The episode involving the bank bill is described at some length in McDonald, *Hamilton*, 202-210. See also Kenneth R. Bowling, "The Bank Bill, the Capital City, and President Washington," *Capital Studies* 1 (1972): 59-71; Washington to Arthur Young, Dec. 5, 1791, Dec. 12, 1793, in Fitzpatrick, *Writings of Washington*, 31:438, 33:175-176; Boyd, *Papers of Jefferson*, editorial notes, 19:26, 30, 47-49, 281.

emphases on glory and honor. Clearly these were meaningful to Washington; but the military ideal left open the
possibility, under certain circumstances—say, of corruption
and incompetence in the civil authority, with which Caesar
and Cromwell had had to deal—that the successful soldier
take over the power of government. Again, there was the
ideal of republican virtue; but as we have seen, that kind of
virtue demanded almost extrahuman qualities and also
entailed a dogmatism that was foreign to Washington.

But we approach the nub, an ideal guide to behavior
that Washington and no small number of other founders
used as a personal substitute for republican virtue. It seems
likely that the source of the ideal, in Washington's case,
was Joseph Addison's play *Cato*. That he saw the play a
number of times, that it was probably his favorite serious
drama, and that he had had it staged as an inspiration to his
troops are well known. That he identified himself with one
of its characters in a youthful letter, that he repeatedly
quoted from the play (without attribution) in his mature
correspondence, and that he used one of its lines in his
Farewell Address are all documentable. That it offered a
role model that was strikingly similar to the way in which
Washington patterned his life is indicated by a careful
reading of the play.[15]

The drama is set in Utica, where Cato the Younger holds
together the remnants of the Roman republican Senate
against the usurping arms of the all-conquering Caesar.
Already Caesar, "who owes his greatness to his country's

[15] Ford, *Washington and the Theatre*, 1-2, 18, 24-25, 26; Russel Blaine Nye, *The
Cultural Life of the New Nation, 1776-1830* (New York, 1960), 264; Oral Sumner
Coad and Edwin Mims, Jr., *The American Stage* (New Haven, Conn., 1929), 16, 27,
28, 32-33; Flexner, *Washington*, 2:30; Colbourn, *Fame and the Founding Fathers*,
284 n-285 n; Samuel Eliot Morison, *The Young George Washington* (Cambridge,
Mass., 1932), 19-21, 41; Fredric M. Litto, "Addison's *Cato* in the Colonies,"
William and Mary Quarterly 23 (1966): 431-449. This interpretation was developed
in a paper written in Jan., 1983, and circulated for a symposium, sponsored by the
Liberty Fund and the Center for the Study of Federalism, held in Philadelphia on
May 9, 1983. Garry Wills, a participant there, has expressed doubt about one part
of the interpretation (see his *Cincinnatus: George Washington and the Enlightenment*
[Garden City, N.Y., 1984], 135). He has, however, incorporated the larger thesis
into his work (ibid., 8, 125, 127-128, 130, 131, 134-138).

ruin," has "ravaged more than half the globe"; Cato, with "a feeble army, and an empty senate," has vainly fought "the cause / Of honour, virtue, liberty, and Rome." There are ten characters: Cato, his sons Portius and Marcus, Senators Lucius and Sempronius, Prince Juba of Numidia, the Numidian general Styphax, an ambassador from Caesar, and Cato's daughter Marcia and Lucius's daughter Lucia. Against the backdrop of the larger drama of Cato's refusal to bow to Caesar's yoke, there are three subplots, one involving the treachery of Sempronius and Styphax, the other two involving the love of Prince Juba for Cato's daughter and the love of Cato's sons for Lucia. The mutinies of Sempronius and Styphax are suppressed; Marcus dies heroically; and Cato spurns Caesar's overtures, sees to the safe evacuation of his followers, gives the lovers his blessings, and commits suicide.[16]

Two scenes are especially relevant for present purposes. One of these is Cato's confrontation with the mutineers (act 3, scene 5). Contemptuously, Cato faces them saying:

> Where are these bold, intrepid sons of war,
> That greatly turn their backs upon the foe,
> And to their general send a brave defiance?

In an aside, the treacherous Sempronius says "Curse on their dastard souls, they stand astonished," then Cato continues:

> Perfidious men! and will you thus dishonour
> Your past exploits, and sully all your wars?
> Do you confess 'twas not a zeal for Rome,
> Nor love of liberty, nor thirst of honour,
> Drew you thus far; but hopes to share the spoil
> Of conquered towns and plundered provinces?
> Fired with such motives you do well to join
> With Cato's foes, and follow Caesar's banners.

[16] The play is in *The Works of Joseph Addison*, ed. Richard Hurd, 6 vols. (London, 1881), 1:172-226.

Bemoaning that he has lived to see the day, he proceeds:

> . . . why could not Cato fall
> Without your guilt? Behold, ungrateful men,
> Behold my bosom naked to your swords,
> And let the man that's injured strike the blow.

The hero then recalls the campaigns they have endured together and, without boasting, reminds the soldiers that it was always he "who was the first to explore the untrodden path, / When life was hazarded at every step." Swept with remorse and shame, the mutineers break into tears and lay down their weapons.[17]

Washington's confrontation with the mutinous officers at Newburgh in 1783 had been a muted replay of that scene: Addison might have written the lines for the occasion.

The other scene (act 2, scene 5) involves Prince Juba—who, significantly, is the character with whom Washington identified himself in a youthful letter. Juba, as a Numidian, not a Roman, is self-consciously an outsider, though he has in fact absorbed the best of what was Roman. In this scene he is much concerned that he may have earned Cato's disfavor by being preoccupied with his love for Marcia at such an inappropriate time. Juba says, "I'd rather have that man / Approve my deeds, than worlds for my admirers." Just before, he has uttered what were once famous lines:

> Honour's a sacred tie, the law of kings,
> The noble mind's distinguishing perfection,
> That aids and strengthens virtue where it meets her,
> And imitates her actions, where she is not.[18]

Juba's words, properly understood, provide the clue to understanding Washington. Interpreting passages in dramatic and poetic literature can be a problematical affair, but it is not so in the present instance. As it happens, Addison subsequently wrote a little essay in the *Guardian*, explaining

[17] Ibid., 1:207–209.
[18] Ibid., 1:198.

what Juba meant. Addison begins by distinguishing between two kinds of motives to good actions: "What some men are prompted to by conscience, duty, or religion, which are only different names for the same thing, others are prompted to by honour." He is not talking about the kind of honor that attends the military ideal; he calls that "false honour." True honor, he says, "though it be a different principle from religion, is that which produces the same effects. . . . Religion embraces virtue, as it is enjoined by the laws of God; honour, as it is graceful and ornamental to human nature. The religious man *fears*, the man of honour *scorns* to do an ill action." The one considers vice as offensive to the Divine Being, the other as something beneath him; the one as something forbidden, the other as what is unbecoming.[19]

Honor, in these verses, is that principle of human action which operates out of desire for *"the esteem of wise and good men."* Virtue, by contrast, is stoical virtue, "which regulates itself by the sense of the *honestum* simply, or, in other words, *by self-esteem."* These two principles may exist in the same person, and when they do, honor "aids and strengthens virtue where it meets her." But the combination is rare, and where genuine virtue is absent or inadequate, honor "prompts to the same conduct which virtue prescribes."

The line about kings is crucial: it means that public persons are and should be governed mainly "by the law of *honour* or *outward esteem,"* which is "a more obvious, and, generally, more binding law, to men so employed, than that of *virtue* or *self-esteem."* To put it another way, Addison is advising young Washington, through young Juba, to follow precisely the opposite course from that recommended by Shakespeare's Polonius. Polonius says to Laertes: "This above all: to thine own self be true, and it must follow, as the night the day, thou canst not then be false to any man." Shakespeare put the words in the mouth of a prattling fool, and Addison's message is that, for public men, these are foolish words. Rather, he says, in effect: To others be true;

[19] Ibid., 4:308.

seek the esteem of the wise and the virtuous, and it follows that thou canst not then be false to thyself—or to the republic.

Addison's dictum was repeated, after a fashion, by Shaftesbury and by Hume, and it was given a thorough philosophical grounding in Adam Smith's magisterial inquiry into the origins and nature of moral behavior, *The Theory of Moral Sentiments*. As a principle of personal conduct, it provided the means by which the court-party nationalists among the Framers could reconcile the rule by *Optimates*—through the baser passions of most men—of a society that was too open, too acquisitive, and too large to govern itself through classical republican virtue.

Court-party nationalists in the convention were considerably more influential, but only slightly more numerous, than republican ideologues. In attempting to determine which delegates were of the latter description, one key issue is especially useful. Whereas the first group sought to establish a government on Humean-Mandevillean lines, moderated by Addisonian-Smithian "honor," the ideologues, taught by Bolingbroke, Montesquieu, or classical republicanism, shrank with horror at the prospect of admitting the baser passions as operating principles of government. On four occasions during the convention the delegates confronted a question that turned upon beliefs as to whether virtue or the baser passions should be depended upon as the operating principle of government. The issue was the extent to which congressmen should be excluded from holding other offices. Permeating the debates was the question of "corruption," in the British sense of the term. Bolingbroke had raged repeatedly in denunciation of "placemen," and Montesquieu had more moderately warned against entrusting people with power if it was to their personal advantage to abuse it. Both views had been accepted by the Patriots of 1776. Hume, by contrast, had contended that corruption in the form of the power to manage Parliament by passing out lucrative offices was necessary to the balance of the British constitution. Those delegates to the convention who insisted upon the absolute exclusion of congressmen from other offices during and for a time after their service in Congress can be regarded as being in the Bolingbroke-Montesquieu camp; they still hoped to found the republic upon classical principles, which is to say upon public virtue. Those who were willing to forbid dual officeholding, but who would allow congressmen to resign their seats to accept appointive offices, can be regarded as being in the Hume-Mandeville camp; they rejected as chimerical the idea that virtue alone could activate the republic, choosing instead to erect it on new principles, which is to say upon the channeling of self-interested motives. The first group might be roughly described as corresponding to the country party in England. Judging by their positions on the issue of congressional exclusion, the "country party" in the convention included Abraham Baldwin of Georgia; Pierce Butler, John Rutledge, and Charles Cotesworth Pinckney of South Carolina; Hugh Williamson of North Carolina; George Mason and Edmund Randolph of Virginia; Luther Martin and Daniel Jenifer of Maryland; John Lansing and Robert Yates of New York; Roger Sherman of Connecticut; and Elbridge Gerry of Massachusetts. The court party, by that criterion, included John Langdon and Nicholas Gilman of New Hampshire; Nathaniel Gorham, Rufus King, and Caleb Strong of Massachusetts; Oliver Ellsworth of Connecticut; Hamilton of New York; Wilson, Thomas Mifflin, and Gouverneur Morris of Pennsylvania; John Francis Mercer of Maryland; Charles Pinckney of South Carolina; and William Few, William Pierce, and William Houstoun of Georgia. Madison, along with Alexander Martin of North Carolina, favored a modified Humean position which turned out to be close to what was finally adopted. It is to be observed that the personnel of the court party on this issue is similar to but not identical with the group described earlier as court-party nationalists. Moreover, as will be seen, Sherman and the South Carolinians, identified on this issue as being country party, can more properly be described as advocates of a "foederal," as opposed to a national, system.[20]

The court-party nationalists had a number of advantages. They were, for the most part, young, energetic, bold, articulate, and extremely gifted. They knew one another, knew what they wanted to accomplish, had taken the initiative in bringing the convention about, and were able to seize the initiative once the convention had begun. The republican ideologues, or country party, by contrast, were generally older, less imaginative, and on the defensive. They recognized that something must be done to establish order and to strengthen the Union, and they were willing to make a number of concessions toward that end. Only gradually would they become aware of the nature and extent of the designs to create a national government far more high-toned, far more powerful, and far less compatible with traditional dogmas than anything that a Bolingbrokean or Montesquieuan republican could stomach.

The ablest of the ideologues were Gerry, Mason, Luther Martin, and Randolph. Gerry was a disciple of Sam Adams and may almost be considered to have been Adams's surrogate at the convention. Mason, the author of Virginia's bill of rights, was ideologically and politically pretty much at one with Richard Henry Lee, though he was both more principled and more intelligent than Lee. Luther Martin, the attorney general of Maryland, was a tiresome dipsomaniac, but he was also a man of learning and had

[20] The various debates and votes took place on June 22, 23, Aug. 14, Sept. 3, and are recorded in Farrand, *Records*, 1:375–377, 379–382, 386–394, 2:283–289, 489–492. On one or more occasions, twenty delegates expressed their opinions clearly; and those of eleven others can be inferred. Thus, for example, on June 22 Gorham moved to delete the restraint of ineligibility; he was supported by King. Since Gerry vehemently favored such restraints on other occasions, one can assume that he voted nay; and since Massachusetts voted aye, it follows that Caleb Strong, the state's fourth delegate, also voted aye. On the same roll call, New York's vote was divided; Hamilton favored the motion, Lansing was absent, and Yates voted no. And so on.

I have used the archaic spelling "foederal"—and foederalist—to avoid confusing men of this persuasion with the Federalists, who advocated the ratification of the Constitution and subsequently became members of the political party. "Oe" spellings were passing from use at this time, largely, one expects, because Samuel Johnson pointed out (in his definition of economy) that since oe is not a diphthong in English it makes no sense to use it just because of a Greek or Latin original.

great skills as a lawyer. In actuality, he was in the camp of the ideologues more as a matter of opportunism than of temperament or conviction. The same is at least partly true of Randolph, the governor of Virginia, who was the kind of politician known in the eighteenth century as a trimmer.[21]

Though these men were archrepublicans, they were among the most outspoken enemies of democracy in the convention. Randolph declared: "Our chief danger arises from the democratic parts of our constitutions. It is a maxim which I hold incontrovertible, that the powers of government exercised by the people swallows up the other branches. None of the constitutions have provided sufficient checks against the democracy." Gerry echoed, "The evils we experience flow from the excess of democracy." Curiously, he added that the people were not lacking in virtue, but were "the dupes of pretended patriots." Mason agreed "that we had been too democratic," though he was afraid that the convention might "incautiously run into the opposite extreme."[22]

The republican ideologues (except for Martin) were anxious to check the excess of democracy in the state governments by strengthening the central authority, but only on condition that the strengthening be accompanied by attention to several basic principles. Among these were the complete separation of the three departments of government, both in function and in personnel; either a plural executive or a single executive whose power was shared and checked by an executive council; a bicameral legislature, the two houses being chosen by some means that would ensure that they checked one another; explicit

[21] George Athan Billias, *Elbridge Gerry: Founding Father and Republican Statesman* (New York, 1976); Kate Mason Rowland, *The Life of George Mason, 1725–1792*, 2 vols. (New York, 1892); Paul S. Clarkson and R. Samuel Jett, *Luther Martin of Maryland* (Baltimore, Md., 1970); John J. Reardon, *Edmund Randolph: A Biography* (New York, 1975). For an analysis of Martin's speculative and political activities in Maryland which may have influenced his conduct in the convention see McDonald, *E Pluribus Unum*, 158–171. As for Randolph, it appears likely that his unwillingness to sign the Constitution stemmed from considerations of his political future in Virginia, where the powerful Patrick Henry and perhaps a majority of the citizenry were of anti-Federalist inclinations.

[22] Farrand, *Records*, McHenry's Notes, May 29, 1:26–27; ibid., May 31, 1:48, 49.

enumeration of the powers of each branch of government and a declaration that all other powers were reserved to the states; explicit separation of the "power of the purse" from the "power of the sword," an explicit repudiation of standing armies, and an explicit denial of the power of the national government to charter corporations or to create monopolies; and a bill of rights. They were ill disposed to compromise on these points.[23]

Occupying positions somewhere between those of the court-party nationalists and the republican ideologues were James Madison and Charles Pinckney. Madison was an ideologue in search of an ideology: he was a man of doctrinaire temperament, marked by what Jean-Paul Sartre called "a nostalgia for the absolute"; but he had not yet found or formulated a body of doctrine that he could reconcile with his immense range of reading and his ongoing public experience. It is true that in 1787 and 1788 he pronounced with great certainty his theory of refining public servants by means of complex electoral processes and his theory of checking factions by "extending the sphere." But his certainty was predicated partly on temperament—a preference for the untried but theoretically appealing, as opposed to the imperfections of reality—and partly on the reality that the unchecked legislature of his beloved Virginia (in whose virtue he had once believed with equal confidence) was currently under the sway of his hated political rival Patrick Henry. In a short time the inefficaciousness of his theories would, in his own eyes, be abundantly demonstrated by the triumph of Hamiltonianism, and Henry would lose his power; and then Madison would find it necessary to begin theorizing anew.[24]

[23] This checklist is derived from study of their speeches throughout the convention.

[24] Madison's rethinking is to be seen in the series of articles that he penned for the *National Gazette*, most of which were published between Dec. 19, 1791, and Mar. 31, 1792; Rutland, *Papers of Madison*, 14:170, 191, 197, 201, 206, 217, 233, 244, 257, 266, 274, 370, 426. Ralph L. Ketcham, *James Madison: A Biography* (New York, 1971), 329, says that the essay of Jan. 2, 1792 (*Papers of Madison*, 14:178–179) marks

The Madison of the 1780s, however, is generally regarded as having been as solidly entrenched in the nationalist camp as Hamilton was. This view of Madison as
ardent nationalist must be tempered by at least two major
sets of qualifications. One was that throughout his career
on the national stage, at least until Jefferson became president, Madison was always mindful of the interests of his
state and was rarely if ever willing to do anything in the
national interest which he believed to be inconsonant with
the interests of Virginia. That alone repeatedly set him
apart from such nationalists as Gouverneur Morris, Hamilton, and Washington.[25]

The other qualification to Madison's nationalism was that
it was a matter of vital concern with him that the national
government be appropriately balanced and checked and
refined, lest it become an engine of tyranny. The difference
between him and Hamilton in this respect was evident even

a return to the argument of *Federalist* number 10; but it bears no relation to
Federalist number 10. After brief paragraphs on the advantages and disadvantages
of monarchy and aristocracy, the essay reads: "A republic involves the idea of
popular rights. A representative republic *chuses* the wisdom, of which hereditary
aristocracy has the *chance;* whilst it excludes the oppression of that form. And a
confederated republic attains the force of monarchy, whilst it equally avoids the
ignorance of a good prince, and the oppression of a bad one. To secure all the
advantages of such a system, every good citizen will be at once a centinel over the
rights of the people; over the authorities of the confederal government; and over
both the rights and the authorities of the intermediate governments." That is all:
there is not a word about "refining the electorate" by "extending the sphere" or
about the virtual impossibility of a triumphant faction if the republic is large and
diverse—the two central themes of *Federalist* number 10. The distinguished editor
of the Madison Papers, Robert Rutland, suggests that Madison returned "to his
Federalist 10 position some time in winter of 1791–92," and he cites vol. 14, pp.
160–161, 197–198, "and to some extent 371" (Rutland to the author, Aug. 29,
1984). None of these citations, however, recapitulates the central arguments of
Federalist number 10; and the tenor of all the articles that Madison wrote for the
National Gazette is that of an agrarian republican, not of a Humean. Madison *could*
not have believed in the efficacy of the faction-checking machinery that he had
described in *Federalist* number 10 after the spring of 1791, when it had become
evident to his way of thinking that the Hamiltonian "faction" had captured total
control of the national government.

[25] See the perceptive article by Lance Banning, "James Madison and the
Nationalists, 1780–1783," *William and Mary Quarterly* 40 (1983): 227–255; McDon-
ald, *Hamilton,* 174–175, 181–187; Kenneth Russell Bowling, "Politics in the First
Congress, 1789–1791" (Ph.D. diss., University of Wisconsin, 1968), 208–211; and
Ferguson, *Power of the Purse,* 298ff.

during the convention and even as they were cooperating in the writing of *The Federalist*. Hamilton was concerned that the national government be given stability, strength, and energy; and though he had ideas about how this might best be done, it was almost a matter of indifference to him as to how the government's powers should be organized or what ·forms they should take. Madison's attitude is clear from an often-quoted passage: "If men were angels, no government would be necessary. If angels were to govern men, neither external nor internal controls on government would be necessary. In framing a government which is to be administered by men over men, the great difficulty lies in this: you must first enable the government to control the governed; and in the next place oblige it to control itself." Hamilton thought that such precautions were unnecessary: he believed that the states were and ever would be an adequate, and probably an excessive, restraint upon the national authority. At bottom, Hamilton and other court-party nationalists trusted themselves and therefore trusted power if it was in their own hands. Madison and other men of his temperament did not trust themselves and therefore did not trust power in anyone's hands.[26]

One more observation about Madison is in order. The myth that he was the Father of the Constitution is a deeply rooted one. The facts that he kept the fullest records of the proceedings and that those records show him to have spoken often and brilliantly have helped to perpetuate the myth. As importantly, Madison (unlike Pinckney) did not submit to the convention any detailed plan for a constitution, which makes it difficult to know precisely what he had in mind. Nonetheless, by starting with the Virginia Plan and by working carefully through all the particular proposals that Madison offered or spoke strongly in favor of, we can reconstruct a Madisonian constitution. It bears limited

[26]The differences between Madison and Hamilton are analyzed at greater length in McDonald, *Hamilton*, 107–113; see also Lance Banning, "The Hamiltonian Madison: A Reconsideration," *Virginia Magazine of History and Biography* 92 (1984): 3–28, which reaches similar conclusions on a quite different basis.

resemblance to the document that was drafted by the convention.

Madison proposed to establish a government that would be neither federal nor, to employ the phraseology that he would later use in *The Federalist* to describe the actual government, partly federal and partly national. Instead, his government would have been purely national, the states having no agency in it whatsoever.[27]

In Madison's constitution the legislative power would be vested in a bicameral congress, the number of members in each house to be proportioned among the states according to their populations, though one house would be much more numerous than the other.[28] The electorate would be confined to freeholders, and property qualifications (not exclusively land) would be required for members of congress.[29] The more numerous branch would be chosen directly by the freeholders. The "upper house" would be chosen by electors chosen by freeholders, and presumably the property qualification for its members would be considerably higher than that for the other house, since Madison wanted it to be designed to represent wealth.[30]

Congress would be required to review all state legislation and to veto any that it determined not to be in the national interest.[31] It would guarantee each state a republican form of government, regulate the state militias, and appoint the general officers thereof.[32] It would have a general power to legislate on all matters of national concern, for Madison thought it impracticable to enumerate its powers.[33] (After the decision had been made to enumerate powers, Madison proposed several and voiced his opinion in regard to several others. These will be considered later.)

[27] Virginia Plan, in Farrand, *Records*, May 29, 30, 1:20–23, 37.
[28] Ibid.
[29] Ibid., July 26, 2:124, and McHenry's Notes, Aug. 7, 2:210.
[30] Ibid., May 29, 1:20, and King's Notes, June 7, 1:158.
[31] Ibid., May 29, Aug. 28, 1:21, 2:440. See also Charles F. Hobson, "The Negative on State Laws: James Madison, the Constitution, and the Crisis of Republican Government," *William and Mary Quarterly* 36 (1979): 215–235.
[32] Farrand, *Records*, May 29, Aug. 18, 23, 1:22, 2:332, 389.
[33] Ibid., May 29, 31, 1:21, 54.

Acts of congress would be enforced directly upon individuals; Madison wanted the national government to be empowered to coerce states as well, but he could not think of any practical way of attaining that end.[34] Either house could originate all types of bills. Two-thirds of its members would constitute a quorum. Congress would meet at least once a year, convening in May.[35]

The senate would share the treaty-making power with the president. Two-thirds of the senators would be required to ratify all treaties except (a) treaties of alliance, which the president could conclude by himself, and (b) treaties of peace, which could be ratified by a simple majority. With a two-thirds majority, the senate could conclude treaties of peace without the president's approval.[36] The senate would try impeachment cases, except of the president; the lower house would impeach.[37]

The executive power would be vested in a single president and an executive council; there would be no vice-president. Declaring war would require an act of congress, but the president could "make war" without a declaration in the event of invasion.[38] The treaty-making power would be shared with the senate, as above.

The president would be elected by electors chosen by the freeholders at large, electoral votes presumably being distributed to states in proportion to their population. The person who received the most votes, if these were one-third or more of the total, would become president. If no one received one-third of the votes, the senate would choose the president from the list of all who had received any votes. He would serve a six-year term and be eligible for reelection.[39]

The executive council would consist of six men, to serve six-year terms, one-third to leave office every two years.

34 Ibid.
35 Ibid., May 29, Aug. 7, Sept. 8, 1:21, 2:197, 198, 199, 549.
36 Ibid., Aug. 23, Sept. 7, 2:392, 540.
37 Ibid., July 20, Sept. 8, 2:65–66, 551.
38 Ibid., May 29, Aug. 17, 1:21, 2:318.
39 Ibid., July 19, Sept. 5, 2:56–57, 513, 514.

Two of the members would be chosen from the northern states, two from the middle states, and two from the southern states.[40]

The judicial power would be vested in one or more supreme courts and in inferior courts. Their jurisdiction would extend to all cases of a "judiciary nature" (which presumably excluded "political questions") arising under the constitution or laws of the United States and all cases in which the United States was a party. The supreme court would try cases of impeachment of the president. Judges would be appointed by the senate, to serve during good behavior.[41]

The president and supreme court together would constitute a council of revision. All acts and resolves of congress, including acts or resolves that negatived state legislation, would be submitted to the council of revision for its approval. No act or resolve would become law without the approval of the council of revision, except that congress could override a veto with a majority vote of two-thirds in both houses.[42]

As to details, Madison proposed a number of features that were rejected and opposed several that were adopted. He wanted congress to have power to levy duties on exports, to grant charters of incorporation, to establish a university, and to grant bounties to encourage inventions. He wanted a broad, rather than a narrow, definition of treason, wanted to prohibit standing armies in time of peace, and wanted the salaries of all officers to be fixed in the constitution but indexed to the price of wheat or some other commodity. He did not disapprove of the contract clause, but he thought it redundant, erroneously supposing that the ex post facto clause covered civil cases. He also strongly opposed the electoral-college system as adopted. Overall, of seventy-one specific proposals that Madison

[40]Ibid., Sept. 7, 2:542. This proposal was offered by Mason; Madison supported it.
[41]Ibid., May 29, June 5, 13, July 18, Aug. 27, 1:21–22, 120, 232–233, 2:42–44, 430.
[42]Ibid., May 29, June 6, July 21, Aug. 15, 1:21, 138–139, 2:74, 298.

moved, seconded, or spoke unequivocally in regard to, he was on the losing side forty times.[43]

As for Charles Pinckney, his attitudes and ideas about government were apparently close to those of Madison, but the subject is clouded by considerable mystery. Pinckney was a brilliant and somewhat unstable young South Carolinian who had a penchant for political theory and a pathetic craving to be admired, a craving that he was willing to satisfy by outright deceit. He lied about his age, for instance, in order to confirm his later (unfounded) claim that he had been the youngest man in the convention. More to the point, he claimed, in a paper published shortly after the convention, and claimed again many years later, that he had presented, on May 28, 1787, a plan of government that contained most of the features that were ultimately incorporated into the Constitution. The claims on both occasions were demonstrably bogus, though Pinckney did submit a plan, no authentic copy of which has survived. A close approximation of it has been reconstructed, but it is of limited value in trying to understand what Pinckney advocated, for he was a maverick in the convention, aligning himself at one time or another with members of virtually every faction.[44]

Whatever their political philosophies, most (though by no means all) of the delegates sought to pattern the United States Constitution, as closely as circumstances would permit, after the English constitution. It may seem surprising that men of widely divergent views could share this general attitude, until one recalls that the Framers had available at least three distinctly different versions of the English constitution: those of Blackstone, of Bolingbroke/ Montesquieu, and of Hume.

[43] Ibid., June 12, 22, July 18, Aug. 16, 18, 20, 28, Sept. 4, 14, 1:216, 373, 2:45, 306, 324–325, 345, 440, 500, 617. In an as-yet-unpublished essay (kindly shown to me by the author), Lance Banning argues persuasively that ''Madison's constitution'' changed dramatically during the course of the debates, and he skillfully traces this evolution.

[44] ''The Pinckney Plan,'' in Farrand, *Records*, app. D, 3:595–609.

Blackstone's and Montesquieu's descriptions of the British constitution were summarized earlier;[45] but a few additional points about Blackstone's may be helpful. In it, the powers that Montesquieu thought were separate were seen as being thoroughly interwoven: the Crown, the Lords, and the Commons together constituted an all-powerful Parliament, the executive power was a branch of the legislative power, and the judicial power was a subordinate division of the executive. (The courts were the creatures of the Crown, and judges were appointees of the Crown, though to ensure their independent and impartial administration of justice, judges were permitted to serve during good behavior, and their salaries were "ascertained and established.") In this mixed form of government, the king, representing the principle of absolute monarchy ("the one"), provided the necessary energy, power, or force. The Lords Spiritual and Temporal, representing the aristocratic principle ("the few"), supplied the wisdom. The Commons, representing the democratic principle ("the many"), supplied the goodness, virtue, or public spirit. If supreme sovereignty were lodged in any one of the branches, Blackstone said, "we must be exposed to the inconveniences of either absolute monarchy, aristocracy, or democracy, and so want two of the three principal ingredients of good polity." If it were lodged "in any two of the branches; for instance, in the king and house of lords, our laws might be providently made, and well executed, but they might not always have the good of the people in view." King and Commons together, but without the Lords, would lack "that circumspection and mediatory caution, which the wisdom of the peers is to afford," and so on.[46]

Hume's version of the constitution was different both from Blackstone's and from Montesquieu's. To appreciate its significance in the American context, it is useful to place Hume's thinking in its original context. Hume's first political essays were written in 1741, a time when the long and vehement controversy generated by the ministry of Wal-

[45] Above, pp. 81–85.
[46] Blackstone, *Commentaries*, 1:48–52, 266–268.

pole and the opposition of Bolingbroke and his circle was reaching a climax. A central theme of Bolingbroke's charges against Walpole, which Hume thought was believed by most of the great middle rank of people in England, was that Walpole had destroyed the once-perfect "ancient constitution" by introducing a pervasive corruption which replaced public virtue. More specifically, the House of Commons, the "republican" part of Britain's "mixed" form of government—and therefore the part that must, at all costs, be virtuous—had, in Bolingbroke's view, been corrupted.[47]

Hume thought that Bolingbroke was entirely wrong, and—in addition to remarking that if the constitution had been perfect, Walpole would not have been able to corrupt it—Hume set out to demonstrate Bolingbroke's shortcomings in two different but interrelated ways. The first was by his analysis of factions, which led to his pronouncement that public men must be supposed to be knaves. The second was by insisting that it was institutions, not the manners and morals of the people, which primarily determined whether a country would have good government. In his essay "That Politics may be reduced to a Science," he wrote: "Wise regulations in any commonwealth are the most valuable legacy that can be left to future ages. In the smallest court or office, the stated forms and methods, by which business must be conducted, are found to be a considerable check on the natural depravity of mankind," and the same would be true of the governance of a nation. Citing the history of Rome during the period from the beginning of the first of the Punic Wars to the end of the last one—when private depravity was widespread but public spirit was at its highest—he concluded that "the ages of greatest public spirit are not always most eminent for private virtue. Good laws may beget order and moderation in the government, where the manners and customs have

<hr/>

[47]Kramnick, *Bolingbroke and His Circle;* James Moore, "Hume's Political Science and the Classical Republican Tradition," *Canadian Journal of Political Science* 10 (1977): 809–839; Duncan Forbes, *Hume's Philosophical Politics* (Cambridge, Eng., 1975), 193ff.; Green and Grose, *Hume's Philosophical Works,* 2:117 n, 120–121.

instilled little humanity or justice into the tempers of men."[48]

Preoccupied as he was with the party struggles of his time, Hume could not regard either Blackstone's theoretical model or Montesquieu's Bolingbrokean model as bearing any relation to the realities of power in Britain. (Indeed, though he was a friend and admirer of Montesquieu's, he thought *The Spirit of the Laws* would undermine the renown that the Frenchman had won with his *Persian Letters*.) Hume's own analysis of the British constitution was characteristically empirical. Where Blackstone saw one force consisting of three complementary and interdependent parts, and where Montesquieu saw three separate and functionally distinct branches, Hume saw two contending power blocs: the "court party" versus the "country party," or the king and the Lords and the civil list versus the House of Commons. The Commons, having control over taxation and ultimately over the army, was potentially the more powerful: it could destroy the monarchy any time it should see fit to do so. But the court preserved the balance of the system, partly by its prestige and partly by the "corrupt" dispensation of the enormous and lucrative patronage that it had at its disposal. In both ways the court could make or break ministries and keep the Commons divided against itself.[49]

Advocates of adaptations of each of these constitutions were present in the convention. Roger Sherman and others endorsed legislative supremacy; Dickinson and others lauded the separation of powers; Madison and others wanted to join the executive and the judicial so as to prevent the emergence of a too-powerful legislative; and Hamilton and others endorsed "corruption" for the same end. But there was a formidable obstacle to all efforts to model an American constitution upon any version of the English one. As Charles Pinckney pointed out in a long,

---

[48] Green and Grose, *Hume's Philosophical Works*, 3:105–106, 108.

[49] Ibid., 3:119–126, 133–144. Montesquieu notes in passing (*Spirit of the Laws*, bk. 19, chap. 27) that England had "parties" which supported either the "executive" or the "legislative," but he does not develop the theme.

learned, and unnecessary lecture to the delegates, England
had an institutional and social structure which had taken
centuries to evolve and which America lacked; and if the
delegates were agreed upon any of Montesquieu's teach-
ings, it was that government must be suited to the manners, customs, and social institutions of a people. Several
delegates favored making the senators a substitute for the
barons by having them chosen for long terms or during
good behavior and by setting high property qualifications
for them. There was little support for the first idea, however, and the second proved to be impractical because of
the disparity of levels of wealth from state to state: what
would have been an adequate property qualification in the
South would have been prohibitive in New England, and
what would have been suitable in New England would
have been inadequate in the South.

It was John Dickinson—a devotee of Montesquieu—who
came up with an approach that was theoretically sound,
practically sound, and tailored to American realities. Before
considering Dickinson's solution, however, we must look
at another grouping, one concerning the delegates' beliefs
as to the extent to which the revised central authority
should continue to be a confederation of sovereign states.
In broad terms, there were five possible positions, each
containing variants. One was to leave matters as they
were—which no one in the convention openly advocated,
but which Lansing and Yates of New York probably privately favored. A second was to make no changes in the
structure of the Confederation but to vest Congress with
additional powers. This was in keeping with the intentions
of Congress when it sanctioned the convention, with the
intentions of the legislatures when naming delegates, and
with the expectations of many, if not indeed most, of the
delegates during the early phases of the deliberations. It
soon became clear, however, that this approach was impracticable. If Congress were to be given additional powers,
it would also have to be given the means to enforce them;

but to give it power to coerce states would be to invite civil wars, and to give it the power to coerce individuals would mean that Congress would no longer be a confederation but a confederated government.[50]

Just such a government was a third possibility. Congress could remain organized as it was, or it could be divided into two branches; the executive and judicial functions could be conducted by agencies or committees of Congress, or they could be entrusted to separate and independent branches. The only crucial feature, from the point of view of those who favored a confederated government, was that the personnel must be elected by the state governments, so that the central authority be "foederal," the creature and representative of the states as political societies. The ablest and most determined champions of such "foederalism" were Sherman, Rutledge, C. C. Pinckney, Butler, William Paterson, and David Brearley. They were given qualified support by Gerry, Ellsworth, and Charles Pinckney, and they were supported on tactical (as opposed to principled) grounds by a handful of others.

A fourth possibility was to create a purely national government, one that would derive its powers from the people, whose officials would be chosen by the people, and which would operate directly upon the people, without states as states having any role. Almost (but not quite) all of the nationalists, both the court-party and country-party varieties, preferred such an arrangement, though they differed among themselves as to particulars. Only one of them, George Read, was willing to declare that he wanted to abolish the states altogether; Hamilton would have liked to do so but dismissed the idea as impracticable. Most of the nationalists wanted to preserve the states but wanted to draw strict lines between national and state authorities and to ensure, through provision for a national veto of state legislation or some other means, that the supreme authority would reside in the national government. Some who

---

[50]This and the following two paragraphs are derived from study of the first month of the convention. Closer analysis of the subject follows in chaps. 7 and 8 below.

thought along these lines also wanted to make the national government as democratic as possible, meaning based upon as broad an electorate as possible.

There was one more possibility: this was the one that Dickinson proposed. In thinking about devising structural substitutes for the English baronies, Dickinson alone had perceived that the United States already had institutional substitutes in the form of the individual states—which, in a manner of speaking, were permanent and hereditary. He therefore proposed a mixed system, partly national and partly foederal, in which one branch of Congress would "be drawn immediately from the people" and the other would represent the states as states and be elected by the state legislatures for long terms, "through such a refining process as will assimilate it as near as may be to the House of Lords in England." This combination of state governments with a strong national government, he added, was "as politic as it was unavoidable."[51]

When Dickinson so spoke, the deliberations had been under way just over a week. At that point only two delegates, Richard Dobbs Spaight of North Carolina and William Pierce of Georgia, supported him.[52] All the others, blinded by principles or interests, failed as yet to see the merits of Dickinson's perception.

As indicated, delegates disagreed with one another in regard to the question whether government should be designed to utilize men's interests; they also disagreed in their perceptions of what those interests were. Some held that great conflicts of interest lay in the future, in rivalry between seaboard states and those that would arise in the West. Several delegates foresaw that the differences between the North and the South would be the most troublesome. Gouverneur Morris expressed a fairly common attitude when he declared bluntly that the great economic-class distinction was between the rich and the poor, the one

[51] The quotations are in Farrand, *Records*, June 6, 1:136.
[52] Ibid., May 31, June 1, 6, 1:51, 69, 137.

always committed to oppressing and the other to robbing its opposite. Charles Pinckney, whose state had greater extremes of wealth among its citizenry than did any other, nonetheless insisted that wealth was so equally distributed in America that it was meaningless to talk about rich and poor. Rather, he said, the real interest groups were three—the landed, the professional, and the commercial; and he saw the nation's commercial interests as consisting of five distinct subinterests. This was an elaborate version of what was probably the most commonly held categorization of contending interests, that of merchants (including moneyed men and public creditors) versus farmers.[53]

Madison, following Hume closely, drew up an extensive catalog of passions and interests. He declared that participation in public life was almost always marked by divisions into two mutually antagonistic groups. Not having witnessed a Jacobite uprising in Scotland, as Hume had, and not having the seventeenth-century Puritan upheavals as part of his felt heritage, as New Englanders had, Madison mentioned but was disposed to belittle attachments to particular leaders or families and religious zeal as passions that underlay such groupings. Instead, viewing society as a provincial American, he believed that the most common and most durable source of mutual animosities was "the various and unequal distribution of property." Those who had and those who did not have property, as well as creditors and debtors, formed distinct classes, he said, as did a landed interest, a mercantile interest, a moneyed interest, and many lesser interests. Because of the plurality of interests, the mutuality of conflicting passions broke down in complex societies, and therefore Madison could not share Gouverneur Morris's simplistic idea of institutionally separating the rich from the poor. Nor could he share the more sophisticated idea, expressed by Hamilton and others, that all economic interest groups were interdependent.[54]

[53] These and other detailed positions are taken up in chaps. 7 and 8 below.

[54] The Madison quotation is from *Federalist* number 10; regarding Hamilton and the interdependence of economic interests see, among others, *Federalist* number 35 and his later reports on public credit and manufactures.

Hamilton delivered a lengthy analysis, which incorporated treatment of interests but went beyond them. Focusing upon the tension between loyalties to states and to the nation and asking whether the creation of a durable national government was possible, Hamilton outlined what he considered to be the "principles of civil obedience." These, he suggested, were five: interest, opinion, habit, force, and influence. By "interest," he explained, he meant the "active and constant" personal rewards, either tangible or psychic, that were derived from supporting a particular government or party. By "opinion," he meant the general, largely unarticulated assumption that a government was legitimate, useful, and necessary. By "habit," he meant "habitual sense of obligation" and "habitual attachment of the people." By "force," he meant coercion or the threat or fear of coercion, of which there were two kinds: the coercion of law, which was by far the more desirable, and the coercion of arms. Finally, as for "influence," he explained that he did not mean corruption (though what he did mean would have seemed indistinguishable from corruption to Mason or Gerry); he meant regular "honors & emoluments" such as judgeships and militia commissions, which "produce an attachment" in the recipients. The weight of all these forces was on the side of the states, Hamilton pointed out. The objective, he said, was somehow to transfer them to the national government.[55]

Several additional conflicts of interests among the delegates themselves became highly visible as the convention unfolded. The Georgians and the South Carolinians insisted that taxes on exports be prohibited and that congressional interference in the slave trade be forbidden. Tobacco planters from the upper South were largely indifferent regarding the first of these points, but having more slaves than they could profitably employ, they felt rather strongly that the slave trade should be suppressed. Their major economic concern lay elsewhere: as was indicated in chapter 4, they feared that if Congress were empowered to pass "navigation acts," which is to say to regulate international

[55] Speech of June 18, in Farrand, *Records*, 1:282-311.

trade, northerners would see to the enactment of restrictions against foreign shipping, which would send
freight rates and the profits of northern merchants soaring.
To prevent that, they sought to require a two-thirds majority for the passage of navigation acts. The delegates from
Massachusetts and Pennsylvania fiercely opposed such a
provision, for they saw the need for commercial regulation
as among the primary reasons for the existence of the
convention. Inasmuch as the rice growers from the lower
South, to whom freight rates were relatively unimportant,
were indifferent in the matter, the issue would turn upon
such deals as someone might work out with delegates from
disinterested states, those having little international trade.[56]

Far more visible, though not as well understood, was
the conflict between what Madison called "small" states
and "large" states. The description is not altogether accu-
rate. If Virginia, by far the most populous state, and
Delaware, the least populous, are excluded, the average
population in the "large" states was about 307,000, as
compared to about 278,000 in the "small" states. Moreover,
the line-up was sectional: all four states south of the
Potomac voted with the bloc of large states, whereas those
to the north (including New Hampshire, when its delegates
arrived) voted as small states, six to two. The designations
do apply if by them is meant territorial extent or, more
properly, having or not having claims to vast tracts of
habitable but as yet uninhabited land. Massachusetts,
Pennsylvania, Virginia, North Carolina, South Carolina,
and Georgia were "landed" states, and all of them voted in
the convention to apportion representation in the reconstituted Congress upon the basis of population, rather than
equally by states. Connecticut, New York, New Jersey,
Delaware, and Maryland had no such lands; they all voted
as small states, which is to say to preserve equal representation.[57]

[56] Ibid., Aug. 29, 2:449–453.

[57] The population is calculated from the Census of 1790. There would appear to
be one misfit in each camp, South Carolina and New York. But South Carolina,
though it had no claims to interior lands, had ready access to the abundance of
lands in Georgia; and South Carolinians acquired land in Georgia on a grand

Partly what was at stake was power. Most of the delegates who fought for equal representation genuinely feared that a few large states—say, Massachusetts, Pennsylvania, and Virginia—would combine, if proportional representation became the rule, and deprive them of their liberties. In vain did their opponents try to persuade those delegates that the large states had such diverse interests as to preclude any motive for combining; they were too much imbued with the idea that man's love of power is insatiable. Indeed, when delegates from Virginia, Pennsylvania, and Massachusetts demanded that their states have a voice in the national councils that would be commensurate with their population, it was clear that their claims to being more national-minded were spurious and that they were taking a position that would increase the influence of their own states, not the power of the nation.

But greed was an equally potent motive in the struggle: the advocates of equal representation sought for their states a share in the great domain of unoccupied lands. This they at first proposed to obtain by preserving the one-state/one-vote rule of the existing Confederation, and when it became clear that they could not do that, they demanded equal votes by states in the second branch of the national legislature and proposed to give to that branch control over the public domain. Alternatively, as George Read put it, give to the small states equal shares of the common lands which "the great states have appropriated to themselves . . . and then if you please, proportion the representation, and we shall not be jealous of one another."[58]

Remaining to be considered are the economic interests of the delegates as individuals and the influence that these might have had on the positions they took in the conven-

scale, as is attested by the manuscript volume Land Grants, Washington and Franklin Counties, in the Georgia Department of Archives and History. A related consideration is that the South Carolina delegates wanted representation to be based upon wealth rather than population. As for New York, it had lost its claim to Vermont; Massachusetts had title to the land in New York's western third; and much of what was left was held by hostile Indians.

[58] Farrand, *Records*, June 25, 1:412.

tion. Thirty-four of the fifty-five men who participated in the deliberations were lawyers, though several were not active practitioners. Of those who were active, eight had as their main clients merchants who were engaged in interstate and foreign commerce; thirteen were country lawyers (most of whom also derived income from farms); and others received most of their incomes from salaries as public officials. Twenty-seven of the delegates, including nine who doubled as lawyers, were farmers. At least nineteen of the farmers were slave owners, and at least eleven nonfarmers owned slaves as well. The commercial interest was represented, in addition to the eight mercantile lawyers, by seven delegates who were actively engaged in interstate and foreign trade.[59]

The delegates also had a variety of investments, one form of which was speculation in land. Many of the delegates had doubtless taken small plunges, but only eight can be identified as speculators on a grand scale. These were Washington, who owned scores of thousands of acres in all parts of the country; Robert Morris, who had begun the speculations that would see titles to several million acres pass through his hands before he would go bankrupt; Thomas Fitzsimons, who was to be Morris's partner in several ventures; Gorham, who in 1787 was negotiating a contract to buy, with a partner, a million acres of the land that Massachusetts owned in western New York; Jonathan Dayton of New Jersey, who had begun land operations that would ultimately run into hundreds of thousands of acres; Wilson, who operated on a somewhat smaller scale in Pennsylvania; Mason, who had acquired fifteen thousand acres in the upper Potomac region and another sixty thousand in Kentucky; and William Blount of North Carolina, who was in process of acquiring scores of thousands of acres in Tennessee.[60]

[59] The economic interests of the delegates are recited at length in McDonald, *We the People*, 38–92. I am indebted to M. E. Bradford for calling to my attention evidence that a considerable number of northern delegates also held slaves.

[60] See the list of Washington's landholdings in his will, in Jared Sparks, *The Life of George Washington* (Boston, 1842), app. 9; Ellis P. Oberholtzer, *Robert Morris: Patriot and Financier* (New York, 1903), 301–304, 314, and passim; William G.

Apart from the involvement of western lands in the issue of representation, the only important point of contention that directly affected land speculators pertained to the admission of new states. That subject elicited strong emotions and extreme proposals, but none of the large land speculators except Wilson had anything to say on the matter, and Wilson's remarks were desultory.[61] For that reason and also because most of the land speculators, contrary to their interests, favored strong measures to provide for the public debts, it may be inferred that their speculations exerted little significant influence upon their behavior in the convention.

The holding of public securities was another and more complex affair. No fewer than thirty of the delegates owned certificates of the public debt; their combined holdings had a par value of approximately $266,000 and a market value, in 1787, of about $65,000. As a result of the creation of the government under the Constitution and of the subsequent adoption of Hamilton's funding and assumption plans, those securities would appreciate in value by more than $100,000. But the matter was not clear-cut. Three-quarters of the securities were owned by the ten largest holders, nearly ninety-five percent by the sixteen largest holders. Of those sixteen, no fewer than five (Gerry, Randolph, Mercer, Lansing, and Luther Martin, who together held nearly one-third of the total) opposed the Constitution.[62]

And the complexities do not end there. It was generally believed that the interests of state creditors and Continental creditors were mutually opposed. On the one hand, Congress, if it were given the better sources of revenue including duties on imports, might be able to service its debts; but

Sumner, *The Financier and the Finances of the American Revolution*, 2 vols. (New York, 1891), 2:253ff.; Journal of the House of Representatives of the General Court of Massachusetts, Mar. 31, 1788, manuscript in the Massachusetts Archives; *American State Papers: Public Lands*, 1:104–106, 118, 129; *The Correspondence of John Cleves Symmes* . . . , ed. Beverly W. Bond (New York, 1926); Smith, *Wilson*; Rowland, *Mason*, 2:368; William H. Masterson, *William Blount* (Baton Rouge, La., 1954), passim.

[61] Farrand, *Records*, Aug. 29, 30, 2:454–466.

[62] Data on security holdings are derived from the Records of the Loan of 1790, National Archives. Details and particular citations are in McDonald, *We the People*, 38–92.

the capacity of the states to do so, which was already inadequate for most of them, would be undermined. Yet, on the other hand, few believed that the new government could collect enough revenues to assume responsibility for servicing the state debts. To the extent, therefore, that public creditors in the convention were divided into holders of state paper and holders of Continental paper, their interests were antithetical. As it turns out, they were divided almost equally. Of those who held securities with a face value of more than $10,000, five were national and five were state creditors. Of those who held between $5,000 and $10,000, four were creditors of the nation, three of the states. And of those who held between $1,000 and $5,000, four were state creditors and three were Continental creditors.

Given that division, given the fact that it was to the interest of land speculators to keep security prices low, and given the emotional and ideological quality of the issue, it is scarcely surprising that the convention found it difficult to reach an agreement concerning the public debts. When the subject was first seriously considered, several delegates expressed dissatisfaction with the way the resolution providing for the debts was phrased, and the matter was dropped. It arose again later, with similar results. At one point, four delegates suggested that Congress be empowered to assume the states' debts. These included King and Sherman, who were substantial state creditors; but Ellsworth, who also held a sizable amount of state paper, thought that no such provision was necessary. Gerry, who owned more than $50,000 in Continental securities, insisted that Continental creditors be provided for, but he suggested that it would be improper to assume the states' debts. Gouverneur Morris, who said that he had deliberately avoided investing in the public funds so that he could be a disinterested advocate of public credit, argued that it was not enough to empower Congress to provide for the public debts; Congress should be required to do so. The convention then unanimously adopted his motion that Congress "*shall* discharge the debts & fulfil the engagements of the U States." The next day, however, Butler delivered a diatribe against speculators in public paper, insisted that a discrimination between original creditors and speculators be made, and gave notice that he would move for a reconsideration. Tempers flared during two days of reconsideration, whereupon Randolph sought to cool feelings by proposing the neutral wording which, with minor changes, found its way into the finished Constitution: "All debts contracted & engagements entered into, by or under the authority of Congs. shall be as valid agst the U. States under this constitution as under the Confederation."[63]

Because they dodged the issue in that manner, it is impossible to determine the intentions of all the Framers, but it is possible to reconstruct the attitudes of many. We considered earlier Hamilton's intention to use the public debts as the material for fashioning, British style, a system of monetized credit. Among his fellow delegates, perhaps five or six fully shared that aim: the two Morrises, probably King and Wilson, and possibly the Philadelphians George Clymer and Thomas Fitzsimons. Another ten—Langdon, Gerry, Strong, William Samuel Johnson, Sherman, Ellsworth, Paterson, Read, Washington, and (surprisingly) Butler—would give strong support to Hamilton's program when it came before the First Congress. Thus, seventeen viewed or would be persuaded to view with favor the idea of using the public debt to create a capitalist order in America. On the other hand, thirteen delegates indicated during the convention, during the contests over ratification, or by later opposition in the First Congress that they were hostile to that idea: Lansing, Yates, Luther Martin, Mercer, Gilman, Bassett, Carroll, Madison, Mason, Williamson, Spaight, Baldwin, and Few. The attitudes of the remaining twenty-five delegates cannot be ascertained, but from what is known of them, it seems probable that all but six or eight would have been part of the opposition.[64]

[63] Farrand, *Records*, July 18, Aug. 18, 21, 22, 23, 24, 25, 2:46–47, 326ff., 355–356, 377, 392, 400, 412–414.

[64] The attitude of the Morrises is implicit in Hamilton's consultation of them in preparing his "First Report on the Public Credit" (see Syrett, *Papers of Hamilton*, 6:54–59, 62–63). Wilson's attitude is inferred from his intimacy with the Morrises;

It should be obvious from this survey that it is meaningless to say that the Framers intended this or that the
Framers intended that: their positions were diverse and, in
many particulars, incompatible. Some had firm, well-
rounded plans, some had strong convictions on only a few
points, some had self-contradictory ideas, some were
guided only by vague ideals. Some of their differences were
subject to compromise; others were not.

Their undertaking was further complicated by the fact
that they represented states and voted as states, and most
delegates felt obliged to champion the interests of their
states as they perceived them. Several delegations were
divided against themselves. Three of the five Maryland
delegates were absent much of the time, and Luther Martin
and Daniel of St. Thomas Jenifer disagreed often, with the
result that the state's vote was frequently canceled out.
When the convention began, the Massachusetts delegation
was united, but as it wore on, King and Gorham tended to
take one side of an issue and Gerry and Strong the other.
Lansing and Yates canceled Hamilton's vote, and when
they walked out of the convention early in July, he felt
obliged to stay away as well, though he returned as a
nonvoting delegate in September. Two of the Virginia
delegates left early, and Mason and Randolph began to vote
against Washington and Madison on some issues, which
threw the deciding vote into the hands of Judge John Blair,
who wavered from one side to the other.

Burdened by differences and difficulties, the convention
would require a great deal of wisdom, patience, willingness
to compromise, and careful management if it was to produce a plan "to render the constitution of the Foederal
Government adequate to the Exigencies of the Union," as it
had been charged with doing.

King's, from his intimacy with Hamilton; and Clymer's and Fitzsimons's, from
the strong support they (along with King and Robert Morris) gave to Hamilton's
system in Congress. Of the opponents, five opposed the Constitution and eight
others fought against Hamilton's system in the First Congress.

VII

THE CONVENTION:
CONSTITUTING A GOVERNMENT

DRAFTING THE CONSTITUTION, AS Madison wrote long afterward, was "the work of many heads and many hands."[1] Some delegates, to be sure, were more active and influential than others, and some were engaged in artful backstage manipulations; but no delegate or coalition of like-minded delegates was able to dominate the convention except for brief periods and on specific issues. The diversity of interests and points of view among the delegates made for alignments that shifted with circumstances and necessitated repeated compromises. The physical conditions—an average of close to forty men, most of them obese, crowded into a modest-sized and not well ventilated room for five to seven hours a day during an intensely hot and muggy summer—ensured that those compromises would not always be accepted with good grace. The complexity and duration of the undertaking, combined with the absence of a stenographic record, meant that the delegates could not always even be sure just what they had decided.

Despite all that, there was a logic to the proceedings. Before attempting to describe and analyze that logic and to set it in the context of the various currents of thought which were considered in the preceding chapters, it may be helpful to preface the effort by chronicling, in broad outline, the course of events in the convention.

[1] Madison to William Cogswell, Mar. 10, 1834, in Farrand, *Records*, 3:533.

The delegates were scheduled to assemble on Monday May 14. Only a handful showed up on time, however, and no quorum was obtained until the twenty-fifth. Washington was then unanimously elected president, rules were adopted, and finally, on May 29, Governor Edmund Randolph of Virginia "opened the main business." After a speech in which he pointed out the defects of the existing confederation, he offered fifteen resolutions, drafted jointly by the Virginia delegates, to serve as the basis for debate.[2]

The resolutions, variously known as the Randolph, the Virginia, or the large-states plan, called for the establishment of a national government that would consist of an executive branch, a judiciary, and a bicameral legislature. Members of the first branch of the legislature would be apportioned to states according either to their free population or to the quotas of revenues assessed for contribution to the national treasury, and would be elected directly by the people. The members of the second branch, likewise to be so apportioned, would be elected by the first branch from candidates nominated by the state legislatures. The national legislature would have a generalized grant of power "to legislate in all cases to which the separate States are incompetent, or in which the harmony of the United States may be interrupted by the exercise of individual Legislation"; to veto state legislation that violated the new articles of union; and to employ the force of the union against any state that was delinquent in its duties. The executive and judicial, combined, would form a council of revision that would have a provisional veto over national legislation.[3]

The Randolph plan was referred to a committee of the whole house, where it was debated for two weeks. The committee made some modifications—the only important ones being that senators were to be elected directly by the state legislatures, that the power to coerce states was dropped, and that the council of revision was rejected—and

[2] Ibid., May 29, 1:18–19.
[3] Ibid., May 29, 1:20–22.

reported the amended resolutions back to the formal convention.[4]

Attorney General William Paterson of New Jersey then (on June 15) proposed an alternate set of resolutions, known variously as the Paterson, the New Jersey, or the small-states plan. This "purely federal"[5] proposal would retain the existing unicameral Congress and the rule of equal voting by states, but it would establish executive and judicial branches, would bind state courts to annul state laws contrary to the revised articles of union, and would vest Congress with broad but enumerated powers to collect import taxes and other duties and to regulate interstate and foreign commerce.[6] Both plans were returned to the committee of the whole, where, after five days of debates, Paterson's was rejected and Randolph's revised resolutions were adopted for consideration in the formal convention.

For nearly a month the convention made no progress toward fleshing out the resolutions, for the issue of proportional versus equal representation hung over it at all times, threatening to force the delegates from the "small" states to walk out. Two of those delegates, Lansing and Yates of New York, did walk out. Finally, on July 16, it was voted that representation was to be equal in the Senate and proportional to population in the House.[7] Some delegates on the other side now talked of walking out, but none did so.

During the next ten days the remaining general features of a constitution were agreed to, and on July 26 the convention took a recess and turned its resolutions over to a committee of detail, which was instructed to draft a constitution in accordance with its resolutions. The committee, which consisted of Rutledge, Randolph, Gorham, Ellsworth, and Wilson, had its draft ready by August 4, and on Monday August 6 the full convention reassembled.[8]

For just over another month the delegates joined in a new round of debates, using the committee of detail's

[4] Ibid., June 13, 1:235–237.
[5] Ibid., June 14, 1:240.
[6] Ibid., June 15, 1:242–245.
[7] Ibid., July 16, 2:15–16.
[8] Ibid., July 23, 26, Aug. 6, 2:85, 87, 95–97, 128, 177–189.

report as the basis of their deliberations. Two characteristics in particular marked the proceedings at this phase. One was that the delegates engaged in a great deal of trucking and bargaining in behalf of special interests they wanted to have protected by the constitution. The other was that they proved entirely unable to agree on a way of constituting the presidency that was generally satisfactory. At the end of August, to reconcile the conflicting views on this and many another particular, the convention appointed a committee of eleven (one delegate from each state in attendance).[9] That committee produced a number of crucial provisions, including the electoral college, and by September 8 the convention was ready to turn its resolutions over to a committee of style (Gouverneur Morris, Hamilton, Johnson, Madison, and King) for the finished drafting.[10] Two days later the draft was reported. Another week was devoted to final touches, and on September 17 the Constitution was signed by thirty-nine of the forty-two delegates who were still present.[11]

Within this framework, the first and crucial question to be settled concerned the constitution (or reconstitution) of the legislative authority. All the delegates, except for the handful who opposed any changes in existing arrangements, agreed upon this; their underlying disagreements would emerge only after this question had been resolved. The primacy of the question derives ultimately from the connection between the law-making power and sovereignty: in Blackstone's words, "Sovereignty and legislature are indeed convertible terms."[12]

Analyzing the matter more closely, we may say that, given the American commitment to representative govern-

9 Ibid., Aug. 31, 2:481.
10 Ibid., Sept. 8, 2:553.
11 Actually, though there are thirty-nine signatures on the document, there were only thirty-eight signers; George Read signed both for himself and for John Dickinson, who requested him to do so when Dickinson realized that he could not be present at the end (Dickinson to Read, ibid., Sept. 15, 3:81 and n. 2).
12 Blackstone, *Commentaries*, 1:46.

ment, the issue of the constitution of the legislative authority resolved itself into two questions: what representative body (or bodies) was (or were) to have the supreme lawmaking power, and whom would it (or they) represent? Under the Articles of Confederation and under the several state constitutions, sovereignty, as defined, rested in the state legislatures, on the understanding that it had been delegated to them by the people of the several states severally and could be withdrawn by the people at will. Viewed in this light, the Randolph plan had a subtle ambiguity about it. On the one hand, it proposed to reorganize Congress so that its members would represent the people in their capacity as citizens of the several states severally. On the other, it proposed to vest the Congress, thus reconstituted, with power to legislate in all cases in which the states separately were incompetent.

The proposal was debated at great length throughout the first two weeks of the convention, during which time a variety of positions came to light. The initial skirmishing took place on May 30. After some dickering over phraseology, the delegates seemed on the verge of agreeing to a motion offered by Madison and seconded by Gouverneur Morris—"that the equality of suffrage established by the articles of Confederation ought not to prevail in the national Legislature, and that an equitable ratio of representation ought to be substituted"—when the subject was postponed on motion of George Read. Read reminded the members that the instructions of the Delaware delegates prohibited them from assenting to any change in the rule of voting in Congress; he added that if the change were made, they might have to leave the convention.[13] (Read did not reveal, at the time, either that the instructions had been written at his urging or that his stated motive was to secure the "claims of the smaller and bounded States to a proportional share" of the "ungranted lands in most of the larger States.")[14]

[13] Farrand, *Records*, May 30, 1:36–37.
[14] Read to Dickinson, Jan. 17, 1787, ibid., 3:575 n–576 n.

On the next day and again on June 6, the members debated the question, who should elect the members of the first branch, and other dimensions to the question became evident. Six states voted for popular elections (Massachusetts, New York, Pennsylvania, Virginia, North Carolina, and Georgia), but the others followed a mixed pattern. New Jersey voted for elections by the state legislatures, its vote implying a desire to retain the existing system and its motive apparently being in part the one that was privately held (and was soon to be openly professed) by Read. South Carolina also voted no: its delegates favored proportional representation but wanted all branches of the new government to be elected by the state legislatures and therefore to be dependent upon them. Sherman shared the New Jersey position; his colleague Ellsworth favored equal representation but (at this stage) also favored popular election. Therefore, Connecticut's vote was divided. Gerry strongly opposed election by the people, an attitude that Sherman also held. Finally, Delaware's delegation was divided, Dickinson and Read favoring popular election, the others preferring election by the legislatures.[15]

Meanwhile, Dickinson was offering his mixed proposal to use the states as surrogate baronies—which was at once a compromise and something far more positive than a compromise.[16] At this stage the convention accepted only the less important part of Dickinson's recommendation, that providing for the election of senators by the state legislatures. On June 6 the convention rejected Charles Pinckney's motion to reconsider and to have the first branch elected by the legislatures (only Connecticut, New Jersey, and South Carolina supporting it). On the next day, Dickinson moved that the second branch be elected by the state legislatures.

[15] Ibid., May 31, June 6, 1:48–50, 132–138. Dickinson's position is indicated by his proposal for a mixed basis of representation, Read's from his speech at 136–137; since the Delaware delegation voted for legislative election, it follows that Bassett, Bedford, and Broom voted for legislative election.

[16] Ibid., June 2, 6, 7, 1:87, 136, 150, 156–157. See also Dickinson's notes for June 18, scribbled while Hamilton was delivering his day-long speech, in James H. Hutson, "Notes and Documents: John Dickinson at the Federal Constitutional Convention," *William and Mary Quarterly* 40 (1983): 271. Dickinson wrote: "The States will give Play to Aristocracy. Agreed. better than hereditary Courtiers."

Advocates of the Randolph plan argued strongly against this proposal, and a sharp-witted and erudite exchange ensued. Wilson contended that both branches should derive their power from the same source, for otherwise "dissentions will naturally arise between them." Dickinson replied that if all power were "drawn from the people at large, the consequence would be that the national Govt. would move in the same direction as the State Govts. now do, and would run into all the same mischiefs." Madison insisted that if the legislatures were to elect the second branch, "we must either depart from the doctrine of proportional representation; or admit into the Senate a very large number of members," both of which Madison found unacceptable. On the latter point, Madison said: "The example of the Roman Tribunes was applicable. They lost their influence and power, in proportion as their number was augmented." Dickinson, who knew his Roman history quite as well as Madison did, countered that if Madison's reasoning were sound, "it would prove that the number of the Senate ought to be reduced below ten," the highest number the "Tribunitial corps" had ever reached. Whether because of Dickinson's persuasiveness or because of predisposition—probably both were involved—all eleven state delegations voted in favor of Dickinson's motion that the second branch be elected by the legislatures.[17]

A showdown on the larger question—whether representation would be equal or proportional—was soon to follow. On Saturday June 9, Paterson and Brearley moved and seconded that the question be now taken up, and between them the two New Jerseymen spoke almost all day in behalf of equal representation. There was a logical consistency in their position. Both held that if the states were to continue to exist, the federal principle must be adhered to, meaning that their votes in Congress must be equal; if the national principle were adopted, then the states must be abolished or their lines must be redrawn to make them of roughly the same population and territorial extent, either of which options the two men said they would support.[18]

[17] Farrand, Records, June 6, 7, 1:137–138, 150–161.
[18] Ibid., June 9, 1:187–189.

Votes were taken on the following Monday, and the crucial aspect of Dickinson's mixed system was rejected. First, however, came some revealing comments. Sherman began the day's deliberations with a statement indicating that he had come around to Dickinson's way of thinking, significantly likening the states to the English lords. Rutledge and Butler then urged that representation be tied to quotas imposed in congressional requisitions, which Dickinson suggested should be amended to apply to the actual contributions of the states to the national treasury. After Franklin and Gerry had offered irrelevant comments, the delegates voted overwhelmingly in favor of representation based upon population in the first branch, New Jersey and Delaware casting the only negative votes. Then Sherman moved that representation in the second branch be equal. The motion failed, Connecticut, New York, New Jersey, Delaware, and Maryland being for it, the other six states against. Proportional representation was approved immediately thereafter, the same states holding the same positions.[19]

A few important details were agreed upon the next day, June 12. Over the objections of New Englanders who insisted on annual elections and of Carolinians who preferred biennial terms, the other delegations voted that members of the first branch serve three-year terms. They also voted that senators serve seven-year terms, and they rejected efforts to have members of one or both houses be paid by the states or be not paid at all. In the discussion of these matters, the delegates from Connecticut, Delaware, and South Carolina continued to express foederal, rather than national, positions.[20]

It was at this point—after a day of miscellaneous activity and a day of recess—that the Paterson plan was proposed. Nearly a week was consumed in deciding to reject it and to take up in convention the report of the committee of the whole, the modified Randolph plan. From June 20 to July 16

[19] Ibid., June 11, 1:196–206.
[20] Ibid., June 12, 1:214–222.

the delegates addressed themselves exclusively to the constitution of the legislative branch.

Except for decisions to make the terms of the two
legislative branches two and six years instead of three and
seven,[21] the debates throughout this period were largely a
rehash of the less extensive debates in the committee of the
whole; but they reveal something about the ideological
predispositions of several delegates. The Randolph plan had
called for a fundamentally Montesquieuan separation of
powers, and on one occasion Randolph cited Montesquieu
in support of his argument for proportional representation,
and on another he uttered a dictum of Montesquieu's
without attribution.[22] C. C. Pinckney and Madison, among
other advocates of proportional representation, cited approvingly the doctrine of the separation of powers, and
Madison later cited Montesquieu in arguing against equal
representation in the Senate.[23] Yet Dickinson's partly national, partly federal plan was even more clearly Montesquieuan; and in addition to Dickinson himself, Davie,
Pierce, Sherman, Ellsworth, and Johnson had explicitly
endorsed that concept.[24] Wilson, a staunch supporter of
proportional representation in both houses, was far from a
devotee of Montesquieu and indeed said that no version of
the British constitution could serve as a model for America.[25] Pierce Butler, who demonstrated in various connections that he was solidly in the camp of Bolingbroke and
Montesquieu, said the same thing.[26]

[21] Ibid., June 21, 25, 1:362, 408–409.
[22] Ibid., June 22, July 11, 1:372, 579–580. The unattributed Montesquieuan
sentiment concerned the respect due to "popular prejudices" in cases "where
they formed the permanent character of the people."
[23] Ibid., June 2, 30, 1:67, 485.
[24] Ibid., June 6, 11, 29, 30, 1:137, 196, 461–462, 468–469, 484, 487–488.
[25] Ibid., June 7, 1:153.
[26] Ibid., June 13, 23, 1:238, 391. See also Aug. 23 (2:392), where Butler
denounces public creditors as "Blood-suckers who had speculated on the distresses of others," one Bolingbrokean sentiment, and Butler to Weedon Butler,
Oct. 8, 1787, ibid., 3:102, where he says that the delegates had taken "the
Constitution of Britain, when in its purity, for a model," which is another
Bolingbrokean sentiment. In addition, see James H. Hutson, "Pierce Butler's
Records of the Federal Constitutional Convention," Quarterly Journal of the Library
of Congress 37 (1980): 69, where the author suggests that Butler may have been a
"closet anti-Federalist."

Similarly, Hume and Blackstone were quoted or paraphrased, or their ideas were reflected, in observations of delegates on all sides. Madison was eclectic: his celebrated speech of June 6, anticipating *Federalist* number 10, was adapted from Hume; and later, in addition to citing Montesquieu, he also drew upon natural-rights theory and his great learning in the history of confederations to buttress his arguments in favor of proportional representation.[27] But Paterson appealed to Hume's (or Harrington's) idea of a legislature "refined by the mode of election" in support of his plan,[28] and Gunning Bedford of Delaware supported the Paterson plan by applying a Humean theory of the passions to the states, and also with a Blackstonean legislative-supremacy argument.[29] Sherman used legislative supremacy against proportional representation;[30] Hamilton used Blackstone against equal representation.[31] Hume runs through Hamilton's great speech of June 18, though Montesquieu, Necker, and classical authors are cited as well, and Hamilton explicitly endorsed Hume's dictum that corruption was necessary to maintain the balance of the British constitution.[32] Gorham, another court-party nationalist, also endorsed that dictum.[33] Gouverneur Morris, yet another, employed Humean principles in a long and fascinating speech on July 2, and four days later he stated flatly that "we should either take the British Constitution altogether or make one for ourselves"; and it is clear, from remarks he made elsewhere, that he had Blackstone's version of the constitution in mind.[34]

Three observations are in order. One is that the delegates—at least in dealing with the question whether the legislature should be national, federal, or a mixture—did

[27] Farrand, *Records*, June 6, 19, 30, July 14, 1:134–136, 314–315, 319, 485, 2:8.
[28] Ibid., June 16, 1:251.
[29] Ibid., June 4, 30, 1:100, 490–491.
[30] Ibid., June 1, 1:65.
[31] Ibid., June 29, 1:472.
[32] Ibid., June 18, 22, 1:282–311, 376, 381.
[33] Ibid., June 22, 1:375–376, 381.
[34] Ibid., July 2, 6, 1:511–514, 545; and also Aug. 15 (2:299), where Morris makes the Blackstonean observation that the judiciary "was part of the Executive."

not derive their positions from systems of political theory. Rather, they used political theorists to justify positions that they had taken for nontheoretical reasons. Another is that the Framers were politically multilingual: they could speak in the language of Bolingbroke, Montesquieu, Locke, the classical republicans, Hume, and many others, whichever seemed rhetorically appropriate to the particular argument at hand. The third is that if the convention was not to end in failure, a compromise must be worked out and/or extraordinary means of persuasion must be applied.

Precisely what happened cannot be known for certain, but the most important known facts are suggestive. After the committee of the whole had voted to reject equal representation in the second branch, but before the question came up in formal convention, some key changes in the personnel of two delegations took place. James McHenry of Maryland, learning of the illness of his brother, went home and did not return until August. Because Carroll and Mercer had not yet arrived, Maryland was now represented only by Luther Martin, who favored equal representation, and Daniel Jenifer, who did not. William Pierce and William Few of Georgia had gone to New York, the one on personal business and the other to attend Congress, leaving Georgia represented by William Houstoun and Abraham Baldwin. Houstoun stuck by his state's earlier position against equal representation; but Baldwin, who had been born and educated in Connecticut and had only recently moved to Georgia, now began adhering to the position of his native state.[35]

The vote was taken as the first item of business on July 2. Jenifer was late in arriving, so Martin was able to cast Maryland's vote for equal representation, and Houstoun and Baldwin split Georgia's vote, with the result that five states were for, five were against, and one was divided. The convention was, as Sherman put it, "at a full stop." Sherman suggested that a committee consisting of one delegate from each state be appointed to try to work out a

---

[35] For the comings and goings see the Attendance of Delegates, ibid., 3:586–590.

compromise. Wilson and Madison strongly objected, and the New Jersey and Delaware delegates voted against a commitment, but otherwise the idea received general support.[36]

The committee reported its compromise proposal, which was Franklin's brainchild, on July 5. This was that the states should be equally represented in the second branch, but that all bills for raising or spending money should originate in the first branch and that the second branch could concur with or reject such bills but could not amend them in any way. The convention avoided taking a direct vote for eleven days, during which a temporary apportionment of seats in the first branch was worked out, regular reapportionment according to a decennial census of the population was agreed to, and the question whether slaves would count was compromised—it being agreed that they would count as three-fifths of a person for purposes of both representation and direct taxation.[37] Along the way, about half the delegates made clear their attitudes toward the Franklin compromise. Of those who did, all who had previously supported equal representation, except for Paterson, signified their acceptance of the proposal.[38] Of those in the contrary camp, only Franklin himself, Gerry, and Strong indicated their willingness to accept it.[39] That changed only one state's vote, removing Massachusetts from the proportional camp by splitting and thus neutralizing it. All of the ardent advocates of a purely national system—including Madison, Wilson, Gouverneur Morris, Charles Pinckney, King, and Gorham—were adamantly opposed to the compromise.

[36] Ibid., July 2, 1:510–516.

[37] Ibid., July 12, 1:597. That the compromise was based upon a suggestion made by Franklin is recorded by Yates, who was on the committee (ibid., 1:523). There was a great deal of sentiment, especially among southerners, in favor of basing representation upon property holding; several northerners insisted upon population as the sole base of representation and vehemently sought to exclude slaves from the reckoning. The "three-fifths" compromise was based upon an earlier compromise incorporated into congressional resolutions of Apr. 18, 1783.

[38] Ibid., July 5, 6, 7, 10, 14, 1:527, 531–533, 543, 546, 550, 551, 2:4.

[39] Ibid., July 5, 14, 1:532, 2:7–8.

Even so, had all other delegates held to the positions they had been taking, the change in the Massachusetts vote would have turned the balance, for on July 9 Daniel Carroll showed up to side with Luther Martin in favor of the compromise; and if things had worked out that way, it would be evident that Franklin's compromise had been decisive. Such, however, was not the way things worked out. First, Lansing and Yates left for home; New York was therefore unrepresented (Hamilton having previously departed), and the equal-representation camp was thereby deprived of one vote. Second, when the final vote on Franklin's compromise was taken on July 16, Baldwin unaccountably reversed himself and again voted against equality in the Senate, so the opponents picked up another vote.[40]

But third and crucially, three delegates from North Carolina—Williamson, Alexander Martin, and Davie—unexpectedly voted for equality, even though Williamson, when the compromise proposal was first reported, had said that it was "the most objectionable of any he had yet heard."[41] That made the tally five in favor (Connecticut, New Jersey, Delaware, Maryland, and North Carolina), four against (Pennsylvania, Virginia, South Carolina, and Georgia), and one—Massachusetts—divided. In accordance with previous rulings, Washington held that the resolution had passed. The conclusion seems inescapable that extraordinary means of persuasion had been applied to the North Carolina delegates, but I shall not speculate here as to what those means might have been.[42]

[40] Ibid., July 16, 2:15.
[41] Ibid., July 5, 1:532.
[42] Ibid., July 16, 2:15. For an effort to explain the backstage maneuvering that underlay North Carolina's change of votes see McDonald, E Pluribus Unum, 289–302. This explanation was strongly criticized by several reviewers when that book first appeared. Whether it is sound or not, however, it seems certain that (as is argued in E Pluribus Unum) some kind of negotiations among the delegates from Connecticut, North Carolina, and South Carolina were involved. Williamson, on Aug. 9 (Farrand, Records, 2:233), said that North Carolina "had agreed to an equality in the Senate, merely in consideration that money bills should be confined to the other House"; but that assertion seems to contradict what Williamson said on July 5 (n. 41, above).

A few more decisions concerning the constitution of the legislative branch were made before the proceedings were turned over to the committee of detail. On July 17 the convention agreed, by a six to four vote, to vest the legislature with a broad, general grant of power (the alternative, presumably, being to enumerate its powers), and it rejected, by a seven to three vote, the Madison-Pinckney proposal for a negative on state legislation. On the twenty-sixth the delegates voted to instruct the committee to require property-holding qualifications for members of the legislature; but after a debate that reverberated with Mandeville/Hume versus Bolingbroke/Montesquieu undertones and overtones, they rejected proposals that the property qualifications be landholding and that public debtors, persons with unsettled accounts with the government, and pensioners be ineligible for membership.[43]

The committee of detail disregarded the convention's resolutions in three key particulars: by itemizing the legislative powers, by failing to specify property qualifications for congressmen, and by providing that congressmen be paid by their states rather than out of the national treasury. The evolution of the powers of Congress, a complicated affair, will be treated in the next chapter. The other two matters are more directly concerned with the subject at hand, the constituting of the legislative branch.

The committee provided that the qualifications for voters for representatives be the same, "from time to time, as those of the electors in the several States, of the most numerous branch of their own legislatures."[44] That was an ideal solution to the problem arising from the differences in wealth from state to state, and the principle underlying it would be an influential one in regard to the allocation of powers between general and state governments. A few of the delegates objected, insisting that the suffrage should be expressly confined to freeholders. Unsurprisingly, Dickinson, as a republican of the Harrington/Bolingbroke/Montesquieu school, was one of them: the freeholders, said he, were "the best guardians of liberty." Gouverneur Morris

[43] Farrand, *Records*, July 17, 26, 2:25–28, 121–126.
[44] Ibid., Aug. 6, 2:178.

was another, but his grounds were Blackstonean: "Give the votes to people who have no property, and they will sell them to the rich who will be able to buy them." He added that the delegates should not confine their attention "to the present moment. The time is not distant when this Country will abound with mechanics & manufacturers who will receive their bread from their employers. Will such men be the secure & faithful Guardians of liberty? Will they be the impregnable barrier agst. aristocracy?" Most of the delegates, however, accepted the committee's recommendation.[45]

As for the question of property qualifications for membership in Congress, the committee proposed to authorize Congress itself to establish them. This met with opposition on a variety of grounds. Charles Pinckney and Rutledge proposed that high property qualifications be set in the constitution (Pinckney thought that $100,000 clear from debt was the minimum desirable for the president, and half that sum for judges and congressmen). Franklin objected, expressing "his dislike of every thing that tended to debase the spirit of the common people" and adding that "some of the greatest rogues he was ever acquainted with, were the richest rogues." Dickinson did not speak on this occasion, but he had made his position clear earlier: "He doubted the policy of interweaving into a Republican constitution a veneration for wealth. He had always understood that a veneration for poverty & virtue, were the objects of republican encouragement." Gouverneur Morris wanted Congress to be able to set its own qualifications in all respects, not merely in regard to property. Williamson pointed out that this would enable "any particular description of men, of lawyers for example," to set qualifications that would exclude all others. When Morris's motion was narrowly defeated, it was generally agreed that no uniform standard could be adopted, and so the whole clause was dropped.[46]

The proposal that congressmen be paid by the states was a surprising one, and it met with general hostility. The

---

[45]Ibid., Aug. 7, 2:201–206.
[46]Ibid., Aug. 10, 2:248–251; for Dickinson see ibid., July 26, 2:123.

South Carolinians favored it, in keeping with their strong tendency toward foederalism, and so did the Massachusetts delegation, apparently out of concern that senators especially would otherwise lose sight of their constituents. Sherman expressed concern that congressmen would set their wages too low, not too high, in order to keep out all but the rich; he proposed that the constitution set a modest wage on the understanding that state governments could augment the amount if they chose. Instead, it was decided that congressmen would be paid by the national treasury and would establish their own salaries by law.[47]

Reaching agreement about the way in which the executive branch would be constituted was quite as difficult as agreeing about the legislative, but for different kinds of reasons. With the exception of two particulars, what was at issue were matters of principle rather than of power and influence; but the delegates differed considerably in their principles, and even when they agreed in principle, they disagreed as to the best means of achieving the desired ends.

Almost all the delegates agreed that there must be an executive branch, independent of the legislative and judicial branches. Many of them, however, particularly among those who had come of age politically before 1776, were extremely uneasy with the idea. Indeed, at least twelve—more than a fourth of the delegates who were present when the issue was decided—so feared executive power that they sought to diffuse it among several persons. These advocates of a plural executive included Sherman, Randolph, Mason, Blair, Franklin, Dickinson, Williamson, Lansing, Yates, Jenifer, Brearley, and William Churchill Houston. To this list might be added those who supported the Paterson plan, for it contemplated a plural executive.[48]

[47] Ibid., Aug. 14, 2:290–293; observe the change from the position adopted on June 26 (ibid., 1:428).

[48] For Sherman, ibid., June 1, 1:65; for Randolph, Blair, and Mason, June 4, 1:97; for Franklin, June 4, 1:102 n. The positions of Lansing and Yates are inferred from the fact that New York voted for a plural executive, even though Hamilton

On the opposite end of the spectrum, the concern was not with fear that the executive would be dangerously strong but that it would not be strong enough, as Madison phrased it, to resist the "powerful tendency in the Legislature to absorb all power into its vortex."[49] Champions of a vigorous executive (generally, those identified earlier as being nationalists of a Hume/Mandeville persuasion) were not, however, of one mind in regard to the most efficacious way of investing the office with sufficient energy. Several thought the best way lay in a long term of service. As indicated, Hamilton proposed having an executive chosen to serve during good behavior, and his position was supported at one time or another by Read, Gouverneur Morris, Jacob Broom, and a few others. Leaning in the same direction were those who thought the executive ought not to be impeachable, an idea that was endorsed by Morris, Charles Pinckney, Gorham, Strong, and King—the last, curiously, on the ground that giving the legislature the power of impeachment would violate the principle of the separation of powers.[50] (By contrast, early in the convention the Connecticut, South Carolina, and Georgia delegations voted to make the executive removable at the pleasure of Congress, and the Delaware delegation voted in favor of Dickinson's motion that the executive be removable by Congress on request of a majority of the state legislatures.)[51]

favored a single executive (June 4, 1:97). Jenifer's position is inferred: Maryland voted against a single executive on June 4 (1:97), and Jenifer was the only Marylander present. Brearley and Houston were the New Jersey delegates present, and they cast the state's vote against a single executive. Dickinson's position is derived from his notes for June 18–19, in Hutson, "John Dickinson at the Federal Convention," 270. According to Farrand's analysis of the attendance (3:587–590), eight of the fifty-five delegates had not yet arrived on June 4, and two had already departed, meaning that the maximum number in attendance was forty-five.

[49] Farrand, *Records*, July 21, 2:74.

[50] Ibid., July 20, 2:64, 66–67, 69. The position of Gorham and Strong is inferred: Gerry favored impeachment, but the Massachusetts delegation voted against it. Given King's stated position, had either Gorham or Strong voted in favor of impeachment, the state's vote would have been divided.

[51] Ibid., June 2, 1:85, 87. The impeachment process as finally adopted is a good example of the Framers' drawing, neither upon theory nor upon British practice, but upon colonial experience, as is clearly shown in Peter C. Hoffer and N. E. H.

Taking another approach, Madison and Wilson reasoned that no executive who would be acceptable to the people could be given enough power to restrain legislative excesses and therefore that the executive and the judiciary should be combined into a council of revision, with the power to veto legislation. Amidst cries that such a council would be an "improper coalition" of separate branches, the convention rejected the proposal on both occasions when Wilson and Madison brought it up, though the Connecticut and Virginia delegations voted in favor of it both times. New York also supported it on the first occasion, and Maryland (Jenifer and Carroll combining against Martin) and half of the Pennsylvania and Georgia delegations did on the second.[52] Most of the delegates supported a conditional executive veto, subject to overriding by Congress; the exceptions were the Connecticut delegates and Franklin, Bedford, and Jenifer, who opposed any veto power, and Hamilton, Wilson, and King, who favored an absolute veto.[53]

Those who ardently distrusted executive power drew their position, for the most part, from experience, both in the narrow sense of participation in the events leading to 1776 and in the broader sense of history, especially of the Stuart kings of England. The position of the advocates of a strong executive was more nearly ideological or theoretical. Together, these two camps numbered something over half of the delegates. Most of the remainder were governed neither by history nor by ideology, but by considerations of power.

Attitudes were slow to come to light, partly because delegates were loath to speak their minds and partly because, at first, no one knew how far the convention would go in departing from the Articles of Confederation. Accordingly, when the Randolph plan was initially under discussion, only tentative resolutions concerning the execu-

Hull, "Power and Precedent in the Creation of an American Impeachment Tradition: The Eighteenth-Century Colonial Record," *William and Mary Quarterly* 36 (1979): 51–77.

[52] Farrand, *Records*, June 6, July 21, 1:138–140, 2:73–80.

[53] Ibid., June 4, 1:98–100, 104, 108.

tive were adopted, pending the settlement of the structure of the legislative. At that stage, it was agreed that the executive should be a single person, that he should be elected by the legislative for a seven-year term, and that he should be ineligible for a second term. These resolutions were approved by all delegations except those of Pennsylvania and Maryland, which preferred election by electors chosen by the qualified voters at large.[54] Except in the Paterson and Hamilton plans, the subject was not raised again for more than six weeks.

Between July 17 and July 26—between the adoption of Franklin's compromise on representation and the adjournment for the committee of detail—the matter was vigorously debated. Gouverneur Morris led off the debates, attacking the idea of congressional election of the executive on the ground that "it will be the work of intrigue, of cabal, and of faction." He proposed, instead, election by the freeholders. Sherman objected that the people would not be well-enough informed to make an intelligent choice, that they would never give a majority to one man, and that popular election would throw the choice into the hands of the largest states. Charles Pinckney endorsed Sherman's objections and added that the people would "be led by a few active & designing men." Wilson countered Sherman's contention regarding the improbability of a majority by offering as a backup plan an ultimate choice by Congress. Morris declared that designing men would have little chance of succeeding in a nationwide election. As for the danger that large states would combine to swing the election, he said that it would be impossible for the people of such states to combine, though their representatives in Congress could easily do so. If the executive were elected by the legislative, "he will not be independent on it; and if not independent, usurpation & tyranny on the part of the Legislature will be the consequence."[55]

---

[54] Ibid., June 1, 2, 4, 1:64–75, 80–92, 96–97.

[55] Ibid., July 17, 2:29–31. Morris likened legislative election to the choice of kings of Poland by the Polish diet, which had produced notoriously bad selections. Several other delegates also referred to the Polish example, and it must be remembered that the first partition of Poland had only recently taken place.

A flurry of votes and counterproposals ensued. Morris's motion for election by the freeholders was supported only by the Pennsylvania delegation. Luther Martin then moved, Bedford seconding, that the executive be chosen by electors chosen by the state legislatures, but they were supported only by their own delegations, those of Maryland and Delaware. Houstoun of Georgia then moved to strike out the clause making the executive ineligible for reelection, and somewhat surprisingly the motion carried, six states to four. Many thought that this would make the executive unacceptably dependent on the legislative—it would render the legislative the executor as well as the maker of laws, said Madison, and "then according to the observation of Montesquieu, tyrannical laws may be made that they may be executed in a tyrannical manner." To dramatize their position, advocates of an independent executive then proposed that he serve during good behavior, and four of the ten state delegations supported the motion. That vote had a chilling effect, and on the next day the delegates agreed unanimously to reconsider the whole question.[56]

The subject was thrashed out anew on Thursday the nineteenth. Sentiment for a choice by electors now began to grow, and Ellsworth moved that the executive be chosen by electors, who would be appointed by the state legislatures, each state being allotted one, two, or three electors, depending on the size of its population. On the question of choice by electors, Massachusetts was divided, and the three southernmost states voted no, but all states in between voted aye; and therefore that part of the motion carried. On the question of having the state legislatures appoint the electors, all but Virginia and South Carolina approved. Thus, for the first time, the convention voted in favor of election of the executive by somebody other than Congress.[57]

Morris thought the use of Poland as a horrible example had been decisive; see Morris to the President of the New York Senate, Dec. 25, 1802, ibid., 3:394. See also Butler's remarks in the United States Senate, Dec. 2, 1803, ibid., 3:403-404.

[56] Ibid., July 17, 18, 2:33-36, 37.
[57] Ibid., July 19, 2:52-58.

The arrangement, however, did not hold, and when the subject was raised anew on July 24, an additional dimension came to light. It was generally assumed that if a system of electors were resorted to, the electors would gather and vote in the national capital, and it was also assumed that the national capital would be in New York or Philadelphia. But while those cities were centrally located and easily accessible for Americans who lived between Norfolk and Boston, they were remote from the Carolinas, Georgia, and New Hampshire. Houstoun of Georgia, who with Spaight was responsible for bringing about the reconsideration, pointed out that few capable men, chosen as electors "from the more distant States," would undertake the long and arduous trip to cast their ballots. In other words, such states would in effect be deprived of a voice in the election of the executive unless he were chosen by the national legislature. Delegates from the Carolinas and Georgia were supported by those from New Hampshire (who had just arrived) and Massachusetts (who were now reunified) and also, unaccountably, by those from New Jersey and Delaware. Accordingly, the six to three to one vote in favor of electors on July 19 was reversed, the convention now voting seven to four to return to the original plan of having Congress elect the executive. But that decision rekindled the dispute over what means were to be employed to make the executive branch independent, and the day's deliberations ended in rancor and confusion.[58]

The next day was even more rancorous and confused. Ellsworth led off with a cumbersome proposal whereby "a deserving Magistrate may be reelected without making him dependent on the Legislature," namely, that the executive be appointed by Congress for his first term but by electors chosen by the state legislatures if he sought reelection. That proposal was rejected, seven to four. Charles Pinckney then proposed a Harrington-like "rotation": that the executive be elected by Congress "with a proviso that no person be eligible for more than 6 years in any twelve years."

[58] Ibid., July 24, 2:99–101.

Pinckney's motion was favored by the two northernmost and the three southernmost states, but it too failed, six to five.[59]

Between these two votes a great many things were said, two of them being of some influence. One was an observation that Madison made during a long analysis in which he discountenanced every mode of election except by the people, directly or through electors: that ministers of European powers would "have and make use of" the opportunity to intrigue in the election if it were in the hands of Congress. That prospect affrighted a number of delegates into moving toward a decentralized election. The other was a suggestion by Williamson that afforded a positive step toward a solution. Several delegates had observed that electors, however chosen, would tend to vote for citizens of their own states, in which case the large states would have a great advantage over the small ones. That consideration disposed a number of delegates from small states to favor congressional selection, and it left others doubtful as to whether any but a mediocrity would be elected through a decentralized plan. What Williamson suggested was that the electors vote for three candidates; then, he said, they would probably vote for only one person from their own state. Gouverneur Morris instantly took to the idea and offered a refinement: that electors vote for two persons, "one of whom at least should not be of his own State." Madison endorsed the idea and proposed another which, had it been adopted, would later have prevented the emergence of the Virginia Dynasty and probably his own presidency: to provide a mandatory rotation of the executive from state to state. Gerry remarked sourly that an election on such a basis would be "radically vicious," for it would enable "some one set of men dispersed through the Union & acting in Concert"—he named the Society of the Cincinnati—to control the election.[60]

Gerry's comment may have been a telling one. On the next day Mason, who had been much upset by Madison's

[59] Ibid., July 25, 2:108–109, 111–112, 115.
[60] Ibid., July 25, 2:109–114.

observation about the danger of foreign intrigue, indicated
that with him, fear of the danger posed by aristocracy was
even greater; he concurred with Gerry's remark about the
Cincinnati and announced that he had come back to
favoring election by Congress. Others, including Mason's
colleague John Blair, apparently felt the same way. In any
event, New Hampshire and the three southernmost states
were joined by Connecticut and New Jersey; Virginia's vote
was divided; and the original plan—to have an executive
elected by the national legislature for a seven-year term and
ineligible for reelection—was passed and turned over to the
committee of detail on July 26.[61]

The tenth article of the report of the committee of detail
stipulated that "the Executive power of the United States
shall be vested in a single person," to be styled "The
President of the United States of America." During their
debates on the subject the delegates had addressed themselves to form rather than to substance, and except for an
occasional hint that "the executive power" would be
limited, no one made any extensive comments as to just
what it would include. Experience was not an adequate
guide, for their experience with colonial and state governors was largely irrelevant to the task presently at hand.
Hume was silent on the subject, Montesquieu muddled,
Locke too general. That left Blackstone's description of the
royal prerogative as the only readily available account of
what had traditionally been regarded as the executive
power in a mixed form of government.

The executive powers, as itemized by Blackstone, can be
grouped under several headings. One broad heading was
the conduct of relations with foreign nations. The king was
commander in chief of the armed forces, having exclusive
power to raise and regulate fleets, armies, and the militia,
though standing armies were prohibited by law in time of
peace and Parliament could dissolve armies simply by not

[61] Ibid., July 26, 2:119–121.

appropriating money for their support. The Crown also had the exclusive power to send and receive ambassadors, to make treaties, to make war and peace (including the declaring of war), to grant letters of marque and reprisal, and to grant safe conducts. Domestically, the Crown had an absolute power to veto legislation, though it had not exercised that power since the reign of Queen Anne, and it convened and dissolved parliaments within limits established by law. Several of its additional powers were broadly economic: to designate ports and havens for persons and merchandise to pass into and out of the realm, to erect beacons and lighthouses, to coin money and establish the value thereof, to establish markets, and to regulate weights and measures. Related powers were those of prohibiting the exportation of arms and ammunition, prohibiting persons from leaving the kingdom, and issuing proclamations that had the force of law, such as proclaiming embargoes in time of war. Next came powers to enforce the law, which included the powers to establish courts, appoint judges, prosecute law violators in the courts, and grant reprieves and pardons except in cases of impeachment. More personally, the Crown had the exclusive power to appoint persons to civil and military offices, to confer dignities and titles, and to grant privileges such as making denizens of aliens and creating corporations. Finally, the Crown was the head of the Church of England.[62]

Wilson, however, expressly rejected the prerogative as a guide; and the other members of the committee of detail obviously agreed with him. In their draft, certain of the executive powers were not lodged in any part of the government, and the power to confer nobility was specifically withheld. The other executive powers were distributed three ways. The commercial powers, the naturalization power, the power to establish courts, the power to appoint a treasurer, and the power to subdue rebellions, make war, raise armies, build and equip fleets, and call out the militia—all of these were assigned to Congress, not to

<hr>

[62] Blackstone, *Commentaries*, 1:250–280, 334, 408–421, 4:394–402.

the president. More interestingly, the Senate, representing the residual sovereignty that lay in the states, was given the exclusive power to make treaties, to appoint ambassadors, and to appoint the judges of the supreme court. The president was empowered to appoint all other officials except the treasurer, to grant pardons and reprieves except in regard to impeachments, and to receive ambassadors. He was also given a conditional veto and was made commander in chief. So much for the doctrine of the separation of powers.[63]

Inasmuch as the committee had virtually no instructions from the convention in this matter, the roots of its decision to divide and distribute the executive power in this curious manner must be looked for in the attitudes of the committee members themselves. Two of the members, Rutledge and Ellsworth, were foederalists. The other three, Gorham, Wilson, and Randolph, were nationalists; but Randolph was also an agrarian republican who preferred a plural executive. Assigning executive powers to the Senate was consistent with the views of the two foederalists and also with Randolph's preference for a plural executive. Wilson might have agreed because of his intense dislike of the plan for congressional election of the president: he was ill disposed to entrust such an official with any power. As for the executive powers vested in Congress as a whole, some were in keeping with a trend that had been present in Britain; as a practical matter, for example, the powers to regulate weights and measures and to determine what was money had been taken over by Parliament. That the committee went much further in that direction must have reflected, at least in part, the discontent with the mode of choosing the president and with the structure of the office in general.

Being preoccupied with the powers of Congress, the convention was slow in getting around to serious consid-

[63]Farrand, *Records*, June 1, Aug. 6, 1:65, 70, 2:177–189.

eration of the presidency. On August 15 it voted to increase the majority necessary for overriding a veto from two-thirds to three-fourths; on the eighteenth and twentieth there was a brief discussion about providing an executive council; on the twenty-third there was desultory talk about the Senate's treaty-making power. Then, on the twenty-fourth, the method of electing the president came up, and though the debates and votes were indecisive, they indicated considerable discontent with every mode that had been suggested so far. Over the objection of four of the small states, the convention approved a motion to have the election be by a joint ballot of the two houses of Congress. It rejected, six to five, a motion that each state have one vote in such election, rejected by the same margin a motion that the president be chosen by popularly elected electors, and rejected (by a tie vote) an abstract proposal that electors, however selected, should make the choice.[64]

On Friday August 31 a committee composed of one delegate from each state was appointed in an effort to resolve all unsettled questions, and it was in that committee that Pierce Butler came up with a method of electing the president that almost satisfied almost everybody. The proposal was complex. It provided for both a president and a vice-president; this feature satisfied those who had been concerned about the succession in the event of the death or disability of the president. It provided that electors be appointed in such manner as the several legislatures should direct; that took care of the objections of those who feared popular election, for it meant that the legislatures could elect the electors if they chose to do so. Each state was allotted a number of electors equal to the combined number of senators and members of the House of Representatives to which it was entitled; this effected a compromise between proportional and equal allocation. The proposal provided that the electors meet in their respective states, which overcame the problem of distance of travel and also reduced the possibility of intrigue, and provided that they

[64]Ibid., Aug. 15, 18, 20, 23, 24, 2:299–302, 328–329, 342–344, 392–394, 401–404.

vote for two candidates, one of whom must be the resident of another state. The person receiving the most votes, if a majority, would become president, and the one with the second most votes would become vice-president. In the expectation that a president thus elected would be sufficiently independent, the office was now to be entrusted with a share in the executive powers previously vested in the Senate: the president would be empowered to appoint ambassadors, judges, and other officers with the concurrence of the Senate, and to make treaties with the concurrence of two-thirds of the Senate.[65]

That much of the proposal was generally accepted; but there was more. The scheme provided that in the event that two persons had a majority and they had the same number of electoral votes, the Senate should choose between them, and that if no one had a majority, the Senate would elect the president from among the top five candidates. Most of the delegates thought it unlikely, as a rule, that any candidate would have a majority, and therefore they assumed that the Senate would normally elect the president from nominees chosen by the electors. If that should prove to be the case, the partly national, partly foederal government would be strongly tilted on the foederal side, for three of the four branches (including the judicial) would then be chosen directly or indirectly by the state governments. A good many nationalists objected to this feature of the electoral-college system, protesting that it would make the Senate a dangerous aristocracy. After three days of heated discussion, Sherman came up with a motion that undermined the aristocracy argument: he moved that in case of a tie or in the absence of a majority, the decision be made by

---

[65] Ibid., Sept. 4, 2:497–498. Regarding Butler's authorship see Butler to Weedon Butler, May 5, 1788, ibid., 3:302. Several years later, Dickinson said that Madison had sketched out the idea for the electoral college in a committee (Dickinson to George Logan, Nov. 4, 1802, quoted in Milton E. Flower, *John Dickinson: Conservative Revolutionary* [Charlottesville, Va., 1983], 247). Dickinson's memory seems to have been inaccurate; Madison did not like the plan when it was first proposed, and he offered several amendments to it (see Farrand, *Records*, Sept. 4, 5, 2:500, 513, 514, 515).

the House of Representatives, the member or members
from each state having one vote for the occasion.[66]

Even on that basis the states would retain a powerful
voice in the election of the president (it would, in fact, be
the common practice for the legislatures to choose the
electors until after the War of 1812); and the small states
would continue to have a disproportionate voice in the
selection. A bit of backstage maneuvering helped to bring
this about. Early in August the delegates from three small
states (New Jersey, Delaware, and Maryland) had reneged
on the compromise that had won them equal representation in the Senate, and they had joined with four other
states to strike out the provision that money bills must
originate in the House. Champions of the originating clause
strove vainly to have it reinserted, and when the electoral
college came up for consideration, they supported the
electoral college in exchange for votes for reinsertion of the
originating clause. The clause was changed, however, to
allow the Senate to amend money bills after they had been
passed by the House.[67]

As in the matter of constituting the legislative branch,
foederalists and small-state delegates had the better of the
exchange with large-state nationalists in constituting the
executive. The more ideologically oriented of the nationalists were extremely unhappy over the turn of events;
Randolph, Mason, and Gerry would refuse to sign the
Constitution. Wilson, too, was unhappy, especially with
the convention's denial to the House of a share in the
treaty-making power and with the "blending a branch of
the Legislature with the Executive" in requiring senatorial
confirmation of executive appointments—in other words,
with giving greater power to the foederal branch of the
legislative than to the national or popular branch. Charles
Pinckney shared that view. And Madison, on the day that
the electoral-college system was agreed to, wrote to Jefferson, outlining the main features of the proposed constitution and opining that "the *plan, should* it *be adopted*, will

[66] Farrand, *Records*, Sept. 4–6, 2:499–502, 511–515, 522–525.
[67] Ibid., Aug. 8, 9, 13, 15, 21, Sept. 5, 8, 2:222–225, 232–234, 273–280, 297–298,
357–359, 509–510, 552.

neither effectually *answer* its *national object*, [nor] prevent the local *mischiefs* which everywhere *excite disgusts* agst. the State Governments."[68]

The delegates devoted less time to forming the judiciary—and less attention to careful craftsmanship—than they had expended on the legislative and executive branches. In part the judiciary received minimal consideration because it was regarded as the least powerful and least active branch of government.[69] In part, too, it could be disposed of with little contention because the delegates were in general agreement as to the principles that should be embodied in forming it.

One such principle was that the judiciary should be independent. Accordingly, though the proposed mode of appointing the judges varied as the convention progressed—at first they were to be elected by Congress, then by the Senate, and finally by the president with the confirmation of the Senate—it was agreed from the outset that they would hold their positions during good behavior, which is to say for life unless they chose to resign or were impeached and convicted of high crimes and misdemeanors. Only once did anybody propose a departure from that principle: late in August, Dickinson made a motion that the justices be removable by the president upon the petition of both houses of Congress. Gerry seconded the motion, and Sherman spoke in favor of it, pointing out that that was the practice in Britain. Wilson, Gouverneur Morris, Rutledge, and Randolph all spoke against it: Wilson declared that the rule was a safe one in Britain because the Lords and Commons were unlikely to concur on the same occasions, whereas it was entirely probable that the "gust of faction" might prevail in both houses of Congress. In

---

[68] Ibid., Sept. 7, 2:538–539; Madison to Jefferson, Sept. 6, 1787, ibid., 3:77.

[69] Hamilton observed, in *Federalist* number 78, that of the three branches, the "judiciary, from the nature of its functions, will always be the least dangerous to the political rights of the Constitution." This was true in the eighteenth century; and it was true of the Constitution as it was written. The Framers could not have foreseen the development of judicial activism a century later.

any event, the proposal was rejected, Connecticut alone voting in favor of it.[70]

There was minor disagreement over the salaries of the judges, a matter that was directly related to their independence. In the resolutions adopted by the committee of the whole, it was provided that the judges' salaries could not be decreased or increased during their terms of service. Gouverneur Morris moved that "or increased" be stricken; he was seconded by Franklin. Madison strenuously objected, insisting that that would make it possible for Congress to bribe the court, but he was supported only by the Virginia and North Carolina delegations. Several weeks later Madison proposed that the prohibition against increasing the salaries be reinstated; this time he was supported only by his Virginia colleagues and by McHenry and one other delegate from Maryland.[71]

A second fundamental principle on which the delegates were in general agreement was that, despite the shakiness of the precedents for the doctrine, the courts would by the very nature of their function have the power to strike down legislative acts if they were in violation of the Constitution. At least eight delegates of widely divergent political views—Gerry, King, Sherman, Madison, Gouverneur Morris, Luther Martin, Wilson, and Mason—asserted that the courts would have such power, and no one argued to the contrary.[72] Indeed, Madison and Wilson, in contending for a council of revision, wanted to give the judges even greater power, that of vetoing legislation on policy grounds as well as on constitutional grounds. They were supported by the Connecticut, Maryland, and Virginia delegations; those of Pennsylvania and Georgia were divided.[73]

[70] Farrand, Records, Aug. 27, 2:428–429. See also Dickinson's annotated copy of the committee of detail's report, in Hutson, "John Dickinson at the Federal Convention," 281.

[71] Farrand, Records, July 18, Aug. 27, 2:44–45, 429–430.

[72] Ibid., June 4, July 17, 21, 1:97–98, 2:27–29, 73, 76, 78. For a broader perspective on the Framers and judicial review see Walter Berns, "Judicial Review and the Rights and Laws of Nature," in 1982: The Supreme Court Review, ed. Philip B. Kurland et al. (Chicago, 1983), 49–83.

[73] Farrand, Records, June 4, July 21, 1:97–98, 104–105, 2:73–80. Regarding Wilson's advocacy of as strong a judiciary as possible see also The Works of James Wilson, ed. Robert Green McCloskey, 2 vols. (Cambridge, Mass., 1967), 1:293–331.

But the handling of the matter of judicial review was one
of several instances of carelessness in constituting the
judiciary. The courts were not *expressly* given the power to
rule on constitutionality. The nearest thing to a direct
statement on the subject is the supreme-law clause, which
underwent a curious and incomplete evolution. The first
version of the clause was proposed by Luther Martin as an
alternative to the Madison/Pinckney proposal that Congress be empowered to veto state legislation: he moved that
the constitution, acts of Congress passed in pursuance of it,
and treaties be "the supreme law of the respective States
. . . & that the Judiciaries of the several States shall be
bound thereby in their decisions, any thing in the respective laws of the individual States to the contrary notwithstanding." The motion was passed without discussion or
dissent.[74] The committee of detail changed the phraseology
from "the Judiciaries of the several States" (which would
include juries) to "the judges in the several States," which
excluded juries but can be read as including national as well
as state judges; it retained, however, the wording "supreme law of the several States," clearly implying that the
judges were to apply the test of constitutionality to *state*
legislation.[75] The phrasing was changed a bit further when
the clause was adopted by the convention on August 23,
but the quoted passages remained the same.[76]

The committee of style radically altered the import of the
clause by changing "supreme law of the several States" to
"supreme law of the land," the revised phraseology clearly
implying that judges were to apply the test of constitutionality to national as well as to state legislation. Yet
ambiguity remained. When the clause had been adopted in
August, provision for the District of Columbia had not yet
been made, and it was assumed that the national capital
would be located in some state. When provision for the
District of Columbia was added, the implication was that
the Supreme Court would sit there—which meant, in turn,

[74]Farrand, *Records*, July 17, 2:28–29.
[75]Ibid., Aug. 6, 2:183.
[76]Ibid., Aug. 23, 2:389.

that Supreme Court justices would not be included among the "judges in the several States" who were to be bound by the "supreme law of the land."[77]

Another shortcoming of the constitutional arrangements for the judiciary was less a matter of careless workmanship than of shirking responsibility. Early in the convention, Rutledge and Sherman had attacked the Randolph plan's resolution calling for a supreme court and "inferior tribunals." In keeping with their foederalist orientation, they believed that state courts were adequate for most purposes, that those courts should have original jurisdiction in most cases arising under the constitution, and that no national court except a supreme court was necessary. A sufficient number of delegates agreed with them—the vote was five to four, with two states divided—to strike constitutionally mandated lower courts from the plan. Immediately afterward, Wilson and Madison moved that Congress be empowered to create lower courts if it saw fit, and that motion was passed by a sizable majority. The convention never departed from that plan, and therefore, if a national court system was to be created, Congress would have to create it. Moreover, since Congress could establish and abolish lower courts at will, all courts except the Supreme Court were structurally subordinate to the Congress.[78]

Indeed, the arrangements for the judiciary resulted in going the rest of the way, which is to say making the Supreme Court itself subordinate to Congress. In some measure the vulnerability of the Court derived from a more or less conscious decision to allow Congress to determine the number of justices. Only the chief justice is specifically mentioned in the Constitution (in article 1, section 3, regarding impeachment trials of the president); Congress was otherwise left free to increase or decrease the number of justices without limit, which gave it power to "pack" the Court if the Court were not ruling the way Congress liked.

[77] Provision for the District of Columbia was added on Sept. 5 (ibid., 2:509, 510).
[78] Ibid., June 5, 1:124–125.

The greatest vulnerability arose from the fact that Congress is empowered to deprive the Supreme Court of most of its jurisdiction. This entered the scheme of things inadvertently and perhaps against the intention of the Framers. The Court's jurisdiction was given only cursory attention prior to the meeting of the committee of detail.[79] The committee fleshed out the jurisdiction, and its working papers clearly indicate what its members had in mind in giving Congress any voice in the matter. In an early draft, Randolph and Rutledge sketched the kinds of cases in which they believed the Court should have jurisdiction, then scribbled some qualifications: "But this supreme jurisdiction shall be appellate only, except in those instances, in which the legislature shall make it original. and the legislature shall organize it. 8. The whole or a part of the jurisdiction aforesaid according to the discretion of the legislature may be assigned to the inferior tribunals, *as original tribunals.*"[80]

In the committee's final draft the phraseology was more ambiguous. After specifying the kinds of cases over which the Supreme Court would have jurisdiction, the draft listed certain kinds in which "this jurisdiction shall be original." It went on to say: "In all the other cases before mentioned, it shall be appellate, with such exceptions and under such regulations as the Legislature shall make." In light of the earlier draft, the wording would seem to indicate that the committee intended that Congress should be able to change some of the Court's appellate jurisdiction into original jurisdiction; but that reading is not the only possible one, as precisely the reverse might also be implied. Moreover, the committee muddied the question by adding: "The Legislature may assign any part of the jurisdiction above mentioned (except the trial of the President of the United States) in the manner, and under the limitations which it shall think proper, to such Inferior Courts, as it shall constitute from time to time." In the earlier draft it was specified that such assignments would give the lower courts original

[79] Ibid., June 13, July 18, 1:231, 232, 2:46.
[80] Committee of detail, ibid., 2:146–147 (emphasis added).

jurisdiction, meaning that the Supreme Court would retain its appellate jurisdiction. That clarifying phraseology was absent in the final draft; and the words of the final draft do in fact authorize Congress to deprive the Supreme Court of jurisdiction in all cases except those few in which the Court was to be given original jurisdiction.[81]

The convention considered the judicial portions of the committee's draft on August 27 and 28. A motion was made to add, after the specification of cases in which the Court would have original jurisdiction, the words "In all the other cases before mentioned the Judicial power shall be exercised in such manner as the Legislature shall direct." That motion was defeated, Delaware and Virginia alone voting in the affirmative, but the language agreed upon—which found its way into the completed Constitution—amounted almost to the same thing. Article 3 of the Constitution specifies the extent of "the judicial Power," then reads: "In all Cases affecting Ambassadors, other public Ministers and Consuls, and those in which a State shall be Party, the supreme Court shall have original Jurisdiction. In all the other Cases before mentioned, the supreme Court shall have appellate Jurisdiction, both as to Law and Fact, with such Exceptions, and under such Regulations as the Congress shall make."[82] That left the Supreme Court at the mercy of the Congress.

The doctrine of the separation of powers had clearly been abandoned in the framing of the Constitution; as Madison explained in *Federalist* numbers 47–51, mixing powers was necessary to ensure a system of checks and balances. Indeed, in addition to the overlaps and sharings and dependencies already noted, there was another feature in the Constitution—one that resulted from an oversight on the part of the Framers—which made possible a thorough mixing of the legislative and executive powers. For all their care in arriving at a mode of appointing governmental

---

[81] Ibid., Aug. 6, 2:186–187.
[82] Ibid., Aug. 27, 28, 2:431–433, 437–438, 660–661.

officers, the Framers made no provision for removing them except through impeachment. Several delegates made it evident, during discussions of an executive council, that they assumed that presidential appointees would be removable at the president's pleasure, but nothing on the subject was stated in the Constitution. Hamilton, who heartily admired the British constitution and intended to make the American government, in practice, conform as closely as possible to it, saw opportunity in the Framer's neglect. Calling attention to the Senate's power to confirm or reject executive appointments, Hamilton casually noted, in *Federalist* number 77, that "the consent of that body would be necessary to displace as well as to appoint." Administrators would therefore tend to remain in office at the pleasure of the Senate, Hamilton believed, despite the elections of new presidents. "Where a man in any station had given satisfactory evidence of his fitness for it, a new President would be restrained from attempting a change in favor of a person more agreeable to him, by the apprehension that a discountenance of the Senate might frustrate the attempt, and bring some degree of discredit upon himself." Should that interpretation of the removal power prevail, the way would be open for a ministerial/cabinet system after the British mode.[83]

And yet if the Montesquieuans did not have their way in the convention, neither did the Humean nationalists. For the latter group the task of the convention was, to quote Madison again, first to "enable the government to control the governed; and in the next place oblige it to control itself." To attain these ends, the court-party nationalists had sought variously to devise processes of selection that would place as many *Optimates* as possible into government, to distribute and arrange powers in ways that would make it to the interest of men in government to act in the public interest, and to devise a structure of government that

---

[83] *Federalist*, 496–497. It can be argued that Hamilton was only engaging in propaganda to allay fears of a strong executive, which he of course favored. My reasons for interpreting his position otherwise are developed in my *Hamilton*, 125–126, 130–131.

would be as close to the British model as American circumstances would allow. The specific institutional means that such nationalists proposed were almost uniformly rejected by the convention, and yet the convention accomplished just what the nationalists had wanted it to accomplish. Ironically, it was two disciples of Montesquieu, supported by foederalists and interested champions of the states, who were most responsible for giving the court-party nationalists the kind of government they sought. Dickinson, with his understanding that the states, as baronies, could be made to serve as a substitute for the House of Lords, and Butler, with his electoral college, which could make an "elective monarchy" a safe one, provided the crucial conceptual breakthroughs. The practical maneuverings of such foederalists as Rutledge, Sherman, and Ellsworth helped to transform the conceptions into reality.

And in an ultimate sense the Constitution did reflect a Montesquieuan principle, perhaps the most fundamental of them all: it provided for a government that would itself be governed by laws, and by laws that conformed to the genius and circumstances of the people.

VIII

POWERS,
PRINCIPLES, AND CONSEQUENCES

IN THE TRUEST SENSE OF THE TERMS, THE reformation of the Constitution

was simultaneously a conservative and a radical act. The word *conservative* derives from the Latin *conservare*, meaning "to guard, defend, preserve." *Radical* derives from the Latin *radix*, meaning "root, base, foundation"; to be radical is to get at the root of a matter. No abstract speculative doctrines could inform such an undertaking, and both for that reason and because of the incompatibilities amongst the doctrines themselves, the political theories and ideologies at the command of the Framers were, as we have seen, of limited practical use. Those theories and ideologies helped to shape the political perspectives of the Framers and helped to define their goals, to be sure; but as Dickinson said, experience, both their own and that of the mother country, provided the surer guide.

Moreover, restructuring the central authority from a simple unicameral Congress into a complex, self-balancing, four-branched institution was only part of the genius of what the Framers did. Quite as important in their efforts to attain their goals—cementing the Union, providing for the common defense, ensuring domestic tranquility, promoting the general welfare, and securing the citizenry in its rights of life, liberty, and property—were the allocations of powers among the branches of the central government and between it and the state governments. In this portion of their work, theory was even less relevant, and experience itself was inadequate: they could rely ultimately only on common sense, their collective wisdom, and their willingness to compromise.

So it was that the Framers brought a vast knowledge of history and the whole long tradition of civic humanism with them to Philadelphia in May of 1787, and that they departed four months later having fashioned a frame of government that necessitated a redefinition of most of the terms in which the theory and ideology of civic humanism had been discussed. Into the bargain, they introduced an entirely new concept to the discourse, that of federalism, and in the doing, created a *novus ordo seclorum:* a new order of the ages.

It is easy to forget that the convention did not start from scratch, but was building upon an existing constitution. Under the Articles of Confederation, Congress had been vested with a variety of powers. One set concerned the military: Congress could appoint and commission officers in the armed services, build and equip a navy, make rules for governing the armed forces, direct their operations, and issue letters of marque and reprisal. In the matter of international relations, it could declare war and make peace, send and receive ambassadors, make treaties and alliances, prescribe rules for captures, and punish piracies and felonies on the high seas. To enforce its admiralty powers, it could establish courts. In domestic affairs, Congress was empowered to regulate the value of coin, to fix uniform standards of weights and measures, to regulate trade and manage all affairs with Indians who were "not members of any of the states," to establish and regulate post offices, to borrow money on the credit of the United States, and to establish courts for settling disputes between states.

Under the Constitution, Congress retained all those powers (though now sharing, as noted, some of them with the president) and was vested with ten additional powers.

Five of these were of relatively minor importance: the powers to establish uniform naturalization and bankruptcy laws, to punish counterfeiting of United States currency or securities,[1] to grant copyrights and patents, to punish offenses against the law of nations, and to acquire and exercise exclusive jurisdiction over a seat of government and other property of the United States. One was important but conditional: the power to protect the several states against domestic violence, on request of the state legislature or, "when the Legislature cannot be convened," on request of the state's chief executive.

The other new powers—taxation, regulation of commerce, regulation of the militias, and the powers implicit in the necessary and proper clause—want closer scrutiny. The taxing power was obviously the most important, for it gave substance and energy to the others. At the convention there was no serious resistance to vesting Congress with broad powers of taxation, though delegates from the southern states, jealously guarding their particular interests, saw to the insertion of certain restrictions. One was that duties on exports were forbidden: against the arguments of Wilson, Gouverneur Morris, Dickinson, and Madison, southerners insisted that their staples be thus exempted, and with the support of the Massachusetts and Connecticut delegations, they carried the point.[2] Another restriction was that "all Duties, Imports and Excises shall be uniform throughout the United States." On August 25 James McHenry and other Marylanders, concerned lest Congress might favor the ports of other states over those of their own, proposed the restriction as part of a larger restriction on the regulation of commerce.[3] The proposal was committed, separated

---

[1] I qualify the word *minor* with a remark by Samuel Johnson that forgery of bonds or currency was "the most dangerous crime in a commercial country" (James Boswell, *The Life of Samuel Johnson*, ed. Bergen Evans [New York, 1952], 340).

[2] Farrand, *Records*, Aug. 16, 21, 2:305-308, 359-364. Madison's opposition would appear to contradict my earlier statement that he almost never voted against the interests of his state, but the appearance is deceptive: he explicitly indicated that an export tax on tobacco could readily be passed along to consumers.

[3] Ibid., Aug. 25, 2:417-418.

from the commercial restriction, reported out, and, on August 31, passed without dissent.[4] But then the committee of style, whether intentionally or inadvertently, omitted the clause from its draft of a constitution. The oversight was noticed and, on September 14, the restriction was restored.[5]

Still another restriction on the taxing power was that "no Capitation or other direct Tax shall be laid except in proportion to the number of Inhabitants," in which slaves were to be reckoned by the three-fifths rule. As the North Carolina delegates reported to Governor Richard Caswell, that meant not only that slaves would not be fully taxed if Congress should resort to head taxes but also that taxes on land would be the same in the southern states as in the "Eastern States," even though "we certainly have, one with another, land of twice the value that they Possess."[6] Indeed, this restriction was so inequitable that, for practical purposes, it virtually denied Congress the power to levy direct taxes altogether. Southerners were able to win such an advantage because they demanded much more and thus could compromise with a position that still favored them. That is, some of them had adamantly insisted upon counting slaves fully in allocating seats in the House of Representatives, upon prohibiting interference in the slave trade, and upon exempting imported slaves from import duties. When they accepted less than what they had demanded in regard to these three points, the tax advantages seemed to be a fair compensation.

The most important limitation upon the taxing power had a strange history. This was the qualification that taxes could be levied only "to pay the Debts and provide for the common Defense and general Welfare of the United States." The phraseology was derived from the language of the Articles of Confederation and was understood as prohibiting the expenditure of money for such "internal im-

[4]Ibid., Aug. 28, 31, 2:437, 473, 481.
[5]Committee of style, ibid., 2:594, and Sept. 14, 2:614.
[6]Blount, Spaight, and Williamson to Governor Richard Caswell, Sept. 18, 1787, ibid., 3:83–84.

provements" as roads and canals, since those must, of necessity, promote the particular welfare of specific states rather than the "general" welfare. Gouverneur Morris, however, had other ideas. In a private conversation with James McHenry and Nathaniel Gorham, he casually remarked that the general-welfare clause would authorize the construction of piers.[7] McHenry was horrified by the implications of so broad an interpretation of the clause, but Morris made a clever attempt to ensure that it would in fact be so interpreted. In drafting article 1, section 8 (as principal penman for the committee of style), Morris itemized the powers of Congress in clauses, separating the clauses by semicolons. He inserted a semicolon between "To lay and collect taxes, duties, imposts and excises" and the qualifying "to pay the debts and provide for the common defense and general welfare." Given the form of the whole section, that would have made the clause a positive grant of power rather than a limitation on the taxing power. Roger Sherman, however, noticed the semicolon and called it to the attention of the other delegates, whereupon a comma was put in its place.[8]

Two final points about the taxing power need be made. One is that the states were prohibited from levying duties on imports, though they continued to be free to collect all other forms of taxes. Because import duties were by far the most bountiful source of tax revenues, this tipped the federal-state balance of power considerably in the federal direction and all but assured that Congress would find it necessary to assume responsibility for the Revolutionary

[7] McHenry's Notes, Sept. 6, ibid., 2:529–530.

[8] Committee of style, ibid., 2:594; final version, ibid., 2:655. That Sherman discovered Morris's "trick" and was responsible for the change was stated by Albert Gallatin in Congress in 1798 (ibid., 3:379). Gallatin refers only to "a member from Connecticut, now deceased," but Sherman is obviously meant, since he died in 1793 and Johnson and Ellsworth were still alive in 1798. For an elaborate analysis of the general-welfare clause see Madison to Andrew Stevenson, Nov. 17, 1830 (ibid., 3:483–493). It is to be noted that even Hamilton, an advocate of "loose construction" though he was, thought that Congress could not authorize the building of such internal improvements as canals, and he proposed a constitutional amendment granting such power (see Hamilton to Jonathan Dayton, Oct.–Nov., 1799, in Syrett, *Papers of Hamilton*, 23:603).

War debts of the states. The other point is that except for
the restrictions noted above, the taxing power of Congress
was unlimited. This meant, among other things, that
Congress could promote manufacturing through protective
tariffs and could even create a full-fledged mercantilistic
system if it so desired. Thus, as far as systems of political
economy were concerned, the Constitution gave Congress
a blank check.

The statement is no sooner made than it wants qualification because of the restrictions attached to the second great
new power vested in Congress, the power to regulate
interstate and foreign commerce. As has been noted, many
southern delegates in the convention insisted upon a
provision that Congress not be allowed to pass "navigation
acts" except by a two-thirds majority in both houses.
Several New Englanders struck an agreement with South
Carolina and Georgia planters, whereby the planters
helped to defeat the proposed two-thirds clause and New
Englanders supported the arrangements noted earlier concerning slavery and taxation. The delegates from Maryland,
who were most militantly concerned in regard to commercial regulation, then sponsored a limitation on the regulatory power, which was incorporated into article 1, section 9:
"No Preference shall be given by any Regulation of Commerce or Revenue to the Ports of one State over those of
another: nor shall Vessels bound to, or from, one State, be
obliged to enter, clear, or pay Duties in another." That
clause, together with certain restrictions on the powers of
the states, ensured that no matter what system of political
economy was adopted, internally the United States would
be the largest area of free trade in the world.[9]

The third important new power, regulation of the
militias, was fraught with ideological overtones. The republican ideologues in the convention, expressing a view that
would be echoed by many opponents of the Constitution,
objected that congressional control over the militias would

---

[9]Committee of detail, in Farrand, *Records*, 2:181, 183; McHenry's Notes, Aug.
6, 7, ibid., 2:191, 211; ibid., Aug. 16, 22, 24, 25, 28, 29, 31, 2:308, 374–375, 400,
415–418, 437, 449–453, 480–481.

result in tyranny. The Connecticut foederalists Ellsworth and Sherman likewise objected to such control, as did Dickinson, on the ground that the states needed to be able to defend themselves. The ranks of the foederalists were divided, however, for the South Carolina delegates (like those of Georgia and New Hampshire) were acutely concerned about their military vulnerability and wanted even stronger national control of the militias than the Constitution provided. Moreover, the archrepublicans from Virginia had little fear of such control, the discipline of the Virginia militia being notoriously lax. And thus, though the anti-Federalist Richard Henry Lee could declare that "the militia are the people," in the same sense that the Greek army had been the *polis*, provision for congressional power to organize, arm, and discipline the militias and to employ them to enforce the laws of the Union, as well as to suppress insurrections and repel invasions, found its way into the Constitution. Discontent with the provision, however, would later lead to the adoption of the Second Amendment.[10]

The fourth significant new grant of power was the power "to make all Laws which shall be necessary and proper for carrying into execution" the enumerated powers. Some such clause was indispensable, given the decision to itemize the powers of Congress; and in the convention only Gerry, Randolph, and Mason expressed objections to it.[11] In the contests over ratification, however, opponents of the Constitution would repeatedly charge that the clause amounted to an unlimited grant of power to Congress; but then, after ratification, they reversed themselves and, to justify a narrow interpretation of the powers

[10] Ibid., Aug. 18, 21, 22, 23, 2:330-333, 356, 377, 385-388. For anti-Federalist complaints about congressional regulation of the militias see, among others, Storing, *Complete Anti-Federalist*, 2:58, 118, 159-160, 366, 3:36, 202-203, 4:36, 6:35. The Lee quotation is ibid., 2:342. Regarding the Second Amendment see Robert E. Shalhope, "The Ideological Origins of the Second Amendment," *Journal of American History* 69 (1982): 599-614; Lawrence Delbert Cross, "An Armed Community: The Origins and Meaning of the Right To Bear Arms," ibid. 71 (1984): 22-42; Shalhope and Cross, "The Second Amendment and the Right to Bear Arms: An Exchange," ibid. 71 (1984): 587-593.

[11] Farrand, *Records*, Sept. 10, 15, 2:563, 633, 640.

of Congress, insisted that the word "necessary" meant indispensably and absolutely required, which was a test of constitutionality that almost no enactment would be able to pass.[12]

In addition to allocating powers, the Framers restricted or prohibited the exercise of certain powers, as regarded both the central authority and the states. Of the specific limitations on the powers of the national/federal government, six concerned property rights in one fashion or another: the prohibition against interference in the slave trade before 1808, the ban on export duties, the restriction regarding direct taxes, the prohibition against preferential treatment of ports, the ban on taxation of interstate commerce, and the prohibition of corruption of the blood. Six more were protective of liberty: the prohibition of the suspension of the writ of habeas corpus except in times of rebellion or invasion, the prohibition of bills of attainder and ex post facto laws, the provision for impeachment of all civil officers, the provision for jury trials in criminal cases, the narrow definition of treason, and the prohibition of religious qualifications for officeholding. Five more restrictive provisions may be regarded as gestures toward adhering to republican maxims: that money bills must originate in the House of Representatives, that no money be spent except by appropriations voted by Congress, that military appropriations be limited to two years, and that dual officeholding and titles of nobility be forbidden.

None of these elicited much discussion in the convention, except for those already mentioned and the prohibitions against bills of attainder and ex post facto laws. Gerry and McHenry proposed that pair of prohibitions on August 22. There was general agreement about bills of attainder,

[12] For examples of anti-Federalist assertions that the necessary and proper clause gave unlimited powers see Storing, *Complete Anti-Federalist*, 2:365–367, 3:24, 6:17, 113. For the classical argument that *necessary* meant *indispensably necessary* see Jefferson's opinion on the constitutionality of the Bank of the United States, in Commager, *Documents*, 159–160; see also Hamilton's rebuttal, in Syrett, *Papers of Hamilton*, 8:97ff., and especially at 102–103.

but Gouverneur Morris and Ellsworth said it was unnecessary to prohibit ex post facto laws, since every lawyer would agree that they were "void of themselves." Wilson added that to mention ex post facto would "proclaim that we are ignorant of the first principles of Legislation." Daniel Carroll retorted that whatever the light in which ex post facto laws might be viewed by lawyers, "the State Legislatures had passed them, and they had taken effect." Williamson added that a provision against them in the North Carolina constitution had been violated, but that a prohibition was useful anyway because "the Judges can take hold of it." The prohibition was then passed by a comfortable margin.[13]

In placing any such restrictions in the Constitution, the Framers were introducing an element of ambiguity and were opening the door for the charge that they were being inconsistent. They deliberately refrained from putting a bill of rights in the instrument, on the logical grounds that the document established a government of limited, enumerated powers, and thus, as Hamilton put it, that there was no point in declaring "that things shall not be done which there is no power to do." This argument was criticized by pointing to the prohibitions against granting titles of nobility, against suspension of habeas corpus, and the like. Yet all the constitutional prohibitions were of actions that, as British history had shown, could in fact have been legitimately taken in the absence of a specific denial of the authority.[14]

The placing of constitutional restrictions upon the powers of the states was qualitatively a different matter.

[13] Farrand, *Records*, Aug. 22, 2:375–376.

[14] *Federalist* number 84, 559. There was British precedent also for the violation of every manner of rights, and thus the addition of the Bill of Rights was not entirely illogical. Though Rutland's *Bill of Rights* is a good survey of the subject, the origin of the Bill of Rights has not been examined as thoroughly as have the roots of much of the body of the Constitution. For notable exceptions see the articles by Shalhope, cited in n. 10 above; William Cuddihy and B. Carmon Hardy, "A Man's House Was Not His Castle: Origins of the Fourth Amendment to the United States Constitution," *William and Mary Quarterly* 37 (1980): 371–400; Walter Berns, *The First Amendment and the Future of American Democracy* (New York, 1976), 2–32; and Russell L. Caplan, "The History and Meaning of the Ninth Amendment," *Virginia Law Review* 69 (1983): 223–268.

The powers of the state legislatures, within the confines of their territorial jurisdictions, were quite as unlimited as those of the British Parliament, except for a few specific restrictions contained in the state constitutions. As James Wilson put it, in the state constitutions the people did not delegate enumerated powers but rather "invested their representatives with every right and authority which they did not in explicit terms reserve."[15] The legislatures had further limited their own powers by adopting the Articles of Confederation. Thenceforth they could not, without the consent of Congress, send or receive ambassadors or otherwise treat with foreign crowns or states, establish treaties among themselves, maintain armies or ships of war, or engage in war except if invaded; they could not grant letters of marque and reprisal except after Congress had declared war; they could not lay imposts or other duties contrary to treaties negotiated and ratified by Congress; and they could not grant titles of nobility.

The Constitution reaffirmed those restrictions—in most instances making them absolute or nearly so—and added a number of others. The states were, for practical purposes, forbidden to tax or restrain interstate or foreign commerce, which brought about a fundamental shift of power. Like the national/federal government, the states were prohibited from passing ex post facto laws and bills of attainder; in regard to the states, however, these prohibitions were aimed more at protecting property rights (recall the wartime confiscations) than at protecting liberty. The other new restrictions were designed exclusively to prevent infringement upon property rights by the legislatures. Specifically, the states were forbidden to coin money, to emit bills of credit, to make anything but gold or silver coin legal tender in payment of debts, and to pass any law impairing the obligation of contracts.

Few delegates contested any of these restrictions but one, and several wanted in addition to forbid Congress the power to issue paper money. The exception is the contract

---

[15] *Pennsylvania and the Federal Constitution, 1787-1788*, ed. John Bach McMaster and Frederick D. Stone (Philadelphia, 1888), 143-144.

clause, whose history is shrouded in mystery. The first proposal regarding it arose late in the convention. On August 28 the delegates voted to amend an article of the committee of detail's report to read, "No state shall coin money, nor emit bills of credit, nor make any thing but gold & silver coin a tender in payment of debts." King then moved to add, "in the words used in the Ordinance of Congs establishing new States, a prohibition on the States to interfere in private contracts."[16] The language of the Northwest Ordinance to which King referred is significant: "And, in the just preservation of rights and property, it is understood and declared, that no law ought ever to be made, or have force in the said territory, that shall, in any manner whatever, interfere with or affect private contracts or engagements, *bona fide*, and without fraud, previously formed."[17] It is to be observed that the use of the words "*bona fide*, and without fraud" would have left abundant room for preserving the fair-value and just-price theories of contract.

The proposal met with a generally negative reaction, though not at all for that reason. Gouverneur Morris objected that "this would be going too far." The federal courts would prevent abuses within their jurisdiction, he said, but within a state "a majority must rule, whatever may be the mischief done among themselves." Mason agreed with Morris. Madison expressed mixed feelings. Wilson supported the motion but stressed that only *retrospective* interferences were to be banned. Madison responded with a question, "Is not that already done by the prohibition of ex post facto laws." Rutledge picked up on the suggestion and offered as a substitute for King's motion the words "nor pass bills of attainder or ex post facto laws." This was approved by a seven to three vote, and thus the proposed contract clause was dropped.[18] On the

[16] Farrand, *Records*, Aug. 28, 2:439.

[17] Northwest Ordinance, in Commager, *Documents*, 131.

[18] Farrand, *Records*, Aug. 28, 2:439–440. There is some confusion in the record at this point. Madison recorded Rutledge's motion as prohibiting "retrospective laws"; the Journal recorded it as prohibiting ex post facto laws. Presumably Madison was in error: (1) because Madison did not know that ex post facto laws

next day, John Dickinson announced that he had looked up
"ex post facto" in Blackstone and had found that the term
"related to criminal cases only; that they would not consequently restrain the States from retrospective laws in civil
cases, and that some further provision for this purpose
would be requisite."[19]

The convention, however, did not get around to making
"some further provision" or even to considering the subject again. Instead, disregarding the rejection of King's
motion, the committee of style inserted it into the Constitution. That the committee would presume to include in the
finished document features that the convention had either
not approved or had expressly rejected can be explained by
two circumstances. First, the delegates had no list of what
they had agreed to: they had only a general record of the
votes and proceedings, which made detailed checking on
the committee of style tedious and difficult.[20] Second, by
the time the committee had finished its draft, the delegates
were tired, harassed, and eager to finish the work and go
home.[21] In any event, the contract clause was apparently
the work of the five members of the committee of style
rather than of the body of the convention.

But there are other mysteries about the clause. Morris
did most of the work of the draftsmanship, and one might
thus assume that he was the author of the contract clause;
he was obviously audacious enough to do such a thing. But
Morris had outspokenly opposed the contract clause that
King had proposed, and the ground of his objection applied
with equal or greater force to the final version of the clause.
That leaves, as possible originators, the other four members
of the committee: Madison, Johnson, King, and Hamilton.

related only to criminal cases and (2) because if the convention had voted to
prohibit "retrospective" laws, Dickinson's comment on the next day would have
made no sense. In any event, the committee of style had the Journal's record, not
Madison's, to work with.

[19] Ibid., Aug. 29, 2:448-449.

[20] The scholar has the advantage over the delegates in this respect, for Max
Farrand compiled the resolutions from the proceedings (ibid., 2:565-580).

[21] See Mason to Washington, Oct. 7, 1787, Madison to Washington, Oct. 18,
1787, and Madison to Jefferson, Oct. 24, 1787, ibid., 3:102, 129, 135-136, for
descriptions of the mood toward the end of the convention.

The recorded speeches and extant writings of Madison and Johnson contain nothing that would suggest that either of them regarded the contract clause as other than a redundancy, a reemphasis of the constitutional prohibitions against paper money and tender laws; and thus there is no reason to suppose that either would have proposed that it be added.[22] King had proposed the original clause, but as indicated, the qualifications he had placed on it would greatly have reduced its potency. That leaves Hamilton as a possible source.

Hamilton's earlier career as a lawyer, his later conduct as secretary of the treasury, his reasoning in his great reports, and his avid participation in a movement to modernize the law of contractual relationships all accord with an inference that he would have advocated the enshrining in fundamental law of a broad, modern conception of contracts. He had experienced firsthand the advantages of regarding corporate charters as contracts, for he had represented stockholders after Pennsylvania had revoked the charter of the Bank of North America in 1785. Later, in an advisory opinion regarding the Yazoo land purchases, he would formulate the first thoroughly reasoned argument that the contract clause was intended to apply to public grants and charters as well as to private agreements. Hamilton was the only member of the committee who thought along such lines, except insofar as he could persuade the others. He could be persuasive, and in addition to his gifts for argument, he was a long-time intimate friend of Gouverneur Morris's, he held King almost in a hypnotic spell, and he was on intimate political (though not personal) terms with Madison. But to suggest that Hamilton was the source of the contract clause is only a suggestion; we cannot know.[23]

22 Elliot, *Debates*, 3:471–481; *Federalist* number 44, 291.

23 McDonald, *Hamilton*, 80–82, 311–313. Hamilton's opinion in the Yazoo case is published in C. Peter Magrath, *Yazoo: Law and Politics in the New Republic: The Case of Fletcher v. Peck* (Providence, R.I., 1966), 149–150. Hamilton would have allowed setting aside some contracts in equity, but none in law; *Federalist* number 80, in Syrett, *Papers of Hamilton*, 4:671. Wilson, it should be added, is another prospective candidate for author, even though he was not a member of the committee. He

In the public debates on the Constitution, two interpretations of the contract clause were advanced, and neither was the one that Hamilton would offer in his advisory opinion (and that Chief Justice John Marshall would confirm in *Fletcher* v. *Peck*). The most common view was that the prohibition against legislative impairment of contractual obligations was simply a catchall extension of the bans on paper money and legal-tender laws. As James Wilson put it during the Pennsylvania ratifying convention, "There are other ways of avoiding payment of debts," such as "instalment acts, and other acts of a similar effect." Madison regarded the clause in a similar, though somewhat broader, light in *Federalist* number 44. He treated it together with the other restrictions in article 1, section 10, as being designed to stop "the fluctuating policy which has directed the public councils." Madison attributed "legislative interferences, in cases affecting personal rights," to "enterprising and influential speculators" whose activities gained profit for themselves at the expense of "the more-industrious and less-informed part of the community." Luther Martin, himself an enterprising and influential speculator who opposed ratification, interpreted the contract clause in essentially the same way that Wilson and Madison did, but he painted the implications in different colors. The clause, Martin said, would prevent the states from stopping "the wealthy creditor and the moneyed man from totally destroying the poor, though industrious debtor."[24]

Quite a different construction of the contract clause was advanced by opponents of the Constitution in Virginia and North Carolina. In Virginia, George Mason and Patrick Henry interpreted the clause as applying to public as well as private obligations, and they objected that it would necessitate the redemption of old continental bills of credit, which had depreciated to a thousand for one and had long

was on intimate terms with Hamilton and Morris, and he also advanced the argument that a legislative grant was a contract (see the Philadelphia *Evening Herald*, Sept. 7, 8, 1785, Apr. 1, 1786). See also McCloskey, *Works of Wilson*, 1:175–176, where Wilson argues that acts of Parliament were contracts.

[24] Wilson and Martin are quoted from Elliot, *Debates*, 1:376 and 2:492; Madison, from *Federalist* number 44, 291.

since ceased to circulate. The face value of those bills had been over $200 million, and Mason and Henry argued that the resulting tax burden would be crushing. Madison and other defenders of the Constitution insisted, not to the satisfaction of their opponents, that article 5 (making public debts "as valid" under the Constitution as under the Confederation) covered the continental paper and that it was unaffected by article 1, section 10. In North Carolina, opponents of the Constitution reiterated the argument of Henry and Mason but added a twist of their own. North Carolina, like several other states, had issued paper currency and had made it legal tender, and obligations payable in that paper had formed the basis of a large number of contracts. The ban on paper money, anti-Federalists pointed out, would outlaw that currency, and the legal-tender clause would alter those contracts; and yet the contract clause itself prohibited them from being impaired. Champions of ratification could offer no satisfactory rebuttal, for the last-minute insertion of the clause had in fact created a temporary contradiction.[25]

One more point about the restrictions on the powers of the states wants making. Madison's interpretation of the general purpose of article 1, section 10—that it was intended as a check upon "the fluctuating policy which has directed the public councils"—accords with the evidence contained in the records of the Constitutional Convention. That being so, it is possible to regard the supreme-law clause as vesting the judiciary, both federal and state, with the veto power over state legislation which Madison had wanted to vest in Congress or jointly in Congress and the Supreme Court. In other words, article 1, section 10, taken together with the supreme-law clause in article 6, can be interpreted as having been designed to give to the courts the power to review state laws but not acts of Congress. Such an interpretation, to be sure, is contrary to Hamilton's argument in *Federalist* number 78 and to almost all constitutional scholarship. And yet, when the supreme-law clause

25 Elliot, *Debates*, 3:471–481, 4:156–157, 168–175.

was introduced in the convention, it was expressly offered as a substitute for the proposed congressional veto on state legislation;[26] and shortly after the convention had adjourned, Madison tacitly confirmed this interpretation in a letter to Jefferson and repeated his conviction that the substitution would prove to be inadequate.[27] Moreover, the belief that the supreme-law clause established the power of judicial review over state laws but not over acts of Congress obviously had widespread currency, as is attested by the intensely hostile reaction in the Congress and in the press on the two occasions on which, before the Civil War, the Supreme Court dared to declare an act of Congress unconstitutional.

The constitutional reallocation of powers created a new form of government, unprecedented under the sun. Every previous national authority either had been centralized or else had been a confederation of sovereign constituent states. The new American system was neither one nor the other: it was a mixture of both. Madison developed the variations on this theme in *Federalist* number 39. After first calling attention to the checks inherent in having officials in the several branches be elected for periods of differing lengths, he analyzed the Constitution in respect to "the foundation on which it is to be established; to the sources from which its ordinary powers are to be drawn; to the operation of those powers; to the extent of them; and to the authority by which future changes in the government are to be introduced." He concluded that the Constitution was federal in regard to the first and fourth of these criteria, mixed in regard to the second and fifth, and national only in regard to the third. In sum, it was partly national, partly federal—not the purely national form that Madison himself had championed during the convention.[28]

[26] Farrand, *Records*, July 17, 2:27–29; and Luther Martin's Reply to the Landholder, Mar. 19, 1788, ibid., 3:286–287.

[27] Ibid., July 17, 2:27–28; Madison to Jefferson, Oct. 24, 1787, ibid., 3:134.

[28] *Federalist*, 245–250.

If Madison found it expedient not to divulge that he had opposed the very system he was now defending—and it seems probable that a purely national system would never have been ratified—John Dickinson similarly found it prudent not to repeat out of doors his arguments in favor of a mixed system. In his "Letters of Fabius" (notice the pseudonym, which suggested to his readers that the Constitution was a slow, cautious, conservative undertaking), Dickinson made no comments about using the states as structural substitutes for the English baronies or about fashioning the Senate in the mold of the House of Lords, which was indeed the subject of charges made by many opponents of ratification. Rather, he offered another justification of the partly national, partly federal system. The principle underlying it, he wrote, was "that a territory of such extent as that of United America, could not be safely and advantageously governed, but by a combination of republics, each retaining all the rights of supreme sovereignty, excepting such as ought to be contributed to the union." To enable these republics to preserve those sovereignties, they were "represented in a body by themselves, and with equal suffrage."[29]

In defending these arrangements, the Framers had to work their way around a knotty theoretical problem. Blackstone and many another commentator had insisted that sovereignty, the supreme law-making power, was by definition indivisible; the cliché, repeated both in England and in America, was that it was "a solecism in politics for two coordinate sovereignties to exist together," for that would be "*imperium* in *imperio*."[30] Hamilton had advanced the same idea at the convention, declaring flatly that "Two Sovereignties can not co-exist within the same limits." Yet in *Federalist* number 34 he asserted that in the Roman republic sovereignty had in fact been divided between the Comitia centuriata, in which voting "was so arranged as to give a superiority to the patrician interest," and the Comitia

29 Farrand, *Records*, 3:304.
30 See, for examples, Storing, *Complete Anti-Federalist*, 2:99, 3:183–185, 4:79, 5:179.

tributa, in which "the plebian interest had an entire pre-
dominancy." These were not branches of the same legislature, Hamilton said, but were "distinct and independent
legislatures, . . . each having power to *annul* or *repeal* the
acts of the other. . . . And yet these two legislatures
coexisted for ages, and the Roman republic attained to the
utmost height of human greatness."[31]

Hamilton was able to reverse himself in that manner
because he—along with Wilson, Ellsworth, and various
others—had conceived of a means of attacking the problem
in an ingenious new way. The key to the new approach was
the proposition that sovereignty embraced a large number
and a wide variety of different specific powers: obviously
these specific powers could be assigned to different governments, to different branches of the same government, or to
different persons serving within the same branch of a
government. Hamilton spelled out the implications in his
opinion on the constitutionality of the Bank of the United
States. "The powers of sovereignty," Hamilton wrote, "are
in this country divided between the National and State
Governments," and "each of the *portions* of powers delegated to the one or to the other . . . is . . . sovereign *with
regard to its proper objects.*" It followed from this "that each
has sovereign power as to *certain things,* and not as to *other
things.* To deny that the Government of the United States
has sovereign power as to its declared purposes & trusts,
because its power does not extend to all cases," Hamilton
continued, would also be to deny that the states retained
sovereignty "in any case," because they were forbidden to
do a number of things. "And thus the United States would
furnish the singular spectacle of a *political society* without
sovereignty, or of a people *governed* without *government.*"[32]

There was one crucial feature of the scheme of things
which, since it lay beyond the argument he was making on
that occasion, Hamilton declined to address. Sovereignty,
in its eighteenth-century signification, was absolute: sovereignty comprehended the power to command anything

---

[31] Farrand, *Records,* June 18, 1:287; *Federalist,* 204–205.
[32] Syrett, *Papers of Hamilton,* 8:98.

and everything that was naturally possible. No one contended that the combined powers of the state and federal governments were absolute, for there were some powers that remained beyond the reach of both. Logically, those powers must reside somewhere else. The Framers made clear where that was—and incidentally pointed to where sovereignty had devolved upon independence—in the procedure they prescribed for ratification of the Constitution.

Article 7 provided that the "Ratification of the Conventions of nine States, shall be sufficient for the Establishment of this Constitution between the States so ratifying the Same." That provision by-passed the prescribed method for amending the Articles of Confederation, which required that amendments be proposed by Congress and be approved by the legislatures of all thirteen states. It was not, however, as many enemies of the Constitution charged and as some scholars have asserted, either "illegal" or a usurpation.[33] In a resolution appended to the Constitution and "laid before Congress," the convention recommended that Congress forward the document to the states and that "it should afterwards be submitted to a Convention of Delegates, chosen in each State by the People thereof, under the Recommendation of its Legislature, for their Assent and Ratification."[34] Congress unanimously resolved to follow that recommendation,[35] and the legislatures of all thirteen states voted to abide by it. In so doing, Congress and the legislatures approved article 7 of the Constitution and thereby constructively amended the Articles of Confederation in regard to the amendment process; and they did so in accordance with the stipulations in the Articles themselves.

The Constitution was submitted to state conventions for several reasons. One was political: the revised procedure simplified ratification. Another was theoretical: as Madison pointed out during the first week of the convention, a constitution that was ratified by the legislatures could be

---

[33] See, for example, Storing, *Complete Anti-Federalist*, 1:13.

[34] Farrand, *Records*, 2:665.

[35] The Secretary of Congress to the Several States, Sept. 28, 1787, in Burnett, *Letters*, 8:650.

construed as being only a treaty "among the Governments of Independent States," and thus it could be held that "a breach of any one article, by any of the parties, absolved the other parties" from any further obligation. Accordingly, Madison urged that the Constitution be submitted to "the supreme authority of the people themselves."[36] But it could not be submitted to the people of the United States *as* people of the United States because of two prior commitments, one theoretical and one legal. The theoretical commitment was that no matter how Locke is read, the states as political societies, as opposed to the governments thereof, had not ceased to exist upon the declaring of independence. The legal commitment was that each of the states already had a constitution. The Constitution amended each of the state constitutions in a number of ways, and if it were adopted by a majority vote of the whole people, the people in some states would be altering both the political societies and the constitutions of other states. This, in the nature of things, they could not have the authority to do. The Constitution must, then, be submitted for ratification by each of the thirteen political societies, which is to say by the people of the several states in their capacities as people of the several states. This unmistakably implied that the source of sovereignty was the people of the states and that the residue of sovereignty that was committed neither to the national/federal nor to the state governments remained in them—an implication that was subsequently made explicit by the Tenth Amendment.

Such a compact was also something new. It was not Lockean, for the Lockean compact was between the people, on one side, and the prince, sovereign, or rulers on the other. Nor was it a compact among the people to govern themselves, as some modern scholars have contended.[37]

[36] Farrand, *Records*, June 5, 1:122–123.

[37] Herbert Storing, in his *Complete Anti-Federalist*, 1:12–14 and the notes at 1:82, argues that the ratification procedure rested on the "assumption that the American states are not several political wholes . . . but are, and always were from the moment of their separation from the King of England, parts of one whole." His reasoning disregards the prior commitments, is replete with contradictions, and is contrary to the position taken by most Federalists in 1787–1788, as

Rather, it was a compact among political societies, which were themselves, according to a Lockean principle, indissoluble—a principle that is explicitly confirmed in the Constitution itself by the provision in article 4, section 3, which prevents the states from being divided without their consent, and is implicitly confirmed by article 5, which exempts equal suffrage by states in the Senate from the possibility of amendment.

Because it was a new kind of compact, there were no guidelines, either in theory or in history, as to whether the compact could be dissolved, and if so, on what conditions. The Supreme Court would rule in *Texas* v. *White*, almost a century later, that the Constitution "looks to an indestructible Union, composed of indestructible states." No less important a Framer than Gouverneur Morris, however, argued to the contrary: during the War of 1812 he contended that secession, under certain circumstances, was entirely constitutional.[38] So, too, did the southern states in 1860–1861; significantly, those states declared their secession from the constitutional Union by means of precisely the same instrumentality as that by which they had entered it, namely, conventions elected for the purpose. Closer to the founding era, many a public figure during the 1790s declared that the states could interpose their power between their citizens and the power of the federal government, and talk of secession was not unknown.

Storing's own notes indicate. The preamble to the Constitution, to be sure, reads "We the People of the United States . . . do ordain and establish this Constitution," and that language is strikingly different from the listing of the states in the Articles of Confederation. That does not prove anything, however; and it is interesting to note that in the instances in the body of the Constitution in which the construction requires a decision in the matter as to singularity versus plurality, the document opts for the latter.

[38] Morris, "Address to the People of the State of New York" (1814), quoted in Bradford, *Worthy Company*, 92; Max M. Mintz, *Gouverneur Morris and the American Revolution* (Norman, Okla., 1970), 239; Morris to King, Jan. 7, 1815, in King, *Life of King*, 5:458–459, but see also King to Morris, ibid., 5:467–469, in which King disagrees on policy grounds without reference to the constitutional issue; *The Diary and Letters of Gouverneur Morris*, ed. Anne Cary Morris, 2 vols. (New York, 1888), 2:545, 547, 551–552, 556, 557–559, 565, 572, 574, 578, 582. See also James M. Banner, Jr., *To the Hartford Convention: The Federalists and the Origins of Party Politics in Massachusetts, 1789–1815* (New York, 1970), 118–121.

But such a question, like the earlier question of independence, could be settled only by the arbitrament of force,
and the Framers' whole purpose was to establish a government based upon consent. Having been through one Machiavellian return to first principles and having seen the havoc
it had wrought, they were anxious to avoid another. It was
toward that end that they addressed such careful attention
to the niceties of legitimizing the Constitution, and it was
toward the same end that they specified the legitimate
means for constitutional change in future. In that sense, the
establishment of the Constitution completed and perfected
the Revolution.

Another question about the nature of the constitutional
Union is likewise problematical. The compact was among
previously existing political societies, but it was expressly
provided that new political societies might be formed and
admitted to the Union. In contemplation were the creation
of new states in the Northwest Territory and in what would
become Kentucky and Tennessee. That is clear both from
the debates in the convention and from the first paragraph
of article 4, section 3 (though working out that section had
involved considerable rancor and a movement, led by
Luther Martin, to permit Congress to break up the larger
states without their consent). But the new states thus
provided for would be within the existing territorial confines of the United States, and there was an unspoken
assumption among most Americans, including the Framers, that some day the United States would acquire Canada,
Louisiana, and the Floridas. Some of the Framers, most
influentially Gouverneur Morris, wanted to discourage the
expansion of the population into that "remote wilderness,"
partly because expansion would retard intensive economic
development in the older areas and partly because experience had convinced them that frontiersmen were the least
desirable and least governable of citizens. Accordingly,
Morris proposed that territory acquired in future be forever
governed as provinces, with no prospect of statehood.
He was unable to carry the point directly, but
he deliberately phrased the first clause of the second

paragraph of article 4, section 3, in such a way as to make possible permanent central control of new territories: ''The Congress shall have Power to dispose of and make all needful Rules and Regulations respecting the Territory or other Property belonging to the United States.''[39]

Morris's position was entirely contrary to the tenet of agrarian republicanism which held that territorial expansion was essential so as to keep agriculture paramount to other forms of economic activity; but the clause went unnoticed in the contests over ratification of the Constitution. When it at last became relevant, upon the occasion of the Louisiana Purchase, shifts in constitutional positions became necessary. Until that time, agrarian republicans, under the leadership of Jefferson and Madison, had carried the compact-among-states doctrine of the origins of the Constitution far beyond what could be justified historically or logically. To combat various Federalist measures that they regarded as pernicious and to justify state resistance to those measures, they insisted that the Constitution was not merely a compact among members of different political societies but, rather, was one between sovereign states as sovereign states, as the Articles of Confederation had been. When the United States acquired Louisiana, however— which was constitutionally justifiable under the treaty-making power—the Republicans faced a dilemma. Their ideology told them to provide for dividing the Louisiana Territory into states, so as to make settlement attractive. Their theory of the nature of the Union told them to interpret article 4, section 3, as Morris had intended for it to be interpreted, because otherwise the Union would ultimately consist of more states than had been parties to the original compact, and their theory would be reduced to rubble. They followed the dictates of agrarianism over those of constitutional scruples; and when they did so,

[39] Morris to Henry W. Livingston, Nov. 25, Dec. 4, 1803, in Farrand, *Records*, 3:401–404. Regarding the ubiquity of the assumption that the United States would ultimately acquire the areas mentioned see Alexander DeConde, *This Affair of Louisiana* (Baton Rouge, La., 1978).

Federalists reversed themselves and took up the compact-among-states doctrine in resistance.[40]

Federalists and Republicans. It was not entirely true that, as Jefferson would aver in his Inaugural Address, all Americans were simultaneously federalists and republicans, with the lower-case "f" and "r"; but it was nearly so. Both terms, however, with their variants, acquired new meanings upon the establishment of the Constitution. Earlier, *federal*—as well as *foederal, federation, federalist*—had been used in two principal ways in America, one being neutral and nonideological, the other expressing a political stance. The neutral usage was interchangeable with confederation; it was descriptive of a league of otherwise autonomous states for purposes of mutual defense, trade, or any other shared objective. The nonneutral usage was more or less interchangeable with *nationalist* or *continentalist* or *unionist;* as the Pennsylvania anti-Federalist George Bryan wrote, "The name of Federalists, or Federal men, grew up at New York and the eastern states, some time before the calling of the Convention, to denominate such as were attached to the general support of the United States, in opposition to those who preferred local and particular advantage." In that sense it was appropriate for champions of the Constitution to designate themselves as Federalists and to call their opponents anti-Federalists—though it was equally appropriate, in light of the neutral definition and of the transfers of power inherent in ratification of the Constitution, that some Anti-Federalists should insist that they were acting on "true *foederal principles*" and that Federalists might properly be called consolidationists. In any event, after the adoption of the Constitution, a federal system meant one in which sovereignty was divided; thenceforth, only *confederation* was used to describe a league of sovereign entities.[41]

[40] Banner, *To the Hartford Convention,* 109–121.
[41] Storing, *Complete Anti-Federalist,* 1:9–11, provides a careful analysis of the uses of *federal.* See also *Federalist* number 9.

As for *republic* and *republican*, we have surveyed various understandings of those terms; and it should be obvious that none of them is applicable to the national/federal government established by the Constitution. Anti-Federalists repeatedly attacked the Constitution on that ground, in two interrelated ways. One was that history and theory alike taught that republican forms of government were suitable only to small territories and among relatively homogeneous peoples. Only a small republic could maintain the voluntary attachment of the people and a voluntary obedience to its laws, make government responsible to the people, and inculcate the people with republican virtue. In addition, anti-Federalists pointed out that the Constitution violated contemporary republican principles in an assortment of particulars, ranging from an improper mixture of legislative and executive powers to the lack of a bill of rights; and they charged that in the absence of voluntary obedience to the laws, the national government would be compelled to force obedience by means of large standing armies.[42]

Federalists sought to counter such arguments; but to do so, they must coin new definitions of what a republic was. Hamilton faced the issue in *Federalist* number 9. Had it been necessary for the United States to have copied directly from the ancient models, Hamilton wrote, he would have preferred to abandon the republican experiment altogether, for "the petty republics of Greece and Italy . . . were kept in a state of perpetual vibration between the extremes of tyranny and anarchy." Over the centuries, however, "the science of politics . . . has received great improvement." The ancients knew nothing, or knew but imperfectly, about "various principles . . . now well understood," such as the

[42] Storing, *Complete Anti-Federalist*, 1:15–21, gives a thorough summary of anti-Federalist thinking on this subject. Strangely, however, Storing says in a note (1:83 n. 7) that classical republicanism was "strikingly absent from the Anti-Federalist thought" and that anti-Federalists were liberals who sought "individual liberty, not the promotion of virtue or the fostering of some organic common good." That interpretation is directly contrary to what anti-Federalists said endlessly in the text, especially at 1:19–21. Storing's treatment of the role of religion and its role in maintaining republican virtue is especially confused.

separation of powers, checks and balances, "courts composed of judges holding their offices during good behavior," and the "representation of the people in the legislature by deputies of their own election." These "wholly new discoveries," Hamilton contended, were "powerful means, by which the excellences of republican government may be retained and its imperfections lessened or avoided."[43] In actuality, those "new discoveries" had excellent moderating effects upon mixed governments, but they had nothing whatever to do with the question, whether the American national/federal government was or was not republican. Hamilton was able to go part of the way toward connecting republicanism with the constitutional order by pointing out similarities between the American system and the ancient Lycian confederacy, which Montesquieu had regarded as the best of the confederated Greek republics. After that, however, Hamilton abandoned the subject; to him the whole question was one of speculative theory, not "science."[44]

Madison was more persistent. In *Federalist* number 14 he attempted a bald-faced redefinition of terms. One must distinguish between a republic and a democracy, he wrote. "In a democracy, the people meet and exercise the government in person; in a republic, they assemble and administer it by their representatives and agents. A democracy, consequently, will be confined to a small spot. A republic may be extended over a large region." It was a mistake, propagated by "subjects either of an absolute or limited monarchy," to cite as specimens of republics "the turbulent democracies of ancient Greece and modern Italy." Most "of the popular governments of antiquity were of the democratic species," Madison insisted.[45] Knowing full well (and doubtless recognizing that his readers also knew full well) that his argument would not wash—because some of the "popular governments" to which he referred were aristocracies or oligarchies, some employed the representative principle,

[43] *Federalist*, 47–49.
[44] Ibid., 50–53.
[45] Ibid., 80, 81.

and some had elective monarchs—Madison temporarily left the subject there.

He picked it up again and made a second effort in *Federalist* number 39. In seeking to determine "the distinctive characters of the republican form," Madison wrote in that essay, one must disregard "the application of the term by political writers." Holland, "in which no particle of the supreme authority is derived from the people, has passed almost universally under the denomination of a republic." The same was true of Venice, where "a small body of hereditary nobles" exercised "absolute power over the great body of the people." Even Poland, "a mixture of aristocracy and of monarchy in their worst forms, has been dignified with the same appellation." And England, with a mixture of republican, monarchical, and aristocratic principles, had likewise erroneously been so called. All previous writers on politics had been wrong, Madison asserted. A republic, he declared, was nothing more and nothing less than "a government which derives all its powers directly or indirectly from the great body of the people, and is administered by persons holding their offices during pleasure, for a limited period, or during good behavior."[46]

It can be maintained that in setting aside every political writer from Plato to Montesquieu, Madison was, in these two essays, being more than a little presumptuous, even arrogant. But in truth, because the Framers had devised a *novus ordo seclorum*, they had rendered all previous political vocabulary obsolete as it pertained to the government of the United States. That government defied categorization by any existing nomenclature: it was not a monarchy, nor an aristocracy, nor a democracy, neither yet was it a mixed form of government, nor yet a confederated republic. It was what it was, and if Madison was presumptuous in appropriating the word *republic* to describe it, he was also a prophet, for thenceforth *republic* would mean precisely what Madison said it meant.

To treat of republicanism as it pertains to the national/federal government, however, does not exhaust the sub-

---

[46] Ibid., 243–244.

ject, for there remained the state governments. Article 4, section 4, provides that "The United States shall guarantee to every State in this Union a Republican Form of Government." The document offers no hints as to what the operative words mean; indeed, the clause contains the Constitution's only reference to republicanism. But it was understood by all that the "Republican Form of Government" clause neither mandated any structural changes in the state governments nor limited their powers. The only limitations are those in article 1, section 10.

Broadly speaking, the powers that the states retained fell under the rubric "internal police," or simply the police power: the states had the powers of the *polis*. These included not only the definition and punishment of crimes and the administration of justice but also all matters concerning the health, manners, morals, safety, and welfare of the citizenry. Despite the assertions of some anti-Federalists, the states retained the police powers exclusively.[47] These powers were nearly unlimited, and they were not affected by the subsequent adoption of the bill of rights.[48] For example, the states could still, in the interest of public morality, establish the mode and manner of religious worship and instruction, and they could levy taxes for the support of religion—as Connecticut and Massachusetts continued to do for many years. They could stifle dissent, stifle freedom of the press, of speech, of inquiry. They could regulate food, drink, and clothing. They could do all these things and more, in the name of the common weal. They were, in sum, the American republics in the traditional meaning of that term.

But there is a flaw in that description of things. As we have seen, both theory and tradition indicated that re-

[47] For examples of anti-Federalist comments in regard to the police power see Storing, *Complete Anti-Federalist*, 2:228, 233, 393–394, 4:77, 6:62. These comments are half-hearted and vague, however, and do not indicate any general belief that the national/federal government had a police power. It was not until the early twentieth century that the Supreme Court laid claim to such a power (see *Champion* v. *Ames*, 188 U.S. 321 [1903], and *McCray* v. *U.S.*, 195 U.S. 27 [1904]).

[48] See John Marshall's decision in *Barron* v. *Baltimore*, 7 Peters 243 (1833), ruling that the Bill of Rights did not apply to the states.

publics could be viable only in limited territories with homogeneous populations. Anti-Federalists criticized the Constitution on that ground, arguing that only a confederation was suitable for an area so large as the United States. In rebuttal, Hamilton, Madison, Wilson, Dickinson, and other Federalists developed the idea of the extended republic and recited its advantages over earlier forms; and they also pointed out that the states themselves were far too large to be governed as traditional republics.[49]

Their arguments were sound as far as they went, but they tended to overlook the fact that the constitutional order, in the circumstances, confirmed that the country was not to be one republic or even thirteen, but a multitude of them. For the United States was a nation composed of several thousand insular communities, each of which exercised virtually absolute powers over its members through two traditional institutions, the militias and the juries. On a day-to-day basis, it was the militias, not the army of the United States, that protected the public safety; it was the juries, not the president or the state governors, who enforced the law; and it was the juries, and not either judges or legislators, who spoke authoritatively as to what the law was.[50]

Anti-Federalists feared, or professed to fear, that the Constitution would undermine these insular republics by vesting the national/federal government with control over both the militias and the juries. Their arguments regarding the militias were hyperbolic and riddled with self-contradictions, and Federalists had no difficulty in rebutting them—

[49] For anti-Federalist arguments see Storing, *Complete Anti-Federalist*, 2:17, 230, 368, 3:153, 4:93–94, 279–280, 5:122, 288. Regarding the extended republic see *Federalist* numbers 9 and 10. For examples of the proposition that the states were too large to be governed as traditional republics see *Federalist*, 49–50, and Ellsworth's speech of June 25, in Farrand, *Records*, 1:406–407.

[50] I am indebted to William E. Nelson for calling to my attention the crucial role of the juries. He did so at a conference in Williamsburg, Virginia, Oct. 4–6, 1984, sponsored by Liberty Fund, where he presented a paper on the common law and the Constitution (see his book *Americanization of the Common Law*, passim, and "The Eighteenth-Century Background of John Marshall's Constitutional Jurisprudence").

as, for example, Hamilton did in *Federalist* number 29.[51]
Criticism of the Constitution in regard to juries, however,
rested on more solid foundations. One ground of objection
was that though trial by jury in criminal cases was provided
for, the Supreme Court's "appellate Jurisdiction, both as to
Law and Fact," effectively nullified the power of juries in
such cases. The other ground was that the Constitution did
not make any provision for jury trials in civil cases at all.
Hamilton attempted to answer the anti-Federalists on both
counts in *Federalist* number 81, but his arguments were
highly technical and not especially convincing. The first
objection was at least partially overcome by the double-
jeopardy clause of the Fifth Amendment and by the pro-
cedural rights guaranteed in that and in the Sixth Amendment. The second was met with the Seventh Amendment,
but the language of that amendment provided means by
which the unchecked powers of juries would ultimately be
brought under control: it provided that in civil cases, "the
right of trial by jury shall be preserved, and no fact tried by
a jury, shall be otherwise re-examined in any Court of the
United States, than according to the rules of the common
law." Limiting the restriction to reexamination of facts
effectively confirmed the power of appellate courts to set
aside jury findings in matters of law—a striking example of
the truth of Hamilton's warning, in *Federalist* number 84,
that a bill of rights "would afford a colorable pretext" for
"the doctrine of constructive powers." Within a generation
after the adoption of the Constitution, the process of
"Mansfieldizing" American juries would be well under
way, and within another generation, their power to rule on
matters of law would be almost entirely gone.[52]

But the curtailment of the juries, in their capacity as a
multiplicity of small republics, came about not as a conse-

---

[51] *Federalist,* 175–182; for anti-Federalist arguments see Storing, *Complete Anti-Federalist,* 2:58, 341–343, 3:36, 163–164, and the index entries under "militia," 7:63–64.

[52] *Federalist,* 559; Horwitz, *Transformation of American Law,* 28–29, 84–85, 141–143, 155–159, 228; Nelson, *Americanization of the Common Law,* 165–171; Edith Guild Henderson, "The Background of the Seventh Amendment," *Harvard Law Review* 80 (1966): 289–337.

quence of legal niceties but because they had, in that capacity, become anachronistic. They were barriers to the rule of law, in the sense of uniform and predictable rules of conduct within a jurisdiction; they were barriers to the expression of the general will, as voiced through legislative assemblies; and they were barriers to the onward flow of history, for a new world of competitive, acquisitive individualism was beginning to replace the old world of communitarian consensualism which the jury system symbolized and embodied.[53]

On the last two counts the Constitution itself was somewhat anachronistic. That it thwarted the general will was a matter of design. To be sure, the precise blend of powers at the national/federal level, the distribution of powers among different levels of government, and the provisions for choosing officials in different branches for different periods of time were products of negotiation and compromise; but they also reflected the Framers' goal of preventing self-government from degenerating into majoritarian tyranny. The constitutional order could be described as republican only by employing a new definition of a term that had always been broad and imprecise. It could not be described as *democratic* except through a violent distortion of the language, for that term had a more specific meaning; nor could it be properly described even as a *representative democracy,* for parts of it represented nobody and other parts did not represent the *demos.*

From the perspective of what had gone before, the Constitution marked the culmination of a tradition of civic humanism that dated back more than two millenia and of a common-law tradition that dated back many centuries. But the order from which it sprang was already crumbling, and soon it was to be destroyed by a host of minor currents and events and by three developments of monumental force: the adoption of the Hamiltonian financial system, the

[53] Nelson, *Americanization of the Common Law,* passim.

French Revolution, and the enormous commercial expansion that accompanied the long succession of international wars which began in 1792. Together, these ushered in the Age of Liberalism, the Age of Capitalism and Democracy. The ensuing society of acquisitive individualists had neither room for nor need of the kind of virtuous public servants who so abundantly graced the public councils during the Founding Era.

Nevertheless, the Framers looked forward in time as well as backwards. For one thing, their plans and hopes that the *Optimates* might be recruited for national service materialized. For the better part of four decades—except during the late 1790s, when the scurrilousness of partisan politics temporarily made positions in government unattractive—the men who served the nation were of a quality not far beneath that of the Framers themselves. After that, the *Populares* took over, and a race of pygmies came to infest the public councils. By that time, however, it made little difference. The order was firmly established and self-maintaining: constitutional government had become part of the second nature of *homo politicus Americanus*.

That the Framers were able to achieve so mightily may be explained in terms of a model that Adam Smith posited in his *Theory of Moral Sentiments*. In times of civil discontent and disorder, Smith wrote, two kinds of leaders tend to arise. One kind of leader, infected with the "spirit of system," tends to "hold out some plausible plan of reformation," which he pretends "will not only remove the inconveniences and relieve the distresses immediately complained of" but will also prevent such from ever arising again. To that end he proposes "to new-model the constitution" and becomes "so enamoured with the supposed beauty of his own ideal plan of government" that he insists upon establishing it "completely and in all its parts, without any regard either to the great interests or to the strong prejudices which may oppose it: he seems to imagine that he can arrange the different members of a great society . . . as the hand arranges the different pieces upon a chessboard."

The other kind of leader acts "with proper temper and moderation," and will "respect the established powers and privileges even of individuals, and still more those of the great orders and societies into which the state is divided." He will accommodate "his public arrangements to the confirmed habits and prejudices of the people" and thereby will become able to "assume the greatest and noblest of all characters, that of the reformer and legislator of a great state; and, by the wisdom of his institutions, secure the internal tranquillity and happiness of his fellow-citizens for many succeeding generations."[54]

Both kinds of leaders were there in Philadelphia during the summer of 1787, and the second kind prevailed. They devised a new order out of materials prescribed by the ages, and they were wise enough to institutionalize the pluralism with which they worked and to draw their Constitution loosely enough so that it might live and breathe and change with time.

But perhaps that was not it at all. Perhaps, as Bismarck is reported to have said, a special Providence takes care of fools, drunks, and the United States of America. Surely the Founders believed the last of these.

---

[54] Smith, *Theory of Moral Sentiments*, 378–381 (pt. 6, sec. 2, chap. 2).

Appendix A

Delegates Attending the Convention

New Hampshire: Nicholas Gilman
John Langdon

Massachusetts: Elbridge Gerry
Nathaniel Gorham
Rufus King
Caleb Strong

Connecticut: Oliver Ellsworth
William Samuel Johnson
Roger Sherman

New York: Alexander Hamilton
John Lansing, Jr.
Robert Yates

New Jersey: David Brearley
Jonathan Dayton
William C. Houston
William Livingston
William Paterson

Pennsylvania: George Clymer
                    Thomas Fitzsimons
                    Benjamin Franklin
                    Jared Ingersoll
                    Thomas Mifflin
                    Gouverneur Morris
                    Robert Morris
                    James Wilson

Delaware: Richard Bassett
                    Gunning Bedford, Jr.
                    Jacob Broom
                    John Dickinson
                    George Read

Maryland: Daniel Carroll
                    Daniel of St. Thomas Jenifer
                    Luther Martin
                    James McHenry
                    John Francis Mercer

Virginia: John Blair
                    James Madison
                    George Mason
                    James McClurg
                    Edmund Randolph
                    George Washington
                    George Wythe

North Carolina: William Blount
                    William R. Davie
                    Alexander Martin
                    Richard Dobbs Spaight
                    Hugh Williamson

South Carolina: Pierce Butler
                    Charles Pinckney
                    Charles Cotesworth Pinckney
                    John Rutledge

Georgia: Abraham Baldwin
                    William Few
                    William Houstoun
                    William Pierce

Appendix B

The Constitution of the United States

WE THE PEOPLE of the United States, in Order to form a more perfect Union, establish Justice, insure domestic Tranquility, provide for the common defence, promote the general Welfare, and secure the Blessings of Liberty to ourselves and our Posterity, do ordain and establish this Constitution for the United States of America.

Article. I.

Section. 1. All legislative Powers herein granted shall be vested in a Congress of the United States, which shall consist of a Senate and House of Representatives.

Section. 2. The House of Representatives shall be composed of Members chosen every second Year by the People of the several States, and the Electors in each State shall have the Qualifications requisite for Electors of the most numerous Branch of the State Legislature.

No Person shall be a Representative who shall not have attained to the Age of twenty five Years, and been seven Years a Citizen of the United States, and who shall not, when elected, be an Inhabitant of that State in which he shall be chosen.

Representatives and direct Taxes shall be apportioned among the several States which may be included within this Union, according to their respective Numbers, which shall be determined by adding to the whole Number of free Persons, including those bound to Service for a Term of Years, and excluding Indians not taxed, three fifths of all other Persons. The actual Enumeration shall be made within three Years after the first Meeting of the Congress of the United States, and within every subsequent Term of ten Years, in such Manner as they shall by Law direct. The Number of Representatives shall not exceed one for every thirty Thousand, but each State shall have at Least one Representative; and until such enumeration shall be made, the State of New Hampshire shall be entitled to chuse three, Massachusetts eight, Rhode-Island and Providence Plantations one, Connecticut five, New-York six, New Jersey four, Pennsylvania eight, Delaware one, Maryland six, Virginia ten, North Carolina five, South Carolina five, and Georgia three.

When vacancies happen in the Representation from any State, the Executive Authority thereof shall issue Writs of Election to fill such Vacancies.

The House of Representatives shall chuse their Speaker and other Officers; and shall have the sole Power of Impeachment.

Section. 3. The Senate of the United States shall be composed of two Senators from each State, chosen by the Legislature thereof, for six Years; and each Senator shall have one Vote.

Immediately after they shall be assembled in Consequence of the first Election, they shall be divided as equally as may be into three Classes. The Seats of the Senators of the first Class shall be vacated at the Expiration of the second Year, of the second Class at the Expiration of the fourth Year, and of the third Class at the Expiration of the sixth Year, so that one third may be chosen every second Year; and if Vacancies happen by Resignation, or otherwise, during the Recess of the Legislature of any State, the Executive thereof may make temporary Appointments until the next Meeting of the Legislature, which shall then fill such Vacancies.

No Person shall be a Senator who shall not have attained to the Age of thirty Years, and been nine Years a Citizen of the United States, and who shall not, when elected, be an inhabitant of that State for which he shall be chosen.

The Vice President of the United States shall be President of the Senate, but shall have no Vote, unless they be equally divided.

The Senate shall chuse their other Officers, and also a President pro tempore, in the Absence of the Vice President, or when he shall exercise the Office of President of the United States.

The Senate shall have the sole Power to try all Impeachments. When sitting for that Purpose, they shall be on Oath or Affirmation. When the President of the United States is tried, the Chief Justice shall preside: And no Person shall be convicted without the Concurrence of two thirds of the Members present.

Judgment in Cases of Impeachment shall not extend further than to removal from Office, and disqualification to hold and enjoy any Office of honor, Trust or Profit under the United States: but the Party convicted shall nevertheless be liable and subject to Indictment, Trial, Judgment and Punishment, according to Law.

Section. 4. The Times, Places and Manner of holding Elections for Senators and Representatives, shall be prescribed in each State by the Legislature thereof; but the Congress may at any time by Law make or alter such Regulations, except as to the Places of chusing Senators.

The Congress shall assemble at least once in every Year, and such Meeting shall be on the first Monday in December, unless they shall by Law appoint a different Day.

Section. 5. Each House shall be the Judge of the Elections, Returns and Qualifications of its own Members, and a Majority of each shall constitute a Quorum to do Business; but a smaller Number may adjourn from day to day, and may be authorized to compel the Attendance of absent Members, in such Manner, and under such Penalties as each House may provide.

Each House may determine the Rules of its Proceedings, punish its Members for disorderly Behaviour, and, with the Concurrence of two thirds, expel a Member.

Each House shall keep a Journal of its Proceedings, and from time to time publish the same, excepting such Parts as may in their Judgment require Secrecy; and the Yeas and Nays of the Members of either House on any question shall, at the Desire of one fifth of those Present, be entered on the Journal.

Neither House, during the Session of Congress, shall, without the Consent of the other, adjourn for more than three days, nor to any other Place than that in which the two Houses shall be sitting.

Section. 6. The Senators and Representatives shall receive a Compensation for their Services, to be ascertained by Law, and paid out of the Treasury of the United States. They shall in all Cases, except Treason, Felony and Breach of the Peace, be privileged from Arrest during their Attendance at the Session of their respective Houses, and in going to and returning from the same; and for any Speech or Debate in either House, they shall not be questioned in any other Place.

No Senator or Representative shall, during the Time for which he was elected, be appointed to any civil Office under the Authority of the United States, which shall have been created, or the Emoluments whereof shall have been encreased during such time; and no Person holding any Office under the United States, shall be a Member of either House during his Continuance in Office.

Section. 7. All Bills for raising Revenue shall originate in the House of Representatives; but the Senate may propose or concur with Amendments as on other Bills.

Every Bill which shall have passed the House of Representatives and the Senate, shall, before it become a Law, be presented to the President of the United States; If he approve he shall sign it, but if not he shall return it, with his Objections to that House in which it shall have originated, who shall enter the Objections at large on their Journal, and proceed to reconsider it. If after such Reconsideration two thirds of that House shall agree to pass the Bill, it shall be sent, together with the Objections, to the other House, by which it shall likewise be reconsidered, and if approved by two thirds of that House, it shall become a Law. But in all such Cases the Votes of both Houses shall be determined by yeas and Nays, and the Names of the Persons voting for and against the Bill shall be entered on the Journal of each House respectively. If any Bill shall not be returned by the President within ten Days (Sundays excepted) after it shall have been presented to him, the Same shall be a Law, in like Manner as if he had signed it, unless the Congress by their Adjournment prevent its Return, in which Case it shall not be a Law.

Every Order, Resolution, or Vote to which the Concurrence of the Senate and House of Representatives may be necessary (except on a question of Adjournment) shall be presented to the President of the United States; and before the Same shall take Effect, shall be approved by him, or being disapproved by him, shall be repassed by two thirds of the Senate and House of Representatives, according to the Rules and Limitations prescribed in the Case of a Bill.

Section. 8. The Congress shall have Power To lay and collect Taxes, Duties, Imposts and Excises, to pay the Debts and Provide for the common Defence and general Welfare of the United States; but all Duties, Imposts and Excises shall be uniform throughout the United States;

To borrow Money on the credit of the United States;

To regulate Commerce with foreign Nations, and among the several States, and with the Indian Tribes;

To establish an uniform Rule of Naturalization, and uniform Laws on the subject of Bankruptcies throughout the United States;

To coin Money, regulate the Value thereof, and of foreign Coin, and fix the Standard of Weights and Measures;

To provide for the Punishment of counterfeiting the Securities and current Coin of the United States;

To establish Post Offices and post Roads;

To promote the Progress of Science and useful Arts, by securing for limited Time to Authors and Inventors the exclusive Right to their respective Writings and Discoveries;

To constitute Tribunals inferior to the supreme Court;

To define and punish Piracies and Felonies committed on the high Seas, and Offences against the Law of Nations;

To declare War, grant Letters of Marque and Reprisal, and make Rules concerning Captures on Land and Water;

To raise and support Armies, but no Appropriation of Money to that Use shall be for a longer Term than two Years;

To provide and maintain a Navy;

To make Rules for the Government and Regulation of the land and naval Forces;

To provide for calling forth the Militia to execute the Laws of the Union, suppress Insurrections and repel Invasions;

To provide for organizing, arming, and disciplining, the Militia, and for governing such Part of them as may be employed in the Service of the United States, reserving to the States respectively, the Appointment of the Officers, and the Authority of training the Militia according to the discipline prescribed by Congress;

To exercise exclusive Legislation in all Cases whatsoever, over such District (not exceeding ten Miles square) as may, by Cession of Particular States, and the Acceptance of Congress, become the Seat of the Government of the United States, and to exercise like Authority over all Places purchased by the Consent of the Legislature of the State in which the Same shall be, for the Erection of Forts, Magazines, Arsenals, dock-Yards, and other needful Buildings;—And

To make all Laws which shall be necessary and proper for carrying into Execution the foregoing Powers, and all other Powers vested by this Constitution in the Government of the United States, or in any Department or Officer thereof.

Section. 9. The Migration or Importation of such Persons as any of the States now existing shall think proper to admit, shall not be prohibited by the Congress prior to the Year one thousand eight hundred and eight, but a Tax or duty may be imposed on such Importation, not exeeding ten dollars for each Person.

The Privilege of the Writ of Habeas Corpus shall not be suspended, unless when in Cases of Rebellion or Invasion the public Safety may require it.

No Bill of Attainder or ex post facto Law shall be passed.

No Capitation, or other direct, Tax shall be laid, unless in Proportion to the Census or Enumeration herein before directed to be taken.

No Tax or Duty shall be laid on Articles exported from any State.

No Preference shall be given by any Regulation of Commerce or Revenue to the Ports of one State over those of another: nor shall Vessels bound to, or from, one State, be obliged to enter, clear, or pay Duties in another.

No Money shall be drawn from the Treasury, but in Consequence of Appropriations made by Law; and a regular Statement and Account of the Receipts and Expenditures of all public Money shall be published from time to time.

No Title of Nobility shall be granted by the United States: And no Person holding any Office of Profit or Trust under them, shall, without the Consent of the Congress, accept of any present, Emolument, Office, or Title, of any kind whatever, from any King, Prince, or foreign State.

Section. 10. No State shall enter into any Treaty, Alliance, or Confederation; grant Letters of Marque and Reprisal; coin Money; emit Bills of Credit; make any Thing but gold and silver Coin a Tender in Payment of Debts; pass any Bill of Attainder, ex post facto Law, or Law impairing the Obligation of Contracts, or grant any Title of Nobility.

No State shall, without the Consent of the Congress, lay any Imposts or Duties on Imports or Exports, except what may be absolutely necessary for executing it's inspection Laws: and the net Produce of all Duties and Imposts, laid by any State on Imports or Exports, shall be for the Use of the Treasury of the United States; and all such Laws shall be subject to the Revision and Controul of the Congress.

No State shall, without the Consent of Congress, lay any Duty of Tonnage, keep Troops, or Ships of War in time of Peace, enter into any Agreement or Compact with another State, or with a foreign Power, or engage in War, unless actually invaded, or in such imminent Danger as will not admit of delay.

Article. II.

Section. 1. The executive Power shall be vested in a President of the United States of America. He shall hold his Office during the Term of four Years, and, together with the Vice President, chosen for the same Term, be elected, as follows

Each State shall appoint, in such Manner as the Legislature thereof may direct, a Number of Electors, equal to the whole Number of Senators and Representatives to which the State may be entitled in the Congress: but no Senator or Representative, or Person holding an Office of Trust or Profit under the United States, shall be appointed an Elector.

The Electors shall meet in their respective States, and vote by Ballot for two Persons, of whom one at least shall not be an

Inhabitant of the same State with themselves. And they shall make a List of all the Persons voted for, and of the Number of Votes for each; which List they shall sign and certify, and transmit sealed to the Seat of the Government of the United States, directed to the President of the Senate. The President of the Senate shall, in the Presence of the Senate and House of Representatives, open all the Certificates, and the Votes shall then be counted. The Person having the greatest Number of Votes shall be the President, if such Number be a Majority of the whole Number of Electors appointed; and if there be more than one who have such Majority, and have an equal Number of Votes, then the House of Representatives shall immediately chuse by Ballot one of them for President; and if no Person have a Majority, then from the five highest on the List the said House shall in like Manner chuse the President. But in chusing the President, the Votes shall be taken by States, the Representation from each State having one Vote; A quorum for this Purpose shall consist of a Member or Members from two thirds of the States, and a Majority of all the States shall be necessary to a Choice. In every Case, after the Choice of the President, the Person having the greatest Number of Votes of the Electors shall be the Vice President. But if there should remain two or more who have equal Votes, the Senate shall chuse from them by Ballot the Vice President.

The Congress may determine the Time of chusing the Electors, and the Day on which they shall give their Votes; which Day shall be the same throughout the United States.

No Person except a natural born Citizen, or a Citizen of the United States, at the time of the Adoption of this Constitution, shall be eligible to the Office of President; neither shall any Person be eligible to that Office who shall not have attained to the Age of thirty five Years, and been fourteen Years a Resident within the United States.

In Case of the Removal of the President from Office, or of his Death, Resignation, or Inability to discharge the Powers and Duties of the said Office, the Same shall devolve on the Vice President, and the Congress may by Law provide for the Case of Removal, Death, Resignation or Inability, both of the President and Vice President, declaring what Officer shall then act as

President, and such Officer shall act accordingly, until the Disability be removed, or a President shall be elected.

The President shall, at stated Times, receive for his Services, a Compensation, which shall neither be encreased nor diminished during the Period for which he shall have been elected, and he shall not receive within that Period any other Emolument from the United States, or any of them.

Before he enter on the Execution of his Office, he shall take the following Oath or Affirmation:—"I do solemnly swear (or affirm) that I will faithfully execute the Office of President of the United States, and will to the best of my Ability, preserve, protect and defend the Constitution of the United States."

Section. 2. The President shall be Commander in Chief of the Army and Navy of the United States, and of the Militia of the several States, when called into the actual Service of the United States; he may require the Opinion, in writing, of the principal Officer in each of the executive Departments, upon any Subject relating to the Duties of their respective Offices, and he shall have Power to grant Reprieves and Pardons for Offences against the United States, except in Cases of Impeachment.

He shall have Power, by and with the Advice and Consent of the Senate, to make Treaties, provided two thirds of the Senators present concur; and he shall nominate, and by and with the Advice and Consent of the Senate, shall appoint Ambassadors, other public Ministers and Consuls, Judges of the supreme Court, and all other Officers of the United States, whose Appointments are not herein otherwise provided for, and which shall be established by Law: but the Congress may by Law vest the Appointment of such inferior Officers, as they think proper, in the President alone, in the Courts of Law, or in the Heads of Departments.

The President shall have Power to fill up all Vacancies that may happen during the Recess of the Senate, by granting Commissions which shall expire at the End of their next Session.

Section. 3. He shall from time to time give to the Congress Information of the State of the Union, and recommend to their consideration such Measures as he shall judge necessary and expedient; he may, on extraordinary Occasions, convene both Houses, or either of them, and in Case of Disagreement between them, with Respect to the Time of Adjournment, he may adjourn them to such Time as he shall think proper; he shall receive Ambassadors and other public Ministers; he shall take Care that the Laws be faithfully executed, and shall Commission all the Officers of the United States.

Section. 4. The President, Vice President and all civil Officers of the United States, shall be removed from Office on Impeachment for, and conviction of, Treason, Bribery, or other high Crimes and Misdemeanors.

ARTICLE III.

Section. 1. The judicial Power of the United States, shall be vested in one supreme Court, and in such inferior Courts as the Congress may from time to time ordain and establish. The Judges, both of the supreme and inferior Courts, shall hold their Offices during good Behaviour, and shall, at stated Times, receive for their Services, a Compensation, which shall not be diminished during their Continuance in Office.

Section. 2. The judicial Power shall extend to all Cases, in Law and Equity, arising under this Constitution, the Laws of the United States, and Treaties made, or which shall be made, under their Authority;—to all Cases affecting Ambassadors, other public Ministers and Consuls;—to all Cases of admiralty and maritime Jurisdiction;—to Controversies to which the United States shall be a Party;—to Controversies between two or more States;— between a State and Citizens of another State;—between Citizens of different States,—between Citizens of the same State claiming Lands under Grants of different States, and between a State, or the Citizens thereof, and foreign States, Citizens or Subjects.

In all Cases affecting Ambassadors, other public Ministers and Consuls, and those in which a State shall be Party, the supreme Court shall have original Jurisdiction. In all the other Cases before mentioned, the supreme Court shall have appellate Jurisdiction, both as to Law and Fact, with such Exceptions, and under such Regulations as the Congress shall make.

The Trial of all Crimes, except in Cases of Impeachment, shall be by Jury; and such Trial shall be held in the State where the said

Crimes shall have been committed; but when not committed within any State, the Trial shall be at such Place or Places as the Congress may by Law have directed.

Section. 3. Treason against the United States, shall consist only in levying War against them, or in adhering to their Enemies, giving them Aid and Comfort. No Person shall be convicted of Treason unless on the Testimony of two Witnesses to the same overt Act, or on Confession in open Court.

The Congress shall have Power to declare the Punishment of Treason, but no Attainder of Treason shall work Corruption of Blood, or Forfeiture except during the Life of the Person attainted.

ARTICLE. IV.

Section. 1. Full Faith and Credit shall be given in each State to the public Acts, Records, and judicial Proceedings of every other State. And the Congress may by general Laws prescribe the Manner in which such Acts, Records and Proceedings shall be proved, and the Effect thereof.

Section 2. The Citizens of each State shall be entitled to all Privileges and Immunities of Citizens in the several States.

A Person charged in any State with Treason, Felony, or other Crime, who shall flee from Justice, and be found in another State, shall on Demand of the executive Authority of the State from which he fled, be delivered up, to be removed to the State having Jurisdiction of the Crime.

No Person held to Service or Labour in one State, under the Laws thereof, escaping into another, shall, in Consequence of any Law or Regulation therein, be discharged from such Service or Labour, but shall be delivered up on Claim of the Party to whom such Service or Labour may be due.

Section. 3. New States may be admitted by the Congress into this Union; but no new State shall be formed or erected within the Jurisdiction of any other State; nor any State be formed by the Junction of two or more States, or Parts of States, without the Consent of the Legislatures of the States concerned as well as of the Congress.

The Congress shall have Power to dispose of and make all needful Rules and Regulations respecting the Territory or other Property belonging to the United States; and nothing in this Constitution shall be so construed as to Prejudice any Claims of the United States, or of any particular State.

Section. 4. The United States shall guarantee to every State in this Union a Republican Form of Government, and shall protect each of them against Invasion; and on Application of the Legislature, or of the Executive (when the Legislature cannot be convened) against domestic Violence.

Article. V.

The Congress, whenever two thirds of both Houses shall deem it necessary, shall propose Amendments to this Constitution, or, on the Application of the Legislatures of two thirds of the several States, shall call a Convention for proposing Amendments, which, in either Case, shall be valid to all Intents and Purposes, as Part of this Constitution, when ratified by the Legislatures of three fourths of the several States, or by Conventions in three fourths thereof, as the one or the other Mode of Ratification may be proposed by the Congress; Provided that no Amendment which may be made prior to the Year One thousand eight hundred and eight shall in any Manner affect the first and fourth Clauses in the Ninth Section of the first Article; and that no State, without its Consent, shall be deprived of it's equal Suffrage in the Senate.

Article. VI.

All Debts contracted and Engagements entered into, before the Adoption of this Constitution, shall be as valid against the United States under this Constitution, as under the Confederation.

This Constitution, and the Laws of the United States which shall be made in Pursuance thereof; and all Treaties made, or which shall be made, under the Authority of the United States, shall be the supreme Law of the Land; and the Judges in every State shall be bound thereby, any Thing in the Constitution or Laws of any State to the Contrary notwithstanding.

The Senators and Representatives before mentioned, and the Members of the several State Legislatures, and all executive and judicial Officers, both of the United States and of the several States, shall be bound by Oath or Affirmation, to support this Constitution; but no religious Test shall ever be required as a Qualification to any Office or public Trust under the United States.

Article. VII.

The Ratification of the Conventions of nine States, shall be sufficient for the Establishment of this Constitution between the States so ratifying the Same.

BIBLIOGRAPHY

PRIMARY SOURCES

NEWSPAPERS

Boston Gazette
Connecticut Courant (Hartford)
Connecticut Gazette (New London)
Connecticut Journal (New Haven)
Daily Advertiser (New York)
Evening Herald (Philadelphia)
Fowle's New-Hampshire Gazette (Portsmouth)
Freeman's Journal (Philadelphia)
Maryland Gazette (Annapolis)
Maryland Journal (Baltimore)
Massachusetts Centinel (Boston)
Middlesex Gazette (Connecticut)
National Gazette (Philadelphia)
New Hampshire Gazette (Portsmouth)
New-Hampshire Mercury and General Advertiser (Portsmouth)
New Hampshire Spy (Portsmouth)
New York Packet
Pennsylvania Journal (Philadelphia)
Pennsylvania Packet (Philadelphia)
Providence Gazette and Country Journal (Rhode Island)
Virginia Gazette (Richmond)
Virginia Journal (Alexandria)

PERSONAL PAPERS

Welcome Arnold Papers, John Carter Brown Library
Brown Family Papers, John Carter Brown Library
Moses Brown Papers, Rhode Island Historical Society
George Bryan Manuscripts, Historical Society of Pennsylvania
William Constable Papers, New York Public Library
Andrew Cragie Papers, American Antiquarian Society
Nicholas Gilman Papers, Library of Congress
William Hemsley Papers, Library of Congress
Henry Knox Papers, Massachusetts Historical Society
John Langdon Papers, Historical Society of Pennsylvania
Frederick S. Peck Collection, Rhode Island Historical Society
Pinckney Family Papers, Library of Congress
Philip Schuyler Papers, New York Historical Society
Charles Simms Papers, Library of Congress
James Wadsworth Papers, Connecticut Historical Society
James Wilson Papers, Historical Society of Pennsylvania

PUBLIC MANUSCRIPT RECORDS

Abstract of Imports Previous to 1792, Customs Office Records, Port of Salem, Fiscal Section, National Archives
Account of the Exports and Clearances of the Port of Boston for the Years 1787–1788, Massachusetts Miscellaneous Collection, Manuscripts Division, Library of Congress
Baltimore Import and Export Books, National Archives
Beverly Customs Office Records, Beverly (Mass.) Historical Society
Commissioners' Ledger and Journal, Maryland Hall of Records, Annapolis
Finance and Currency, vol. 5, Connecticut Archives, Hartford
Journal of the Council of Censors, Public Records Division, Pennsylvania Historical and Museum Commission
Journal of the House of Representaives of the General Court of Massachusetts, Massachusetts Archives
Maritime Papers, Rhode Island Archives
Microfilm Collection of Early Town Records, New Hampshire State Library, Concord

Miscellaneous Votes, Massachusetts Archives
Naval Officer Returns, Virginia State Library, Richmond
Records of the Loan of 1790, Fiscal Section, National Archives
Sale-Book of Confiscated British Property, 1781–1785, Maryland Hall of Records, Annapolis
Sale-Book of Confiscated Estates, 1782, 1785, Georgia Department of Archives and History, Atlanta

PUBLISHED COLLECTIONS OF PUBLIC DOCUMENTS

American Archives: A Documentary History of the Origin and Progress of the North American Colonies. Edited by Peter Force. 9 vols. Washington, D.C., 1837–1853.

American State Papers: Documents, Legislative and Executive of the Congress of the United States. 38 vols. Washington, D.C., 1832–1861.

Connecticut. *The Public Records of the Colony of Connecticut, 1636–1776.* Edited by James H. Trumbull and Charles J. Hoadly. 15 vols. Hartford, 1850–1890.

———. *The Public Records of the State of Connecticut.* Edited by Charles J. Hoadly and Leonard W. Labaree. 9 vols. Hartford, 1894–1953.

Delaware. *Laws of the State of Delaware, 1770–1797.* 2 vols. Newcastle, 1797.

Diplomatic Correspondence of the United States. Edited by Jared Sparks. 5 vols. Washington, D.C., 1832–1833.

Documents of American History. Edited by Henry Steele Commager. 7th ed. New York, 1963.

Documents of the American Revolution, 1770–1783. Edited by K. G. Davies. 21 vols. Dublin, 1972–1981.

The Federal and State Constitutions, Colonial Charters, and Other Organic Laws. . . . Edited by Francis N. Thorpe. 7 vols. Washington, D.C., 1909.

Georgia. *Colonial Records of the State of Georgia.* Compiled by Allen D. Candler. 26 vols. Atlanta, 1904–1916.

Journals of the Continental Congress, 1774–1789. Edited by W. C. Ford et al. 34 vols. Washington, D.C., 1904–1937.

Maryland. *The Laws of Maryland.* Edited by William Kilty. Annapolis, 1800.

————. *Votes and Proceedings of the House of Delegates of the State of Maryland*. Annapolis, 1788, 1789.

Massachusetts. *Acts and Laws of the Commonwealth of Massachusetts*. 13 vols. Boston, 1781–1789.

————. *The Popular Sources of Political Authority: Documents on the Massachusetts Constitution of 1780*. Edited by Oscar Handlin and Mary Handlin. Cambridge, Mass., 1966.

New Hampshire. *Documents and Records Relating to the State of New-Hampshire. . . from 1776 to 1783. . . .* Compiled by Nathaniel Bouton. Concord, 1874.

————. *The Provincial and State Papers of New Hampshire*. Edited by Nathaniel Bouton et al. Concord, 1876–1943.

New Jersey. *The Archives of the State of New Jersey*. Edited by William A. Whitehead et al. 36 vols. Newark, 1880–1941.

New York. *Laws of the State of New York Passed at the Sessions of the Legislature Held in the Years 1777* [to 1801]. . . . 5 vols. Albany, 1886–1887.

North Carolina. *The Colonial Records of North Carolina*. Edited by William L. Saunders. Raleigh, 1886–1890.

————. *The State Records of North Carolina* Vol. 23: *Laws, 1715–1776*. Edited by Walter Clark. Goldsboro, 1904.

Ohio Company. *The Records of the Original Proceedings of the Ohio Company*. Edited by Archer B. Hulbert. 2 vols. Marietta, 1917.

Pennsylvania. *Colonial Records of Pennsylvania*. 16 vols. Philadelphia and Harrisburg, 1852–1853.

————. *Pennsylvania and the Federal Constitution, 1787–1788*. Edited by John Bach McMaster and Frederick D. Stone. Philadelphia, 1888.

————. *Pennsylvania Archives*. Edited by Samuel Hazard et al. 138 vols. Philadelphia and Harrisburg, 1852–1935.

————. *Statutes at Large of Pennsylvania from 1682 to 1801*. Compiled by James T. Mitchell and Henry Flanders. 17 vols. Harrisburg, 1896–1915.

The Revolution in America, 1754–1788: Documents and Commentaries. Edited by J. R. Pole. Stanford, Calif., 1970.

Rhode Island. *At the General Assembly . . . of Rhode Island and Providence Plantations. . . .* Providence, 1776–1785.

————. *Records of the Colony of Rhode Island and Providence Plantations, in New England*. Edited by John Russell Bartlett. 10 vols. Providence, 1856–1865.

South Carolina. *The Statutes at Large of South Carolina.* Edited by
Thomas Cooper and D. J. McCord. 10 vols. Columbia,
1836–1841.
Susquehanna Company Papers. Edited by Julian P. Boyd and
Robert J. Taylor. 11 vols. Ithaca, N.Y., 1962–1971.
United States Commercial and Statistical Register. Vol. 1. Edited by
Samuel Hazard. Philadelphia, 1839.
Virginia. *Journal of the House of Delegates of the Commonwealth of
Virginia, 1781–1787.* Richmond, 1828.
————. *The Statutes at Large: Being a Collection of All the Laws of
Virginia.* . . . Compiled by William W. Hening. 13 vols.
Richmond, 1809–1823.

OTHER PRIMARY PRINTED SOURCES

Adams, John. *Familiar Letters of John Adams and his wife Abigail
Adams, during the Revolution.* Edited by Charles Francis
Adams. Boston, 1875.
————. *The Works of John Adams.* Edited by Charles Francis
Adams. 10 vols. Boston, 1850–1856.
Addison, Joseph. *The Works of Joseph Addison.* Edited by Richard
Hurd. 6 vols. London, 1881.
American Political Writing during the Founding Era, 1760–1805.
Edited by Charles S. Hyneman and Donald S. Lutz. 2 vols.
Indianapolis, Ind., 1983.
Ames, Fisher. *Works of Fisher Ames: As Published by Seth Ames.*
Edited by W. B. Allen. 2 vols. Indianapolis, Ind., 1983.
Anti-Federalists. *The Complete Anti-Federalist.* Edited by Herbert
J. Storing. 7 vols. Chicago, 1981.
Aristotle. *The Politics of Aristotle.* Translated by Ernest Barker.
New York, 1958.
————. *The Works of Aristotle.* Edited by W. D. Ross. 11 vols.
London, 1908–1931.
Backus, Isaac. *An Address to the Inhabitants of New-England,
Concerning the Present Bloody Controversy Therein.* Boston,
1787.
Barbé-Marbois, François, *Our Revolutionary Forefathers* (Letters
of 1779–1785). Translated by Eugene P. Chase. Freeport,
N.Y., 1969.

Beawes, Wyndham. *Lex Mercatoria Rediviva, or the Merchant's Directory.* London, 1758.

Belknap, Jeremy. *The History of New Hampshire.* 3 vols. Boston, 1791–1792.

Blackstone, Sir William. *Commentaries on the Laws of England.* 12th ed. 4 vols. London, 1793–1795.

Bolingbroke, Henry St. John, Viscount. *A Dissertation upon Parties.* London, 1744.

———. "The Idea of a Patriot King." In *The Works of . . . Henry St. John Viscount Bolingbroke.* Edited by David Mallet. Vol. 3. London, 1754.

Boswell, James. *The Life of Samuel Johnson.* Edited by Bergen Evans. New York, 1952.

Brooke, Henry. *Gustavus Vasa, the Deliverer of his Country. A tragedy, . . .* London, 1739.

Burgh, James. *Political Disquisitions: or, an Enquiry into Public Errors, Defects, and Abuses.* New York, 1971; reprint of 1774 London edition.

Burke, Aedanus. *Considerations on the Society or Order of the Cincinnati. . . .* Philadelphia, 1783.

Burlamaqui, Jean Jacques. *Principles of Natural and Politic Law. . . .* Translated by Thomas Nugent. 2d ed. London, 1763.

Burnaby, Andrew. *Travels through the Middle Settlements in North-America in the years 1759 and 1760.* Ithaca, N.Y., 1960.

Cantillon, Richard. *Essai sur la Nature du Commerce en général.* Paris, 1755.

Cicero, Marcus Tullius. *Cicero's Brutus, or, History of Famous Orators. . . .* Translated by E. Jones. London, 1776.

———. *The Morals of Cicero. . . .* Translated by William Guthrie. London, 1744.

Clinton, George. *The Public Papers of George Clinton, First Governor of New York, 1777–1795.* Edited by Hugh Hastings. 10 vols. New York and Albany, 1899–1914.

Coke, Sir Edward. *The Institutes of the Lawes of England, In Four Parts.* 15th ed. London, 1794.

Crèvecoeur (J. Hector St. John). *Letters from an American Farmer.* Garden City, N.Y.; reprint of 1782 edition.

Davenant, Charles. *The Political and Commercial Works of Dr. Charles D'Avenant.* Edited by Sir Charles Whitworth. 6 vols. London, 1771.

Deane, Silas. *Correspondence between Silas Deane, His Brothers, and Their Business and Political Associates, 1771–1795.* Hartford, Conn., 1930.

The Debates in the Several State Conventions on the Adoption of the Federal Constitution. Edited by Jonathan Elliot. 5 vols. Washington, D.C., 1830–1836.

Defoe, Daniel. *The Fortunes and Misfortunes of the Famous Moll Flanders, &.* Originally published in 1722; New York, 1964.

———. *The Life and Strange Surprising Adventures of Robinson Crusoe.* Originally published in 1719; New York, 1981.

Dickinson, John. *Empire and Nation: Letters from a Farmer in Pennsylvania, John Dickinson, Letters from the Federal Farmer, Richard Henry Lee.* Edited by Forrest McDonald. Englewood Cliffs, N.J., 1962.

———. *The Political Writings of John Dickinson, 1764–1774.* Edited by Paul L. Ford. New York, 1970.

The Federalist. Edited by Edward Mead Earle. New York, 1937.

Ferguson, Adam. *An Essay on the History of Civil Society.* Edinburgh, 1767.

———. *Institutes of Moral Philosophy.* Edinburgh, 1772.

Fielding, Henry. *The History of Tom Jones, A Foundling.* London, 1749.

Filmer, Robert. *Patriarcha, or the Natural Power of Kings.* London, 1680.

Franklin, Benjamin. *The Political Thought of Benjamin Franklin.* Edited by Ralph L. Ketcham. Indianapolis, Ind., 1965.

———. *The Writings of Benjamin Franklin.* Edited by Albert H. Smyth. 10 vols. New York, 1907.

Freedom of the Press from Zenger to Jefferson: Early American Libertarian Theories. Edited by Leonard Levy. Indianapolis, Ind., 1966.

Gerry, Elbridge. *A Study in Dissent: The Warren-Gerry Correspondence, 1776–1792.* Edited by C. Harvey Gardiner. Carbondale, Ill., 1968.

Goldsmith, Oliver. *The Collected Works of Oliver Goldsmith.* Edited by Arthur Friedman. 5 vols. Oxford, Eng., 1966.

Grotius, Hugo. *The Rights of War and Peace, in Three Books. . . .* With notes by Barbeyrac. London, 1738.

Hale, Sir Matthew. *The History of the Common Law of England.* Edited by Charles M. Gray, Chicago, 1971.

———. *A Treatise De Jure Maris.* London, 1787.

Hamilton, Alexander. *The Law Practice of Alexander Hamilton: Documents and Commentary.* Edited by Julius Goebel, Jr. 2 vols. New York, 1964, 1969.

———. *The Papers of Alexander Hamilton.* Edited by Harold C. Syrett et al. 26 vols. New York, 1961–1979.

Harrington, James. *The Political Works of James Harrington.* Edited by J. G. A. Pocock. Cambridge, Eng., and New York, 1977.

Hervey, John, Lord. *Ancient and Modern Liberty Stated and Compared.* London, 1734.

Hobbes, Thomas. *Leviathan.* Edited by Michael Oakeshott. Oxford, Eng., n.d.

———. *The Moral and Political Works of Thomas Hobbes of Malmesbury,* . . . London, 1750.

Hume, David. *History of England from the Invasion of Julius Caesar to The Revolution in 1688.* 2 vols. Indianapolis, Ind., 1983.

———. *Philosophical Works.* Edited by Thomas Hill Green and Thomas Hodge Grose. 4 vols. London, 1886.

Hutcheson, Francis. *A System of Moral Philosophy.* 2 vols. London, 1755.

Jacob, Giles. *A New Law Dictionary.* 3d ed. London, 1736.

Jay, John. *Correspondence and Public Papers of John Jay.* Edited by Henry P. Johnston. 4 vols. New York, 1890.

Jefferson, Thomas. *The Best Letters of Thomas Jefferson.* Edited by J. G. deRoulhoc Hamilton. Boston, 1926.

———. *Notes on the State of Virginia.* Edited by William Peden, Chapel Hill, N.C., 1955.

———. *The Papers of Thomas Jefferson.* Edited by Julian P. Boyd et al. Multiple vols. Princeton, N.J., 1950–.

Johnson, Samuel, *A Dictionary of the English Language.* . . . 2 vols. London, 1755.

Kames, Henry Home, Lord. *Essays on the Principles of Morality and Natural Religion.* Edinburgh, 1751.

———. *Principles of Equity.* 2d ed. London and Edinburgh, 1767.

Kent, James. *Commentaries on American Law.* 3d ed. 4 vols. New York, 1836.

King, Rufus. *The Life and Correspondence of Rufus King.* . . . Edited by Charles R. King. 6 vols. New York, 1894–1900.

Lansing, John, Jr. *The Delegate from New York or Proceedings of the Federal Convention of 1787*. Edited by Joseph Reese Strayer. Princeton, N.J., 1939.

Law, John. *Oeuvres Complètes*. Edited by Paul Haisin. Paris, 1934.

Lee, Nathaniel. *The Rival Queens; or the Death of Alexander the Great*. London, 1677.

Lee, Richard Henry. *The Letters of Richard Henry Lee*. Edited by James C. Ballagh. 2 vols. New York, 1911, 1914.

Letters of Members of the Continental Congress. Edited by Edmund C. Burnett. 8 vols. Gloucester, Mass., 1963.

Livingston, William. *The Papers of William Livingston*. Edited by Carl E. Prince et al. 3 vols. Trenton, N.J., 1979–.

Livius, Titus. *A History of Rome: Selections*. Translated by Moses Hadas and Joe P. Poe. New York, 1962.

Locke, John. *An Essay Concerning Human Understanding*. Edited by Alexander C. Fraser. 2 vols. New York, 1959.

————. *Two Treatises of Government*. Edited by Peter Laslett. 2d ed. Cambridge, Eng., 1967.

Mably, Gabriel Bonnot de. *De L'Étude de L'Histoire, à Monseigneur le Prince de Parme*. New ed. Mastreicht, 1778.

Machiavelli, Niccolò. *The Prince and the Discourses*. Edited by Max Lerner. New York, 1940.

Maclay, William. *Journal of William Maclay United States Senator from Pennsylvania, 1789–1791*. Edited by Edgar S. Maclay. New York, 1890.

Madison, James. *The Papers of James Madison*. Edited by Robert A. Rutland et al. Multiple vols. Chicago, 1962–.

Mandeville, Bernard. *The Fable of the Bees*. Edited by F. B. Kaye. 2 vols. Oxford, Eng., 1924.

Mason, George. *The Papers of George Mason, 1725–1792*. Edited by Robert A. Rutland. 3 vols. Chapel Hill, N.C., 1970.

Millar, John. *A Historical View of the English Government*. . . . 4th ed. 4 vols. London, 1819.

————. *The Origins of the Distinction of Ranks*. 3d ed. London, 1779.

Minot, George Richards. *The History of the Insurrections, in Massachusetts*. Worcester, Mass., 1788.

Molloy, Charles. *De Jure Maritimo et Navali: or a Treatise of Affairs Maritime, and of Commerce*. 10th ed. London, 1778.

Montesquieu, Charles Louis de Secondat, Baron de. *The Persian Letters.* Translated by George R. Healy. Indianapolis, Ind., 1964.

———. *The Spirit of the Laws.* Translated by Thomas Nugent. New York, 1949.

Morris, Gouverneur. *The Diary and Letters of Gouverneur Morris.* Edited by Anne Cary Morris. 2 vols. New York, 1888.

Morris, Robert. *The Papers of Robert Morris, 1781–1784.* Edited by E. James Ferguson and John Catanzariti et al. 6 vols. Pittsburgh, Pa., 1973–1984.

Mun, Thomas. *England's Treasure by Forraign Trade.* London, 1664.

Necker, Jacques. *A Treatise on the Administration of the Finances of France.* Translated by Thomas Mortimer. 3 vols. London, 1785.

Nedham, Marchmont. *The Case of the Commonwealth of England Stated.* Edited by Philip A. Knachel. Charlottesville, Va., 1969.

———. *The Excellance of a Free State.* Edited by R. Baron. London, 1767.

Neville, Henry. *Plato Redivivus.* In *Two English Republican Tracts,* edited by Caroline Robbins. Cambridge, Eng., 1969.

Old South Leaflets. 9 vols. Boston, 1896–1922.

Otway, Thomas. *Venice Preserv'd, or, the Plot discover'd.* London, 1682.

Paine, Thomas. *The Complete Writings of Thomas Paine.* Edited by Philip S. Foner. 2 vols. New York, 1945.

———. *Selections from the Works of Thomas Paine: The American Crisis, The Age of Reason, Common Sense.* Edited by Arthur Wallace Peach. New York, 1928.

Paley, William. *The Principles of Moral and Political Philosophy.* 4th ed. Boston, 1801.

Pamphlets on the Constitution of the United States. Edited by Paul L. Ford. New York, 1968.

Petty, Sir William. *The Economic Writings of Sir William Petty, . . .* Edited by Charles Henry Hull. 2 vols. New York, 1963–1964.

Plato. *The Laws of Plato.* Edited by E. B. England. New York, 1976.

———. *The Republic.* Translated by Allan Bloom. New York, 1968.

Plutarch. *The Lives of the Noble Grecians and Romans.* Translated by John Dryden. Rev. ed., by Arthur Hugh Clough. New York, 1932.

Polybius. *The Histories.* Translated by E. S. Shuckburgh, edited by F. W. Walbank. Bloomington, Ind., 1962.

Pope, Alexander. *Alexander Pope: Selected Poetry.* Edited by Martin Price. New York and Toronto, 1970.

Postlethwayt, Malachy. *The Universal Dictionary of Trade and Commerce.* . . . 2 vols. London, 1757.

Powell, John. *Essay upon the Laws of Contracts and Agreements.* London, 1790.

Pownall, Thomas. *The Administration of the Colonies.* 3d ed. London, 1766.

Price, Richard. *Observations on the Nature of Civil Liberty, the Principles of Government, and the Justice and Policy of the War with America.* London, 1776.

Principles and Acts of the Revolution in America. Edited by Hezekiah Niles. New York, 1876.

Pufendorf, Samuel Freiherr von. *The Law of Nature and Nations.* Translated by Basil Kennet, with notes of Barbeyrac. 5th ed. London, 1749.

Puritan Political Ideas, 1558–1794. Edited by Edmund S. Morgan. Indianapolis, Ind., 1965.

Quesnay, François. *The Oeconomical Table,* . . . *with explanations, by* . . . *the Marquis de Mirabeau.* London, 1766.

Ramsay, David. *History of the American Revolution.* Dublin, 1793.

Rapin-Thoyras, Paul de. *History of England.* Translated by Nicholas Tindal. 5 vols. Boston, 1773.

The Records of the Federal Convention of 1787. Edited by Max Farrand. 4 vols. New Haven, Conn., 1937.

Reed, Joseph. *Life and Correspondence of Joseph Reed.* Edited by William B. Reed. 2 vols. Philadelphia, 1847.

Reid, Thomas. *An Inquiry into the Human Mind, on the principles of Common Sense.* Edinburgh, 1764.

Robertson, William. *The History of America.* 2d ed. Edinburgh, 1778.

Rollin, Charles. *The Ancient History of the Egyptians, Carthagenians, Assyrians, Babylonians, Medes and Persians, Macedonians and Grecians.* . . . 8th ed. 10 vols. London, 1788.

Rush, Benjamin. *The Autobiography of Benjamin Rush.* Edited by George W. Corner. Princeton, N.J., 1948.

———. *Letters of Benjamin Rush.* Edited by Lyman H. Butterfield. 2 vols. Princeton, N.J., 1951.

Rutherforth, Thomas. *Institutes of Natural Law; being the Substance of a Course of Lectures on Grotius' de Jure Belli ac Pacis.* 2 vols. Cambridge, Eng., 1754–1756.

Schöpf, Johann David. *Travels in the Confederation* (1783–1784). Translated by Alfred J. Morrison. 2 vols. Philadelphia, 1911.

Sidney, Algernon. *Discourses Concerning Government.* London, 1698.

Smith, Adam. *Essays on Philosophical Subjects.* Edited by W. P. D. Wightman and J. C. Bryce. Indianapolis, Ind., 1980; reprint of London, 1795 edition.

———. *Inquiry into the Nature and Causes of the Wealth of Nations.* Edited by R. H. Campbell, A. S. Skinner, and W. B. Todd, 2 vols. Indianapolis, Ind., 1981.

———. *Lectures on Jurisprudence.* Edited by R. L Meek, D. D. Raphael, and P. G. Stein. Indianapolis, Ind., 1978.

———. *Theory of Moral Sentiments.* Edited by R. H. Campbell, A. J. Skinner, and W. B. Todd. 2 vols. Indianapolis, Ind., 1981.

Smyth, John Ferdinand Dalziel. *A Tour in the United States of America.* 2 vols. New York, 1968; reprint of 1784 edition.

Steuart, Sir James. *An Inquiry into the Principles of Political Oeconomy.* Edited by Andrew S. Skinner. 2 vols. Chicago, 1966.

Story, Joseph. *Commentaries on the Constitution of the United States.* 3 vols. New York, 1970; reprint of Boston, 1833 edition.

Swift, Jonathan. *Gulliver's Travels.* Edited by Robert A. Greenberg. New York, 1970.

Symmes, John Cleves. *The Correspondence of John Cleves Symmes.* . . . Edited by Beverly W. Bond. New York, 1926.

Tacitus. *The Works of Tacitus.* Translated by Thomas Gordon. 2 vols. London, 1728, 1731.

Taylor, John, of Caroline. *An Enquiry into the Principles and Tendency of Certain Public Measures.* Philadelphia, 1794.

———. *An Inquiry into the Principles and Policy of the Government of the United States.* . . . Fredericksburg, Va., 1814.

Temple, Sir William. *Observations upon the United Provinces of the Netherlands.* London, 1673.

Travelers in America. *A Mirror for Americans: Life and Manners in the United States, 1790–1870. . . .* Edited by Warren S. Tyron. 3 vols. Chicago, 1952.

Trenchard, John. *A Short History of Standing Armies in England.* London, 1698.

Trenchard, John, and Gordon, Thomas. *The English Libertarian Heritage from the Writings of John Trenchard and Thomas Gordon in* The Independent Whig *and* Cato's Letters. Edited by David L. Jacobson. Indianapolis, Ind., 1965.

Vattel, Emmerich de. *The Law of Nations, Or, Principles of the Law of Nature, Applied to the Conduct and Affairs of Nations and Sovereigns.* Philadelphia, 1817; from revised Neuchâtel ed., 1773.

Washington, George. *The Writings of George Washington.* Edited by John C. Fitzpatrick. 39 vols. Washington, D.C., 1931–1944.

Webster, Noah. *An American Dictionary of the English Language.* 2 vols. New York and London, 1970; reprint of 1828 edition.

Wilson, James. *Considerations on the Nature and Extent of the Legislative Authority of the British Parliament.* Philadelphia, 1774.

———. *The Works of James Wilson.* Edited by Robert Green McCloskey. 2 vols. Cambridge, Mass., 1967.

Woodmason, Charles. *The Carolina Backcountry on the Eve of the Revolution: The Journal and Other Writings of Charles Woodmason, Anglican Itinerent.* Edited by Richard J. Hooker. Chapel Hill, N.C., 1953.

SECONDARY SOURCES

BOOKS

Adams, Willi Paul. *The First American Constitutions: Republican Ideology and the Making of the State Constitutions in the Revolu-*

tionary Era. Translated by Rita Kimber and Robert Kimber. Chapel Hill, N.C., 1980.

Aldridge, Alfred Owen. *Franklin and His French Contemporaries*. New York, 1957.

Allen, David Grayson. *In English Ways: The Movement of Societies and the Transferal of English Local Law and Custom to Massachusetts Bay in the Seventeenth Century*. Chapel Hill, N.C., 1981.

Anderson, Dice Robins. *William Branch Giles: A Study in the Politics of Virginia and the Nation from 1790 to 1830*. Gloucester, Mass., 1965.

Anderson, Patricia A., ed. *Promoted to Glory: The Apotheosis of George Washington*. Northampton, Mass., 1980.

Andrews, Matthew P. *Virginia: The Old Dominion*. Richmond, Va., 1949.

Angell, Joseph K. *A Treatise on the Law of Watercourses*. Boston, 1854.

Ashe, Samuel A., et al., eds. *Biographical History of North Carolina from Colonial Times to the Present*. 6 vols. Greensboro, N.C., 1907.

Ashton, Robert. *The Crown and the Money Market: 1603–1640*. Oxford, Eng., 1960.

Bailyn, Bernard. *The Ideological Origins of the American Revolution*. Cambridge, Mass., 1967.

Bailyn, Bernard, and Hench, John B., eds. *The Press & the American Revolution*. Worcester, Mass., 1980.

Baker, J. H. *An Introduction to English Legal History*. London, 1971.

Banner, James M., Jr. *To the Hartford Convention: The Federalists and the Origins of Party Politics in Massachusetts, 1789–1815*. New York, 1970.

Banning, Lance. *The Jeffersonian Persuasion: Evolution of a Party Ideology*. Ithaca, N.Y., 1978.

Beard, Charles A. *An Economic Interpretation of the Constitution of the United States*. New York, 1913.

Becker, Robert A. *Revolution, Reform, and the Politics of American Taxation, 1763–1783*. Baton Rouge, La., 1980.

Beer, George Louis. *The Old Colonial System, 1660–1754*. 2 vols. New York, 1912.

Bemis, Samuel Flagg. *Pinckney's Treaty: A Study of America's Advantage from Europe's Distress, 1783–1800.* Baltimore, Md., 1926.

Berns, Walter. *The First Amendment and the Future of American Democracy.* New York, 1976.

Bidwell, Percy Wells, and Falconer, John I. *History of Agriculture in the Northern United States, 1620–1860.* New York, 1941.

Billias, George Athan. *Elbridge Gerry: Founding Father and Republican Statesman.* New York, 1976.

Bradford, M. E. *A Worthy Company: Brief Lives of the Framers of the United States Constitution.* Marlborough, N.H., 1982.

Brown, Imogene. *American Aristides: A Biography of George Wythe.* Madison, N.J., 1980.

Brown, Richard Maxwell. *The South Carolina Regulators.* Cambridge, Mass., 1963.

Brown, Robert E. *Middle-Class Democracy and the Revolution in Massachusetts, 1691–1780.* Ithaca, N.Y., 1955.

Brown, Robert E., and Brown, B. Katherine. *Virginia, 1705–1786: Democracy or Aristocracy?* East Lansing, Mich., 1964.

Brown, Stuart Gerry. *The First Republicans: Political Philosophy and Public Policy in the Party of Jefferson and Madison.* Syracuse, N.Y., 1954.

Bruce, Philip A. *Institutional History of Virginia in the Seventeenth Century.* . . . 2 vols. New York, 1910.

Brunhouse, Robert L. *The Counter-Revolution in Pennsylvania, 1776–1790.* Harrisburg, Pa., 1942.

Bryson, Gladys. *Man and Society: The Scottish Inquiry of the Eighteenth Century.* Princeton, N.J., 1945.

Buel, Richard. *Securing the Revolution: Ideology in American Politics, 1789–1815.* Ithaca, N.Y., 1972.

Burnett, Edmund Cody. *The Continental Congress.* New York, 1941.

Bushman, Richard L. *From Puritan to Yankee: Character and the Social Order in Connecticut, 1690–1765.* Cambridge, Mass., 1967.

Campbell, John C. *The Lives of the Chief Justices of England.* . . . Vol. 3. London, 1857.

Chitnis, Anand C. *The Scottish Enlightenment: A Social History.* London, 1976.

Clarkson, Paul S., and Jett, R. Samuel. *Luther Martin of Maryland*. Baltimore, Md., 1970.

Coad, Oral Sumner, and Mims, Edwin, Jr. *The American Stage*. New Haven, Conn., 1929.

Cobb, Sanford H. *The Rise of Religious Liberty in America: A History*. New York, 1902.

Cohen, Patricia Cline. *A Calculating People: The Spread of Numeracy in Early America*. Chicago, 1982.

Colbourn, Trevor, ed. *Fame and the Founding Fathers: Essays by Douglass Adair*. New York, 1974.

————. *The Lamp of Experience: Whig History and the Intellectual Origins of the American Revolution*. Chapel Hill, N.C., 1965.

Cook, Elizabeth Christine. *Literary Influences in Colonial Newspapers, 1704–1750*. New York, 1912.

Crowl, Philip. *Maryland during and after the Revolution: A Political and Economic Study*. Baltimore, Md., 1943.

Dawidoff, Robert. *The Education of John Randolph*. New York, 1979.

Defebaugh, James E. *History of the Lumber Industry of America*. 2 vols. Chicago, 1906, 1907.

DeMond, Robert O. *The Loyalists in North Carolina during the Revolution*. Hamden, Conn., 1964.

Dickerson, Oliver M. *The Navigation Acts and the American Revolution*. Philadelphia, 1951.

Dickson, P. G. M. *The Financial Revolution in England: A Study in the Development of Public Credit, 1688–1756*. London, 1967.

Dickson, R. J. *Ulster Emigration to Colonial America, 1718–1775*. Belfast, 1966.

Diggins, John Patrick. *The Lost Soul of American Politics: Virtue, Self-Interest and the Foundations of Liberalism*. New York, 1984.

Dodgshon, R. A., and Butlin, R. A., eds. *An Historical Geography of England and Wales*. London and New York, 1978.

Dorfman, Joseph. *The Economic Mind in American Civilization, 1606–1865*. 2 vols. New York, 1946.

Duker, William F. *A Constitutional History of Habeas Corpus*. Westport, Conn., 1980.

Dunaway, Wayland F. *A History of Pennsylvania*. New York, 1935.

Dunbar, Louise Burnham. *A Study of "Monarchical" Tendencies in the United States from 1776 to 1801.* New York and London, 1970.

Dunn, John. *The Political Thought of John Locke: An Historical Account of the Argument of the 'Two Treatises of Government.'* London, 1969.

Ellis, Joseph J. *After the Revolution: Profiles of Early American Culture.* New York, 1979.

Ernst, Robert. *Rufus King: American Federalist.* Chapel Hill, N.C., 1968.

Everdell, William R. *The End of Kings: A History of Republics and Republicans.* New York, 1983.

Ferguson, E. James. *The Power of the Purse: A History of American Public Finance, 1776–1790.* Chapel Hill, N.C., 1961.

Fifoot, Cecil H. S. *Lord Mansfield.* Oxford, Eng., 1936.

Fink, Zera S. *The Classical Republicans: An Essay in the Recovery of a Pattern of Thought in Seventeenth Century England.* Evanston, Ill., 1949.

Flexner, James T. *George Washington.* 4 vols. Boston, 1965–1972.

———. *Washington: The Indispensable Man.* Boston, 1974.

Fliegelman, Jay. *Prodigals and Pilgrims: The American Revolution against Patriarchical Authority, 1750–1800.* Cambridge, Eng., 1982.

Flower, Milton E. *John Dickinson: Conservative Revolutionary.* Charlottesville, Va., 1983.

Forbes, Duncan. *Hume's Philosophical Politics.* Cambridge, Eng., 1975.

Ford, Paul Leicester. *Washington and the Theatre.* New York, 1899.

Fox-Genovese, Elizabeth. *The Origins of Physiocracy: Economic Revolution and Social Order in Eighteenth-Century France.* Ithaca, N.Y., 1976.

Freeman, Douglas Southall. *George Washington: A Biography.* 7 vols. New York, 1948–1957.

Galenson, David. *White Servitude in Colonial America.* New York, 1981.

Goebel, Julius, Jr. *History of the Supreme Court of the United States.* New York, 1971.

Goldwin, Robert A., and Schambra, William A., eds. *How Capitalistic Is the Constitution?* Washington, D.C., and London, 1982.

———. *How Democratic Is the Constitution?* Washington, D.C., and London, 1980.

Gray, Lewis Cecil. *History of Agriculture in the Southern United States to 1860.* 2 vols. Gloucester, Mass., 1958.

Greven, Philip. *The Protestant Temperament: Patterns of Child-Rearing, Religious Experience, and the Self in Early America.* New York, 1977.

Gummere, Richard M. *The American Colonial Mind and the Classical Tradition.* Cambridge, Mass., 1963.

Gunn, J. A. W. *Beyond Liberty and Property: The Process of Self-Recognition in Eighteenth-Century Political Thought.* Kingston and Montreal, 1983.

Hamilton, J. G. deRoulhoc. *William Richardson Davie: A Memoir. . . .* Chapel Hill, N.C., 1907.

Handlin, Oscar, and Handlin, Mary F. *Commonwealth: A Study of the Role of Government in the American Economy: Massachusetts, 1774–1861.* New York, 1947.

Haraszti, Zoltan. *John Adams & the Prophets of Progress.* Cambridge, Mass., 1952.

Harper, Lawrence A. *The English Navigation Laws: A Seventeenth-Century Experiment in Social Engineering.* New York, 1939.

Harrell, Isaac S. *Loyalism in Virginia: Chapters in the Economic History of the Revolution.* Durham, N.C., 1926.

Harvey, Ray Forrest. *Jean Jacques Burlamaqui: A Liberal Tradition in American Constitutionalism.* Chapel Hill, N.C., 1937.

Hatch, Nathan O. *The Sacred Cause of Liberty: Republican Thought and the Millennium in Revolutionary New England.* New Haven, Conn., 1977.

Head, John M. *A Time to Rend: An Essay on the Decision for American Independence.* Madison, Wis., 1968.

Heckscher, Eli F. *Mercantilism.* 2d ed. 2 vols. London and New York, 1962.

Hedges, James B. *The Browns of Providence Plantations: Colonial Years.* Cambridge, Mass., 1952.

Holdsworth, William S. *A History of English Law.* 7th ed.; revised vols. 6–8. London, 1966.

Holliday, John. *The Life of William, Late Earl of Mansfield.* London, 1797.

Horwitz, Morton J. *The Transformation of American Law, 1780–1860.* Cambridge, Mass., 1977.

Isaac, Rhys. *The Transformation of Virginia, 1740–1790.* Chapel Hill, N.C., 1982.

James, Sydney V. *Colonial Rhode Island: A History.* New York, 1975.

Jensen, Merrill. *The Articles of Confederation: An Interpretation of the Social-Constitutional History of the American Revolution, 1774–1781.* Madison, Wis., 1940.

———. *The New Nation: A History of the United States, 1781–1789.* New York, 1950.

Kamenka, Eugene, and Neale, R. S., eds. *Feudalism, Capitalism, and Beyond.* New York, 1975.

Kammen, Michael G. *Colonial New York: A History.* New York, 1975.

———. *People of Paradox: An Inquiry Concerning the Origins of American Civilization.* New York, 1973.

Kerber, Linda K. *Women of the Republic: Intellect & Ideology in Revolutionary America.* Chapel Hill, N.C., 1980.

Ketcham, Ralph L. *James Madison: A Biography.* New York, 1971.

Kettner, James H. *The Development of American Citizenship, 1608–1870.* Chapel Hill, N.C., 1978.

Kramnick, Isaac. *Bolingbroke and His Circle: The Politics of Nostalgia in the Age of Walpole.* Cambridge, Mass., 1968.

Lefler, Hugh Talmage, and Newsome, Albert Ray. *North Carolina: The History of a Southern State.* Chapel Hill, N.C., 1963.

Levy, Leonard W. *The Law of the Commonwealth and Chief Justice Shaw.* Cambridge, Mass., 1957.

———. *Legacy of Suppression: Freedom of Speech and Press in Early American History.* Cambridge, Mass., 1960.

Lovejoy, Arthur O. *Reflections on Human Nature.* Baltimore, Md., 1961.

McCaughey, Elizabeth P. *From Loyalist to Founding Father: The Political Odyssey of William Samuel Johnson.* New York, 1980.

McCoy, Drew R. *The Elusive Republic: Political Economy in Jeffersonian America.* Chapel Hill, N.C., 1980.

McDonald, Forrest. *Alexander Hamilton: A Biography.* New York, 1979.

———. *E Pluribus Unum: The Formation of the American Republic, 1776–1790.* Indianapolis, Ind., 1979 edition.

———. *The Presidency of George Washington.* Lawrence, Kans., 1974.

———. *The Presidency of Thomas Jefferson.* Lawrence, Kans., 1976.

———. *We the People: The Economic Origins of the Constitution.* Chicago, 1958.

Macpherson, C. B. *The Political Theory of Possessive Individualism: Hobbes to Locke.* Oxford, Eng., 1962.

Main, Jackson Turner. *The Antifederalists: Critics of the Constitution, 1781–1788.* Chapel Hill, N.C., 1961.

Mansfield, Harvey C., Jr., *Machiavelli's New Modes and Orders: A Study of The Discourses on Livy.* Ithaca, N.Y., 1979.

———. *Statesmanship and Party Government: A Study of Burke and Bolingbroke.* Chicago, 1965.

Masterson, William H. *William Blount.* Baton Rouge, La., 1954.

Matthews, Richard K. *The Radical Politics of Thomas Jefferson: A Revisionist View.* Lawrence, Kans., 1984.

Meek, Ronald L. *The Economics of Physiocracy: Essays and Translations.* Cambridge, Mass., 1963.

———. *Social Science and the Ignoble Savage.* Cambridge, Eng., 1976.

Mendle, Michael. *Dangerous Positions: Mixed Government, the Estates of the Realm, and the Making of the* Answer to the xix propositions. Tuscaloosa, Ala., 1985.

Minchinton, Walter, ed. *Mercantilism: System or Expediency?* Lexington, Mass., 1969.

Mintz, Max M. *Gouverneur Morris and the American Revolution.* Norman, Okla., 1970.

Morison, Samuel Eliot. *Harrison Gray Otis, 1765–1848: The Urbane Federalist.* Boston, 1969.

———. *The Young George Washington.* Cambridge, Mass., 1932.

Morrill, James R. *The Practice and Politics of Fiat Finance: North Carolina in the Confederation, 1783–1789.* Chapel Hill, N.C., 1969.

Namier, Lewis. *Monarchy and the Party System. . . .* Oxford, Eng., 1952.

Nelson, William E. *Americanization of the Common Law: The Impact of Legal Change upon Massachusetts Society, 1760–1830.* Cambridge, Mass., 1975.

Nye, Russel Blaine. *The Cultural Life of the New Nation, 1776–1830.* New York, 1960.

Oberholtzer, Ellis P. *Robert Morris: Patriot and Financier.* New York, 1903.

O'Connor, John E. *William Paterson: Lawyer and Statesman, 1745–1806.* New Brunswick, N.J., 1979.

Onuf, Peter S. *The Origins of the Federal Republic: Jurisdictional Controversies in the United States, 1775–1787.* Philadelphia, 1983.

Perelman, Michael. *Classical Political Economy: Primitive Accumulation and the Social Division of Labor.* Totowa, N.J., 1984.

Plumb, J. H. *England in the Eighteenth Century.* Harmondsworth, Middlesex, Eng., 1950.

———. *The Origins of Political Stability: England 1676–1725.* Boston, 1967.

Pocock, J. G. A. *The Ancient Constitution and the Feudal Law: English Historical Thought in the Seventeenth Century.* New York, 1967.

———. *The Machiavellian Moment: Florentine Political Thought and the Atlantic Republican Tradition.* Princeton, N.J., 1975.

———. *Politics, Language, and Time: Essays on Political Thought and History.* New York, 1971.

Pole, J. R. *Political Representation in England and the Origins of the American Republic.* New York, 1966.

Rankin, Hugh F. *The Theater in Colonial America.* Chapel Hill, N.C., 1960.

Rawson, Elizabeth. *The Spartan Tradition in European Thought.* Oxford, Eng., 1969.

Reardon, John J. *Edmund Randolph: A Biography.* New York, 1975.

Rendall, Jane. *The Origins of the Scottish Enlightenment.* New York, 1978.

Risjord, Norman K. *The Old Republicans: Southern Conservatism in the Age of Jefferson.* New York, 1965.

Robbins, Caroline. *The Eighteenth-Century Commonwealthman: Studies in the Transmission, Development, and Circumstance of*

English Liberal Thought from the Restoration of Charles II until the War with the Thirteen Colonies. Cambridge, Mass., 1959.

Roeber, A. G. *Faithful Magistrates and Republican Lawyers: Creators of Virginia Legal Culture, 1680–1810.* Chapel Hill, N.C., 1981.

Rowland, Kate Mason. *The Life of George Mason, 1725–1792.* 2 vols. New York, 1892.

Rutland, Robert Allen. *The Birth of the Bill of Rights, 1776–1791.* Chapel Hill, N.C., 1955.

Sanderson, John, ed. *Biographies of the Signers to the Declaration of Independence.* 5 vols. Philadelphia, 1831.

Sawyer, Timothy Thompson. *Old Charlestown: Historical, Biographical, Reminiscent.* Boston, 1902.

Schumpeter, Joseph. *A History of Economic Analysis.* New York, 1954.

Seilhamer, George O. *History of the American Theatre.* 2 vols. New York, 1888, 1889.

Seton-Watson, R. W., ed. *Tudor Studies.* London, 1924.

Shalhope, Robert E. *John Taylor of Caroline: Pastoral Republican.* Columbia, S.C., 1980.

Siebert, Fredrick Seaton. *Freedom of the Press in England, 1476–1776.* Urbana, Ill., 1952.

Sims, Henry H. *Life of John Taylor.* Richmond, Va., 1932.

Slichter, Sumner H. *Economic Growth in the United States: Its History, Problems, and Prospects.* New York, 1966.

Smith, Abbot Emerson. *Colonists in Bondage: White Servitude and Convict Labor in America, 1607–1776.* Chapel Hill, N.C., 1947.

Smith, Charles Page. *James Wilson: Founding Father, 1742–1798.* Chapel Hill, N.C., 1956.

Sparks, Jared. *The Life of George Washington.* Boston, 1842.

Sumner, William G. *The Financier and the Finances of the American Revolution.* 2 vols. New York, 1891.

Swanson, Donald F. *The Origins of Hamilton's Fiscal Policies.* Gainesville, Fla., 1963.

Swigett, Howard. *The Extraordinary Mr. Morris.* Garden City, N.Y., 1952.

Szatmary, David P. *Shays' Rebellion: The Making of an Agrarian Insurrection.* Amherst, Mass., 1980.

Taylor, Overton H. *A History of Economic Thought: Social Ideals and Economic Theories from Quesnay to Keynes.* New York, 1960.

Taylor, Robert J. *Western Massachusetts in the Revolution.* Providence, R.I., 1954.

Thayer, Theodore. *Pennsylvania Politics and the Growth of Democracy, 1740–1776.* Harrisburg, Pa., 1953.

Thirsk, Joan, ed. *The Agrarian History of England and Wales.* Vol. 4: *1500–1640.* Cambridge, Eng., 1967.

Thorpe, Francis Newton. *The Constitutional History of the United States, 1765–1788.* Vol. 1. Chicago, 1901.

Trakman, Leon E. *The Law-Merchant: The Evolution of Commercial Law.* Boulder, Colo., 1983.

Tully, James. *A Discourse on Property: John Locke and His Adversaries.* Cambridge, Eng., 1980.

Upton, Richard F. *Revolutionary New Hampshire: An Account of the Social and Political Forces Underlying the Transition from Royal Province to American Commonwealth.* Hanover, N.H., 1936.

Van Tyne, Claude H. *The Loyalists in the American Revolution.* New York, 1902.

Ver Steeg, Clarence L. *Robert Morris: Revolutionary Financier.* New York, 1976.

Viner, Jacob. *The Long View and the Short: Studies in Economic Theory and Policy.* Glencoe, Ill., 1958.

Wallace, Paul A. W. *Pennsylvania: Seed of a Nation.* New York, 1962.

Weeden, William B. *Economic and Social History of New England, 1620–1789.* 2 vols. New York, 1890.

Wharton, Leslie. *Polity and the Public Good: Conflicting Theories of Republican Government in the New Nation.* Ann Arbor, Mich., 1980.

Whitaker, Arthur P. *The Spanish-American Frontier, 1783–1795.* . . . Boston, 1927.

White, Morton. *The Philosophy of the American Revolution.* New York, 1978.

Williamson, Chilton. *American Suffrage: From Property to Democracy, 1760–1860.* Princeton, N.J., 1960.

Wills, Garry. *Cincinnatus: George Washington and the Enlightenment.* Garden City, N.Y., 1984.

———. *Inventing America: Jefferson's Declaration of Independence.* Garden City, N.Y., 1978.

Wood, Gordon S. *The Creation of the American Republic, 1776–1787.* Chapel Hill, N.C., 1969.

Wormald, Jenny. *Court, Kirk, and Community: Scotland, 1470–1625.* Toronto, 1981.

Yoshpe, Harry \B. *The Disposition of Loyalist Estates in the Southern District of the State of New York.* New York, 1939.

Young, Alfred F. *The Democratic Republicans of New York: The Origins, 1763–1797.* Chapel Hill, N.C., 1967.

Younger, Richard D. *The People's Panel: The Grand Jury in the United States, 1634–1941.* Providence, R.I., 1963.

ARTICLES AND DISSERTATIONS

Alymer, G. E. "The Meaning and Definition of 'Property' in Seventeenth-Century England." *Past and Present* 86 (1980): 87–97.

Appleby, Joyce. "Commercial Farming and the 'Agrarian Myth' in the Early Republic." *Journal of American History* 68 (1982): 833–849.

———. "What Is Still American in the Political Philosophy of Thomas Jefferson?" *William and Mary Quarterly* 39 (1982): 287–309.

Ashcraft, Richard, and Goldsmith, M. M. "Locke, Revolution Principles, and the Formation of Whig Ideology." *Historical Journal* 26 (1983): 773–800.

Banning, Lance. "The Hamiltonian Madison: A Reconsideration." *Virginia Magazine of History and Biography* 92 (1984): 3–28.

———. "James Madison and the Nationalists, 1780–1783." *William and Mary Quarterly* 40 (1983): 227–255.

Berns, Walter. "Judicial Review and the Rights and Laws of Nature." In *1982: The Supreme Court Review,* edited by Philip B. Kurland et al. Chicago, 1983.

Bourne, Edward G. "Alexander Hamilton and Adam Smith." *Quarterly Journal of Economics* 8 (1894): 328–344.

Bowling, Kenneth R. "The Bank Bill, the Capital City, and President Washington." *Capital Studies* 1 (1972): 59–71.

———. "Politics in the First Congress, 1789–1791." Ph.D. diss., University of Wisconsin, 1968.

Boyd, Julian P. "Attempts to Form New States in New York and Pennsylvania, 1786-1796." *Quarterly Journal of the New York State Historical Association* 12 (1931): 258-263.

———. "Connecticut's Experiment in Expansion: The Susquehanna Company, 1753-1803." *Journal of Economic and Business History* 4 (1931-1932): 38-69.

———. "The Susquehanna Company." *Connecticut Tercentenary Commission Publications.* New Haven, Conn., 1935.

Branson, Roy. "James Madison and the Scottish Enlightenment." *Journal of the History of Ideas* 40 (1979): 235-250.

Caplan, Russell L. "The History and Meaning of the Ninth Amendment." *Virginia Law Review* 69 (1983): 223-268.

Chafee, Zachariah, Jr. "Colonial Courts and the Common Law." *Proceedings of the Massachusetts Historical Society* 68 (1952): 132-159.

Chinard, Gilbert. "Polybius and the American Constitution." *Journal of the History of Ideas* 1 (1940): 38-58.

Cohen, Charles L. "The 'Liberty or Death' Speech: A Note on Religion and Revolutionary Rhetoric." *William and Mary Quarterly* 38 (1981): 702-717.

Colvin, Milton. "Property That Cannot Be Reached by the Power of Eminent Domain for a Public Use or Purpose." *University of Pennsylvania Law Review* 78 (1929): 1-26, 137-178.

Cross, Lawrence Delbert. "An Armed Community: The Origins and Meaning of the Right to Bear Arms." *Journal of American History* 71 (1984): 22-42.

Cuddihy, William, and Hardy, B. Carmon. "A Man's House Was Not His Castle: Origins of the Fourth Amendment to the United States Constitution." *William and Mary Quarterly* 37 (1980): 371-400.

Dunn, John. "Justice and the Interpretation of Locke's Political Theory." *Political Studies* 16 (1968): 68-87.

Ferguson, E. James. "Political Economy, Public Liberty, and the Formation of the Constitution." *William and Mary Quarterly* 40 (1983): 390-398.

Fiala, Robert Dennis. "George III in the Pennsylvania Press: A Study in Changing Opinions, 1760-1776." Ph.D. diss., Wayne State University, 1967.

Govan, Thomas P. "Alexander Hamilton and Julius Caesar: A Note on the Use of Historical Evidence." *William and Mary Quarterly* 32 (1975): 475–480.

Gribbin, William. "Republican Religion and the American Churches in the Early National Period." *Historian* 35 (1972): 61–74.

Griffith, David. "Catherine II: The Republican Empress." *Jahrbücher für Geschichte Osteuropas* 21 (1973): 323–344.

Hamowy, Ronald. "Jefferson and the Scottish Enlightenment: A Critique of Garry Wills's *Inventing America: Jefferson's Declaration of Independence*." *William and Mary Quarterly* 36 (1979): 503–523.

Henderson, Edith Guild. "The Background of the Seventh Amendment." *Harvard Law Review* 80 (1966): 289–337.

Hobson, Charles F. "The Negative on State Laws: James Madison, the Constitution, and the Crisis of Republican Government." *William and Mary Quarterly* 36 (1979): 215–235.

———. "The Recovery of British Debts in the Federal Circuit Court of Virginia, 1790 to 1797." *Virginia Magazine of History and Biography* 92 (1984): 176–200.

Hoffer, Peter C., and Hull, N. E. H. "Power and Precedent in the Creation of an American Impeachment Tradition: The Eighteenth-Century Colonial Record." *William and Mary Quarterly* 36 (1979): 51–77.

Hulme, Harold. "The Winning of Freedom of Speech by the House of Commons." *American Historical Review* 61 (1956): 825–853.

Hutson, James H. "Notes and Documents: John Dickinson and the Federal Constitutional Convention." *William and Mary Quarterly* 40 (1983): 256–282.

———. "Pierce Butler's Records of the Federal Constitutional Convention." *Quarterly Journal of the Library of Congress* 37 (1980): 64–73.

Jaffa, Harry V. "Inventing the Past: Garry Wills's *Inventing America* and the Pathology of Ideological Scholarship." *St. John Review* 33 (1981): 3–19.

Jensen, Merrill. "The Creation of the National Domain, 1781–1784." *Mississippi Valley Historical Review* 25 (1939): 323–342.

Kammen, Michael. "A Different 'Fable of the Bees': The Problem of Public and Private Sectors in Colonial America." In *The American Revolution: A Heritage of Change*, edited by John Parker and Carol Urness. Minneapolis, Minn., 1975.

Keim, C. Ray. "Primogeniture and Entail in Colonial Virginia." *William and Mary Quarterly* 25 (1968): 545–586.

Klein, Rachel N. "Ordering the Backcountry: The South Carolina Regulation." *William and Mary Quarterly* 38 (1981): 661–680.

Kramnick, Isaac. "Republican Revisionism Revisited." *American Historical Review* 87 (1982): 629–664.

Leder, Lawrence H. "The Role of Newspapers in Early America: 'In Defense of their Own Liberty.'" *Huntington Library Quarterly* 30 (1966): 1–16.

Lenhoff, Arthur. "Development of the Concept of Eminent Domain." *Columbia Law Review* 42 (1942): 596–638.

Liddle, William David. "A Patriot King, or None: American Public Attitudes toward George III and the British Monarchy, 1754–1776." Ph.D. diss., Claremont Graduate School, 1970.

———. "A Patriot King, or None: Lord Bolingbroke and the American Renunciation of George III." *Journal of American History* 65 (1979): 951–970.

Litto, Fredric M. "Addison's *Cato* in the Colonies." *William and Mary Quarterly* 23 (1966): 431–449.

Lynn, Kenneth S. "Falsifying Jefferson." *Commentary* 66 (1978): 66–71.

McCoy, Drew R. "Benjamin Franklin's Vision of a Republican Political Economy for America." *William and Mary Quarterly* 35 (1978): 605–628.

McDonald, Forrest, and McWhiney, Grady. "The Antebellum Southern Herdsman: A Reinterpretation." *Journal of Southern History* 41 (1975): 147–166.

———. "The South from Self-Sufficiency to Peonage: An Interpretation." *American Historical Review* 85 (1980): 1095–1118.

McDonald, Forrest, and Mendle, Michael. "The Historical Roots of the Originating Clause of the United States Constitution: Article I, Section 7." *Modern Age* 27 (1983): 274–281.

Moore, James. "Hume's Political Science and the Classical Republican Tradition." *Canadian Journal of Political Science* 10 (1977): 809–839.

Morgan, Edmund S. "The Puritan Ethic and the American Revolution." *William and Mary Quarterly* 24 (1967): 3–43.

Morgan, Philip D. "Work and Culture: The Task System and the World of Lowcountry Blacks, 1700 to 1880." *William and Mary Quarterly* 39 (1982): 563–599.

Nelson, William E. "The Eighteenth-Century Background of John Marshall's Constitutional Jurisprudence." *Michigan Law Review* 76 (1978): 904–917.

Nussbaum, Frederick L. "American Tobacco and French Politics, 1783–1789." *Political Science Quarterly* 40 (1925): 497–516.

Parker, Rodger D. "The Gospel of Opposition: A Study in Eighteenth-Century Anglo-American Ideology." Ph.D. diss., Wayne State University, 1975.

Pocock, J. G. A. "Virtue and Commerce in the Eighteenth Century." *Journal of Interdisciplinary History* 3 (1972): 119–134.

Rahe, Paul A. "The Primacy of Politics in Classical Greece." *American Historical Review* 89 (1984): 265–293.

Rashid, Salim. "Adam Smith's Rise to Fame: A Reexamination of the Evidence." *Eighteenth Century: Theory and Interpretation* 23 (1982): 64–85.

Robbins, Caroline. "Algernon Sidney's *Discourses Concerning Government*: Textbook in Revolution." *William and Mary Quarterly* 4 (1947): 267–296.

Rosenberg, Norman. "Mandeville and Laissez-Faire." *Journal of the History of Ideas* 24 (1963): 183–196.

Ryan, Alan. "Locke and the Dictatorship of the Bourgeoisie." *Political Studies* 13 (1965): 219–230.

Shackleton, Robert, "Montesquieu, Bolingbroke, and the Separation of Powers." *French Studies* 3 (1949): 25–38.

Shalhope, Robert E. "The Ideological Origins of the Second Amendment." *Journal of American History* 69 (1982): 599–614.

Shalhope, Robert E., and Cross, Lawrence Delbert. "The Second Amendment and the Right to Bear Arms: An Exchange." *Journal of American History* 71 (1984): 587–593.

Sheridan, Richard B. "The British Credit Crisis of 1772 and the American Colonies." *Journal of Economic History* 20 (1960): 161–186.

Statom, Thomas R. "Negro Slavery in Eighteenth-Century Georgia." Ph.D. diss., University of Alabama, 1982.

Wilson, Charles, "The Other Face of Mercantilism." *Transactions of the Royal Historical Society* 9 (1959): 81–101.

Wood, Gordon S. "Conspiracy and the Paranoid Style: Causality and Deceit in the Eighteenth Century." *William and Mary Quarterly* 39 (1982): 401–441.

Wright, Benjamin F., Jr. "The Origins of the Separation of Powers in America." *Economica* 13 (1933): 169–185.

Yoder, Paton. "Tavern Regulation in Virginia: Rationale and Reality." *Virginia Magazine of History and Biography* 87 (1979): 259–278.

INDEX

We the People

Article I

...